Computing Fundamentals with C++

Using, Modifying, and Implementing Object Classes

Rick Mercer

Penn State Berks

Franklin, Beedle & Associates, Incorporated
8536 SW St. Helens Drive, Suite D
Wilsonville, Oregon 97070
(503) 682-7668

Publisher	Jim Leisy
Developmental Editor	Samantha Soma
Manuscript Editor	Sheryl Rose
Production Manager	Bill DeRouchey
Proofreader	Jeff Tade
Cover Design	BLT Graphics
Cover Photograph	Ian Shadburne
Manufacturing	R.R. Donnelley Norwest, WCP Division
	Tigard, Oregon

Rights and Permissions
Franklin, Beedle and Associates Incorporated
8536 SW St. Helens Drive, Suite D
Wilsonville, Oregon 97070

Mercer, Rick
     Computing fundamentals with C++: using, modifying, and implementing object classes / Rick Mercer.
        p.   cm.
     Includes index.
     ISBN 0-938661-72-8
     1. C++ (Computer program language) 2. Electronic digital computers--Programming.   I. Title.
QA76.73.C153M46 1994
005.13'3--dc20   94-29110
                                   CIP

Preface

Computing Fundamentals with C++ is written for students with no prior programming experience. It is intended for students majoring in computer science, the physical sciences, engineering, or business. A working knowledge of high school mathematics is assumed.

Students familiar with another programming language can use this textbook as well. Although a background in programming provides advantages, C++ and the objects-early approach of this textbook provide a more level playing field. Consequently, coverage of the topics in this textbook should be interesting and challenging to students with some programming experience.

Above all else, this book helps anyone wishing to develop and refine their problem-solving and program-development skills. C++ is a tool.

Extensively Tested in the Classroom

The manuscript has been class tested with a wide range of student abilities and backgrounds over eight consecutive terms, from Spring 1992 to Summer 1994. Students supplied many useful comments and suggestions concerning the manuscript's clarity, organization, lab projects, and examples. This comprehensive field testing and development are unique among most of the books available on this subject.

A Gentle Objects-Early Approach:
Use, Modify, then Implement Object Classes

The book begins by placing the student in the role of a consumer—a user of object classes. While students hone problem-solving and program-development skills, they learn to use, modify, and ultimately, design and implement their own classes. Experience with several topic organizations has demonstrated that students more easily master the topics when presented in this manner. This approach alleviates the mental "bump" (referred to by some as "the paradigm shift") often encountered when learning the object model.

Carefully Chosen Subset of Analysis, Design, and C++

Because students using this textbook might have little or no software development experience, several C++ features and subtleties are not covered. Students concentrate on a solid subset of this feature-rich language.

Some of C++'s trickier topics are delayed until the later chapters. For example, an accompanying string class avoids early coverage of pointers (see Chapter 9 for char * objects). Reliance on the cin and cout objects avoids coverage of C style I/O with the address of operator & (see Appendix D for the printf and scanf functions). Some features are left as optional topics, such as operator overloading and the break statement.

There are a few examples of low-level object-oriented analysis in Chapters 1 and 8, but most program development examples use other accessible analysis tools. One involves determining the input and output. Simple design tools include: input, process, and output algorithms; stepwise refinement; and recognizing and locating beneficial classes that already exist. Student-accessible testing tools include test oracles and branch coverage testing.

Pointers and dynamic memory management (Chapter 9) are additional topics or ancillary material in a second course.

Carefully Chosen Subset of Object-Oriented Programming

This textbook does not cover inheritance or polymorphism. However, the major object-oriented concept of encapsulation plays an important role throughout. Data is an integral part of any object, as are the functions that manipulate that data. This approach gives students a chance to become accustomed to using objects and designing and implementing individual classes before classification of larger systems. Students have a good grasp of C++ class design and implementation by the end of Chapter 8. Chapters 9, 10, and 11 illustrate encapsulation with examples of safe array classes and a list class that stores any type (class) of element. The C++ class and encapsulation prove to be important during the first course.

The recent addition of templates could prove genericity is at least as important as inheritance and polymorphism in the first year. Templates provide an alternative approach to data structure implementation. To this end, Chapter 10 provides examples of a generic (parameterized) array class, a list class that stores objects of any class (data type), and a generic stack.

Case Studies Provide Analysis, Design, and Implementation

A basic pedagogical technique employed in each chapter is the use of case studies to enforce constructs of recently covered material. The case studies stress the importance of problem analysis, provide examples of design, and address implementation issues, such as coding and program testing, to ensure the program implementation meets the specification. This three step strategy provides a positive, digestible model right from the beginning.

Abundant Self-Check Questions and Exercises

In each chapter, every section contains self-check questions (with answers). These questions and answers provide a checklist-like opportunity to review and digest the material just covered. A complete set of exercises (with answers in the Instructor's Manual) exists at the conclusion of all chapters. Most chapters include an additional set of exercises at the midpoint.

Numerous Self-Contained (and Tested) Lab Projects

Because hands-on computer use is a key component to learning program design and implementation, programming topics are reinforced with assigned lab projects, at the end of each chapter, or in most cases, in the middle of the chapter.

The lab projects were developed and tested over an extensive period of time. Feedback from students in the lab and from other instructors has led to important refinements. This feedback contributed significantly towards developing each lab project as a self-contained lab, free of entanglement.

Not Tied to a Specific System

In this book, there is no bias toward a particular operating system or compiler. All material applies to any computer system with C++. All software has been tested on the following systems: MS-DOS/Turbo C++ versions 3.0 and 3.1; MS-Windows/Borland C++ and Turbo C++ for Windows; MS-Windows/Microsoft Visual C++ version 1.0 (template classes excluded); Symantec/Macintosh C++; UNIX/Sun C++ (template classes excluded); and UNIX/GNU g++.

Acknowledgments

No textbook is developed in a vacuum. Critical feedback from students and other instructors is essential to creating a solid book. Thanks to my students at Penn State Berks and Pete Petrie's students at Wilkes Community College in North Carolina who class-tested various iterations of the manuscript over the last two years, especially Barry in Fall 1992 and Natasha and Maryann in Spring 1993.

Reviewers spend countless hours poring over material with a critical eye. Because of the high quality of reviewers that worked on this textbook, criticisms and recommendations were always considered seriously. No comment was ignored. Thanks to all of the following reviewers who helped to cohesively organize the content and presentation of the text:

Seth Bergman	*Rowan College of New Jersey*
Tom Bricker	*University of Wisconsin, Madison*
Ed Epp	*University of Portland*
James Heliotis	*Rochester Institute of Technology*
Vijaya Krishnamurthy	*Montgomery College*
Al Lake	*Oregon State University*
Michael Lutz	*Rochester Institute of Technology*
James Murphy	*California State University, Chico*
Rich Pattis	*University of Washington*
David Teague	*Western Carolina University*
Jerry Weltman	*Louisiana State University, Baton Rouge*

Ed Epp, Rich Pattis, David Teague, and Jerry Weltman in particular were extremely helpful.

There are many people who contributed to this textbook through electronic and personal conversations such as the 215 participants of the international discussion group "Teaching and Learning Object-Oriented Programming in the First Year" (CS1OBJ-L@PSUVM.PSU.EDU). Other individuals whose conversations resulted in important contributions and helped to shape opinions include Robert Stroud, Russel Winder, David Teague, E. T. "Pete" Petrie, Rich Pattis, Mitchell Model, John McCormick, Joseph Bergin, Dalton Hunkins, Linda Northrop, Jim Heliotis, Michael Lutz, Tim Budd, Mark Headington, John Barr, Frank Friedman, Joe Lambert, Suzanne Gladfelter, Dave Richards, and Michael Berman.

Publishers play key roles throughout the entire development, marketing, and support of a textbook. For an excellent job, and constant enthusiasm and support, thanks to the crew at Franklin, Beedle, and Associates: Jim Leisy, Ann Leisy, Samantha Soma, Bill DeRouchey, Christina Burress, Sean Lowery, Sandra Cho, Tom Sumner, Victor Kaiser, Daniel Stoops, Steve Klinetobe, and Jeff Tade, especially Sam, Jim, and Bill.

And as always, thanks to my family for the most important support that made this whole thing possible: Diane, Chelsea, Austen, and Kieran.

Table of Contents

Chapter 3
Abstractions   73

Chapter 4
Implementations   131

Chapter 5
Selections

Chapter 6
Repetitions   **239**

Chapter 7
Arrays

Chapter 8
Class Design and Implementation

Chapter 9
Pointers

Chapter 10
Templates

1

Program Development with Objects

First there is a need for a computer-based solution to a problem, or there is a desire to automate some existing process. The problem may be: Prove the existence of quarks. The process to be automated may be: Let the antilock brake system detect and avoid wheel lockup. From analysis of such problems and processes, we must progress toward *program implementation*—computer-based solutions. The progression from the analysis of the *problem specification* (the details of the problem) to the computer-based implementation is known as *program development.* Our study of computing fundamentals begins with an example of this process. In particular, the following three-step strategy embodies many problem-solving and program implementation issues that form a major focus of this text:

A Program Development Strategy

1. *Analysis*   Understand the problem, determine what the software is to do, and specify what the user needs to supply (input) to obtain the desired information (output).

2. *Design*   Plan a solution, order the steps that solve the problem, refine the design strategy through iteration, decompose a problem into smaller problems, look for existing software as building blocks for the new software, and identify objects.

3. *Implementation*   Use computer software and hardware to achieve an executable program that correctly solves the problem or automates the task. Verify that the program does what it is supposed to and that it does it correctly.

You are encouraged to remember and apply this three-step program development strategy to the lab projects. You are also encouraged to begin to view the world as a collection of interacting entities known as objects. The computer programming language we will be using, C++ (pronounced C plus plus), allows these real-world entities to be modeled in software.

After studying this chapter, you will be able to:
1. Understand how analysis and design help us progress toward a C++ implementation.
2. Implement simple C++ programs (after completing certain other lab activities).
3. Recognize and use three objects that appear in many programs.

1.1   Case Study: Grade Assessment

A computer is a system of *hardware*—the physical components—and *software*, automated versions of real-world processes and models of real-world objects. The process that will be automated in this case study is computation of a course grade. The existing objects modeled in software include the computer screen, the computer keyboard, and floating-point numbers (like 76.5). The discussion on floating-point numbers for computations, keyboard input, and screen output leads to opportunities to create simple programs that obtain input data from the user, compute numeric solutions, and display results to the computer screen.

Program development begins with a study, or *analysis,* of the problem. In order to determine what a program is to do, the problem must first be understood. If the problem is written down, the analysis phase can begin with a reading of the problem statement. It may be necessary to reread it, ask questions, and perhaps paraphrase the problem before ascertaining the input required by the program and the output the program is to generate. Specification of the input and output helps provide an overview of what the program is supposed to do. In textbook problems, input and output is either provided or is fairly easy to recognize. In real-world problems of significant scale, a great deal of effort may be expended in the analysis stage of program development. This case study presents a much simpler problem that relates to a situation you might have seen on a course syllabus.

Grade Assessment: Your final course grade is computed as a weighted average using this scale:

Item	*Percent of Final Grade*
Test 1 (0.0 to 100.0)	25%
Test 2 (0.0 to 100.0)	25%
Final Exam (0.0 to 100.0)	50%

Note: Whereas an average or mean is defined as the sum of a set of numbers divided by the number of elements in that set, a *weighted average* has some elements in the set with lesser or greater significance than others.

1.1.1   Analysis: Compute a Course Grade for One Course

From these grade assessment criteria, let us derive a problem:

Problem: *Using the grade assessment scale above, compute a course grade as a weighted average for any combination of two tests and one final exam.*

The analysis of this problem continues by establishing the required input and the desired output. The input is usually supplied at the keyboard by the user of the program, and the output is usually displayed on the computer screen. Determining what output is required from the problem statement is a good place to start. The output summarizes what the program is supposed to do. For this problem, the desired output is the course grade computed as a weighted average.

A problem specification may provide example output, like the following sample output that relates to this case study. When the course grade is computed as 80.25%, the output should look like this:

```
──────── Output ────────
    Course grade: 80.25%
```

This answer could be computed with paper and pencil and/or a calculator. The process could also be automated as a computer-based solution. In either circumstance, the input still needs to be stated more clearly.

Self-Check

1. Paraphrase the problem just given (rephrase the problem of grade assessment in your own words).
2. In general, what output must the computer-based solution generate?
3. Generally speaking, what input is required to compute the course grade?

Answers
1. Many answers are possible.
   Here's one: "Compute a course grade according to the scale given on the syllabus."
2. The label "Course grade: " followed by the final course grade as a percentage.
3. Two test scores and one final exam.

You will often be given a sample *dialogue* that also summarizes the input that must be supplied by the user. Such dialogues help answer questions about what the user is to see while the program is running (the user may be you, a lab assistant, a grader, or your instructor) and what is expected to complete the program. The dialogue consists of output generated by the program combined with user input. In this text, dialogues show input in italic and boldface (*74.0*, for example) to distinguish it from the program output (Final Exam:, for example). Here is one sample dialogue for the analysis at hand:

```
──────── Dialogue ────────
        Test 1: 74.0
        Test 2: 79.0
    Final Exam: 84.0
  Course Grade: 80.25%
```

The box represents a computer screen (or monitor).

From this dialogue we acquire the output the program is to generate. This includes the prompts `Test 1:`, `Test 2:`, and `Final Exam:`. The bold italic text represents the user-supplied input. In this sample dialogue, the person using the program entered *74.0*, *79.0*, and *84.0*. Next we have the solution expressed as the label `Course Grade:` followed by the course grade computed as a weighted average, followed by the percent symbol `%`.

These sample dialogues provide another benefit. They show an answer (80.25%) for one particular set of inputs. This information proves useful when the program undergoes testing. The input and the output are specified more precisely as follows:

Input: Test 1: 74.0   *Output:*   The course grade.
           Test 2: 79.0
           Final: 84.0

In addition to specifying input and output, sample dialogues provide other useful information. This one shows that all three inputs are numeric values with decimal points. This has implications for the choice of objects used to represent these tests that are input by the user. We will use several *float objects* that each store exactly one floating-point number for test1, test2, the final exam, and the course grade. Float objects are used because they are capable of storing a floating-point number (numeric values with decimal points), can be set to hold any numeric value we want through keyboard input, and may have arithmetic operations applied to them. Specifically, some float objects will have addition and multiplication operations applied while computing the course grade. Also, the result of computation (the course grade) is a float object that can be displayed to the computer screen as requested in the problem statement.

Two other objects that help develop this program include the keyboard object for input and the computer screen object for output. If we know beforehand that these objects exist, we are saved from the hassle of implementing floating-point arithmetic, generating computer screen output, and obtaining keyboard input. The proper objects and operations already exist (and we will see them previewed later in the implementation).

Now we have analyzed the problem, specified the input and output, and understood what the computer-based solution is to do. However, a critical component of the solution is still missing: We should also know how to do it! Next we move to the design phase of program development.

1.1.2 Design: An IPO Algorithm

The goal of this particular design is to have the correct number of instructions appear in the proper order. During the design phase of program development in this textbook, a variety of simple design tools are used to help provide proper and effective structuring of programs. These design tools will help us model, or plan, software solutions. They allow us to do something before sitting down at the computer and writing the code. In turn, we are more likely to find a correct solution to the problem. We now look at one design tool to help plan our program: an input, process, and output algorithm.

An *algorithm* is a set of instructions that solves a problem or accomplishes a task. Algorithms may be expressed as the instructions of a programming language. Algorithms may also be expressed in *pseudocode*—instructions expressed in a noncomputer language. Pseudocode is meant to be understood by humans, not by the computer. Pseudocode may also be more expressive since one pseudocode instruction may represent several programming language instructions. Also, using pseudocode means we do not have to be so concerned about such issues as misplaced punctuation marks or lack of implementation detail. In fact, a pseudocode solution will make our job easier by allowing details to be deferred. With pencil-and-paper pseudocode, we begin to design programs without a computer.

In this, the first of many analysis, design, and implementation case studies, the algorithm is based on an Input, Process, Output (IPO) model. The IPO algorithm provides a generic three-step solution to many problems.

IPO Model	A Generic IPO Algorithm
Input:	I Obtain the necessary input data
Process:	P Manipulate the data in some meaningful way
Output:	O Display the results of processing the data

When applied to our problem, this simple model helps us design a more specific algorithm.

IPO Model	One Specific IPO as Applied to This Case Study
Input:	I Obtain test 1, test 2, and the final exam
Process:	P Compute the course grade
Output:	O Display the course grade

By assuming that input and output operations are already implemented in the C++ programming language (and they are), we can implement the Input and Output portions of this algorithm by following the input and output specifications provided earlier. After we learn how to control the keyboard and screen objects through the C++ programming language, the Input and Output steps prove fairly easy to implement. However, the middle step needs further refinement. Specifically, how do we Process the input data to compute the course grade?

Self-Check
1. How many items are used to determine the final grade?
2. Is the final grade determined by a simple average, or a weighted average where items have different rather than equal weights?
3. Using pencil and paper, supply a reasonable set of inputs (between 50 and 100 points each, for example). Then compute the course grade as a weighted average based on your input data.

Answers
1. Three.
2. Weighted average.
3. There are many possible answers. When Test 1 = 74.0, Test 2 = 79.0, and the Final Exam = 84.0, the average is 0.25*74.0 + 0.25*79.0 + 0.50*84.0. The course grade = 18.5+19.75.0+42.0 = 80.25.

Since the three input items comprise varying portions of the final grade, we must compute a weighted average. For example, the simple average of the set 74.0, 79.0, and 84.0 is 79.0. With equal weights, each number is counted equally. However, the weighted average computes differently for this problem. Recall that the first two items are worth 25%, and the third (Final Exam) is 50% of the final grade. Using this input:

Test 1 = 74.0   Test 2 = 79.0   Final Exam = 84.0

the weighted average is computed to 80.25 as follows:

$$(0.25 \times 74.0) + (0.25 \times 79.0) + (0.50 \times 84.0) = 18.5 + 19.75 + 42.0 = 80.25$$

With the same exact grades, we see that the weighted average of 80.25 is computed differently from the simple average (79.0). Failure to follow the specification could result in students receiving grades lower than they earned.

Here is a more detailed version of the second step in our algorithm that computes a *weighted*, not simple, average. This is the Process step between the Input and Output portions of the algorithm.

One Refinement of the Input, Process, Output (IPO) Algorithm:

(I)   Obtain Test 1, Test 2, and the Final Exam from the user of the program.
(P)   Compute Course Grade as 25% of Test 1 plus 25% of Test 2 plus 50% of the Final Exam.
(O)   Display "Course grade" followed by the value of Course Grade, followed by "%".

It has been said that good artists know when to put away the brushes, paint, and easel. Deciding when a painting is complete is critical for its success. With this in mind, we must decide when to stop designing. Although we may need to return to either the analysis and/or the design phase, we will stop here and move to the third phase: program implementation. After all, a step-by-step pseudocode solution has now been established to compute the weighted average, and we have a set of test data with a known result (80.25%). This algorithm will now be translated into a C++ implementation.

1.1.3 Implementation

The implementation phase of program development requires both software and hardware to achieve an executable program that solves the problem or automates the task. For example, with the help of a text editor (software that allows us to create, save, and edit files containing programs), we translate algorithmic solutions such as the one shown above into the C++ programming language. The programs we write are translated into a lower level program understood by the computer by another piece of software known as the *compiler*. The C++ programs we write cannot be run directly on the computer. The programs must go through some transformations first, and the compiler is a vital part of the transformation to the executable program. Along the way, the compiler also detects and reports as many coding errors as possible.

These hardware components of a computer are also used: *memory* to store objects and executable programs while the computer is turned on, *disk drives* to store objects and executable programs more permanently (when the computer is off), the computer keyboard for data input, the screen for output, and so on. While the computer is running, an *operating system* (DOS, UNIX, or MacOS, for example) is another piece of software that is continuously performing many behind-the-scenes operations.

In this book, we will spend some time learning to control the computer with the C++ programming language. A *program* is a set of instructions that allows one to alter data stored in computer memory, display computations on the computer screen, and obtain input from the keyboard. These operations are implemented as the many C++ instructions that make up a program. We can view the computer as a machine controlled by the C++ instructions that we will learn to write. See Figure 1.1.

But the problem we now have is this: Do we learn small parts of this language and build up to a complete program that does something useful, or do we look at an entire program and then learn the coding details? Subsequent case studies will summarize recently covered concepts and constructs. However, in this particular case study, the C++ program instead acts as a preview to the language and as a springboard into some of the elements present in this program. In particular, we'll use the following C++ implementation of the problem solution to show the objects used to aid program development. You are not expected to understand any of the many details of C++ programs that are present—and there are many things to cover. In fact, it will take until the end of Chapter 2 to cover them.

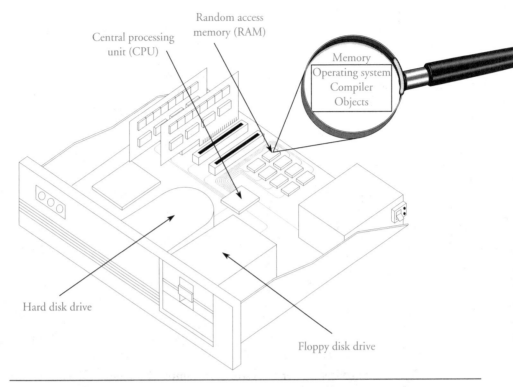

Figure 1.1   Computer components

Instead, just peruse this C++ program and observe the highlighted names that represent the three classes (categories) of objects present in this program. They are: the float objects named test1, test2, finalExam, and courseGrade; the computer screen object referred to as cout; and the keyboard object referred to as cin.

```
// Compute a final course grade percentage with user-supplied input
#include <iostream.h>

int main()
{
  // Declare (bring names into the program), some float objects for
  // input of numeric data and for computation of the course grade:
  float test1 = 0.0;
  float test2 = 0.0;
  float finalExam = 0.0;
  float courseGrade = 0.0;

  // I)nput: Interactively obtain input:
  cout << "     Test 1: ";
  cin >> test1;    // Reset test1's state through keyboard input
```

```
cout << "      Test 2: ";
cin >> test2;
cout << "  Final Exam: ";
cin >> finalExam;

// P)rocess: Compute the weighted average and store it in courseGrade:
courseGrade = 0.25 * test1 + 0.25 * test2 + 0.50 * finalExam;

// O)utput: Display final grade percentage:
cout << endl;      // Generate a new line on the screen
cout << "Course grade: " << courseGrade << "%" << endl;

   return 0;
}
```

```
───────────────────────── Dialogue ─────────────────────────
        Test 1: 74.0
        Test 2: 79.0
    Final Exam: 84.0

Course Grade: 80.25%
```

1.1.3.1   Objects

Objects can be viewed as entities stored in computer memory. Objects are things that we can apply operations to. Every object has its own identity (a name), a well-defined state (value(s) stored in computer memory), and operations (such as assignment =, multiplication *, addition +, input >>, and output <<). For example, the preceding program *declares*—brings names into a program—four `float` objects named `test1`, `test2`, `finalExam`, and `courseGrade`. Each `float` object maintains the value of exactly one floating-point number (a numeric value with a decimal component such as 1.23 or -99.876). Each of these `float` objects is given an initial value of 0.0 when it is declared. Some of these `float` objects store values entered by the user. They are then used to help compute the final course grade. The computed answer, stored in the `float` object named `courseGrade`, is then sent to the screen as output.

Here are the three attributes of objects—identity, state, and operations—as they apply to the `float` objects in the previous program.

Attributes of Objects

Identity	All four `float` objects have their own *identity* because each has its own name.
State	The *state* of all four `float` objects is arbitrarily initialized to 0.0 like this:

```
float test1 = 0.0;
```

Attributes of Objects (continued)

Operations   The state of an object may be altered or examined through a variety of other *operations*. For example, the state of test1 (a float object) was altered through the keyboard input operation like this:

```
cin >> test1; // Alter test1's state with input operation
```

Multiplication and addition operations were applied and courseGrade was altered like this:

```
courseGrade = 0.25 * test1 + 0.25 * test2 ...
```

The state of courseGrade (a float object) was examined through this output operation:

```
cout << "Course grade: " << courseGrade << "%" << endl;
```

Input, output, multiplication, and addition represent only a portion of the operations that can be applied to float objects. The multiplication operation, symbolized as *, allows for computations such as 0.25 * test1. Any float object may have the addition operation, symbolized as +, applied to it (the details of these and other float operations are provided in Chapter 2)[1]. And shortly we will see how this program contains objects to model the computer screen for output (cout) and the keyboard for input (cin).

1.1.4   Testing the Implementation

Each case study in this textbook consists of the following sections:

1. Analysis
2. Design
3. Implementation
4. Testing the Implementation

The section titled "Testing the Implementation" is at the end of each case study. But don't let the placement of this fourth section make you think testing must be deferred until implementation. The important process of testing may, can, and should occur at any moment during program development. Testing takes the form of asking questions during the analysis phase (testing our understanding of the problem), walking through the algorithm (verifying that the proper steps are in the correct order), and establishing a *test oracle*—a collection of inputs and the predicted outputs. A test oracle should be

---

[1] float objects are also called float variables. The terms *object* and *variable* are interchangeable.

complete before the program is coded, not after. When the C++ implementation finally does generate output, the output prediction can be compared to the actual program output. Adjustments must be made any time the predicted output of the test oracle does not match the program output. This would indicate that the test oracle, the program output, or both have been computed incorrectly. The use of test oracles in program analysis and design helps to avoid the misconception that a program is correct just because there is output.

After a program has been successfully compiled, converted into an executable program, and run, it must be tested. One simple testing procedure involves supplying data that produces a known result. For example, we could use the test oracle established earlier during program analysis. With the given data, the average of 80.25 was computed. With the same data entered by the user during program execution, the same result should be displayed. If we get different answers, either the test oracle is incorrect, or the program is incorrect. If the program output matches the predicted test oracle output, confidence that the implementation is correct is improved by expanding the test oracle to include other sets of input data and predicted outputs.

For example, an additional set of input that is easy to test is three equal values. With test1 = 80.5, test2 = 80.5 and a finalExam of 80.5, the weighted average is easily predicted to be 80.5. With this specific test data entered as user input, the program should generate the same output (80.5). The following test oracle summarizes these first two test cases with two additional ones:

	Weights	Prediction #1	Prediction #2	Prediction #3	Prediction #4
Test 1	25%	*74.0*	*80.5*	*60.0*	*80.0*
Test 2	25%	*79.0*	*80.5*	*70.0*	*70.0*
Final Exam	50%	*84.0*	*80.5*	*80.0*	*60.0*
	Grade	80.25	80.5	72.5	67.5

Test Oracle

Before we conclude that rigorous testing proves a program correct, one more point must be made. E. W. Dijkstra has shown that testing only reveals the presence of errors, not the absence of errors. Even with a test oracle in place and matching program output, the program is not proven to be correct. Instead, our confidence is increased that the algorithm (implemented as a program) appears to be reliable. But if you begin to think that you can find all the errors in every one of your programs yourself, try letting another programmer (friend, lab consultant, teacher assistant, or instructor) "break" your program. He or she is likely to uncover errors of which you were unaware, especially as your programs grow in complexity.

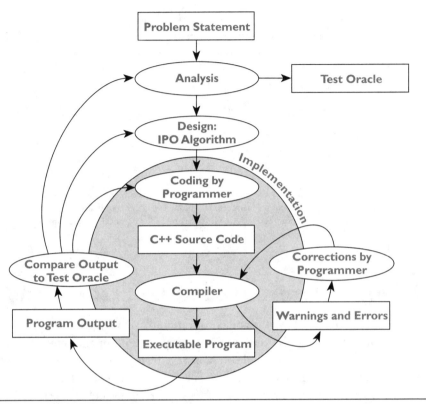

Figure 1.2   Software Development—Analysis, Design, and Implementation

Self-Check

1. Write a test oracle with two predictions for the weighted average case study. Use the grade assessment scale given at the beginning of this case study.

2. Determine the final grade percentage using this scale:

Midterm Exam	20%
Final Exam	30%
Quiz Average	30%
Lab Projects	20%

and this data:

Midterm Exam	87.0
Final Exam	82.0
Quizzes (equal weight)	90.0, 80.0, 100.0
Lab Projects (equal weight)	90.0, 90.0, 90.0, 100.0, 100.0, 100.0

3. Can we prove a program is correct if no errors are found during testing?
4. Why should we test our programs?
5. Why should we let a friend or instructor test our programs?

Answers

1. There are many possible solutions. This question was asked to let you practice predicting program output before the program is implemented.

   Test Oracle

Test 1	70	90
Test 2	80	80
Final Exam	90	70
Course Grade	82.5	77.5

2. 88.0
3. No, testing detects the presence of errors, not the absence of errors.
4. We can detect and correct many errors while increasing our confidence in the program.
5. Another person can view the code with detachment and not make assumptions about anything being correct. They might find errors you don't.

1.2   Input and Output Objects: cin and cout

A program must have the ability to communicate with the user. Such communication is provided through (but not limited to) keyboard input and screen output. This two-way communication is a critical component of many programs. For example, a program that proves the existence of quarks, yet fails to inform anyone of the results is a waste of time and energy. A program that computes when to apply and release the brakes of an antilock brake system is dangerous unless input and output are communicated in a proper manner. We now look at an object to which we can send data for screen display. We can do several things to this object named cout (common output). For example, the appearance of output can be controlled (number of significant digits, column width of each displayed object, and so on). But for now, let's concentrate on the operation symbolized as <<. First, we must consider the notion of a programming language statement.

A C++ *statement* is composed of several components that have been legally grouped together to perform some action. One frequently seen statement uses cout and the operator << to generate screen output. The general form is given as

cout   << *expression-1* << *expression-2* ... << *expression-N* ;

where cout represents the computer screen object and *expression-1* through *expression-N* may take the form of float objects or string constants such as " Final Exam: ". The *insertion operator*, <<, indicates the direction in which data is flowing—toward the screen object named cout. Finally, a semicolon (;) is used to terminate the statement. For example:

```
cout << "This text appears on the computer screen";
```

Unless we do something special, all output appears on the same line of the computer screen. With only one cout object and multiple occurrences of the insertion operator <<, many expressions will appear on the same line. For example, the following statement uses cout once to display a *string constant* (a collection of characters delimited by the double quote marks " and "), an arithmetic expression (the floating-point constants with division and multiplication operators, symbolized as / and *, respectively) and another string constant:

```
cout << "One day represents "
     << (1.0 / 365.0 * 100.0)
     << "% of a non-leap year";
```

--- **Output** ---
```
One day represents 0.273973% of a non-leap year
```

Any subsequent output would appear immediately to the right of "year" because no new line is encountered at the end of this cout statement. New lines are generated when the C++ expression endl is sent to the output device.

1.2.1   New Lines with endl

During a cout insertion operation, the expression *endl* will generate a new line on the computer screen. The cursor is sent to the beginning of the next line on the screen. For example, in the following C++ program, endl is used several times within one cout statement that is long enough to require several new lines for readability (notice that there is only one semicolon after the last endl):

```
// This program contains one very long cout statement. A total
// of 17 expressions (including endls) are inserted
// into the output stream identified as cout (the screen).
#include <iostream.h>

int main()
{
  cout << "One day is " << (1.0/365.0*100) << '%'          << endl
       << "of a year, but in a leap year, one day is"      << endl
       << "only " << (1.0/366.0*100) << "% of a year."     << endl
                                                           << endl
       << "Incidentally, is the year 2000 the first year"  << endl
       << "of the next century or does the 21st century"   << endl
       << "begin on January 1, 2001?"                      << endl;

  return 0;
}
```

```
─────────────────── Output ───────────────────
One day is 0.273973%
of a year, but in a leap year, one day is
only 0.273224% of a year.

Incidentally, is the year 2000 the first year
of the next century or does the 21st century
begin on January 1, 2001?
```

1.2.2   Keyboard Input with cin >>

The state of certain objects is frequently altered through keyboard input. This is accomplished by using the input object named cin (common input) and the *extraction* operator >>. For example, the following statement alters the state of the float object finalExam with data supplied by the user:

```
cin >> finalExam; // Change finalExam's state through keyboard input
```

The general form of the cin statement to extract float objects is:

cin >> *float-object-1* >> *float-object-2, ... ,* >> *float-object-N* ;

where cin >> *float-object-N* may be followed by other float objects so long as they are separated by the extraction operator. For example:

```
cin >> test1 >> test2;
```

The cin and cout objects are examples of *streams*—abstractions referring to the flow of data from some source to some destination. Characters are inserted into output streams and extracted from input streams.

To write even the simplest input/output program, we need to know several details of C++. One involves the inclusion of the file iostream.h (*iostream* is an abbreviation for input/output stream) into our programs. To make the cin and cout objects available, the following code must be added at the beginning of a file containing the program:

```
#include <iostream.h>
```

This automatically makes cout available as the screen object and cin available as the keyboard object.

Programming Tip ─────────────────────────────────

If the file iostream.h is not included, the compiler will object with error messages such as Undefined symbol 'cout'. The appearance of cin and endl would also be undefined and the program would not run.

1.2.3 Interactive I/O

The cin and cout objects are often used in concert to prompt the user for input. This is called interactive input/output (I/O) and it goes something like this:

1. Prompt the user for a value using the cout statement.
2. Extract the value(s) from the keyboard using the cin object to alter the state of certain objects.

```
cout << " Final exam: ";
cin >> finalExam;
```

To summarize, here is a complete program that uses interactive I/O to determine the average of three test scores (*Note:* The float division operation is symbolized as /):

```
// Display a prompt, read three test scores,
// compute the average, display the average.
#include <iostream.h>

int main()
{
  float x, y, z, average;

  // Prompt:
  cout << "Enter three floating point values separated by spaces: ";

  // Input:
  cin >> x >> y >> z;

  // Process:
  average = (x + y + z) / 3.0;

  // Output:
  cout << endl
       << "Average: " << average
       << endl;

  return 0;
}
```

Dialogue

```
Enter three floating point values separated by spaces: 4.1  5.2  6.0

Average: 5.1
```

After the three numeric values are typed, the user must press the Enter (or Return) key. Only then can the extraction operation processes the entire line of input containing three floating-point constants.

Programming Tip

Consider what happens if the user enters invalid data, or the incorrect number of inputs. If less than three numbers are entered, the program waits for a third. If more than three numbers are entered, the fourth is not processed—at least not at first. Any additional values are still waiting to be processed (they are part of cin's state) and they will be the first to be extracted with the next cin statement. Finally, if a bad numeric data value is entered (BAD rather than 4.1, for instance), the input stream is corrupted and subsequent cin statements are skipped.

A few more programming details (covered formally in the next chapter) are previewed here without explanation to allow you to complete all end-of-chapter lab projects. Every C++ program should have a line like this:

```
int main()
```

with statements residing between curly braces, { and }. The last statement should be

```
return 0;
```

and if your program is to perform any input and output operations, #include <iostream.h> must be placed at the beginning of your program. You may also want to include documentation such as your name, the project number, or a description of what the program does. This information may be in the form of comments, which is any text after //. Much more will be said about comments and these other elements in Chapter 2, so for now, these details are summarized with the following code, which does nothing but provide an outline of the minimum code necessary for a program.

```
// Your Name
// Lab 1D
// Due date: Day-Month-Year
//
// Description: This program computes the course grade as ...
//
#include <iostream.h>
```

```
int main()
{
  // Place your declarations and statements here
  // ...

  return 0;
}
```

Self-Check

1. Write the output generated by the following program:

    ```
    #include <iostream.h>
    int main()
    {
        cout << "+--+"
             << "+   +"
             << "+   +"
             << "+--+";
        return 0;
    }
    ```

2. Write the output generated by the following program:

    ```
    #include <iostream.h>
    int main()
    {
        cout << "+--+" << endl
             << "+   +" << endl
             << "+   +" << endl
             << "+--+" << endl;
        return 0;
    }
    ```

3. Write the entire dialogue generated by the following program when *5.2* and
    6.3 are entered at the prompt. Make sure you include write the user-supplied
    input as well as all program output including the prompt:

    ```
    #include <iostream.h>
    int main()
    {
        float x, y;
        cout <<" Enter two floats: ";
        cin >> x >> y;
        cout << (x * (1 + y)) << endl;
        return 0;
    }
    ```

4. Write a complete program that inputs two `floats` and outputs their sum.

Answers

```
1.  +--++  ++  ++--+
2.  +--+
    +  +
    +  +
    +--+
3.  Enter two floats: 5.2 6.3
    37.96
4.  #include <iostream.h>
    int main()
    {
      float x, y;
      cout <<"Enter two floats: ";
      cin >> x >> y;
      cout << "Sum: " << (x + y) << endl;
      return 0;
    }
```

Chapter Summary

Program development consists of three phases: analysis, design, and implementation. This same three-step program development strategy, introduced within the context of a case study, will continue to be used in subsequent chapters. During each case study, testing is explored as a tool to build confidence that our solution satisfies the problem specification.

Objects are entities that have an identity (name), state (value), and operations. Only a few of the many available `float` operations were shown, including addition and subtraction. We also saw how insertion operations symbolized as `cout <<`, and extraction operations symbolized as `cin >>`, are used in concert to prompt for interactive input, a frequently used technique to alter the state of objects in meaningful ways. Knowledge of existing objects aids the program development process. For example, knowing about `cin`, `cout`, and `float` objects allows us to avoid implementation of operations such as input, output, addition, and multiplication, since these operations are already defined for us. The objects named `cout` and `cin` are so frequently used that they are made available for easy screen (or window) output and for keyboard input.

Objects also interact with each other. For example, `float` objects can be displayed on the screen by interacting with the `cout` object. Also, the state of `float` objects are altered through interaction with the `cin` object.

Exercises

1. *Problem: With input of three unique digits (0 through 9), display all possible orderings of those three digits.*
   a. Analyze the problem and write down the required input and output.
   b. Design a solution using an algorithm written in pseudocode. This problem requires input and output, but no processing. *Hint:* One float object can store exactly one digit such as 0, 1, or 9.
   c. Develop a test oracle.

2. *Problem: For any two floating-point inputs for float objects a and b, display the sum (a+b) and the product (a x b).*
   a. Analyze the problem and write down the required input and output.
   b. Design a solution using an IPO algorithm written in pseudocode.
   c. Develop a test oracle.

3. *Problem: Find the average of five tests of equal weight.*
   a. Analyze the problem and write down the required input and output.
   b. Design a solution using an IPO algorithm written in pseudocode.
      Hint: One process step might be "Compute sum."
   c. Develop a test oracle.

4. *Problem: You happen to know that a store has a 50% markup on all merchandise. If the retail price (what you pay) of a compact disc (CD) player is 300.00, how much did the store pay for the CD player (the wholesale price)? What is the wholesale price for any item given the retail price?*
   a. Paraphrase the problem.
   b. Identify the known quantities (float objects).
   c. Identify all input that is required.
   d. Identify the value that must be computed.
   e. Write a complete IPO algorithm that solves the problem. You do not need the formula to compute the unknown value. At this point, it is enough to say this: "Compute the unknown value *x*," where *x* is your answer to question 10d.
   f. Now express any relationships in the form of an algebraic expression.
   g. Express the algebraic equation with the unknown on one side of the equal sign.
   h. Write a test oracle for the wholesale cost of the CD player.
   i. Rewrite your entire algorithm using your formula. Be consistent with the names for all objects involved.
   j. Using program examples from Chapter 1 as a guide, write a complete C++ program that implements your solution.

5. Using program examples from Chapter 1 as a guide, write a complete C++ program that prompts for a number from 0.0 through 1.0 and stores this input value into the `float` object named `relativeError`. Echo the input. The dialogue generated by your program should look like this:

```
Enter relativeError[0.0,1.0]:  0.341
You entered: 0.341
```

Lab Projects

I A   Getting Prepared

Obtain the instructions necessary to create, compile, link, and execute a C++ program on your system. You may need a log-in procedure and basic editing commands such as one to save a file. After this, write a complete algorithm that provides all necessary steps to successfully guide a novice to complete a program through testing. Your algorithm may contain steps such as "Create a new file," "Save the source code," or "Compare test oracle predictions to program output."

I B   Using Objects

Create a new file, using the naming conventions appropriate for your system, and carefully retype the following program exactly as shown. Make sure you run it too:

```
#include <iostream.h>
int main()
{
  cout << "Hello world!";
  return 0;
}
```

- Modify this program so that it displays your name with one blank line before and after the line that only contains your name. Compile, and if necessary edit, the program until successful.
- Run the program and verify that your name appears as output on its own line.

I C   Using Objects

One small coding error may cause the report of many errors at compiletime. For the beginning programmer, this can be misleading. For example, a missing semicolon may result in dozens of errors throughout a program. You are now asked to observe what happens when a brace is left out of the program.

- Create a new file and prepare to edit a new program.

- Carefully retype the following program.

```
// Your Name
#include <iostream.h>
int main()
// <- Leave off {
  float x = 2.3;
  float y = 4.5;
  cout << "x: " << x << endl;
  cout << "y: " << y << endl;
  return 0;
}
```

- Compile this program and write the number of errors that occurred at compile-time.
- Add the missing { on a new line after int main() and compile the source code again.
- If necessary, edit, save, and compile this program until there are no compiletime errors.

Various versions of C++ allows a wide variety of skeleton programs. These include, but are not limited to, the following (some do not work on all systems):

```
main()          main()          void main()     void main(void)
{               {               {               {
  // ...          // ...          // ...           // ...
}                 return 0;      }               }
                }
```

The one you use depends on the system that you are using. But there is no single "right" way. However, it does help to pick one style and stay with it consistently. The approach consistently used in this textbook,

```
int main()
{
  // ...
  return 0;
}
```

should be accepted by every system. It avoids certain warnings and errors the other styles may cause. On the other hand, forgetting return 0; or using void may cause the compiler to generate an error or warning. Find out how your system handles a few of these different situations.

- Delete the line with return 0; and compile the program.
- Your compiler may have generated an error or a warning such as Function

should `return a value.` You can eliminate this warning (and some systems will not let the program run) by keeping the line `return 0;` as the last statement in every program. If you have to do this now, remember to include "`return 0;`" as the last statement in future programs:

```
...
cout << "k: " << k << endl;
 return 0; // Removes compiler warning
}
```

• Change the line `int main()` to `void main()`, delete the line with `return 0;` (because `void` means `return` cannot be used), and compile the program. Your system may generate a warning, or it may run without error or warning.

Although you may use several styles, it is recommended that you follow the convention used in this textbook. Remember to use `int main()` and `return 0;`.

Now for one last excursion in a sea of compiletime error messages, try this:

• Delete the entire line with the include directive `#include <iostream.h>`. Compile the program and record all error messages.

I D   Using Objects

Write a C++ program that displays your initials to the screen in large letters. There are no input or process steps, only output. For example, if your initials are E.T.M, the output should be

```
EEEEE   TTTTTTT     M     M
E          T        M M M M
EEEEE      T        M   M   M
E          T        M     M
EEEEE o    T   o    M     M o
```

I E   Using Objects

Write a complete C++ program that declares (brings names into the program) two `float` objects named `op1` and `op2` and initializes them to 0.0. Then extract values for these objects from the keyboard and show the sum of the two. If the user enters *2.67* and *1.23*, your dialogue should look *exactly* like this:

```
Enter two floats: 2.67  1.23
Sum: 3.9
```

2

Programs

We have now seen one example of program development while observing a few useful objects: cin, cout, and some float objects. In this chapter we turn to some details of program coding. We begin with a discussion of *tokens*—the smallest recognizable units of a programming language. Next, our attention turns to some more simple yet complete C++ programs. This involves a study of C++ syntax and the manner in which tokens form expressions, statements, and other larger units such as complete programs. After studying this chapter, you will be able to:

1. Understand the basic structure of simple C++ programs.
2. Recognize C++ tokens such as special symbols, identifiers, constants, and keywords.
3. Create valid programmer-defined identifiers.
4. Declare and manipulate int, float, and char objects.
5. Use assignments and initializations to alter the state of objects.
6. Evaluate a variety of arithmetic expressions.
7. Understand the types of errors that occur during program development.
8. Implement simple input/output programs.

2.1 Tokenizing a C++ Program

A C++ program is a sequence of characters created with a text editor and stored as a file. The names of files containing C++ programs typically end with .C, .cc, or .CPP (first.C, first.cc, or FIRST.CPP, for example). Some programming environments require or assume certain file-naming conventions. Therefore the extensions you should—or must— use depend on your operating system and compiler. The text contained in a program file is referred to as the *source code*.

The following short C++ program is presented here to show how the compiler views source code as a collection of tokens:

```
// Comment: This is a complete C++ program
#include <iostream.h>

int main()
{
   cout << "Hello, World!";
   return 0;
}
```

The C++ compiler translates source code into an executable program. This source code represents input to the compiler. Along the way, the compiler may generate error and warning messages. The errors are detected as the compiler scans the source code of the program and any "include" files that represent additional source code. For example, the file named `iostream.h` precedes the code beginning at `main()` and so the source of that other file becomes part of the program.

Every C++ program uses more than one file to take advantage of the code produced by other programmers. In fact, C++ compilers are delivered with a large number of files. Here is one general form that makes other code become part of our programs:

```
#include < include-file >
```

where `#include` and the angle brackets `< >` are used exactly as written and *include-file* is any valid system filename. (*Note:* Some compilers require that # be in column 1.) For example, our small program contains the following include directive in order to furnish the output object named `cout`:

```
#include <iostream.h>
```

The C++ compiler reads the source code and identifies the tokens, the smallest recognizable components of a program. Tokens include special symbols such as ( ) { << ; and }, and identifiers such as `main`. Programs also contains *white space*—the name given to spaces, tabs, and the invisible newline characters embedded in the source code. The compiler reads source code in a character-by-character fashion, so it begins to process the source code of the Hello World program by first recognizing the two consecutive characters `//` as the beginning of a *comment:*

```
// Comment: This is a complete C++ program
```

The next line causes the compiler to process the source code from the file `iostream.h`:

```
#include <iostream.h>
```

Include directives are neither tokens nor white space. Rather, they are instructions telling the compiler to use the source code stored in another file, specifically, the file named `iostream.h`. The compiler continues to parse the source code by stripping out all white space until the "i" in `int` is encountered.

```
int main()
```

The "i" begins a C++ keyword (a word reserved for a specific purpose). This is separated from the next token with white space (the blank before "m"). The next token, "main", is a name that must be part of every C++ program. This name is terminated by the occurrence of a special symbol—the open parentheses "(". The open parentheses and the close parentheses ")" are followed by the left brace, "{", which is another special symbol. The compiler continues to scan the source code in a character-by-character fashion.

The next token found in the source code is the identifier cout, followed by the special symbol <<, followed by the string constant "Hello, World!".

Figure 2.1   Tokens in the "Hello, World" program

The compiler continues to tokenize (break up the source code) until the end of the file to establish the following list of tokens (notice that blanks, comments, and include directives are not part of this token list):

Tokens in the "Hello, World" program

1.	int	keyword
2.	main	identifier
3.	(	special symbol
4.	)	special symbol
5.	{	special symbol
6.	cout	identifier
7.	<<	special symbol
8.	"Hello, World!"	string constant
9.	;	special symbol
10.	return	keyword
11.	0	int constant
12.	;	special symbol
13.	}	special symbol

2.1.1   Special Symbols

In C++, tokens consist of special symbols, identifiers, keywords, and constants. Special symbols are used as operators and to separate other tokens. A special symbol is a sequence of one or two characters with one or possibly many specific meanings. Here is a partial list of single-character and double-character special symbols frequently seen in C++ programs:

(.   +   -   /   *   =   <   >=   //   {   }   ==   ;   <<   >>   )

2.1.2   Identifiers: Standard and Programmer-Defined

All C++ compilers are required to declare certain identifiers. An *identifier* is a wordlike token that can be used with little effort so long as we are aware of its existence and purpose. As shown earlier, one such identifier, cout, is the program name for the computer screen object. Another identifier, cin, is the program name for the computer keyboard object. Here are some other *standard identifiers* made available through the proper include files:

```
cin   cout   endl   exit   precision   width   pow   rand   sqrt
```

We declare our own identifiers for use in almost all C++ programs. Such *programmer-defined identifiers* have meaning to the programmer who created the program, to others who might later use it, and to those who must maintain the program. We saw some of these programmer-defined identifiers in previous code (testOne, finalExam, courseGrade, and main, for example). Here are some rules that govern the creation of C++ identifiers:

- Identifiers begin with upper- or lowercase letters (the underscore character (_) may be used as the first character of an identifier, but this should be avoided).
- The first letter may be followed by a number of upper- and lowercase letters, digits, and underscore characters.
- Identifiers are case sensitive. For example, Ident, ident, and iDENT represent three different identifiers.
- The number of significant characters used to distinguish identifiers is compiler dependent, but we can always count on at least eight significant characters. In this textbook, a maximum length of 32 characters is used. Here are some examples of valid identifiers:

Valid Identifiers

name	incomeTax	j	MAX_SIZE
PIN	employee	x	top_employee
balance	string	n	worldInMotion

- Here are a few invalid identifiers:

Invalid Identifier   Reason

Invalid Identifier	Reason
1A	Begins with a digit
miles/Hour	"/" is unacceptable
first Name	(blank) is unacceptable
pre-shrunk	"-" is unacceptable inside a program

Programming Tip ───

Don't ignore the case sensitivity of C++. For example, every complete program must include the identifier `main` followed by `()`. `MAIN` or `Main` won't do; the program will not run.

Also note that several conventions may be used for upper- and lowercase letters. Some programmers prefer avoiding uppercase letters, others prefer to use uppercase letters for each new word. The convention used in this textbook is the `camelBack` style where each *new* word has an uppercase letter. For example, you will see `letterGrade` rather than `lettergrade`, `LetterGrade`, or `letter_grade`. Certain other identifiers will be written with all uppercase letters like this: `MAXIMUM`.

2.1.3   Keywords

Keywords are wordlike tokens that exist for a specific purpose—they may not be used for anything else. All keywords are said to be reserved. They are predefined identifiers whose meaning is fixed by the language. Unlike standard identifiers such as `cout`, `endl`, and `cin`, keywords cannot be redeclared to mean anything else. So far we have only seen the keywords `float` and `return`. Here is a partial list that covers the majority of keywords used throughout this textbook:

auto	default	for	operator	switch
break	do	goto	return	typedef
case	double	if	short	unsigned
char	else	int	sizeof	void
class	float	long	struct	while

The case sensitivity of C++ applies not only to identifiers, but also to keywords. For example, there is a difference between `float`, `Float`, and `FLOAT`. The only proper reference to `float` is the one with all lowercase letters.

2.1.4   Constants

The C++ compiler recognizes several types of *constants* (also called literals). These include string, integer, floating-point, and character constants. A string constant is a set of zero or more characters enclosed within a pair of double-quote special symbols (finished on the same editing line):

```
"Double quotes are used to delimit string constants."
"Hello, World!"
```

Also allowed in string constants are escape sequences to control the appearance of output. An escape sequence is the backslash character (\) followed by one or more other characters. For example, the *newline escape sequence* "\n" is used to send the cursor to the beginning of a new line:

```
"\n This string is guaranteed to be on its very own line \n"
```

In addition to string constants, C++ programs may contain constants that represent integer, floating-point, or character values. Some of these constants were introduced in Chapter 1, but here is a summary of tokens that represent valid constants in C++:

Integer constants	Floating-point	Character constants	String constants
-32768	-1.0	'A'	"A"
-1	0.0	'a'	"Hello"
0	39.95	'1'	"1"
1	1.3e-5	'$'	"\n\n"
32767	1.234e02	'\n'	"Bob's Cafe"

Floating-point constants may be expressed in exponential notation where the e means "times 10 raised to the power of." For example, 1.3e-2 is 1.3 times 10 raised to the power of -2, or 0.013. 1.2e02 can also be expressed as 120.0. Letters, digits, special characters like @ or :, and escape sequences enclosed in single quotes (apostrophes) are considered to be character, not string constants. The difference is subtle.

Programming Tip ────────

Numeric constants have a limited range, so all possible (an infinite number) integer and floating-point values cannot be represented on a computer. The range varies among systems (compiler/computer combinations). The range of int on some systems is -32768..32767, whereas on other systems the range of ints is -2147483648..2147483647. A situation like this, where results vary between computers or compilers, is referred to as *system dependent*.

2.1.5 Comments

Comments are portions of text that annotate a program. They fulfill any or all of the following functions:

- Provide internal documentation to help one programmer read another's program (assuming the comments clarify the meaning of the more obscure code).
- Help a programmer understand his or her own program, especially during program implementation.
- Explain certain code fragments or the reason an object is declared as part of a program.

- Indicate the programmer's name and the goal of the program for grading purposes.
- Help explain the programs in this textbook.

Comments may be added anywhere throughout the program, including to the right of any C++ statement, on a separate line, or over several lines. They may begin with the two-character special symbol /* when closed with the corresponding symbol */:

```
/* Update Customer Record */
/*
   A comment may extend
   over many lines
*/
```

An alternate form for comments is to use // before the text. Such a comment may appear on a line by itself or at the end of a line:

```
// -----------------------------------------------
// This is a complete C++ program that does nothing
// -----------------------------------------------
int main()
{ // These types of comments terminate at the end of the line
   float distance; // Store travel to the nearest tenth of a kilometer
   // ... Indicates additional statements
   return 0;       // Tell the operating system everything is okay
}
```

Programming Tip

Within the context of the programs in this textbook, comments are most often written as one-line comments like //Comment rather than /*Comment*/. The one-line comments are a personal preference because they make it more difficult to accidentally comment out large sections of code. Because all code after /* is a comment until */ is encountered, using those special symbols may accidentally turn a large portion of the program into a comment—text in the source code that is ignored by the compiler.

Comments can also be used in place of code during program development. This allows details to be deferred while simpler portions of the code are written. These comments may remain to help explain to other programmers (or graders) the more difficult-to-understand portions of the source code:

```
//
// Add documentation later ...
//
#include <iostream.h>

int main()
{
  float answer;
  // I'll determine if any more objects are needed later
  // Obtain input    (Figure out how to do this later)
  // Compute answer (Defer the details)
  cout << answer;
}
```

Comments are added to help clarify and document the purpose of the source code. The goal is to make the program more understandable, easier to *debug* (correct errors), and easier to maintain (change when necessary). Programmers need comments to understand programs that may have been written days, weeks, months, or years ago.

Self-Check

1. List two special symbols that are one character in length.
2. List two special symbols that are two characters in length.
3. List two standard identifiers.
4. Create two programmer-defined identifiers.
5. Which of the following are invalid identifiers?

   a. abc   e. float   i. sales Tax
   b. 123.0   f. (j. sales_tax
   c. ABC   g. 123   k. a
   d. #include   h. mispellted   l. _

6. Which of the following are valid identifiers?

   a. my Age   e. H.P.   i. salesTax
   b. #define   f. jaykay   j. Mile/Hour
   c. Abc!   g. 55_mph   k. 1
   d. int   h. mispellted   l. #

7. Which of these tokens

   234   1.0   1.0e+03   "H"   'H'   "integer"   '\n'   -123

   a. are valid string constants?
   b. are valid integer constants?
   c. are valid floating-point constants?
   d. are valid character constants?

8. Which of the following are valid C++ comments?

   a. `//  Is this a comment?`

   b. `/ / Is this a comment?`

   c. `/* Is this a comment?`

   d. `/* Is this a comment? */`

Answers

1. `+, - (*, /)`
2. `==, /* (++, //, /*, */, <=, >=, >>, <<)`
3. `cout, cin (endl, exit)`
4. `oneIdent, anotherIdent (others_are_possible)`
5. b, d, e, f, g, i
6. f, h, i (*Note:* `int` is not an identifier because `int` is a keyword)
7. a. `"H", "integer"`   b. `234, -123`   c. `1.0, 1.0e+03`   d. `'H', '\n'`
8. a, d (b: / is separated from / by a space, c: */ is missing)

2.2 float, int, and char Objects

Objects are entities stored in memory. The state of any particular object is initialized, examined, or altered through the operations defined for the class (category) of objects and the particular object name.

The set of values that an object may store during program execution along with the operations that manipulate that object is said to be a *class* or *data type*[1]. The class, or data type, acts as model to create many objects of the class. For example, `float` is one class that allows us to declare many floating-point objects.

Objects are so important to input, processing, and output that they are used in virtually all programs. If we need an object to store a numeric value with a fractional part, we can specify the `float` class. If a single character or an escape sequence needs to be stored, the `char` class could be used. If we are interested in whole numbers (integers), the `int` class of object can be used. So how is all of this accomplished?

The easy way to use objects of any class is to let the compiler do the work for us through a process known as object declaration. In general, a *declaration* refers to the introduction of one or more names into a program. So the term *object declaration* is given to the introduction of one or more objects into a program. An object declaration reserves and names computer memory to store the state (value) of a specific object. One form of object declaration is

    class-name   object-identifier-list ;

---

[1]The terms *class* and *data type* are used interchangeably. Although these two items are not exactly the same thing, distinguishing the two serves no useful purpose at this point. So it is acceptable to say `float`, `int`, and `char` are class names. They are also called data types.

where the *class-name* includes, but is not limited to, the `float` class (numbers with a decimal point), the `int` class (whole or integer numbers, with no fractional part), or the `char` class (a single character or escape sequence). The *object-identifier-list* consists of one or more valid C++ identifiers separated by commas. For example,

```
int quiz1;
float average;
```

declares two objects named `quiz1` and `average`. C++ offers an alternate *initialization* operation for setting the state of object when it is declared. Here is the general form followed by two example initializations:

class-name identifier = *expression* ;

For example:

```
float sum = 0.00;
int MAX = 999;
```

Objects are often declared or initialized immediately after the beginning of the left brace {, but they may be declared at any point in a program.

```
// Show some object initializations
int main()
{
  int quiz1 = 93;
  int quiz2 = 90;
  float average = (quiz1 + quiz2) / 2.0;
  char letterGrade = 'A';
  // ... Use the float objects

  return 0;
}
```

The initializations reserve enough memory to store two integer values (`quiz1` and `quiz2`), a floating-point value (`average`), and a single-character value (`letterGrade`). The class, name, and values of these four objects are summarized as follows:

Class (or Type)	Name	State
int	quiz1	93
int	quiz2	90
float	average	91.5
char	letterGrade	'A'

To properly use objects in a program, all three attributes must be considered:

- An object must be given a name in an object declaration.
- An object must have a specific class associated with it.
- An object should be given a meaningful value.

We have just seen how objects are declared—the name and class attributes are satisfied—and initialized to give the object value. We now look at another technique for placing a meaningful value into the memory that stores the object's state.

Programming Tip

Be wary of uninitialized objects! These garbage values can cause unpredictable errors. An old saying is: garbage in, garbage out (GIGO). Make sure you initialize all objects through initialization or other operations such as keyboard input.

2.2.1 Assignments

The *assignment operation*, symbolized as =, is frequently used to alter the state of the computer memory. It is one of several methods that alters the state of a particular object. Objects may initially have meaningless values sometimes referred to as *garbage*. This is shown in the following program that outputs the garbage values stored for quiz1, quiz2, and letterGrade when these objects have an *undefined* state—a garbage or meaningless value. The actual values stored for these objects are completely arbitrary. The state is represented by whatever that memory happens to have stored from some previous unrelated operation or program run. The same object may even have varying initial states from one program run to the next.

```
// This program illustrates that object declarations
// do not automatically satisfy the state attribute.
// Objects may have undefined state (meaningless values).
#include <iostream.h>

int main()
{
  int quiz1, quiz2;
  char letterGrade;

  cout << " Quiz 1: " << quiz1 << endl;
  cout << " Quiz 2: " << quiz2 << endl;
  cout << "  Grade: " << letterGrade << endl;

  return 0;
}
```

Output

```
Quiz1: 7628
Quiz2: 2578
Grade:
```

The above output could have been anything.

During one sample run of this program, the garbage values stored at `quiz1` and `quiz2` were 7628 and 2578, respectively, and `letterGrade` was a blank space ' '. On another program run, the undefined states were 9558, 0, and the character '♥'. At some other time, the values could be something completely different (try retyping this program and run it in your system to see what values you get). Assignment statements that give meaningful values to objects have several forms, including this one.

object-name = *expression* ;

When an assignment statement is encountered, the expression on the right, sometimes called an *rValue* (for right value), is evaluated and then stored into the storage location reserved for the object on the left, sometimes called the *lValue* (for location value or left value). These assignment operations alter the state of `quiz1` and `quiz2`:

```
quiz1 = 90;
quiz2 = quiz1;
quiz1 = 65;
```

An object name to the right of = denotes its value. But the object name to the left of = denotes the location of the object in memory or the place where the value will be stored. For example, in the first assignment statement above, 90 is stored into the memory for the object named `quiz1`. The second assignment retrieves the value of `quiz1` (now set to 90) and stores it into the memory used to store the value of `quiz2`. The third assignment sets the value of `quiz1` to 65; destroying its former value of 90.

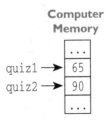

Computer
Memory

2.2.2 Altering the State of an Object

The assignment operation stores new values into an object, effectively destroying the old value. Another common assignment operation involves *modification* of the object to change its value in a meaningful way. This occurs when the same object name appears on both the left side and right side of the assignment operator =. For example, the int object total is incremented by 1 and then decremented by 1 with these two assignment operations:

```
total = total + 1;  // Increment total by 1
total = total - 1;  // Decrement total by 1
```

This common operation is implemented in a variety of ways in C++, but for the time being, assignment with the object name on both sides of = is general enough to perform object modification. Consider, for example, adding a value-added tax of 17.5% to the cost of an item:

```
// Modify an object
#include <iostream.h>
int main()
{
  float itemCost = 100.00;
  cout << "    Cost of item: " << itemCost << endl;
  // Add 17.5% Value added tax
  itemCost = itemCost + 0.175 * itemCost;
  cout << "Value added cost: " << itemCost << endl;
  return 0;
}
```

```
------------------------- Output -------------------------
      Cost of item: 100
Value added cost: 117.5
```

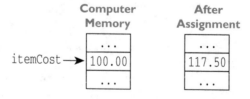

2.2.3   Type Conversions

During assignment, it is usually preferable to have an expression (rValue) that evaluates to the same type as the object. Assignment is meant to alter the state of the memory, not the type of value stored there. However, there are times when this is perfectly natural. For every integer, there is an equivalent floating-point number (with .0 as the fractional part). Thus, C++ lets us store an int into a float:

```
int intObject;
float floatObject;
intObject = 100;
floatObject = intObject;    // Convert the int value to a float
```

The assignment intObject = 100 resets the state of intObject to 100. Storing this integer constant into an int object is perfectly natural. But the assignment of intObject to floatObject is an attempt to store an int value into a float object. So first the integer value 100 is promoted to the equivalent float value of 100.0. In C++ parlance, this is called *implicit type conversion.*

Unfortunately, C++ type conversions permit some rather unintuitive transformations of memory. For example, floats can be converted to ints, but truncation occurs. Also, a float may look like an int when it is output.

```
// This program demonstrates that some rather unintuitive
// alterations may occur during assignment operations
#include <iostream.h>

int main()
{
  // Use the int and float classes to declare two objects
  int intObject;
  float floatObject;

  // Perform two assignment operations
  intObject = 1.999;  // Truncation occurs, 1 is stored at intObject
  floatObject = 5;    // 5 is stored as a float, 5.0

  cout << "intObject: " << intObject  << endl;
  cout << "floatObject: " << floatObject  << endl << endl;

  return 0;
}
```

——————————— **Output** ———————————

```
intObject: 1
floatObject: 5
```

The first line of output shows that the floating-point constant 1.999 was truncated in the assignment to intObject. Although floatObject stores 5.0, the second line of output (floatObject: 5) makes it look like an int. This is because C++ shows the minimum number of significant digits and will not display the decimal unless there is a fractional part other than 0.

Programming Tip ──────────────────────────────

Although some implicit type conversions are either perfectly acceptable (int to float), and other "wrong" assignments (char to int) may be convenient to experienced programmers, for the time being care is recommended when writing assignment statements. Try to have the rValue evaluate to the same type as the lValue.

2.2.4   Constant Objects

The state of any object can be, and usually is, altered during program execution. But sometimes it is convenient to have data with values that cannot be altered during program execution. The C++ keyword const is used for this purpose. Constant objects are created by specifying and associating an identifier with a value preceded by the keyword const. In essence, this is an object whose state cannot be changed through assignment or stream extraction operations. The general form used to declare a constant object is a combination of an initialization preceded by the keyword const:

> const *class-name identifier* = *expression* ;

For example, the value stored in the constant object pi is the floating-point number 3.14159, and TAX_RATE is 7.51%:

```
const float pi = 3.14159;
const float TAX_RATE = 0.0751;
const float primeRate = 6.5;
const float loanRate = primeRate + 2.0;
```

These constant objects represent values that cannot be changed while the program is executing; therefore a statement such as pi = pi * r * r; generates an error because pi is declared as constant.

Programming Tip

In the absence of a data type, C++ often assumes we meant to write int. For example, if we want a constant object that is a float and we forget to include float, we get an int and the implicit conversion that causes a lost value, such as a tax rate of 0.00% as shown here:

```
#include <iostream.h>
int main()
{
  const TAX_RATE = 0.0751;    // Without float, int is assumed and
  cout << TAX_RATE << endl;   // the output is 0 rather than 0.0751
  return 0;
}
```

Objects represent values that change while the program is executing. If the state of an object is not changed at least once in a program, it should probably be declared as a constant object instead.

Self-Check

1. List three attributes of an object that we should keep in mind while using them in a program.
2. Write code that declares totalPoints as an object capable of storing one integer value.
3. Write code that changes to 100, the state of totalPoints in the preceding question.
4. Write code that declares totalSales as a float object and at the same time initializes it to 123.45.
5. Add a 6% tax to totalSales.
6. Write a constant object identified as year that stores the integer 1996.
7. What value is stored into x with the expression const x = 1.99; ?
8. Write the code to initialize a constant object named sentinel as an integer equal to -1. Make sure it is impossible to alter the identifier sentinel.

Answers

1. class, name, and state
2. int totalPoints;
3. totalPoints = 100;
4. float totalSales = 123.45;
5. totalSales = totalSales + (0.06 * totalSales);
6. const int year = 1996;
7. 1 (0.99 is truncated because the data type of x is assumed to be int)
8. const int sentinel = -1;

2.3 Arithmetic Expressions and Operator Precedence

Several of the previous programs have used some arithmetic operations that may look somewhat familiar. Specifically, the / (division) and * (multiplication) operators were used to compute the percentage of one day in a year. We also saw floating-point numbers displayed with a number of decimal places. We now look at other arithmetic expressions, the simplest of which is a single integer or floating-point constant, which may be preceded with the unary minus sign "−" or the unary plus sign "+":

```
-2   -1   0   1   2   +3   +1234   1.234   1.234e-12   1e5   -0.9
```

Arithmetic expressions are also frequently written with two components: operators and operands. An *operator* is one of the arithmetic operators like +, −, /, or * that specifies the operation to be applied to the operands. An *operand* is the object or constant that determines the meaning of the operator and the final value of the arithmetic expression. For example, + adds two integers if both operands are integer constants or int objects, but + adds two floating-point values if either one or both of the operands are floating-point constants or float objects. In the expression 3 + 4, the integer constants 3 and 4 are called the operands and + is the operator.

An arithmetic expression is defined as:
    a numeric value (object or a constant)
    or *expression* + *expression*
    or *expression* − *expression*
    or *expression* * *expression*
    or *expression* / *expression*
    or *expression* % *expression*
    or (*expression*)

The following table lists the five arithmetic operators in terms of the precedence rules necessary for the proper evaluation of expressions with more than one operator.

Precedence Rules of C++ Binary Arithmetic Operators

`*  /  %`   In the absence of parentheses, the multiplication and division operators have precedence over addition and subtraction. If more than one of these operators appear in an expression, the leftmost operator takes precedence.

`+   -`   `+` and `-` are performed after all `*`, `/`, and `%` operators, with the leftmost operator taking precedence. Parentheses may override these precedence rules.

The operators of the following expression are applied to their operands in this order: `/`, `+`, and `-`:

```
2 + 2 - 8 / 4     // Evaluates to 2
```

Parentheses may alter the order in which arithmetic operators are applied to their operands. For example, the same expression with parentheses causes the operators to evaluate in a different order: `+`, `-`, and `/`. Now `/` evaluates last, rather than first. The same set of operators and operands with parentheses results in a different value (-1 rather than 2):

```
(2 + 2 - 8) / 4   // Evaluates to -1
```

Addition (`+`), subtraction (`-`), and multiplication (`*`) represent three of the four basic arithmetic operations. (*Note:* x is not used for multiplication since it would specify a valid C++ identifier.) However, the `%` operator shown above is probably not as familiar, and `/` has different meanings for int and float objects. The result of `18 % 4` is the integer remainder after dividing 18 by 4, or 2. In the following example, `403 % 4` is 3 and `403 / 4` is the integer quotient 100:

$$
\begin{array}{r}
100 \leftarrow\!\!\!-\!\!\!- \ 403 \ / \ 4 \\
4\overline{)403} \\
\underline{100} \\
3 \leftarrow\!\!\!-\!\!\!- \ 403 \ \% \ 4
\end{array}
$$

It must also be noted that integer division is not the same operation as floating-point division. Whereas the result of `3.0 / 4.0` is 0.75, the result of `3 / 4` is the quotient obtained from dividing 3 by 4, or 0. This implies that the operands may give different meanings to the `/` operator. These differences are illustrated in the following program, which shows `%` and `/` operating on integer expressions and `/` operating on floating-point operands:

```
// This program provides an example of int division
// with '/' for the quotient and '%' for the remainder
#include <iostream.h>

int main()
{
  cout << 254 << " minutes can be rewritten as "
       << (254 / 60) << " hours and "  // evaluates to 4
       << (254 % 60) << " minutes"     // evaluates to 14
       << endl                         // start a new line
       << "or 254 minutes is "
       << (254.0 / 60.0) << " hours "  // shown as floating-point
       << endl;

  return 0;
}
```

Output

```
254 minutes can be rewritten as 4 hours and 14 minutes
or 254 minutes is 4.233333 hours
```

This preceding program indicates that even though int and float objects are similar, there are times when float is the more appropriate class than int, and vice versa. The float class should be specified when you need a numeric object with a decimal component. If your interest is only in whole numbers (integers), you may use the int class. With the class chosen, you must consider the differences in some of the arithmetic operators. For example, although the +, -, /, and * operations can be applied to float objects, the % operator is not defined as a float operation. The expression 5.1 % 2.0 will not evaluate, nor will 5 % 2.0. The compiler will flag both of these expressions as errors.

There are a few other details concerning output of arithmetic expressions that should be mentioned here. Whenever int and float objects are on opposite sides of an arithmetic operator, the int object is implicitly converted to its float equivalent (3 becomes 3.0, for example). The entire expression then has a floating-point result.

$$1 + 2.3$$
$$\downarrow$$
$$\underline{1.0 + 2.3}$$ Promote 1 to its float equivalent
$$\downarrow$$
$$3.3$$

Some floats do not need the decimal point. In this case, the float value is shown as its int equivalent. For example, cout << 2 * 2.5 displays 5 rather than 5.0. This is the default situation that reigns unless we make the effort always to show a decimal point and trailing zeros (this will be shown later). C++ displays floating-point in exponential notation (1.2345678e7 rather than 12345678.0) when there is more than a certain number of significant digits (the number of significant digits needed to trigger exponential notation is system dependent). These points are summarized in the following program, which displays a variety of expressions:

```
// Provide examples of output using a variety
// of single-operator arithmetic expressions.
#include <iostream.h>

int main()
{
  cout << "a. " << 2 + 5.7         << endl   // Mix of int and float
       << "b. " << 2.34 + 5.67     << endl   // Show minimum decimals
       << "c. " << 2 * 2.5         << endl   // No decimal shown
       << "d. " << 2e3 * 5.7e4     << endl   // Exponential output
       << "e. " << 9999.0 * 9999.0 << endl   // Exponential output
                                   << endl;
  return 0;
}
```

--- **Output** ---
```
a. 7.7
b. 8.01
c. 5
d. 1.14e+08
e. 9.998e+07
```

2.3.1   Evaluating Expressions with Object Names

The expressions shown above all have constant operands. But arithmetic expressions almost always have object names as operands. When C++ evaluates this type of expression, it conceptually replaces each object name with its stored value. The following examples demonstrate this, assuming the state of the int objects j, k, l, and m are as shown (values are substituted for all objects in the first step).

Object Name	State
j	1
k	2
l	3
m	4

Example 1

```
j + k * l / m
```

1 + <u>2 * 3</u> / 4   Reference the state of all objects and substitute the names with the values
        ↓

1 + <u> 6 / 4</u>   2 * 3 evaluated to 6 (* has precedence over +)
            ↓

<u>1 +   1</u>   6 / 4 evaluated to 1, not 1.5 (/ occurs before +)
      ↓

  2   1 + 1 evaluated to 2

Example 2

```
j - k % l * m
```

1 - <u>2 % 3</u> * 4   Reference the state of all objects and substitute the names with the values
        ↓

1 - <u> 2   * 4</u>   2 % 3 evaluated to 2 (% has precedence over -)
            ↓

<u>1 -   8</u>   2 * 4 evaluated to 8 (* has precedence over -)
     ↓

  -7   1 - 8 evaluated to -7

Self-Check

1. Predict the output of the following programs:

   a.
   ```
   #include <iostream.h>
   int main()
   {
     cout << (5 / 2.0);
     return 0;
   }
   ```

   b.
   ```
   #include <iostream.h>
   int main()
   {
     cout << "Remainder: "
          << (11 % 2)
          << ", Quotient: "
          << (11 / 2);
     return 0;
   }
   ```

   c.
   ```
   #include <iostream.h>
   int main()
   {
     cout << (1+2) << "  " << (3/4);
     return 0;
   }
   ```

   d.
   ```
   #include <iostream.h>
   int main()
   {
     cout << "  " << (1.0 + 5.5);
     cout << "  " << (3+3 / 3);
     cout << "  " << ( (1 + 2)/
                       (3 + 4) );
     cout << "  " << (1 + 2 * 3 / 4);
     return 0;
   }
   ```

2.   Evaluate the following expressions and state the resulting type of constant (int or float):

   a.   5 / 2   c.   5.0 / 2.0

   b.   5 % 2   d.   1 + 2 - 3 * 4

3.   Assuming int j = 5, k = 7;, evaluate the following expressions:

   a.   j / k   c.   2 - j * k

   b.   j % k   d.   (j * k) / (j + k)

Answers

1. a. 2.5 (implicit conversion from int to float occurs)
    b. Remainder 1, Quotient 5   c. 3 0   d. 6.5 4 0 2
2. a. 2 (int)   b. 1 (int)   c. 2.5 (float)   d. -9 (int)
3. a. 0 (int)   b. 5 (int)   c. -33   d. 2

Exercises

1.   List four types of C++ tokens and give two examples of each.

2.   What capabilities are provided with #include <iostream.h>?

3.   Tokenize the following program by listing each token followed by the type of token (special symbol, identifier, constant, or keyword):

```
// List the tokens
#include <iostream.h>
int main()
{
  int j;
  float x = 10.0;
  cout << ( 2 * j + 2.0 / x ) << endl;
  return 0;
}
```

4.   Which of the following are valid identifiers?

   a.   a-one   e.   1Header   i.   all right

   b.   R2D2   f. $money   j.   'intVar'

   c.   registered_voter   g.   1_2_3   k.   {Right}

   d.   BEGIN   h.   A_B_C   l.   Mispelt

5. Write the output generated by the following program:

```cpp
#include <iostream.h>
int main()
{
  int j, k;
  float x, y;
  j = 5;
  j = j + 1;
  k = 7 / 2;
  k = k + 1;
  x = 1.4;
  y = 3.2 * (1 + x);
  cout << j << "  " << k << "  " << x << "  " << y << endl;
  return 0;
}
```

6. Write a complete C++ program that displays your full name on the screen followed by your age (will this program be correct on this date next year?).

7. Write C++ code to declare j and k as int objects with an undefined state.

8. Write C++ code to declare j and k as int objects with both initialized to zero.

9. Write C++ code to define tolerance as a float object (leave it as garbage), letter as a char object initialized to 'A', and total as an int object initialized to 5.

10. Write a statement that displays the current value of an object named total.

11. Write the output generated by the following program:

```cpp
#include <iostream.h>
int main()
{
  int minutes, hours;
  minutes = 865;
  hours = minutes / 60;
  minutes = minutes % 60;
  cout << "Time = " << hours << ':' << minutes << endl;
  return 0;
}
```

12. Write the output generated by the following program:

```cpp
#include <iostream.h>
int main()
{
  float sales = 10.0;
  cout << sales << endl;
  // Add 5%
  sales = sales + 0.05 * sales;
```

```
    cout << sales << endl;
    return 0;
}
```

13. Write the output generated by the following program:

```
#include <iostream.h>
int main()
{
  int j = 5, k = 10;
  float x = 1.4, y = 3.7;
  cout << ( 2 / j + 2 / k )        << " ";
  cout << ( 2 * ( j + 2 ) / k )    << " ";
  cout << ( 3 * ( x + y ) / 10 )   << " ";
  cout << ( x / 2 + y / k )        << " ";
  cout << ( ( j + k + x + y ) / 4 ) << endl;
  return 0;
}
```

Lab Projects

2A   Using Objects

To complete this lab project, complete the following bulleted instructions in sequence:

- First predict the output that will be generated by the following program if the user enters *3667* at the prompt:

```
// Programmer: _____
// This program computes the number of seconds,
// minutes, and hours in a given number of seconds
#include <iostream.h>

int main()
{
  // Start with a given number of seconds:
  int totalSeconds, hours, minutes, seconds;

  cout << "Enter totalSeconds: ";
  cin >> totalSeconds;
  hours   = totalSeconds / 3600;        // 3600 seconds in an hour
  minutes = totalSeconds % 3600 / 60;   // 60 seconds in a minute
  seconds = totalSeconds % 3600 % 60;   // The remaining seconds
```

```
    cout << totalSeconds << " written as hours:minutes:seconds = "
        << hours << ':' << minutes << ':' << seconds << endl;

    return 0;
}
```

- Create a new file and use your editor to retype the preceding program exactly as shown.
- Save the file containing your source code.
- Compile, link, and run this program using the instructions particular to your system (if necessary, fix any errors).
- Does your prediction match the program output? Change your prediction or your program, whichever is appropriate, until your prediction matches the program output.

2B   Using Objects

Write a complete C++ program that declares two float objects named op1 and op2. Then extract values for these objects from the keyboard and show the sum and the difference (op1-op2). If the user enters *2.67* and *1.23*, the sum and difference of the two variables and the dialogue should look *exactly* like this:

```
Enter two floats: 2.67  1.23

2.67 + 1.23 = 3.9
2.67 - 1.23 = 1.44
```

Hint: The first line output statement should look like this:

```
cout << op1 << " + " << op2 << " = " << (op1 + op2);
```

Now input different values for op1 and op2 (555.55 and 666.6, for example), and run the program again. Verify that your output looks *exactly* like this:

```
555.55 + 666.66 = 1222.21
555.55 - 666.66 = -111.11
```

2C   Using Objects

Using the following formula that converts Fahrenheit temperatures to Centigrade:

$$C = \frac{5}{9}(F - 32)$$

Complete this test oracle:

```
┌──────────────────────── Test Oracle ──────────────────────────┐
│                                                                │
│        F          C                                            │
│       85.5       ___                                           │
│       -40        ___                                           │
│        32        ___                                           │
│       212        ___                                           │
│                                                                │
└────────────────────────────────────────────────────────────────┘
```

Then write a C++ program that extracts a `float` representing a Fahrenheit temperature. Display the centigrade equivalent of the Fahrenheit input. Follow this algorithm for the `main` program:

Algorithm to Convert Fahrenheit to Centigrade

1. Declare F and C as `float` objects.
2. Extract F with `cin >>`
3. Compute C
4. Display the value for F, "`degrees Fahrenheit = `", the value for C, and finally "` degrees centigrade`"
5. Your dialogue should look exactly like this when 85.5 is entered for F:

```
Enter F: 85.5
85.5 degrees Fahrenheit = 29.7222 degrees centigrade
```

After you obtain the preceding program, run the program and enter each different value of F verifying that your output matches each prediction in the test oracle. For example, when F is input as 212.0, you should get this exact output (you probably will not see decimal points in your output):

```
212 degrees Fahrenheit = 100 degrees centigrade
```

2D   Using Objects

Use algebra and the formula of the preceding lab project to solve for F. Then complete this test oracle:

```
┌──────────────────────── Test Oracle ──────────────────────────┐
│                                                                │
│        C          F                                            │
│       29.7       ___                                           │
│       -40        ___                                           │
│        0         ___                                           │
│       100        ___                                           │
│                                                                │
└────────────────────────────────────────────────────────────────┘
```

Next, write a C++ program that extracts and displays the Fahrenheit equivalent of 29.7 degrees centigrade. Your dialogue should look like this:

```
Enter C: 29.7
29.7 degrees centigrade = ?.? degrees Fahrenheit
```

After you obtain this dialogue, modify your program so that the memory for degrees centigrade is reset to each value of C in the test oracle. Run the program and enter each value of C. Verify that your output matches each prediction. For example, when C is entered as 100.0, you should see this exact output (you probably will not see decimal points in your output):

```
100 degrees centigrade = 212 degrees Fahrenheit
```

2E   Using Objects

Write a C++ program that extracts a value for the radius of a circle (r) from the keyboard and then displays the diameter, circumference, and area of a circle. Use these formulas:

$$d = 2 \times r$$
$$c = \pi \times d$$
$$a = \pi \times r \times r$$

where r is the radius, d the diameter, c the circumference, and a the area of a circle. Use π = 3.14159. First, complete this test oracle using paper and pencil or a calculator:

	Test Oracle	
	Radius = 2.0	Radius = 2.5
d =	_____	_____
c =	_____	_____
a =	_____	_____

Your dialogue should look like this (exact output for float objects varies between C++ compilers, so your output might be slightly different—especially with the number of decimal places shown for Circumference and Area):

```
   Enter Radius: 1.0
      Diameter: 2
 Circumference: 6.28318
          Area: 3.14159
```

Run your program when radius is extracted as 1.0 and make sure your output matches the preceding dialogue. After this, run your program to input the remaining two radii given in the test oracle. Make sure your output matches both predictions.

2.4   Programming Errors

In general, four types of errors occur during program development:

1. **Compiletime**: Errors that occur during compilation.
2. **Linktime**: Errors that occur during the linking process used to create executable files.
3. **Runtime**: Errors that occur while the program is executing.
4. **Intent**: When the program does what we told it to do, not what we intended.

Many of these errors occur during the transformation of the C++ programs we write into the executable program.

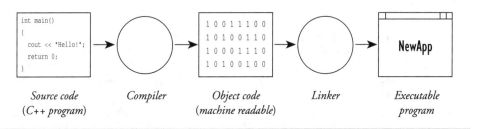

Figure 2.2   Compiling and linking

The compiler translates source code (our C++ programs) into object code (code that can be processed by the computer system). Almost always, many object code files need to be *linked* together. On many systems compilations and linking are combined into one step and so linking may appear to be hidden (until a linktime error occurs, that is).

2.4.1   Compiletime Errors

Programming language requires strict adherence to its own set of formal syntax rules. It is difficult to always adhere to them due to mistakes made during the coding phase of program development. As the C++ compiler translates source code into a program that can be run on the computer, it also

•   Locates and reports as many errors as possible.
•   Warns of potential problems that are legal, but might cause errors later.

A *compiletime error* occurs when the C++ compiler recognizes the violation of one of these syntax rules during compilation. The program will not execute until all compile-time errors have been removed from the program. While you are compiling programs, you are likely to discover many strange-looking error messages. Unfortunately, deciphering these compiletime error messages takes practice, patience, and unfortunately, a fairly complete knowledge of the language. So in an effort to improve this situation, here are some examples of compiletime errors and how they are corrected. *Note:* Your compiler will generate different error messages.

Compiletime Error	Incorrect Code	Correction
Accidentally splitting an identifier	`int Total Weight;`	`int total_Weight;` `// or totalWeight;`
Misspelled keyword	`integer total;`	`int total;`
Misspelled standard identifier	`out << "Hello";`	`cout << "Hello";`
Misspelled identifier	`int studentNumber;` `studentNum = 1;`	`// missing 'ber'` `studentNumber = 1;`
Leaving off a required semicolon	`float x` `x = 1.23;`	`float x;` `x = 1.23;`
Not closing a string constant	`cout << "Hello;`	`cout << "Hello";`
Failing to define an object	`cin >> testScore;`	`int testScore;` `cin >> testScore;`
Ignoring the case sensitivity of C++	`int j;` `J = 0;`	`int j;` `j = 0;`

Other compiletime errors you might encounter include:

- Attempting to reference an identifier when it is declared in a separate file and the proper include directive is not present.
- Failing to include `()` after `int main`.
- Failing to include an opening or closing brace to mark the objects and statements that belong to `main`.
- Failing to include a `>>` or `<<` operator when it is necessary (or using , instead of `<<`).
- Using `>>` with `cout` or `<<` with `cin`.

Unfortunately, you might spend a good deal of time deciphering compiletime error messages and warnings, which might take the form of "Invalid indirection" or "type mismatch in call to sqrt" and warnings such as "converted main function to int" or "possibly suspicious assignment". Only with time and further study will such compiler output make sense and become beneficial.

Programming Tip

Whenever your compiler appears to be a nagging piece of software, remember that the compiler is not our enemy: *The compiler is our friend.*

The output generated by a compiler includes error messages and warnings intended to help us avoid other errors that are more difficult to correct. Unfortunately for the beginning programmer, compiler messages are meant to be read by programmers. They include programming jargon that beginners must learn to decipher.

The following program attempts to show numerous errors detected at compiletime. Some compilers will stop after finding a few errors, others may generate a screen full of errors. Also, the error messages output by the compiler vary among systems. The comments indicate the reason for the error—again, your compiletime error messages will look quite different.

```
// When this program is compiled, many compiletime errors
// are detected and many error messages are displayed
int main // 1. no () after main
{        // 2. All occurrences of cin and cout are errors because
         //    the directive #include<iostream.h> is missing
    int pounds;

    cout << "Begin execution" << endl      // Missing ; after endl
    cout >> "Enter weight in pounds: ";    // >> should be <<
    cin << pounds;                         // << should be >>
    cout << "In the U.K., ";               // extra ;
        << "you weigh " << ( Pounds / 14 ) // Pounds is not declared
        << " stone, " ( pounds % 14 )      // Missing << after "stone, "
        << endl                            // Missing ; after endl
    return 0;                              // Return is misspelled
                                           // Missing right brace }
```

Programming Tip

Compilers generate some rather cryptic messages, especially to those not accustomed to the language. When the program shown above was compiled with one particular compiler, six errors occurred, all reporting "Type name expected" (the manner in which errors are presented varies among systems). On another system, a different crop of errors may occur. Compiletime error messages take some getting used to, so try to be patient and observe the location where the compiletime error occurred (the error is usually in the vicinity of the line where the error was detected, although you may have to fix preceding lines).

Also note that one small compiletime error can result in a cascade of errors. For example, by adding the () after main, six completely different error messages were detected by the same compiler. It is also possible that fixing the first error might correct many other errors. So try to concentrate on the first error your compiler reports. The compiler usually, but not always, will be able to correctly point out the location of the error in your program.

The corrected source code, without error, is given next, followed by an interactive dialogue:

```
// When this program is compiled,
// NO compiletime errors are detected
#include <iostream.h>

int main()
{
    int pounds;

    cout << "Begin execution" << endl;
    cout << "Enter your weight in pounds: ";
    cin >> pounds;
    cout << "In the U.K., "
         << "you weigh "  << ( pounds / 14 )
         << " stone, "    << ( pounds % 14 )
         << endl;
    return 0;
}
```

-------------------------- **Dialogue** --------------------------
```
Begin execution
Enter your weight in pounds: 146
In the U.K., you weigh 10 stone, 6
```

Programming Tip

Go back and examine the general forms of the cout statement, object declaration, initialization, cin statement, and assignment operation. Note that each statement and declaration is terminated by a semicolon (;). Exclusion of this terminator or its presence where it does not belong are common syntax violations resulting in compile-time errors.

2.4.2 Linktime Errors

To create an executable program, a piece of software called a *linker* usually puts together several files. Among other things, the linker must resolve such details as locating the identifier "main" in one of these files. If main is not found during the linking process, the linker generates an error that may look like "Undefined symbol _main". If this transpires, verify that your program starts with void main or int main:

```
void main()          or          int main()
{ ...                                 ( ...
```

and that "main" is not misspelled as "mane," "maine," "Main," "MAIN," or "man". The causes and fixes of other linktime errors are system dependent.

2.4.3 Runtime Errors

Program execution may begin after all compiletime errors have been removed and the linker has created an executable program. But errors may still occur while the program is executing. Such *runtime errors* may cause the program to terminate abnormally (before it should have) because an event occurs that the computer can't handle. Examples of runtime errors include: division by 0, square root of a negative number, and input of invalid numeric data. First, consider the following program that runs without error:

```
// When this program is run and 0 is entered for n,
// a runtime error occurs (division by 0)
#include <iostream.h>

int main()
{
  float sum;
  int n;
  // Obtain input:
  cout << "Enter sum: ";
  cin >> sum;
  cout << "  Number: ";
  cin >> n;
  // Calculate the average:
  cout << "  Average: " << (sum / n) << endl;

  return 0;
}
```

When valid numeric constants are entered from the keyboard, correct values are stored into memory set aside for sum and n. For example, when the input data is 291 followed by 3, the program would execute until it is terminated normally.

```
Enter sum: 291
    Number: 3
   Average: 97
```

However, if after the prompt `Number:`, 0 is entered, we have division by zero. Since this is not defined mathematically, the program may terminate abnormally. And we usually want our programs to terminate normally—under the control of the user. The dialogue shown here indicates that the output for average never occurred—`sum / n` caused abnormal program termination before any of the expressions in the final `cout` statement appear on the screen.

```
Enter sum: 291
    Number: 0
 <ERROR>
```

Note: `<ERROR>` indicates that the error message is system dependent. Two errors encountered on two particular compilers included: "`Arithmetic exception (core dumped)`" and "`Floating point error: Divide by 0 Abnormal program termination`". So remember that your system may deal with this error differently.

Using the same program with invalid numeric input results in a different type of runtime error. The input stream is corrupted with invalid numeric input, and subsequent input operations may be ignored. In at least two environments, this does occur and `cin >> n` is ignored. This results in a garbage value for `sum / n`:

```
Enter sum: BadData
    Number:     Average: 6.56360e-20
```

Your environment may handle this situation differently. For example, another system generated this rather strange runtime error: "`Square root of a negative number`".

2.4.4 Intent Errors

Even when no compiletime errors are found and no runtime errors occur, the program still may not execute properly. A program may run and terminate normally, but it may not be not correct. In such a case, the processing steps probably contain an error in intent. One example requires a small change to one of the expressions from the preceding program:

```
cout << "  Average: " << n / sum;
```

The interactive dialogue may now look like this:

```
Enter sum: 291
   Number: 3
  Average: 0.010309
```

Intent errors occur when the program does what we typed, not what we intended. Unfortunately, the compiler does not locate such intent errors. The expression n / sum is syntactically correct—the compiler just has no way of knowing that this programmer intended to write sum / n instead.

Of the four types of errors encountered so far, intent errors are the most insidious and usually the most difficult to correct. They are also the most difficult to detect—we may not know they even exist. Consider the program controlling the Therac 3 cancer radiation therapy machine. Patients received overdoses of radiation while the indicator displayed everything as normal. Another infamous intent error involved a program controlling a probe that was supposed to go to Venus. Because a period was used instead of a comma, an American Viking Venus Probe was lost. Both controlling programs had compiled successfully and were running at the time of the accidents—they did what the programmers had written, certainly not what was intended.

Even when a process has been automated and delivered to the customer in working order as per the perceptions of the developers, there may still be errors. There have been many instances of software working, but not doing what it was supposed to do. This is a failure to meet the problem specifications. We will see an example of this type of intent error in the case study that follows.

A related error occurs when the requester of a program specifies the problem incorrectly. This could be the case when the requester isn't sure what she or he wants. A trivial or critical omission in specification may occur, the request may not be written clearly, or—as is often the case—the requester may change his or her mind after program development has begun.

For the most part, the lab projects in this textbook simply ask you to fulfill the problem specification. But if you think there is an omission or there is something you don't understand, don't hesitate to ask questions. It is better to understand the problem and know what it is you are to trying to solve, before getting to the design and implementation phases of program development.

Self-Check

1. Assuming a program is supposed to find an average given the total sum and number of objects in the set, then the following dialogue is generated. What clue reveals the presence of an intent error?

```
Enter sum: 100
   Number: 4
  Average: 0.04
```

2. Assuming the following code was used to generate the dialogue above, how is the intent error to be corrected?

```
cout << "Enter sum: ";
cin >> n;
cout << "    Number: ";
cin >> sum;
// Calculate the average:
cout << "  Average: " << (sum / n) << endl;
```

3. List the type of error (compiletime, runtime, linktime, or intent) that exists when the last statement in the preceding program is changed to:

a. `cout << "  Average: " << "sum / n";`

b. `cout << "  Average: " << sum / (n - n);`

c. `cout << "  Average: ", sum / n;`

d. `cout << "  Average: " << sum / n`

Answers

1. 100 divided by 4 should be 25, not 0.04
2. Change `cin >> n` to `cin >> sum` and `cin >> sum` to `cin >> n`
3. a. Intent: The output would be: `Average: sum / n`
   b. Runtime: Division by 0
   c. Compiletime: Used , after `"Average:"` instead of `<<`
   d. Compiletime: Missing statement terminator ;

2.5   Case Study: Grade Point Average

Question: Before beginning to read this case study, use the following data to determine the grade point average (GPA) for a student taking three courses for a term. Write down your answer now! Don't look ahead to the problem specification. The answer is given later.

Course	Numeric Grade	Credits
CmpSc 101	4.0	3.0
ESACT 257	3.0	1.0
Math 141	2.0	4.0

Answer: Grade Point Average = _____

2.5.1   Analysis

Problem: *Write a program that determines a grade point average given three numeric grade equivalents and the number of credits for each of the three courses taken (the program should work only for three courses). For example, if a student received a 4.0 in a 3-credit course, a 3.0 in a 1-credit course, and a 2.0 in a 4.0 credit course, the dialogue should look exactly as follows with ?.? replaced by the correct grade point average (Note: 4.0 = A, 3.0 = B, and 2.0 = C):*

```
Enter grade equivalent for three classes: 4.0  3.0  2.0
Enter credits for each class, respectively: 3.0  1.0  4.0
                 Grade Point Average: ?.?
```

We should allow entry of floating-point numbers for both grade equivalents and class credits. Some grading systems equate a B- with the value 2.67 while others grant grades in one-tenth increments. Also, some courses are assigned values such as 0.5 or 1.5 credits.

We begin our analysis by reading and understanding the problem. The problem may then be paraphrased like this: *Calculate the grade point average for any three courses.* Next the input and output should be identified. The output is easy; it's the prompts as shown and the labeled grade point average. As for input, each course needs the numeric grade and the number of credits. The grades are entered on the first line, the credits on the second.

Input:
- Three term grades ranging from 0.0 through 4.0 identified as g1, g2, and g3 (these objects must be able to store floating-point values)
- Three values for credits ranging from 0.0 through 15.0 identified as c1, c2, and c3 (these should be able to store floating-point values)

Output:
- Prompts as shown: Colons should line up
- The GPA preceded by the label: Grade Point Average:

2.5.2   Design: IPO Algorithm

This problem can be viewed as matching the IPO model introduced in Chapter 1. The three-step algorithm may begin as follows:

   I   Obtain three grades and the three associated credits per grade
   P   Compute the grade point average (GPA)
   O   Display the GPA

The first Input step involves interactive input: two prompts followed by three user inputs for each prompt. This is straightforward and so is the Output step. The second step, Process, needs some work, however. We first need to determine what a grade point average is. In a recent three-year survey it was found that two-thirds of students who were asked did not correctly compute the GPA. If you answered 3.000 to the question posed earlier, count yourself among the majority who got it incorrect. If you answered 2.875, count yourself among the minority who got it correct. The difference is in the terms. The average grade is 3.000 but the GPA is 2.875. This implies a weighted average, not a simple average. Recall that the problem specification states "Grade Point Average"—not "Average grade." If we go ahead and design a program that computes the average grade, we end up with an intent error—the correct solution to the wrong problem! So let us proceed with our design by refining the Process step with the goal of meeting the program's specification.

Recall from Chapter 1 that a weighted average is one in which some values are worth more (have more weight) than others. So the grade point average in the example is not $(4+3+2)/3 = 3.000$; it is 2.875, a bit lower than 3.0 because the grade of 2 (C) was for a course worth four credits and the 4 (A) was for a course worth only three credits. So assuming we have values for all objects:

g1	g2	g3	c1	c2	c3	GPA
4	3	2	3	1	4	?.?

a grade point average (GPA) is computed as :

```
GPA = qualityPoints / totalCredits
```

where `qualityPoints` is the sum of each numeric grade multiplied by the credits for each course. This gives us the "weight" factor. Now the Process step may be refined as follows:

1. Compute `qualityPoints` as $(g1 * c1) + (g2 * c2) + (g3 * c3)$
2. Compute `totalCredits` as $(c1 + c2 + c3)$
3. Compute `GPA` as `qualityPoints/totalCredits`

This refinement is tested with the data of the previous example:

1. `qualityPoints` = (g1 * c1) + (g2 * c2) + (g3 * c3)
   (4 * 3) + (3 * 1) + (2 * 4)
       12   +   3   +   8
                  23

2. `totalCredits` = (c1 + c2 + c3)
                  8

3. GPA = qualityPoints/totalCredits
                23 / 8
                  2 **whoops!**

One int divided by another int results in an int and a terribly wrong answer. If we pick the wrong class, the GPA might be computed as 2 rather the correct 2.875—an error that could mean the difference between obtaining or retaining a scholarship or student loan, or it could mean you don't get that job or cooperative education position with your dream employer.

One way to fix this error is to declare all objects as float rather than int. This is shown in the C++ program below. Once again, it is important to keep in mind the differences between the int and float classes, and in particular, the division operation symbolized as /.

2.5.3 Implementation

The following program is one computer-based solution to the problem specified earlier. Notice that it does indeed compute a grade point average as specified in the problem (and not an average grade). Also notice that all objects are from the float class.

```cpp
// Compute the grade point average for exactly three courses
#include <iostream.h>

int main()
{
  // These objects store data for three courses
  float g1, g2, g3, c1, c2, c3;

  // I)nput:
  cout << "  Enter grade equivalent for three classes: ";
  cin >> g1 >> g2 >> g3;
  cout << "Enter credits for each class, respectively: ";
  cin >> c1 >> c2 >> c3;

  // P)rocess
  float qualityPoints, totalCredits, GPA;
  qualityPoints = (g1 * c1) + (g2 * c2) + (g3 * c3);
  totalCredits  = c1 + c2 + c3;
  GPA = qualityPoints / totalCredits;

  // O)utput:
  cout << "                        Grade Point Average: " << GPA << endl;

  return 0;
}
```

—————————————— **Dialogue** ——————————————

```
        Enter grade equivalent for three classes: 4  3  2
        Enter credits for each class, respectively: 3  1  4
                              Grade Point Average: 2.875
```

Programming Tip ————————————————————————

The input, provided as integer constants rather than float, might cause you to wonder why we did not get an error. It just so happens that when C++ attempts to extract a float from the input stream, and an int is encountered, the integer value is promoted to its float equivalent. So 4 is converted to 4.0 and 1 to 1.0.

It should also be noted that the inverse operation does not apply. When an attempt is made to extract an int from the input stream, and a floating-point constant is encountered, the input stream (cin) is corrupted. Subsequent extractions are likely to fail.

The float class of objects was used for several reasons:

1. To avoid integer division such as 23 / 8 that produces a wrong answer.
2. To allow for credits and grades other than integers.
3. The problem input specified float (4.0 was written rather than 4).

The problem specification stated floats were to be allowed as input. For example, a plus/minus system may have numeric grade equivalents such as A- = 3.67, B+ = 2.34, and so on. We might also have schools with courses that have 0.5, 1.0, or 1.5 credits, or with grades ranging from 0.8 to 4.0 in increments of 0.1. The implementation given here could handle these different situations.

2.5.4   Testing the Implementation

If the GPA had been displayed as 3, we might have assumed that the program works properly. After all, the average grade is 3.0. But this is an intent error disguising itself as output—the wrong problem is solved correctly. In an attempt to implement the correct solution, we are left with the question of how to test the program adequately. There are many possible combinations of credits and grades, and we cannot possibly try all of them. However, a few sets of GPA computations should increase our confidence in the program's viability. We could create a test oracle to predict GPAs separately, and then run the program for each set of data. The computer-generated GPA output should match our predictions (to three decimals). Here is one test oracle and some possible combinations of grades and credits with predicted GPAs shown rounded to three decimals:

						Test Oracle
g1	*g2*	*g3*	*c1*	*c2*	*c3*	*GPA*
2	3	4	4	3	2	*2.778*
4	3	2	2	3	4	*2.778*
4	4	4	1	1	1	*4.000*
3	3	3	1.5	3.0	4.0	*3.000*

Now the implementation can be tested with each set of data in the test oracle. The computer output of GPA should match each one of our predictions. If this does not occur, the test oracle could be incorrect, the program may have an intent error, or the input may have been entered incorrectly. In either case, we stick with the comparisons until output matches prediction.

Self-Check

1. What type of error occurs when all three values for credits are interactively input as 0.0?

2. What type of error (if any) would occur when all parentheses are omitted from the assignment to qualityPoints:

   ```
   qualityPoints = g1 * c1 + g2 * c2 + g3 * c3;
   ```

3. What type of error (if any) would occur if the parentheses were omitted after int main:

   ```
   int main
   ```

4. What type of error (if any) would occur if qualityPoints and credits had been declared as int rather than float?

5. What type of error (if any) would occur if we had used the following alternate method for computing grade point average? (*Hint:* Carefully evaluate the expression using one of the test data set.)

   ```
   GPA = (g1 * c1) + (g2 * c2) + (g3 * c3) / (c1 + c2 + c3);
   ```

6. What type of error (if any) would occur if int main() had been written like this?

   ```
   int Main()
   ```

7. Complete this test oracle by predicting the GPA for each set of grades and credits.

───────── **Test Oracle** ─────────

g1	g2	g3	c1	c2	c3	GPA
1	2	3	4	4	4	a. _____
4	4	4	3	2	1	b. _____
3	3.34	2.67	1.5	3	4	c. _____

Answers

1. Runtime division by 0.0 (actual error message is system dependent—some compilers evaluate 0.0 to 0 instead).
2. None: * already has higher precedence than +.
3. Compiletime.
4. An intent error because all GPAs would be truncated; the only possible GPAs would be: 0, 1, 2, 3, or 4.
5. Intent: This is not the correct expression for GPA because another set of parentheses is required to avoid the numerator of only (g3 * c3). The value stored into GPA would typically be much higher than a 4.0 maximum.
6. Linktime: The linker would report an error indicating main was not found. Remember that C++ is case sensitive and that Main and main are two unique identifiers.
7   a.   2.0   b.   4.0   c.   2.965

Chapter Summary

We started this chapter with the include directive that brings in code written by other programmers. We then tokenized the simple "Hello World" program and ended with a case study that reviewed the program development process while exposing us to examples of the wide variety of errors that may occur in even the simplest of programs. In between, source code was viewed as a collection of tokens.

You have now been confronted with a large variety of details concerning the C++ programming language, program development, and the types of errors that occur during program development. This can be a bit overwhelming at first, but most of these details are necessary for implementation of even the simplest input/output program. Many of the concepts covered in this chapter are common to many programming languages: the concept of an object (variable); the existence of constants (integers, floating-points, strings); larger arithmetic expressions using the four basic arithmetic operations; memory assignment; use of tokens such as special symbols, identifiers, keywords, and constants; and interactive I/O.

C++ tokens include special symbols such as + and {, identifiers such as cin and cout, keywords such as int and float, and constants (literals) such as "String-Constant", 'A', 123, and 0.0751. We also saw two new classes. Stream insertable expressions now include int, float char, string constants, object names, expressions with arithmetic operators, and identifiers such as endl. We also learned that many of the familiar rules of arithmetic and algebra are applicable to a programming language.

Some time was spent on object declaration, altering an object's state through initialization, assignment, and extraction operations.

We also studied the four general types of programming errors and how they may occur at various phases of program development, including analysis and design. We worked through another case study using the analysis, design, and implementation approach to program development. We saw specific examples of errors that may occur even in a relatively straightforward and simple problem (complete the case study's Self-Check section if you have not already done so). With all that can go wrong, you should allow yourself to feel good about successfully implementing a computer program. It is recommended that you complete as many lab projects as your schedule permits until you feel comfortable with the material in the chapter. This applies to all chapters of this textbook.

Exercises

14. Give one example of code that causes at least one compiletime error. Then supply the correct version of the code that does not generate a compiletime error.
15. Write C++ code that generates a runtime error and give the reason.
16. What type of error occurs when we attempt to run this program:

```
#include <iostream.h>
int MAIN()
{
    cout << "Hello world";
    return 0;
}
```

17. Explain the error we get with this attempt at a program:

```
int main()
{
    cout << "Hello world";
    return 0;
}
```

18. Describe the phrase *intent error*.
19. Does the following code always correctly assign the average of the three floats x, y, and z to average?

```
float average = (x+y+z/3.0);
```

20. What value is stored into average in this expression?

```
float average = (81+90+83)/3;
```

21. Answer these questions using the data shown below:
   a.   Write appropriate prompts and input statements to obtain values for all objects (the identifiers in the left column below) except `finalGrade`.
   b.   Write the statement that computes the final term percentage and stores that value into `finalGrade`: `testOne` and `testTwo` are both worth 15% of the final grade, `finalExam` is worth 30%, and the lab project average is worth 40%.
   c.   Write the output statement that displays this final grade. Include an appropriate label.

Float Object (Variable)	*Stored Value*
testOne	97.0
testTwo	85.0
finalExam	92.0
lab1, lab2, lab3, lab4	80.0, 80.0, 100.0, 100.0
finalGrade	??.?

Lab Projects

2F   Using Objects

Write a C++ program that interactively prompts for an integer in the range of 1 through 10. Although we can't yet stop anyone from entering an `int` outside of this range, display the input on a line after the prompt "`You entered: `" (don't forget the space after the colon). The dialogue should look exactly like this when the user inputs 7:

```
Enter a number from 1 to 10: 7
You entered 7
```

1. Make sure the object to store the input is defined as an `int`, not a `float`.
2. Run the program and input the valid int 5. Write down the value output after "`You Entered: `".

During one of the next two modifications, you should observe what is known as an overflow error—failure to properly store what appears to be a valid integer constant. Because of the limited range of `int` objects, either 99999 or 9999999999 (or both) cannot be stored in an `int` object (the exact range is system dependent).

3. Enter the number 99999 (five nines) and write down the value output after "`You Entered: `".
4. Enter the number 9999999999 (ten nines) and write down the value output after "`You Entered: `".

5. Enter the floating-point value 0.9 and write down the value output after "You En-tered: ".

6. Run the program and enter the characters NG instead of a valid integer. Describe what occurs.

7. Modify your program such that main is written with an uppercase M as Main. Try to compile or run your program and describe what occurs. *Note:* You may see "_main" on screen indicating that the underscore character may begin an identifier. This is true, but don't start your identifiers with _. The accepted convention is to allow these names within other parts of C++, not in application programs like the ones you are writing.

2G   Using Objects

Compute the slope of a line given any two points (x1,y1) and (x2,y2) to define the line. Use the rise over run formula for the slope of a line:

```
slope = (y2 - y1) / (x2 - x1)
```

First, complete the predictions of this test oracle, writing ERROR if an error would occur:

				Test Oracle
x1	y1	x2	y2	slope
0.0	0.0	1.0	1.0	_____
0.0	0.0	-1.0	1.0	_____
6.0	5.2	6.0	-14.5	_____

Then implement the program. Make sure your dialogue appears exactly as shown below. Run your program with each set of input data to verify that your program output matches the test oracle predictions.

```
Enter (x1,y1): 0.0  0.0
Enter (x2,y2): -1.0  1.0
        Slope: -1
```

2H   Using Objects

First, develop an algorithm that determines the final grade percentage using the weighted scale shown below. Add two additional sets of test data of your own choosing to the test oracle below. Then closely trace your algorithm with each set of data to verify that the result is the same as your hand-calculated results. Use your algorithm to implement a program that computes the percentage.

	Weights	──── Test Oracle ──── Test #1	Test #2	Test #3
Test One	20%	80.0	_____	_____
Test Two	20%	85.0	_____	_____
Final Exam	25%	90.0	_____	_____
Lab Projects	35%	92.0	_____	_____
	Percentage:	87.7	_____	_____

2I   Using Objects

Write a C++ program that prompts for an integer that represents the amount of change (in cents) to be handed back to a customer in the United States. First, display the minimum number of half dollars, quarters, dimes, nickels, and pennies that will make the correct change. *Hint:* With increasingly longer expressions, you could use / and % to evaluate the number of each coin. Or you could calculate the total number of coins with / and the remaining change with %. Test your program with cents equal to 16, 91, and 83. When *83* is input, your dialogue should look exactly like this:

```
Enter change [0..99]: 83
The minimum coins required to return 83 cents
=================================================
 Half(ves): 1
Quarter(s): 1
   Dime(s): 0
 Nickel(s): 1
Penny(ies): 3
```

2J   Using Objects

Write a C++ program that prompts for an integer that represents the amount of change in pence to be handed back to a customer in the United Kingdom. Display the minimum number of coins that will make the correct change. The available coins are (p represents pence) 1p, 2p, 5p, 10p, 20p, 50p, and 100p (the one-pound coin). Verify that your program works correctly by running it with change in pence equal to 0, 1, 2, 5, 10, 15, 20, 50, and 298. When *298* is input, your dialogue should look exactly like this:

```
Enter change: 298
The minimum coins required to return 298 pence
=============================================

100p  50p  20p  10p   5p   2p   1p
====  ===  ===  ===  ===  ===  ===
  2    1    2    0    1    1    1
```

2K   Using Objects

Write a program that computes a weighted average to determine a final grade that consists of two tests, a quiz average, and a program average. The final grade is computed using the following weights: each test is worth 25%, the quiz average is worth 15%, and the program average is 35%. One dialogue should look as shown below with ??.? replaced with the correct answer. Before coding your solution, predict the output using the input shown below.

```
        Enter two tests: 78  88
     Enter quiz average: 82.5
  Enter program average: 92.7
             Final Grade: ??.?
```

3

Abstractions

Through include directives like #include <iostream.h>, we add code that has been written by other programmers. We benefit as consumers of existing software. In this chapter, we gain access to even more software such as mathematical functions, a few author-supplied functions, and some new classes. We will also learn more about input and output streams and extracting input from disk files. We learn to use this software through *abstraction*—ignoring details to concentrate on essentials. In the process we learn to use existing functions via comments describing what the function assumes and what it promises to do. In the second part of this chapter, we learn to use some more existing objects such as output streams, input file streams, strings, and bank accounts.

The major theme of this chapter is how to use functions and objects through abstraction. The abstractions are provided to us in the form of individual function declarations or entire class declarations, which are essentially a collection of function declarations. These abstractions allow us to use many functions, cout operations, and several new objects while ignoring their detailed implementations. Mostly, we will be learning to call functions, which may or may not be part of a C++ class.

After studying this chapter, you will be able to:

1. Use some of the nonmember functions declared in math.h (sqrt, sin, ceil, and pow) and the double class.
2. Use a few author-supplied functions.
3. Use some member functions of the ostream (output stream) class.
4. Use ifstream (input file stream) objects to extract input from files.
5. Use string and bankAccount objects through their own sets of member functions.

3.1   Function Abstractions

Some programming tasks are required by many different programs. These tasks include such things as finding the square root of a number, determining the sine or cosine of an angle, searching a list for a specific value, managing a collection of values, obtaining keyboard and file input, and generating screen output. Through existing software, C++ provides all programmers with the ability to perform such tasks. The next bit of software we look at is a collection of mathematical functions including these two:

```
sqrt(x)      Return the square root of the argument x.
pow(x,y)     Return the value of x to the yth power.
```

Many functions are *called* by specifying the name of the function, followed by the appropriate number and class of arguments within parentheses. One general form of a function call is as follows (we will see two other forms later in this chapter):

function-name (*argument-list*)

where *function-name* is a previously declared identifier representing a function name and *argument-list* is a set of zero or more expressions separated by commas. In the following function call, the function name is sqrt (square root) and the argument is 81.0:

```
sqrt(81.0)
```

Many functions may have zero, one, or more arguments. Although most math functions require exactly one argument, others—such as the power function—require exactly two arguments. In the following function call, the function name is pow (power), the arguments are base and power, and the function call pow(base, power) is replaced with base^power, which with the initial value of these two int objects is 8:

```
int base = 2;
int power = 3;
cout << pow(base, power);    // Output: 8
```

Any argument used in a function call must be an expression from an acceptable class. For example, the function call sqrt("Bobbie"); results in a compiletime error because the argument is not one of the numeric classes. The function call sqrt(2.0, 3.0) is also an error because sqrt requires exactly one argument, not two.

The function must also be supplied with reasonable arguments so we receive a correct evaluation. For example, the function call sqrt(-4.0); generates a runtime error because -4.0 is not in the *domain* of function sqrt. The square root function is not defined for negative numeric values. The sqrt function operates correctly only if certain conditions are met (i.e., argument ≥ 0). Here is a summary of sqrt and some of the other functions that are made available through the following compiler directive (*Note:* double is a new class described below):

```
#include <math.h>
```

Partial List of Functions Declared in math.h

Function	Argument Type (class)	Return Type	Value Returned	Example	Returned Value
ceil(x)	double	double	Smallest int ≥ x	ceil(2.1)	3.0
cos(x)	double	double	Cosine of x radians	cos(1.0)	0.5403
fabs(x)	double	double	Absolute value of x	fabs(-1.5)	1.5
floor(x)	double	double	Largest int ≤ x	floor(2.9)	2.0
pow(x,y)	double	double	x to the yth power (x^y)	pow(2,4)	16.0
sin(x)	double	double	Sine of x radians	sin(1.0)	0.84147
sqrt(x)	double	double	Square root of x	sqrt(4.0)	2.0

These are but a few of the functions available in math.h. Figure 3.1 is the first example of an *interface diagram*—a modified version of Grady Booch's module diagram. Interface diagrams summarize the functions in ovals (exp and tan are added), classes in rectangles (there are none shown in this example), and named constants in rectangles (M_PI defined as 3.14159265358979323846) that are available through the include file (math.h shown as the heading). The three dots indicate that there are more functions, classes, or named constants available. The shaded box represents a *module*—the unit of code that serves as a building block for programs.

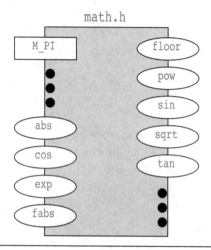

Figure 3.1   *Partial interface diagram for module math.h*

3.1.1   The double Class

Notice that double is specified for each argument and each function return type. The double class is very similar to the float class. A double object stores floating point values and has the same set of operations. The difference between float and double is in the number of significant digits the two respective classes can handle. There are many classes of numeric objects. (See Appendix C for a complete list of the numeric classes). However, the double class of numbers is frequently used for several reasons.

First, double objects usually store approximately double (twice) the number of significant digits of a float counterpart. The double class is specified by designers of the math library because sometimes the precision (the number of significant digits) provided by the float class is just not enough. Values too large, or very close to 0.0 that are stored as a float object may result in a loss of precision (or value). In general, using double objects rather than float objects improves the accuracy of the stored floating-point value. The double class of objects produces more precise results (a truer answer of 3.0 rather than 2.99998, for example). Another benefit of the specification of double as the argument and return type is that the double class of objects allows mathematical functions to take any numeric argument such as int, float, or double.

When a math.h function name is encountered, the function gets a copy of the arguments. For example, sqrt(16.0) copies 16.0 to the sqrt function. The function executes and then a value replaces the function call. As shown in the following program, these returned values are sent to the output object named cout.

Programming Tip

Virtually all C++ programs use one or more include files. Failure to include the proper files results in compiletime errors. For example, if the #include directives are deleted from the beginning of the following program, many errors and warnings are generated usually related to the use of the math functions and cout. This omission means we don't have access to the function declarations.

```
// Show some of the many mathematical functions available with math.h
#include <iostream.h>
#include <math.h>

int main()
{
   cout << "1. Function Call   Return Result" << endl << endl
        << "   pow(2, 10)     " << pow(2, 10)    << endl
        << "pow(4.0, 0.5)     " << pow(4.0, 0.5) << endl
        << "    sqrt(4.0)     " << sqrt(4.0)     << endl
        << "     sin(1.0)     " << sin(1.0)      << endl
        << "     cos(1.0)     " << cos(1.0)      << endl
        << endl;

   double x = -2.1;
   cout << "2. Function Call   Return Result" << endl
        << "     fabs(x)      " << fabs(x)       << endl
        << "     ceil(x)      " << ceil(x)       << endl
        << "    floor(x)      " << floor(x)      << endl;

   return 0;
}
```

─── **Output** ───

```
1. Function Call   Return Result

   pow(2, 10)      1024
pow(4.0, 0.5)      2
    sqrt(4.0)      2
     sin(1.0)      0.841471
     cos(1.0)      0.540302
```

```
2. Function Call   Return Result

     fabs(x)         2.1
     ceil(x)        -2
    floor(x)        -3
```

Programming Tip

Even though the values of ceil and floor are returned as double values (floating point numbers), by default, C++ shows the minimum number of significant digits. And if there is no fraction to show, the decimal point does not appear. This means that the return value of sqrt(4.0) is displayed as 2 rather than 2.0. Unless some extra work is done, a lot of float and double output looks like integer values as the result of stream insertion operations.

Although many math functions typically have only one argument, the pow function requires two arguments. The first argument represents the base and the second argument represents the power. For example, pow(2.0, 3.0) returns 8.0, which is 2.0 raised to the 3.0 power. The function call pow(3.0, 2.0) returns 9.0, which is 3.0 squared. As another example, the function call pow(4.0, 0.5) returns 2.0, which is the square root of 4.0 or 4.0 raised to the 0.5 power.

3.1.2 Evaluating Expressions with Functions

When functions are used in expressions, they are evaluated before any of the arithmetic operators are applied, as shown in the next example:

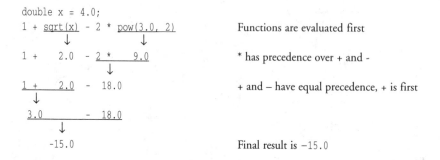

If the argument of the function is an expression with operators or other functions, that argument expression is evaluated first, as shown in this expression:

```
1 + sqrt(floor(9 + 9.9) - 2 * ceil(6.2))
                ↓
1 + sqrt(floor( 18.9  ) - 2 * ceil(6.2))
                              ↓
1 + sqrt(    18          - 2 *    7     )
                              ↓
1 + sqrt(    18          -    14        )
                         ↓
1 + sqrt(                4              )
         ↓
1 +   2
  ↓
3
```

3.1.3   Function-Related Errors

There are several kinds of errors related to functions. Specifying the incorrect number of arguments in a function call usually results in a compiletime error. For example, the compiler will detect sqrt(1,2,3); as having too many arguments and sqrt() as too few. Type mismatch errors occur when the argument does not match the class. For example the sqrt("x"); is an attempt to use a string constant when a numeric argument (int, float, or double) is expected. Function-related errors may also occur when the argument is not in the domain of the function. Even if the value is acceptable to the expected class (double with math functions) and the correct number of arguments are specified (one or two expressions between the parentheses), the function may not be defined for the value of the expression supplied as the argument. For example, the function call sqrt(x); results in a runtime error when x is negative because the square root of a negative number is undefined. The argument x must be in the domain of the function. The domain of the sqrt function is 0.0 or any positive numeric value.

An argument in a function call may be too large to be represented as a double. For example, ceil(1e1000) has an argument that causes trouble because an attempt is made to copy the argument to the function. The exponent (1000) is larger than allowed for the double class.

Even if the arguments can be passed to the function, the result may be outside of the double range. The function call pow(999.0, 999.0) is an example that has a result outside the range of the double type.

Examples of Function-Related Errors

Function Call	Comment
floor(2.5, 4.0)	Too many arguments, floor requires one argument
sin()	Too few arguments, sin requires one argument
floor("1.76")	floor requires an int or float argument, not a string
sqrt(-1.0)	Negative numbers are not in the domain of the square root function
pow(999.0, 999.0);	Result is not in the range of doubles. A runtime error occurs

The following program demonstrates a few function-related errors that occur at runtime because of the arguments and the limited range of doubles.

```
#include <math.h>
#include <iostream.h>
int main()
{
  double x = -1.23;
  cout << "    fabs(x): " << fabs(x)      << endl; // Okay
  cout << " pow(2,1024): " << pow(2,1024)  << endl; // Results are
  cout << "ceil(1e1000): " << ceil(1e1000) << endl; //    too big
  return 0;
}
```

Output

Note: Try running the previous program on your system. You may experience different results. The two results shown next demonstrate just two of many different possibilities):

One UNIX-Based Compiler

```
    fabs(x): 1.23
 pow(2,1024): 0
ceil(1e1000): Infinity
```

One DOS-Based Compiler

```
    fabs(x): 1.23
pow: OVERFLOW error
 pow(2,1024): 1.797693e+308
ceil(1e1000): Floating point error: Overflow
Abnormal program termination
```

3.1.4 Preconditions and Postconditions

For a function to behave properly, certain conditions are presumed. For example, the sqrt function assumes the argument is a numeric value greater than or equal to 0.0. The assumptions stated about the argument(s) to a function are referred to as the *preconditions* of the function. If the preconditions are not met, all bets are off and the result is system dependent. Some systems cause program termination with an arithmetic over-flow error; others may return values such as the largest float available or NaN (not a number). The user must satisfy the preconditions.

Other comments that describe a function are the *postconditions*—the statements that describe what the function does if the preconditions are met. Here is the sqrt function described in terms of preconditions and postconditions:

```
double sqrt(double x);
//  Precondition: x ≥ 0
// Postcondition: Returns the square root of x
```

The comments indicate that sqrt requires the arguments to be greater than or equal to 0.0. If this precondition is met, the square root of that argument is returned. If this is not met, the result is undefined.

Function Call	Return Result
sqrt(-1.0)	Precondition not met. The result is undefined and system dependent (e.g., the largest double or NaN, not a number)

If we know what type of data is required to call the function, we sometimes do not need to satisfy any preconditions. For example, the ceil function takes one double argument. We could state the obvious by saying a valid double in the range of double is required as an argument. But this information is specified as the parameter and it would be redundant to repeat it. The argument must be a valid double. The preconditions could be written as "None":

```
double ceil(double x);
//  Preconditions: None
// Postconditions: Returns the smallest integer ≥ x
```

From now on, function preconditions will be included only if necessary. In this text, the label for preconditions will be abbreviated as PRE: and for postconditions as POST:. The same function (ceil) may now be documented as follows:

```
double ceil(double x);
// POST: Returns the smallest integer >= x
```

3.1.5 Function Prototypes

The previous descriptions of sqrt and ceil can be useful in determining how to use those functions. In fact, any function can be documented with the *function prototype* in this general form:

return-type   function-name   (parameter-list) ;

to completely describe the manner in which function calls must be made. The definition of the function (the complete implementation) is not present. Also, based on the information supplied by the function prototype, a compiler can determine what is a valid function call and what is not. Prototypes reveal many things to users of this function, including the number and class of arguments required to properly invoke the function, and the all-important function name and the type of object returned by the function.

Now, consider the `floor` function prototype:

```
double floor(double x);
// POST: Returns the largest integer <= x
```

Here we see that the return type is `double`. So a `double` numeric value will replace a valid function call. The function name is `floor`. The parameter list consists of one `double` named x. This means that we must supply exactly one numeric argument in all calls to the `floor` function.

The parameter list shown in function prototypes is a collection of zero or more parameters separated by commas where each parameter may have one of these general forms:

class-name   identifier
class-name & identifier

So a function prototype may list 0, 1, 2, or more parameters separated by commas between the parentheses. Here is a function prototype with three parameters:

```
double threeParms(char ch, int j, float x);
```

The arguments are the values that match the parameters when the function is called. Exactly one argument of an acceptable type is required for each parameter listed in the function prototype. So in the case of `threeParms`, exactly three arguments must be present in the call. Function calls to `threeParms` with two or four arguments results in an error.

We must also pay attention to the class of parameters. Specifically, we must supply arguments that can be assigned to the parameter. Each argument in the function call is copied to its associated parameter. Here are some examples of correct calls of `threeParms` used to initialize some `double` objects:

Valid Calls of threeParms

```
double result1 = threeParms('a', 10, 1.2);
double result2 = threeParms('$', -2,  15);
double result3 = threeParms('t',  1, 2.3);
```

The following attempts to call `threeParms` result in compiletime errors:

Errors	Reason for Error
`threeParms('a', 1 );`	Need three arguments
`threeParms("$", -2, 15);`	`String` can't be assigned to `char`
`threeParms(2.3, 1, 't');`	`Float` can't be assigned to `char`
`threeParms('a', 1, 2, 9);`	Too many arguments
`threeParms;`	Need parentheses and three proper arguments

Arguments match parameters by position—first argument to the first parameter, second argument to the second parameter, and so on. For example, when `threeParms` is called, the first parameter is assigned the value of the first argument, the second parameter gets the value of the second argument, and the third argument to the function is copied into the third parameter x. When `threeParms` is called with arguments 'a', 100, and 1.2, like this:

```
int threeParms(       char ch, int j, float x);
                       ↑       ↑      ↑
double result4 = threeParms('a',   100,    1.2);
```

it's as if these three assignment operations occur:

```
ch = 'a';  j = 100;  x = 1.2;
```

Much can be deduced from a function prototype when it is accompanied with the function pre- and postconditions. For example, from the `sin` function prototype complete with pre- and postconditions,

```
double sin(double x);
// POST: Returns the sine of x radians in the range of -1 to 1
```

the following information is ascertained:

return-type	`double`
function-name	`sin`
parameter name	`x`

number of arguments	1
data type of argument	double (or any numeric such as int)
general usage comment	Return value computed as though the argument is expressed in radians rather than degrees—sin(45) does *not* return the sine of 45 degrees.

We should also be able to determine the return results (with the help of a calculator in radian mode):

Function Call	Return Result
sin(3.1415926/2.0)	1.0
sin(1.0)	0.8421 (approximately)
sin(3.1415926)	0.0

Self-Check

1. Write the value returned for each of the following function calls, or write ERROR if any type of error results. (*Note:* A calculator may be required for sin and cos.)

   a. sqrt(16)
   b. sqrt(2,4)
   c. sqrt(-1.0)
   d. sqrt("-1")
   e. floor()
   f. ceil(3, 4)
   g. ceil(3.4 - 0.5)

   h. floor(-1.5)
   i. floor(1.5)
   j. floor(-1)
   k. ceil(pow(100,100))
   l. pow(4.0,0.5)
   m. pow(2,3)
   n. sqrt(14 % 3 - 1)

   o. pow(3.0, 2.0)
   p. cos(0.0)
   q. sin(0.0)
   r. sin()
   s. ceil(-1.9)
   t. sqrt 16.0
   u. 1 % ceil(-0.9)

2. Given the math.h pow function complete with some rather complicated preconditions and postconditions, determine the following information from the function prototype:

   a. return type
   b. function name
   c. number of arguments

   d. class of first argument
   e. class of second argument
   f. class of third argument

   ```
   double pow(double x, double y)
   //  PRE: When y is a real, x is positive
   //       When y is an integer, x may be negative
   // POST: Return value is x to the y power
   ```

3. Write the return result for each function call or explain the error.

a. pow(3, 2)   d. pow(16.0, 0.5)

b. pow(-2, 5)   e. pow(-16.0, 2)

c. pow(1, 1)   f. pow(10.0)

Answers

1. a. 4
   b. ERROR (sqrt must have one argument)
   c. ERROR (-1.0 is undefined for sqrt)
   d. ERROR (sqrt needs one numeric argument)
   e. ERROR (floor must have one argument)
   f. ERROR(ceil must have one argument)
   g. 3
   h. -2
   i. 1
   j. -1
   k. ERROR (argument too large)
   l. 2.0 (same as sqrt(4.0))
   m. 8
   n. 1
   o. 9
   p. 1
   q. 0

   r. ERROR (sin needs one argument)
   s. -1
   t. ERROR: Missing (and)
   u. ERROR (division by 0)

2. a. double
   b. pow
   c. 2
   d. double (any numeric class)
   e. double (any numeric class)
   f. There is no third argument.

3. a. 9
   b. -32
   c. 1
   d. 4.0 ($x^{0.5}$ is the square root of x)
   e. 256
   f. This is a compiletime error since pow needs two arguments.

3.2 Function decimals(cout, n)

You may have already noticed float objects displayed on the screen with a seemingly uncontrollable number of decimal places. The *default* situation—the one that occurs unless we do something else—for floating-point output is to show the minimum number of decimal places. With float x = 1.2, cout << x displays 1.2. With float x = 1.23, cout << x displays 1.23. If more than seven digits (six on some systems) are required, exponential notation kicks in. This means with float x = 12345678.9, cout << x displays 1.23457e+07. Additionally, 1.0 appears as an int (1) with no trailing zeros. So if we want to represent a currency value of 1056.00, we might see only 1056.

The output could be controlled through a sequence of function calls that alter the state of the ostream object cout. Or we could use one function call that performs the necessary operations with a simpler interface. And so, a function declared in ourstuff.h is provided to more easily control the appearance of output and avoid repetition of the several function calls. The decimals function is called with code such as decimals(cout, 2) or decimals(cout, 3). Its prototype is previewed here because it has a few new elements:

```
void decimals(ostream & cout, int n);
```

One new element is the keyword void, which means the function returns nothing. In other words, we must call the function as a stand-alone statement because there is no expectation of a return value. Another element introduced here is the class name *ostream*. Because the function prototype shows an ostream (output stream class) parameter named cout (the same name as the object with which we are familiar), the first argument to decimals must be an ostream object (and cout is the only ostream object we have so far). The second parameter is an int, so the second argument to function decimals should be an int object. Because there is no return value, the decimals function is called as a stand-alone statement where the first argument (cout) is the ostream object to which formatting changes are made:

```
decimals(cout, 2);
```

The third new element in the function prototype is the *reference* symbol &. Whenever you see & between the class name and the parameter name, it means the state of the associated argument may be altered. Since cout is the first argument, it is cout that is altered—specifically, the default formatting characteristics of cout are modified to show a decimal (possibly trailing zeros) and to avoid exponential notation. Subsequent insertions into cout are displayed differently on the screen.

The entire function prototype for decimals with pre- and postconditions is now given:

```
void decimals(ostream & cout, int n);
//   PRE: n >= 0. The argument associated with cout is initialized.
//
// POST: The state of the ostream object is altered such that all
//        floating-point values are displayed on the output screen
//        with exactly n decimals places. Trailing zeros are output
//        when necessary. The state of the output stream is affected
//        until the end of the program or decimals(cout, n) is
//        called again with a different value for n.
//        No value replaces the function call. However, the
//        first argument--usually the output stream cout--is affected.
//        When n = 0, the stream is set back to default formatting.
```

The file named ourstuff.h (on the accompanying disk) declares a collection of functions used occasionally throughout this text. Some of these functions should also prove useful for completion of lab projects. They are made available with the following include directive:

```
#include "ourstuff.h"   // Note: " " instead of <  >
```

Notice that the include filename is delimited by the double quote special symbol (" ") rather than the angle brackets (< >). This different notation causes the C++ compiler to first look in the working or current directory for this source code. If < and > are used, a search may not be made, and the search is confined to where your compiler stores the other include files, such as iostream.h. All include files that are part of this textbook (those that begin with "our") will be included using " " rather than < >. This allows you to have these files in your own working or current directory.

Self-Check

1. Using the function prototype, the preconditions, and the postconditions of the decimals function, ascertain the following information:
   a.   What does the function do?
   b.   What type of value is returned?
   c.   What is the function name?
   d.   How many arguments are required in each call to decimals?
   e.   Name one object that may be used as the first argument to decimals.
   f.   What class of argument should be used for the second argument?
2. What happens if the second argument is negative?
3. Write a valid call to function decimals.

Answers
1. a. Alters the state of an output stream to show n decimals with trailing zeros if necessary.
   b. None   c. decimals   d. Two   e. cout   f. int
2. Because the argument fails to meet the precondition, effects upon cout are undefined.
3. decimals(cout,3);

3.2.1   Using decimals to Alter cout's State

The decimals function alters the default formatting state of cout. The following program shows the differences between this default and the change in the appearance of subsequent floating-point output after decimals is called to alter the state of cout:

```
// A few practical uses which show output with 2 and 3 decimals
#include "ourstuff.h"
#include <iostream.h>

int main()
{
  float GPA = 8.0/3.0;
  cout << "        GPA with default output = " << GPA << endl;
  decimals(cout, 3);
  cout << "Same GPA after decimals(cout, 3); = " << GPA << endl << endl;
```

```
float cost = 9.99;
// Apply a 6.52% tax to cost:
cost = cost + 0.0652 * cost;

// Reset state of cout to original formatting defaults (n=0)
decimals(cout, 0);
cout << "     Currency with default output = " << cost << endl;
decimals(cout, 2);
cout << "Currency after decimals(cout, 2); = " << cost << endl;
return 0;
}
```

— Output —

Note: Exact appearance of output is system dependent.

```
          GPA with default output = 2.6666667
Same GPA after decimals(cout, 3); = 2.667

      Currency with default output = 10.641348
Currency after decimals(cout, 2); = 10.64
```

Programming Tip

The state of some arguments is altered by the function call. The state of other arguments is not altered. For example, when sqrt(x) is encountered, it may appear as though x is altered. But it is not. The sqrt prototype is

```
double sqrt(double x);
```

indicating that the argument is copied to the parameter x. The return value replaces the entire function call. The argument x is not changed. On the other hand, a reference parameter (&) is an indication that the state of the associated object argument will be altered. Such is the case with decimals, which has this prototype:

```
void decimals(ostream & cout, int n);
```

to indicate the argument associated with the first parameter may have altered state (but n does not). Therefore in this function call:

```
decimals(cout, n);
```

the state of cout will be altered, but n's state cannot be altered. The only purpose of the second argument is to supply information to the function, just like x and y in pow(x,y).

Self-Check

1. Write the output generated by the following program:

```
#include "ourstuff.h"
#include <iostream.h>
int main()
{
   double x = 123.45555;
   cout << x << endl;
   decimals(cout, 2);
   cout << x << endl;
   decimals(cout, 0);
   cout << x << endl;
   return 0;
}
```

Answer
  1. 123.45555
      123.46
      123.45555

3.3   Case Study: Height and Distance of a Projectile

In this case study, the height and distance of a projectile are computed for a given moment in time. Assuming no wind resistance, the distance and height at a given time during its flight are given as follows:

```
distance = (velocity * cos(angle)) * seconds
height = -0.5 * gravity * seconds² + (velocity * sin(angle)) * seconds
```

where `velocity` is the initial velocity of the projectile at takeoff, `angle` is the takeoff angle from level ground, `gravity` is the acceleration due to gravity (9.8 meters per second per second), and `seconds` is the length of time the projectile has been in flight. The path of the projectile might look like this, where each dot represents the projectile at 1.0, 2.0, 3.0, 4.0, and 5.0 seconds using a takeoff angle of 45°:

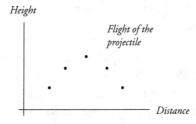

Height

Flight of the projectile

Distance

3.3.1 Analysis

Problem: *Write a program that displays the height and distance of a projectile at a given moment in time for any given takeoff angle (in degrees) and any initial velocity.*

Given a value for `seconds`, the takeoff `angle`, and an initial `velocity`, the `distance` and `height` at one particular moment must be displayed. The input and output are summarized as follows:

Input
- `angle`   a numeric value representing degrees (45 for example)
- `velocity`   a numeric speed in meters per second (35 for example)
- `seconds`   a floating point value (0.0 through 10.0 seconds for example)

Output
- `height`   at the given `seconds` into the flight (rounded to 1 decimal place)
- `distance`   at the given `seconds` into the flight (rounded to 1 decimal place)

The program must have an interactive dialogue. For example, when the takeoff angle is 45 degrees and the initial velocity is 35 meters per second, at 0.0 seconds, the dialogue should look exactly like this:

```
───────────────────── Dialogue ─────────────────────
   Takeoff angle in degrees: 45.0
     Initial velocity (m/s): 35.0
    Seconds into the flight: 0.0

   After 0 seconds, the projectile is at (in meters)
     height = 0
   distance = 0
```

3.3.2 Design

This program can be designed by starting with an algorithm based on the IPO algorithmic model:

> Input: Obtain takeoff angle, initial velocity, and seconds
> Process: Compute height and distance
> Output: Display height and distance

The Input and Output steps are easily accomplished with the help of the `cout` and `cin` objects. The Process step requires application of the formulas for height and distance. When we look at those formulas, we should recognize the need for the existing arithmetic operators -, *, and +. You are also asked to consider that if the `sin` and `cos` functions did not exist, we would have to spend a considerable amount of time implementing the functions. But in this design phase, we should ask ourselves if these functions have already been implemented. By legally using someone else's software, we save ourselves from the effort of implementation and testing. So the design decision is to use existing functions for the **Process** step. The program should accurately implement the formulas for height and distance, but not the functions for cos and sin. But we must know how to use them and read the function documentation, which states that the return value assumes the angle was specified in radians. If we express the angle in degrees, an intent error occurs—the result is not what we want.

```
double cos(double x);
// POST: The cosine of x radians is returned (-1.0 through 1.0)
```

Programming Tip

The sin and cos functions assume that the argument is provided in radians. If you wish to determine the sin and cos of an angle given in degrees, the angle must first be converted from degrees to radians by multiplying the number of degrees by $\pi/180.0$ where $\pi \approx 3.1415926$. For example,

```
const float degToRad = 3.1415926 / 180;
float angle = 90.0;
cout << "sine of 90.0 degrees: " << sin(angle*degToRad);
```

Output

```
sine of 90.0 degrees: 1
```

Before we begin to implement a computer-based solution, it would be helpful to determine the height and distance for several values of seconds—a test oracle. Both height and distance formulas are multiplied by seconds, so when seconds is 0.0, height and distance are easily computed to 0.0. For all other values of seconds (1, 2, 3, 4, 5, and 6), a calculator is required. You are not asked to compute these values. They are supplied to track the projectile's flight in tabular form.

Test Oracle

Takeoff Angle	Velocity m/s	Seconds	Height	Distance (Meters)
45.0	35.0	0.0	0.0	0.0
"	"	1.0	19.8	24.7
"	"	2.0	29.9	49.5
"	"	3.0	30.1	74.2
"	"	4.0	20.6	99.0
"	"	5.0	1.2	123.7
"	"	6.0	−27.9	148.5

Self-Check ────

Assuming the above input data tracks the path of a golf ball (and the input data reasonably does), answer the following questions.

1. For which value of seconds is the height of the golf ball closest to its maximum?
2. Between which two values for seconds did the golf ball height pass from positive to negative?
3. For which value of seconds is the height closest to ground level (zero)?

Answers
1. 3
2. 5 and 6
3. 5

3.3.3 Implementation

The following program is one possible translation of the IPO algorithm, complete with the necessary overhead such as the include directives to allow references to cout, cin, cos, pow, and sin, and the object declarations to represent the variables from the formulas:

```
// Given an initial velocity, a takeoff angle, and using an
// input value for seconds, this program determines the
// height and distance (in meters) of a projectile.
#include <iostream.h>   // for cout and cin
#include <math.h>       // for sin, cos, and pow
#include "ourstuff.h"   // for decimals(cout, 1)

int main()
{
    // Acceleration due to gravity in meters per second per second
    const double gravity = 9.8;
    // Conversion factor for converting from degrees to radians
    const double degToRad = 3.1415926 / 180.0;

    // Declare Objects
    double velocity;            // Takeoff speed in meters/second
    double aDegrees;            // Angle as input
    double aRadians;            // Angle in its radian equivalent
    double seconds;             // Time in flight in seconds
    double height, distance;    // Computer and then displayed

    // I)nput:
    cout << "Takeoff angle in degrees: ";
    cin >> aDegrees;
```

```
cout << " Initial velocity (m/s): ";
cin >> velocity;
cout << " Seconds into the flight: ";
cin >> seconds;

// P)rocess: Compute height and distance
aRadians = aDegrees * degToRad;
distance =(velocity * cos(aRadians)) * seconds;
height = -0.5 * gravity * pow(seconds, 2)
            +(velocity * sin(aRadians)) * seconds;

// O)utput: Display height and distance
// This is intentionally written as a comment:   decimals(cout, 1);
cout << endl
     << "After " << seconds
     << " seconds, the projectile is at (in meters)"  << endl
     << "  height = " << height                        << endl
     << "distance = " << distance                      << endl;

return 0;
}
```

―――――――――――――――― **Dialogue** ――――――――――――――――

```
Takeoff angle in degrees: 45.0
   Initial velocity (m/s): 35.0
 Seconds into the flight: 5.05

After 5.05 seconds, the projectile is at (in meters)
   height = 0.018872
distance = 124.981125
```

Given the input value of 5.05 for seconds, the output indicates that the height is only about 18.9 millimeters above the ground. This indicates that a golf ball would hit the ground (assuming a level fairway) at approximately 5.05 seconds. Incidentally, at this time the golf ball would have traveled approximately 125 meters.

Now if you return to the analysis section, you should see that the output specification stated height and distance are to be shown with one decimal place. To produce this output, the file ourstuff.h was included. But the decimals function call was intentionally commented out to show the difference between the default output above, and the following output that has each floating-point value displayed to the nearest tenth with decimal point and trailing zero displayed:

```
After 5.05 seconds, the projectile is at (in meters)
   height = 0.0
distance = 125.0
```

3.3.4   Testing the Implementation

We have already seen separately calculated values for height and distance when values for seconds were 0.0, 1.0, 2.0, 3.0, 4.0, 5.0, and 6.0 for the same velocity and takeoff angle. This program can be tested by comparing the hand-calculated results shown in the test oracle with the output produced from a series of program runs using the various values of seconds. It is good practice to determine some test data and the expected results before moving to the implementation phase. This helps us understand the problem better. We may also find that the program executes, but not correctly. In other words, an intent error (bug) may exist. We should compare the expected results with the program output; if they match, there is a possibility that the program works correctly. Just remember that if the program output doesn't produce the expected results, the hand-calculated results may be wrong.

One final point: It is helpful to know the difference between reasonable input that produces reasonable answers and improbable input that may result in strange results. For example, if you have ever witnessed a golf ball in flight, it would be unreasonable to think that the height of a golf ball would be positive before 0.0 seconds or after 30.0 seconds.

Self-Check

1. Why are gravity and degToRad good candidates to be constant objects?
2. Why must we call sin and cos with angles expressed in radians rather than degrees?
3. To the nearest tenth, compute the height and distance of a soccer ball after 1.7 and 1.8 seconds using a takeoff angle of 20.0 degrees and an initial velocity of 25 meters per second.

Answers

1. The gravitational constant does not change, nor does the degrees to radians conversion factor ($\pi/180$). Also, using const prevents accidental changes. If declared as non-const objects, we could accidentally alter the object's state.
2. cos and sin presume arguments are in radians.
3. At 1.7 seconds height = 0.4 meters, distance = 39.9 meters. You provide the answer for 1.8 and predict how far the soccer ball travels before hitting the ground.

Exercises

1. Predict the value returned by each of the following function calls:

   a. sqrt(pow(1.234,2))   d. pow(-2, 5)   g. fabs(5-9)
   b. ceil(2.001)   e. pow(pow(2,2),5)   h. sqrt(16.0)
   c. floor(1.999)   f. decimals(cout, 2)   i. sqrt(sqrt(16))

2. Describe the error in each of these attempts at calls:

   a. `pow(2)`

   b. `sqrt(-2)`

   c. `fabs("-1")`

   d. `decimals(2, 3)`

   e. `pow(1000, 9999)`

   f. `sin(sin)`

   g. `FLOOR(6.5)`

   h. `SqRt(16.0)`

   i. `pow 2,4`

   j. `sqrt(sqrt(16)`

   k. `sqrt("4")`

   l. `decimals(cout, -1)`

3. Convert 90° to radians.

4. Declare a constant object g that represents gravity at 32 feet per second per second.

5. Using the function prototype, the preconditions, and the postconditions of the `floor` function, ascertain the information requested below:

```
double floor(double x);
// POST: floor returns the largest integer <= x
```

   a. What does this function return?

   b. What type of value is returned?

   c. What is the function name?

   d. How many arguments are required?

   e. May the argument be negative?

   f. Write a valid function call for `floor()`.

6. Write a statement that alters the state of the output stream cout such that exactly 5 decimal places are always shown for float and double output.

7. Identify the include file where each function is located:

   a. `ceil`

   b. `floor`

   c. `sqrt`

   d. `pow`

   e. `decimals`

   f. `sin`

8. The header file `ourstuff.h` contains two other functions described as follows:

```
void clearScreen()
// POST: All screen output is cleared and the cursor
//       is positioned in the upper left corner

void causeApause();
// POST: Displays a message and pauses the program
//       until the user presses the Enter key
```

   a. How many arguments are required to call function `clearScreen`?

   b. What does `clearScreen` return?

   c. Write a valid function call to `clearScreen`.

   d. How many arguments are required to call function `causeApause`?

   e. What does `causeApause` return?

   f. Write a valid function call to `causeApause`.

Lab Projects

Note: If you are using GNU g++, you must link to the math library for any program using any of the functions from math.h. If your file is named 3a.cc, try using the UNIX command g++ 3a.cc -lm

3A   Using Objects

Copy the following program exactly as shown (*Note:* The endl insertions are there for blank lines to make it easier to read your output):

```
#include <math.h>
#include <iostream.h>
int main()
{
    cout << endl << endl;
    cout << sqrt(-1) ;
    return 0;
}
```

Compile, link, and run this program and on a separate piece of paper, write down the output or describe what happens if a runtime error occurs.

Next, edit your file and replace the function call sqrt(-1) with each of the following function calls. Recompile, link, and run the program and observe the errors. On a separate piece of paper, write the letters of the function calls that cause:

1. compiletime errors
2. runtime errors (*Note: Different systems may treat some functions differently.*)
3. incorrect results
4. correct results

a. sqrt("-1") ;   e. pow(2.0, 0.5) ;
b. pow(10000, 10000) ;   f. pow(-2.0, 0.5) ;
c. floor() ;   g. sin(1.0) ;
d. ceil(1.23e555) ;   h. myfun(3) ;

3B   Using Objects

Write a program that extracts any double input and an integer representing the number of decimal places to show. Use this test oracle and the sample dialogue (below) to test your implementation.

double Input	Number of Decimals	Value
4.56789	2	4.57
4.56789	3	4.568
4.56789	1	4.6
9.9999	6	10

──────── Test Oracle ────────

──────── Dialogue ────────

```
Enter double: 4.56789
Decimal places: 2
Rounded output: 4.57
```

3C   Using Objects

Write a program that extracts any double input, which after an appropriate label shows the return value from the following functions (assume x is the extracted double object):

1. the square root of x
2. x to the 0.5 power
3. x to the 2.5 power
4. the ceiling of x
5. the floor of x
6. the absolute value of x

Here is the beginning of a sample dialogue (always show 2 decimals places with trailing zeros):

──────── Dialogue ────────

```
        Enter x: 2.4
     Square root: 1.55
To the 0.5 power: 1.55
     ...
```

Once your output matches your test oracle, try running your program with a negative input like -2.4.

3D   Using Objects

Write a program that outputs the range of a projectile to the nearest tenth of a meter. The formula is:

```
range = sin(2 * angle) * velocity² / gravity
```

where

angle   = the angle of the projectile's path (in radians)
velocity = the initial velocity of the projectile (in meters per second)
gravity = acceleration at 9.8 meters per second per second

The takeoff angle must be input in degrees so you must convert this angle to its radian equivalent. This is necessary because the trigonometric functions cos(x) and sin(x) assume the argument (x) is an angle expressed in radians. An angle in degrees can be converted to radians by multiplying the number of degrees by π / 180 where $\pi \cong 3.14159$. For example, 45° = 45 * 3.14159 / 180, or 0.7853975 radians. The velocity input is presumed to be in meters per second. Make your interactive output look like this (your output for Range must be rounded to the nearest tenth—one decimal place):

```
       Takeoff Angle (in degrees):   45.0
Initial Velocity (meters per second): 100.0
                        Range: ?.? meters
```

Test Oracle

Takeoff Angle	Initial Velocity	Range
45	100 m/s	_____
45	200 m/s	_____
60	200 m/s	_____

3E   Using Objects

The monthly payment on a loan is computed using the amount borrowed, the duration of the loan, and the interest rate. Write a program that reads the necessary data, calculates, and then displays the monthly loan payment. The first task consists of obtaining values for the amount borrowed, the length of the loan in years, and the annual interest rate. Your dialogue should look exactly like this with the output for Monthly Payment rounded to the nearest hundredth—two decimal places:

```
        Amount Borrowed: 106000.00
   Rate (1 to 35 percent): 11.5
   Years (1 to 35 years): 30.0

   Monthly Payment: 1049.71
```

The formula used to calculate monthly payments on a loan given the Amount, Rate, and the number of Months can be written as:

$$Payment = Amount \times Rate \times \frac{(Rate+1)^{Months}}{(Rate+1)^{Months}-1}$$

Note: Make sure your function payment converts the annual interest rate and the years into the equivalent monthly interest rate (divide Rate [11.5 above] by 1200) and number of months (multiply Years [30 above] by 12), respectively.

3.4   Member Function Abstractions

Classes and objects are the salient feature of object-oriented programming (OOP). We have used the float class to declare many float objects, cout is an object of the ostream class, and cin is an object of the istream (input stream) class. Every program requiring interactive input relies on the cout and cin objects. We will continue to see many programs developed with objects. So here is a review and preview of all nine classes that will have been used by the end of this chapter:

Class[1]	Brief Description
float	Floating point storage and arithmetic operations
double	Similar to float with more significant digits
int	Integer storage and arithmetic operations
char	Stores one character or sequences such as the newline char:'\n'
ostream	Provides convenient output stream operations such as << and formatting
istream	Provides convenient input stream operations such as >>
ifstream	Manages input file streams to extract data from a disk
string	Manages string data (storage, I/O) such as "Lee Iglasias"
bankAccount	Manages a bank account with withdraw, deposit, and balance functions

The first seven of these classes are part of all C++ systems. The last two classes, string and bankAccount, are supplied on disk. But the common characteristics of all of these classes is that they exist to declare objects with a name, state, and a collection of

---

[1]Recall that float, int, and char are data types which are not exactly the same thing as a class. However, conceptually they can be considered as a class. If you are accustomed to the terms *type* and *variable*, remember that type is interchangeable with class and variable is interchangeable with object.

operations. The operations are often implemented as functions. When functions are declared as part of a class, they are called member functions.

3.4.1 Member Functions of the ostream Class

Besides stream insertion (cout <<), there are many other operations available to ostream objects like cout. These operations are often implemented in the form of *member functions*—functions that are declared to be part of a C++ class. Functions like pow, sqrt, and decimals are called *free functions* because they do not belong to one particular class.

To illustrate some member function calls, consider the function decimals, which alters the formatting characteristics of cout. One of those changes is accomplished with the setf (<u>set</u> format <u>flags</u>) member function, which alters the appearance of floating-point output inserted to cout. It is used inside the function decimals to ensure that float objects always show a decimal point. The same function ensures that all output is fixed point rather than exponential. Here is what the decimals function looks like as stored in the file ourstuff.cpp, where setf is one of several calls to member functions.

[*Note:* Because cout is an object, there is a difference in how functions are called when they are the part of the class member function. For example, the function name setf is preceded with the name of the output stream (cout) and a period (.). We will look at this new form of member function call later.]

```
void decimals(ostream & cout, int n)
{ // This function alters the state of the ostream object
  // to show fixed point values with the decimal up to n
  // decimal places using trailing zeros if necessary.
  long oldFlags = cout.flags();
  if(n == 0)
  {
    // Reset format state of cout to original defaults
    cout.flags(defaultFlags);
    cout.precision(defaultPrecision);
    cout.setf(default_x_flags);
  }
  else if(n > 0)
  {
    // Change the output stream to show decimal point and
    // n decimal places for any subsequent float or double
    cout.setf(ios::fixed, ios::floatfield);
    cout.setf(ios::showpoint);
    // By itself, this function call does not produce the desired effect
    cout.precision(n);
  }
```

This implementation of the decimals function contains many elements not yet covered, so hopefully your reaction to this complete function definition will be something like this: "It's easier to call decimals through its interface (function name, number, and class [type] of arguments), than it is to remember and write all of this." It is easy to understand the abstraction decimals(cout, 2); instead.

With decimals available, we do not need to study the ostream member functions setf, precision, flags, and the enumerated constants ios::fixed, and so on. Instead, we will concentrate on two other ostream member functions, width and fill, as an introduction to calling member functions (there is a different syntax for this).

Output is formatted using ostream member functions such as ostream::width(int n) and ostream::fill(char ch). Here are the function prototypes written with the *scope resolution operator* :: to signal that the function is a member of the class that precedes it:

```
int ostream::width(int n);
// POST: The width characteristic of the ostream object is
//       reset. The very next output to the ostream object
//       is displayed in a minimum of n columns.
//       The default width is 0--the minimum columns.
//       The old width is returned but it may be ignored.


char ostream::fill(char ch);
// POST: The fill character of the ostream object is reset
//       to the argument ch. The very next output is preceded
//       with ch's to fill up to the output width if necessary.
//       The default fill character is ' ' (a blank character).
//       The old fill char is returned but it may be ignored.
```

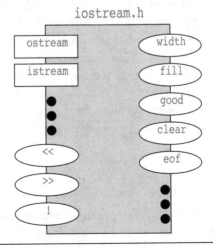

Figure 3.2   *Partial interface diagram for module iostream.h*

The member function `ostream::width` resets the number of columns that will be used to display the very next `cout` insertion (and only the very next output). The member function `ostream::fill` resets the `char` used to fill any extra columns that precede the value (the default `char` is a blank space). Calls to these two member functions are shown in the following program. These function calls alter the default formatting characteristics of `cout`:

```
#include <iostream.h>  // Include the width and fill member functions
#include "ourstuff.h"  // Include the decimals function

int main()
{
  double netPay = 123.4577777;
  cout << netPay      // Show with default formatting, output varies
       << endl;
  decimals(cout, 2); // Show '.', 2 decimal places and trailing zeros
  cout.width(10);    // Show next insertion to cout in 10 columns
  cout.fill('*');    // Precede netPay with '*' rather than default ' '
  cout << netPay << endl;
  return 0;
}
```

```
———————————————— Output ————————————————
 123.457778
****123.46
```

In the preceding program, the value of `netPay` (123.4578) is inserted into the output stream, but the preceding function calls (`decimals`, `ostream::width`, and `ostream::fill`) first alter the format state of `cout`. Therefore, the value of `netPay` is displayed in 10 columns rounded to two decimals. The four columns that would otherwise be blank are filled with leading asterisks to prevent someone from writing a few leading digits on his or her paycheck.

The preceding program that calls two `ostream` member functions, `width` and `fill`, shows a syntactic difference between free (nonmember) function calls—such as `sqrt(x)` and `decimals(cout,2)`—and *member* function calls—such as `cout.width(5)`.

———————————————— Rule ————————————————
The object name and a period must precede the call to a member function.

Free functions are called without a preceding object and period—`pow(2,10)`, for example. However, member functions such as `ostream::width`, and `ostream::fill` require an object name and a period before the function name. Here is the general form used to call certain member functions of a class:

object-name . member-function-name (argument-list) ;

Free functions are not members of a class, so they have no object name preceding the call. However, member functions such as `ostream::width` and `ostream::fill` must be called with an object name in front. For example,

```
cout.width(8);  // Correct
```

is valid, but

```
width(8);       // Error
```

is not. The function prototype itself indicates the class to which the member function belongs. For example, this prototype with the scope resolution operator `::` indicates that the function (`width`) is a member of a class (`ostream`):

```
int ostream::width(int n); // Width is a member of the ostream class
```

The member function prototype, very similar to the nonmember prototype, has this general form:

return-type class-name :: member-function-name (parameter-list) ;

This syntactic difference represents one of the differences between an object and a variable. The state of an object is managed by member functions. On the other hand, because `int`, `float`, and `char` have different implementations, they are more likely to be *passed* to functions as arguments (the differences are historic: `ints` and `floats` existed before the C++ class). If `double` were implemented exactly like a C++ class, we might see math member function calls like this:

```
double x = 1.2;
cout << x.sqrt();  // Call sqrt as a member function
```

rather than:

```
double x = 1.2;
cout << sqrt(x);  // Pass the double object to a free function
```

Because of this syntactic difference, most C++ programs contain free function calls (without the object name/dot in front) along with member function calls.

3.4.2 Operator Member Functions

Now that we have seen several member functions called by name, we can look at some member functions that are called whenever certain mixes of objects and operators are encountered. Such is the case with the ostream insertion operator <<. Whenever an ostream object is followed by the insertion operator << and an "insertable" object (and that is everything we've seen so far), one of the ostream operator member functions is called. For example, the function that inserts a floating-point value into an output stream is called with this code:

```
cout << 1.23;
```

The function that inserts an int value into an output stream is called with this code:

```
cout << 123;
```

And the function that inserts a char value into an output stream is called with this code:

```
cout << 'U';
```

In each case, the same operator has an object of the ostream class on the left (cout to be precise) and an insertable object to the right. The compiler decides which function to call based on the operand to the right of <<. For example, when the compiler encounters code such as this:

```
cout << 123;
```

a search is made for a function matching the sequence of ostream object, followed by the << operator, and the operand to the right of <<, which may be float, int, or char. The iostream.h header file includes declarations for these three functions to allow each object to be displayed in a manner appropriate to that object.

The same approach is used for the stream extraction operator >>. For example, the function that extracts a floating-point value from an input stream is called with this code:

```
cin >> floatVar;        // assume float floatVar;
```

The function that extracts an integer value from an input stream is called with this code:

```
cin >> intVar;          // assume int intVar;
```

And the function that extracts a `char` value from an input stream is called with this code:

```
cin >> charVar;          // assume char charVar;
```

In each case, the same operator has an `istream` object on the left (`cin` to be precise). The compiler decides which function to call based on the operand to the right of `>>`. This allows objects to be extracted in an appropriate manner. When the compiler encounters code such as this:

```
cin >> anyObject;
```

a search is made for a function matching this sequence of `istream` object, followed by the `>>` operator, and an operand to the right of `>>`, which may be a `float`, `int`, or `char` object. The `istream` class has a member function declared for each data type to the right of the `istream` object `>>`: one function for `int`, one for `float`, one for `char`, and so on.

Self-Check

1. *True or False:* `cout.width(3)` alters the formatting characteristics of the output stream `cout`.
2. *True or False:* `ostream` is a class.
3. *True or False:* `cout` is a class.
4. *True or False:* `fill` and `width` are objects of the `ostream` class.
5. *True or False:* We may have many classes of the same object.
6. List one operator member function of the `ostream` class.
7. List one operator member function of the `istream` class.
8. Write the output generated by the following program:

```
#include <iostream.h>
#include "ourstuff.h"
int main()
{
    double x = 123.4 ;
    cout.width(8) ;
    cout.fill('X') ;
    cout << x ;
    x = x + 0.175 * x ;
    cout.width(12) ;
    cout.fill(' ') ;
    cout << x << endl ;
    return 0;
}
```

9. What must be done to call the member functions of a class?

10. Approximately how many function calls occur in this code?

```
cout << "Enter x ";
cin >> x;
cout << "x: ";
cout.width(10);
cout.fill('*');
cout << x;
```

11. Write the output generated by the following program:

```
#include <iostream.h> // for cout <<
#include "ourstuff.h" // for decimals(ostream & cout, int n);
int main()
{
    double x = 765.56789;
    decimals(cout, 2);
    cout.width(10);
    cout.fill('0');
    cout << x << endl;
    return 0;
}
```

Answers
1. True
2. True
3. False: cout is an object
4. False: These are member functions of the ostream class
5. False: We may have many objects of the same class
6. <<
7. >>
8. XXX123.4   144.995
9. Precede the function name with the object name and a period
10. 5
11. 0000765.57

3.5 The ifstream class

Since keyboard input is fairly common, inclusion of iostream.h has been designed to make cin immediately available. The cin object is automatically initialized for us and associated with the keyboard. But input may also be obtained from many other sources, such as a mouse, a graphics tablet, or a file stored on disk. We now look at a class that is closely related to istream—the *ifstream* class—for the following reasons:

1. ifstream is another standard C++ class that allows us to obtain input from other sources.

2. ifstream illustrates the consistency of stream input; ifstream objects use the same operators as cin.
3. The ifstream class will allow us to test programs with less interactive input. This saves time.

The ifstream (input file stream) class is declared in the include file fstream.h. So this compiler directive must be added:

```
#include <fstream.h>
```

to programs intended to obtain input from a disk file. The ifstream class is similar to the istream class, so ifstream objects share many istream member functions and operators. Therefore, we are already familiar with many ifstream operations. For example, to input data from a file stored on a disk we use the extraction operator >>. The same rules that apply to istream input for int, floats, chars, and strings also apply to ifstream objects.

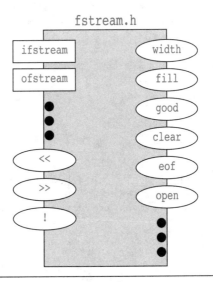

Figure 3.3   Partial interface diagram for module fstream.h

An ifstream object is initialized with this general form:

ifstream *object-name* = "*file-name*" ;

where *file-name* is the operating system file name written as a string constant. Among other things, this initialization associates *object-name* with the disk file stored in the operating system as *"file-name."* In the next example, inFile is the object name and "in.dat" is the associated operating system file name:

```
ifstream inFile = "in.dat"; // Initialize an ifstream object
```

Now a function call like this:

```
inFile >> intVar;
```

extracts input from the file in.dat rather than from the keyboard.

We can now look at a complete program that extracts three ints from a file. The difference lies in the name and class of the object. Before, we used cin—an istream object—for keyboard input. Now we use inFile—an ifstream object—for file input:

```
// Include fstream.h for I/O streams dealing with disk files
#include <fstream.h>    // for the ifstream class
#include <iostream.h>   // for the istream class

int main()
{
    int n1, n2, n3;
    // Initialize an ifstream object so inFile is an input stream
    // associated with the operating system file named "in.dat"
    ifstream inFile = "in.dat";

    // Extract three ints from the file "in.dat"
    inFile >> n1 >> n2 >> n3;
    cout << "n1: " << n1 << endl;
    cout << "n2: " << n2 << endl;
    cout << "n3: " << n3 << endl;
    return 0;
}
```

Assuming the file "in.dat" stores these three integers:

| 70 80 90 | ← A file with three integers stored on disk with the file name "in.dat"

we get this output:

```
n1: 70
n2: 80
n3: 90
```

and if the file "in.dat" is saved with these three integers:

| -45 |
| 77 |
| 23 | ← A file with three integers stored on disk with the file name "in.dat"

we would get this output:

```
n1: -45
n2: 77
n3: 23
```

Input file stream extractions work just like keyboard extractions—spaces and newlines separate the input data. This applies to all data we have seen so far: char, int, float, and double. If an integer is encountered in the file input stream during an attempt to extract a double, the int is promoted to the double. The one input difference is this: With an ifstream object, keyboard input is not necessary for stream extraction. Once the program begins to run, data is extracted from the disk file.

Programming Tip

If your input file is not stored in the current working directory, you may need to use an operating system path to locate it. For the DOS operating system, which uses \ to separate directory names, the escape sequence \\ (two backslashes) must be used to specify full path names. So the file name may appear like this:

```
ifstream inFile = "c:\\mystuff\\in.dat";
```

where \\ indicates only one operating system \. We don't have this problem in UNIX where the / character is used "as is":

```
ifstream inFile = "~/myC++Stuff/in.dat";
```

We should also consider what happens if the file is not found. Chances are, all input operations such as inFile >> will fail. If you don't seem to be extracting input from the file or the values appear to be garbage, chances are the file does not exist as specified; it has a different name, is in a different directory, or uses \ rather than \\.

Self-Check

1. What does ifstream stand for?
2. Write the code that declares an input stream capable of extracting input from a file called "student.dat". Call the object inFile.
3. Which include file must be part of a program that declares input file stream objects?
4. Write the output of the following program when the input file named "input.dat" looks like this:

```
11
  H    22.249   -33

  X

4.4  Ain't no more
<End of file>
```

← A file with the name "input.dat"

```
#include <fstream.h>    // for ifstream
#include <iostream.h>   // for cout
#include "ourstuff.h"   // for decimals
int main()
{
  int anInt;
  double aDouble;
  char aChar;
  ifstream inFile = "input.dat";

  // Get 3 inputs from a file and display them to the screen
  inFile >> anInt >> aChar >> aDouble;
  decimals(cout, 2);
  cout.width(6);    cout << anInt;
  cout.width(4);    cout << aChar;
  cout.width(8);    cout << aDouble << endl;

  // Get 3 more inputs from a file and display them to the screen
  inFile >> anInt >> aChar >> aDouble;
  cout.width(6);    cout << anInt;
  cout.width(4);    cout << aChar;
  cout.width(8);    cout << aDouble << endl;
  return 0;
}
```

Answers
1. Input file stream
2. ifstream inFile = "student.dat";
3. fstream.h
4.   11 H 22.25
     -33 X   4.40

3.6 string Objects

Computers operate on many classes of data. For example, a fair amount of computer processing involves character and string data. Even though such a "string" class is part of some languages and libraries, to date, no standardized string class is distributed with C++ compilers. Some primitive string-handling capabilities are provided, but there are several problems with using them. First, more advanced knowledge of C++ is required (such as pointers, arrays, and dynamic memory allocation). Also, some of the operations we might expect of a class (such as assignment) are not automatically available.

There are other difficulties (such as system crashes) presented by the crude string-processing capabilities of C++ (further discussion of the inherent problems of primitive C++ strings is delayed until Chapter 9). Many of these problems are avoided with string objects. The string class is declared in the file ourstr.h that accompanies this textbook. This *programmer-defined* (not part of the standard C++ package) string class allows us to manage strings as a natural part of the language. For example, string objects are declared and/or initialized in the same fashion as other classes such as int, float, and ifstream. Assignment operations are also allowed.

```
// Demonstrate the string class stored in the file ourstr.h
#include <iostream.h>
#include "ourstr.h"     // This file contains the string class

int main()
{ // Declare a string object
   string strOne;

   // Declare and initialize a string object
   string strTwo = "Initialization is okay";

   // Assignment to string objects is OK
   strOne = "Assignment with = is allowed";

   // Input is defined for string objects
   cout << "Enter a string: ";
   cin >> strOne;

   // Output is also defined
   cout << "strOne: " << strOne << endl;
   cout << "strTwo: " << strTwo << endl;
   return 0;
}
```

Dialogue

Note: The text "separate all data" is still in the input stream waiting to be processed:

```
Enter a string:  Spaces separate all data
StrOne: Spaces
StrTwo: Assignment with = is allowed
```

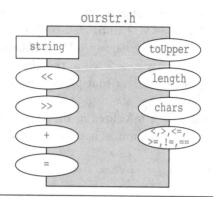

Figure 3.4   Interface diagram for module ourstr.h

string objects store from zero to many characters. The character strings to which you are now accustomed (characters between the double quote " " delimiters) could be the rValue in an assignment to a string object.

```
string str;
str = "A string literal assigned to a string object";
```

The number of characters stored in a string at any given point is the *dynamic length*. For example, after these two object declarations:

```
string str1 = "A string";
string str2;               // Set to default initial value of null: ""
```

the characters of str1 are "A string" and its dynamic length is eight. The object str2 has no characters and a length of zero, which is the string *default value* for objects at declaration (recall that classes such as char and double have no default initial value).

3.6.1   string Input with >>

The extraction operator >> inputs string values from the keyboard. Stream extraction rules for string objects are consistent with other classes, but there is one difference. The double quote mark " required to delimit character strings within a C++ program is simply the same double quote mark when typed in from the keyboard. In other words, the " is not a special symbol on input—it's just one of the many characters that can be stored as part of a string object. As with the other classes of input data, each string input item is separated by one or more blanks, a tab or a newline (the Enter or Return key).

The following program prompts for and stores all characters before the Enter key, or up to but not including the first blank space, whichever occurs first. Therefore, string input is separated by one or more blanks, just like ints, floats, and chars.

```
// Demonstrate the extraction operator >> with string object
#include "ourstr.h"
#include <iostream.h>

int main()
{
  string firstName, lastName;
  cout << "Enter your first and last names separated by a space: ";
  // Need two string objects to get two names (blanks separate data)
  cin >> firstName >> lastName;
  cout << "Hello " << firstName << ' ' << lastName
       << ", how are you?" << endl;
  return 0;
}
```

─────────────────────────── **Dialogue** ───────────────────────────
```
Enter your first and last names separated by a space: Kim Sollie
Hello Kim Sollie, how are you?
```

In the dialogue shown above, the string object firstName stores the value of "Kim" with a dynamic length of three. When strings are extracted from an input stream, leading and trailing blanks are not considered part of the string input. The length of firstName would be three even if one or more blanks were typed before or after the name before the Enter key is pressed. Also, you can press the Enter key as often as you like, but the cin >> firstName function call does not finish executing until you enter a valid string input like Kim, abcdefg, 123, $$$, or some other group of characters. And one last detail: The dynamic length of a string is automatically updated whenever an assignment or cin extraction is used to initialize or change the state of a string object.

3.6.2   Member Function string::length()

The length of a string, returned through the member function string::length(), is a positive int ranging from zero to many. This is the prototype:

```
int string::length();
// POST: The dynamic length of the string is returned
```

This is an example function call:

```
cout << "Length of str1: " << str1.length();
```

Many operators available for other fundamental classes, such as =, <<, and >>, are also declared as free operator functions. All operator functions are available with #include "ourstring.h". For example, strings can be output with the stream insertion operator << and input with the stream extraction operator >>.

3.6.3 Member Function string::toUpper

The following function prototype shows that toUpper is a member of the string class because it is qualified with string::. We also see that toUpper is a void function which must be used as a stand-alone statement. And finally, the prototype tells us that no arguments are required when toUpper is invoked.

```
void string::toUpper();
// POST: The string object is converted to upper case
```

When toUpper is called, the string object preceding the toUpper function is converted. Any lowercase letter in the string object is converted to its uppercase equivalent. This complete C++ program illustrates the effect toUpper has on one string object named s:

```
#include <iostream.h>
#include "ourstr.h"
int main()
{
  string s = "abc*123*xyz";
  cout << "s before conversion: " << s << endl;
  s.toUpper();
  cout << "s after s.toUpper(): " << s << endl;
  return 0;
}
```

──────────────── **Output** ────────────────
```
s before conversion: abc*123*xyz
s after s.toUpper(): ABC*123*XYZ
```

3.6.4 Concatenation

When the binary + operator has string operands, a different type of operation called concatenation is applied. *Concatenation* (also called catenation) is the formation of one string object as the combination of two or more other string objects:

```
str1 = "String literal " + str2;
str2 = str3 + "another string literal";
str3 = str1 + str2;
```

The following program demonstrates string concatenation and the >> operator to obtain string data from the keyboard:

```
// Demonstrate the concatenation operation
// implemented using the + operator for strings.
#include <iostream.h>
#include "ourstr.h"

int main()
{
  string first, last;
  string nameRearranged;

  cout << "Enter your first name and last name " << endl
       << "using at least one space between names: " ;
  cin  >> first >> last;

  nameRearranged = last + ", " + first;
  nameRearranged.toUpper();
  cout << nameRearranged << endl;
  return 0;
}
```

─────── **Dialogue** ───────

Enter your first name and last name
using at least one space between names: *Kellen   Stetson*

STETSON, KELLEN

So far we have seen the + operator used to perform int addition, float addition, and now string concatenation. This is just one example of one operator that has different meaning when different operands are part of the expression.

We will see this string class as a part of many programs and other classes used throughout this textbook.

Self-Check

1. For each of the following, write the characters that are stored into the string object.

   a. string a;   c. string a = "Any name";
   b. string a = "12345";   d. string a = "   ";

2. List two string operator member functions.
3. List two free string functions not symbolized by operators.

4. Write the output generated by this program:

```
#include <iostream.h>
#include "ourstr.h"
int main()
{
    string a, b, c = "abcd";
    a = "xyz";
    b = a;
    a = a + "123" + "lmn";
    a.toUpper();
    cout << endl;
    cout << a << "--" << b << "--" << c << endl;
    return 0;
}
```

5. Which include file must be part of programs that declare string objects?
6. Write code that declares a string object named s, stores the string "My Name" into s, and then displays all characters of s and the length of s.
7. What separates string input values?
8. Write the code that converts the string object named s to its uppercase equivalent.

Answers
1. a. The null string ""   b. "12345"   c. "Any name"   d. "   "
2. =, << (or + or >>)
3. string::toUpper and string:: length
4. XYZ123LMN--xyz--abcd
5. "ourstr.h"
6. string s;
   s = "My Name";
   cout << s << s.length();
7. Spaces, newlines, or tabs (the same as ints, floats, and chars)
8. s.toUpper();

3.7   bankAccount Objects

In this section, we look at one more new class called bankAccount to review the use of objects through abstraction and to introduce two new components of objects:

- Constructor member functions
- Data members

The bankAccount class permits the declaration of many objects, where each object models a checking or savings account. Using our knowledge of real-world bank accounts, we might recognize that each bank account object should at least store an account number and an account balance. We should also be able to quickly determine some banking operations such as creating a new account, making deposits, and making withdrawals, with the ability to access the current balance. Member functions are used for all of these operations.

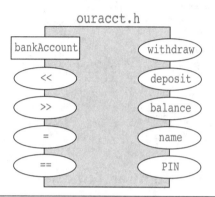

Figure 3.5   *Interface diagram for module ouracct.h*

The bankAccount class is part of an example that will be used in the remaining chapters. It was designed to be part of a program that manages a bank (a collection of bankAccount objects) through an automated teller machine (ATM) interface. (The bank and ATM classes are described in Chapter 4.) The class declaration of bankAccount—a collection of function prototypes and object declarations—is given next to summarize the member functions and objects that store the state of every bankAccount object. Since class declarations are not covered in detail until Chapters 4 and 8, for now just note that the class name is bankAccount and the highlighted member functions include bankAccount—to initialize bankAccount objects—deposit, withdraw, balance, name, and PIN. The data stored for each bankAccount object includes the accountName, accountBalance, and accountPIN.

```
class bankAccount {
public:
  // Initializer constructor
  bankAccount::bankAccount(string initName,
                           string initPIN,
                           double initBalance);
  // POST: A bankAccount object is initialized when three arguments
  //       are used at initialization. Here is an example:
  //          bankAccount anAcct("Hall", "1234", 100.00);

  void bankAccount::deposit(double amount);
  // POST: amount is added to the current balance of the object
```

```
    void bankAccount::withdraw(double amount);
    // POST: amount is deducted from the current account balance

    double bankAccount::balance();
    // POST: The current balance is returned

    string bankAccount::name();
    // POST: The account name is returned

    string bankAccount::PIN();
    // POST: The account PIN is returned

  private:
    double accountBalance;
    string accountName;
    string accountPIN;
  };
```

3.7.1 Constructor Member Functions

The bankAccount class is declared and initialized with a *constructor function*—a special member function that always has the same name as the class and never has a return type. Constructor functions are used to initialize objects of any class. The constructor member function prototype

```
    bankAccount::bankAccount(string  initName,
                             string  initPIN,
                             double  initBalance);
```

describes the function that will be called to initialize a bankAccount object. The difference between object initializations that we have seen (float x = 0.0; for example), and bankAccount object initializations is that every bankAccount object must be initialized with three arguments in this order: accountName, accountPIN, and balance [any (string, string, numeric) combination of arguments]. For example, the object named anAccount is initialized below using the three arguments to bankAccount::bankAccount. The account name becomes "HALL" (names are automatically converted to uppercase with the constructor function), the PIN "1234", and the initial balance is 100.00.

```
    // Call the bankAccount constructor member function
    // to initialize the bankAccount named anAccount
    bankAccount anAccount("Hall", "1234", 100.00);
```

Programming Tip

Because three arguments are required, we can no longer use an initialization like this:

```
bankAccount anAccount = "Hall"; // Where do the other 2 arguments go?
```

Therefore, every `bankAccount` object will have the initialization data enclosed in parentheses. Constructor initializations (with parentheses) are common. In fact, we could initialize `string` and `ifstream` objects with the same syntax:

```
string aString("Initializer");  // Same as aString = "Initializer";
ifstream inFile("in.dat");      // Same as inFile = "in.dat";
```

3.7.2 Other Member Functions

Once an object is constructed, the balance may be modified through withdrawal and deposit operations such as these:

```
anAccount.deposit(145.98);
anAccount.withdraw(50.00);
```

All `bankAccount` objects have three member functions to access the data of the object: name, PIN, and `balance`. For example, the current balance may be inspected at any time through `bankAccount::balance`.

The following program defines two `bankAccount` objects and calls several member functions. A deposit is made to the object identified as `Pat`, a withdrawal is made to the object identified as `Chris`, and the updated balances for both objects are shown last:

```
// Declare and initialize two bankAccount twice (Pat and Chris).
// In order, the 3 arguments are name, PIN, and starting balance.
#include <iostream.h>
#include "ouracct.h"

int main()
{
  bankAccount Pat("Hall", "1234", 100.00);
  bankAccount Chris("Fuller", "5501", 987.65);
  // Pat and Chris are now initialized bankAccount objects.

  Pat.deposit(133.33);
  Chris.withdraw(250.00);

  cout << "  Pat's current balance: " << Pat.balance()   << endl;
  cout << "Chris's current Balance: " << Chris.balance() << endl;
  return 0;
}
```

─────────── **Output** ───────────

```
    Pat's current balance: 233.33
Chris's current Balance: 737.65
```

Pat and Chris are two unique objects of the same bankAccount class. Although they share the same set of member functions, they are distinguished by the object names—Chris and Pat. Notice again that the member functions are preceded by the object name and a period. For example, the statements shown above make a deposit of 133.33 to Pat and a 250.00 withdrawal from Chris. Obviously, it is important that we know the particular bankAccount object to which we are making a deposit and the particular object from which we are making a withdrawal. Also, to check the current balances after these two operations, the object name and a period must precede the call to balance.

Objects store varying degrees of data depending on the class to which they belong. A bankAccount object holds data representing a balance, a name, and a personal identification number (PIN). An employee object might hold name and pay rate data. A robot object may hold a current position, a map, and the state of its arm mechanism. The stored items are referred to as *data members*—the collection of objects (of different classes possibly) that represent the state of the object. For example, Pat's balance data member currently stores the value 737.65, and Chris's PIN is "1234". The data members of any one bankAccount attribute are accessed with the balance function and these two other member functions—name and PIN:

```
string bankAccount::name();
// POST: The name data member is returned

string bankAccount::PIN();
// POST: The PIN data member is returned
```

We can also observe the current values of all three data members with the overloaded stream insertion operator << also declared in ouracct.h. Insertion of a bankAccount object into an output stream displays all three data members in this form:

{ bankAccount: *name, PIN, balance* }

The name, PIN, and << operations are illustrated in the following program:

```
// Operator << is overloaded to output bankAccount objects
#include <iostream.h>
#include "ouracct.h"

int main()
{
  bankAccount anAccount("Hall", "1234", 100.00);
  cout << "Name: " << anAccount.name() << endl;
  cout << " PIN: " << anAccount.PIN()  << endl;
  anAccount.deposit(25.67);
  anAccount.withdraw(50.00);
  // The stream insertion operator is overloaded for bankAccount objects:
  cout << anAccount << endl;
  return 0;
}
```

--------- Output ---------

```
Name: HALL
 PIN: 1234
{ bankAccount: HALL, 1234, 75.67 }
```

3.7.3   Interacting Objects: A Review

This section reviews the new classes of this chapter, ifstream, string, and bankAccount. These objects interact with each other to initialize one bank account object and then to perform one deposit operation and one withdrawal operation. The program extracts data from this input file stored as account.dat:

```
Hall    1234    100.00
34.50
20.00
```

The first line contains the data to initialize one bankAccount object, the second line represents a deposit amount, and the third line stores a constant representing a withdrawal amount.

In all, there are four modules required to complete this program. Besides the standard classes (such as double), classes and operations must be included from iostream.h, fstream.h, ourstr.h, and ouracct.h. The relationships are summarized in the module diagram of Figure 3.6.

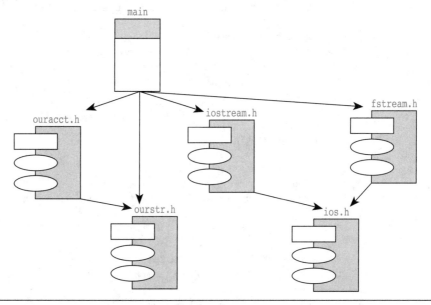

Figure 3.6   A Module Diagram Showing Dependencies in a Small Program

To keep the diagram simple, only the module names are written to label the modules. The ovals and rectangles represent classes and functions exported from the modules. For the main function to compile, the modules must be made visible through #include directives. The directed lines show where one module depends on another. For example, main depends on four modules while ouracct.h depends on only one (ourstr.h). Also shown is a previously hidden relationship. Both iostream.h and fstream.h depend on a module called ios.h.

```
// This program requires no user input. Extractions come from
// a file. New classes include ifstream, string, bankAccount.
#include <iostream.h>
#include <fstream.h>
#include "ouracct.h"
#include "ourstr.h"

int main()
{
  ifstream inFile = "account.dat";
  string initName;
  string initPIN;
  double initBalance;
  double amount;

  // Declare and initialize one bankAccount object using file input
  inFile >> initName >> initPIN >> initBalance;
  bankAccount anAcct(initName, initPIN, initBalance);

  // Show the starting balance
  cout << "Initial balance: " << anAcct.balance() << endl;

  // Make two transactions using file input
  inFile >> amount;
  anAcct.deposit(amount);
  inFile >> amount;
  anAcct.withdraw(amount);

  // Show the current state of the bankAccount object
  cout << " Ending balance: " << anAcct.balance() << endl;
  cout << "The bankAccount object is now " << anAcct endl;
  return 0;
}
```

─────── **Output** ───────
```
Initial balance: 100
 Ending balance: 115.5
The bankAccount object is now { bankAccount: HALL, 1234, 115.50 }
```

3.7 bankAccount Objects   123

Self-Check

Use these two bankAccount declarations for each of the questions that follow:

```
bankAccount acct1("Mikelsen", "4641", 150.00);
bankAccount acct2("Kallester", "5701", 50);
```

1. What type of function is called in both declarations (free function, operator function, or constructor member function)? What is the name of this function?
2. Is the balance of acct1 affected by this member function call? (*Hint:* Review the function's precondition.)

```
acct1.withdraw(-40.00);
```

3. Is the balance of acct2 affected by this member function call? (*Hint:* Review the function's precondition.)

```
acct2.withdraw(250.00);
```

4. Is the balance of acct2 affected by this member function call? (*Hint:* Review the function's precondition.)

```
acct1.withdraw(10.00);
```

5. What class of data is returned by bankAccount::name() and bankAccount:PIN()?
6. Write the output generated by the following program:

```
#include <iostream.h>
#include "ouracct.h"
int main()
{
   bankAccount anAccount("Unger, India", "7112", 1567.90);
   anAccount.withdraw(300.00);
   cout << anAccount << endl;
   return 0;
}
```

Answers

1. A constructor member function. bankAccount.
2. Yes: The postconditions state the argument is added to the balance. It is up to the programmer to avoid negative withdrawal amounts.
3. Yes: The postconditions state the argument is subtracted from the balance, even though 250.00 is greater than the balance of acct2. Someone has determined that withdrawals greater than the balance are allowed. Some bank accounts are like this.
4. No; acct1's balance is affected, however.
5. string
6. { bankAccount: UNGER, INDIA, 7112, 1267.90 }

Chapter Summary

In this chapter we learned that abstraction helps us to utilize existing functions while ignoring implementation details. Function prototypes document the number and class of arguments required, preconditions that describe what the function expects from the programmer, and postconditions that describe what the function will do if the preconditions are met. In addition to free functions, include files also provide useful operators and classes. Include files allow programmers to build virtually unlimited capability into the language. Just knowing that this software exists aids in the program development process.

Some new classes introduced in this chapter include the ifstream class for file input and the string class capable of easily managing string constants. The bankAccount class helped show the need for constructor functions. When more than one value is required for initialization, those values are enclosed in parentheses. This leads to a different initialization syntax for the declaration of bankAccount and other objects:

```
bankAccount Harry("Poland", "2068", 1052.45);
string name ("Harry");
ifstream infile("bank.dat");
```

The extraction >> and insertion << operators that allow insertion into output stream objects and extraction from input stream objects are declared for all the classes covered so far. The extraction operator that extracts input from the istream object cin also extracts data from ifstream objects.

Whereas int and float objects store one value, other objects such as string and bankAccount objects may store many different types of data members (string objects have a length and a varying collection of chars). Every bankAccount object has its own two string objects (accountName and accountPIN) and one double object (accountBalance).

Review of Object Terminology

object   An entity stored in memory that has identity (name), state (value), and behavior (the collection of operations that may be applied to the object). The terms *variable* and *object* are interchangeable.

class   The set of values that an object may store during program execution along with the operations that define the behavior of those objects. The class acts as a model to create many objects of the class. The terms *class* and *data type* are interchangeable.

identity   The unique name of an object. Two objects of the same name cannot exist in the main function.

state	The value of an object as it is stored in memory. The state of an object may be altered through operations such as keyboard input, assignment, or calls to member functions. Care must be taken to avoid undefined states, which cause intent errors.
operations	The collection of actions (implemented as functions and operators) that manipulate an object. Each class has its own set of operations to define the behavior of the objects in that class.
abstraction	The practice of ignoring implementation details while concentrating on a function prototype to determine how to call that function. The practice of focusing on the essential characteristics of an object in order to effectively use that object.
member functions	The operations of a class that require the object name and a period to precede the function call. Free functions may also manipulate objects, but the calling syntax is different. Both member and nonmember (free) functions exist in the same program.
constructor	An operation (implemented as a member function) that is used to declare an object and initialize its state.
operator function	The operations of a class where a mix of C++ operators and object operands achieve the desired actions. The operand's class often determines which operator function is called when one operator represents many operator functions. This is the case for the +, << and >> operators.

Exercises

9. How many individual objects of a class may exist in a program?
10. cin is an object of which class?
11. cout is an object of which class?
12. List one special symbol operator available to the cout object.
13. List one special symbol operator available to the cin object.
14. What do the *i* and *f* in ifstream stand for?
15. Describe how member functions of a class are called.
16. Approximately how many member function calls occur in this code:

```
string name("?");
cout << "Enter your name ";
cin >> name;
name.to Upper();
cout << name;
```

17. Write a minimal program that inputs an `int`, a `double`, and a `char` from the file "my.dat."
18. Write the contents of a file that can be used as input for the program in Exercise 17.
19. Write the output generated by the following program:

```
#include <iostream.h>
#include "ourstr.h"
int main()
{
  string a;
  string b = "123";
  cout << "Enter a string: ";
  cin >> a;
  a = a + b + a;
  cout << "a = " << a << endl;
  cout << "length of a = " << a.length() << endl;
  return 0;
}
```

20. Declare two `string` objects and initialize both using any identifiers you desire.
21. Name two member functions of the `string` class.
22. Write the function call that returns the dynamic length of the `string` object named `aString`.
23. Write C++ code that concatenates "end of string" to the `string` object named `aString`.
24. How is the state of a `string` object altered?
25. List two member functions available to `bankAccount` objects.
26. Name two data members of `bankAccount`.
27. Write the output generated by the following program:

```
#include <iostream.h>
#include "ouracct.h"
int main()
{
  bankAccount Justin("Shmeal", "0907", 500.00);
  cout << Justin.balance() << endl;
  Justin.deposit(50.00);
  Justin.withdraw(20.00);
  cout << Justin.balance() << endl;
  return 0;
}
```

Lab Projects

3F   Using Classes

Write a program that reads exactly four floating-point values and displays the sum of all four floats. The input must come from a disk file stored as "float.dat". First create the input file using the editor you use to create program files. The file must contain at least four valid numeric values, but it does not matter how each is placed in the file. For example, you could use a file that looks like this:

```
1.23   4.56
7.89   5.43
```

─────────── **Test Oracle** ───────────

Contents of "in.dat"				Output
1 2 3 4				10
1.1				
2.2				
3.3	4.1			_____
443.5678	-101.243	+65.65	-65.76	_____
123	456	789	BAD	<ERROR>

3G   Using Objects

Write a program that:

- Inputs three strings from the keyboard.
- Concatenates them into a fourth string object.
- Converts the fourth object to uppercase.
- Displays the concatenated string and its dynamic length on screen.

─────────── **Test Oracle** ───────────

Three Strings Input	Output
Able	String: ABLEBAKERCHARLIE
Baker	Length: 16
Charlie	

3H   Using Objects

Write a program that inputs exactly seven `string` values and displays the `strings` in reverse order with no space between the `string` output. Remember to separate `string` values with a space, tab, or newline:

```
Enter 7 strings: a man a plan a canal panama
panamacanalaplanamana
```

3I   Using Objects

Write a program that inputs exactly seven `string` values from one line of a text file and displays them in reverse order. Repeat this process three times. This means your disk input file must be edited to have exactly three lines where each line must contain exactly seven `string` values.

```
1 2 3 4 5 6 7
a b c d e f g
a man a plan a canal panama
```

When your program is executed with input from this file, your output should look exactly like this:

```
7654321
gfedcba
panamacanalaplanamana
```

Note: There is no interactive input to this problem, only output to the screen.

3J   Using Objects

Examine the following program and predict the output:

```cpp
#include <iostream.h>
#include "ouracct.h"
#include "ourstr.h"

int main()
{
    bankAccount anAcct("Hall", "1234", 100.0);
    bankAccount anotherAcct;
    string name = "Filbert";
    string PIN = "9999";
    float amount = 0.00;
    anotherAcct = bankAccount(name, PIN, amount);
```

```
anAcct.withdraw(25.00);
anotherAcct.deposit(123.45);
anAcct.withdraw(50.00);
anotherAcct.withdraw(50);
anAcct.deposit(9.99);
cout << anAcct.name() << "  "
     << anAcct.balance() << endl;
cout << anotherAcct.name() << "  "
     << anotherAcct.balance() << endl;
return 0;
}
```

Copy, compile, link, and run the previous program to check if your prediction was correct.

3K   Using Objects

Write a program that performs the following actions:

- Inputs name and PIN as string objects and startingBalance as a float.
- Uses the input to create a bankAccount as bankAccount anAcct(name, PIN, startingBalance).
- Shows the beginning balance. Don't display the object named startingBalance! Instead make sure you call the bankAccount::balance member function.
- Makes a 100.00 deposit using the bankAccount::deposit member function.
- Makes a 40.00 withdrawal using the bankAccount::withdraw member function.
- Displays the ending balance with the balance method.

One dialogue should look like this:

—————————— **Dialogue** ——————————
```
Enter Name, PIN, and starting balance: Anyname  7789  1000.00
Starting Balance: 1000
  Ending Balance: 1060
```

4

Implementations

In the previous chapter, we learned to use existing functions and objects. We also discovered that functional level preconditions and postconditions explain what a function expects and what that function will do. In this chapter, we will implement our own functions. We will also gain the ability to read C++ class declarations, which provide a summary of member functions and data members for any given class. As we continue our study of computing fundamentals, we will see a persistent use of functions and classes as they relate to other goals of this textbook. These goals involve the following program development methods:

1. Building up programs involving existing and programmer-defined functions and classes.
2. Breaking down problems into subproblems, which are then implemented as programmer-defined functions.
3. Building up classes as a collection of data members and programmer-defined member functions.

All three processes involve functions and/or classes. After studying this chapter, you will be able to:

- Implement programmer-defined functions that return nothing (void functions).
- Return values from functions with the return statement.
- Understand argument/parameter associations.
- Read and understand class declarations.
- See how a bank object interacts with an ATM object.

4.1   Programmer-Defined Functions

Abstraction is important in computer science. *Abstraction* is the process of understanding something without full knowledge of the details. Abstraction is our weapon against complexity. For example, we understand and use functions such as sqrt and pow without knowing too much about their code, which was written by some other programmer. It is also abstraction that allows us to quickly use classes such as int, float, and string. We can understand the characteristics of int data (a specific range of integer values) and int operations (such as addition, multiplication, and cout << intObject;) without knowing the details of those operations or even how those values are stored in the computer.

A class can be understood through its interface—the functions and operators that may be applied to the objects of the class. In the case of int or float, operations include sqrt, pow, +, -, *, and so on. In this manner, we can ignore many details and concentrate on the big picture. Although C++ is delivered with a large set of functions and classes, we will eventually need other classes and their associated operations (functions and operators). These abstractions are usually built from existing classes, operations, and algorithms implemented as C++ code. We now begin to create our own simple abstractions implemented as programmer-defined functions. Let us set a goal to build these abstractions as though they were among the functions that come with the compiler. Then we can use abstraction to concentrate on the larger tasks at hand. We use the function because we know what it does. Once it is implemented, we don't have to remember how it does it.

We have already seen a programmer-defined function in every program. In fact, you have even written several programmer-defined functions. This is because the portion of the program beginning at int main and ending with the closing right brace, }, is one example of a programmer-defined function. Our view of program execution can be this: The first function executed is function main. If the main function is not present, the program will not run. This error is detected at linktime. Let's now look at the syntax of programmer-defined functions, of which main is an example.

A programmer-defined function is composed of a function heading followed by a block:

function-heading
block

A *block* starts with { and ends with }. It contains components such as object declarations and executable statements:

```
{ // <- BEGIN block
  declarations
  statements
} // <- END block
```

The function heading contains the type of value the function is to return, the name of the function, and the parameters (discussed later) between parentheses.

return-type identifier (*parameters*)

For example, the return type may be int for functions that return an integer value. In this case, a return statement (discussed later) should be included as one of the statements in the function. Using the main function as an example, we see the return type is int and that so far, the value of 0 has always been returned to the caller. The caller, in the case of main, is always the operating system. Returning 0 signals everything is okay; a nonzero integer is a signal to the operating system that something went wrong. This detail can be ignored except that it helps explain the appearance of all the C++ programs seen so far. The use of int and return 0 is a standard method for implementing even the smallest of C++ programs and it works on all systems.

```cpp
int main()
{
  // This function executes first...
  //
  // Report normal program termination to the operating system
  return 0;
}
```

The return type may be void if the function is not meant to return anything. The following example of a programmer-defined function from ourstuff.cpp has a void return type to indicate that no value is returned:

```cpp
void clearScreen()
{ // This implementation of clearScreen writes 25 new lines,
  // which does not look nice and it clears the screen slowly
  // (but it works on all systems)

  cout << "\n\n\n\n\n\n\n\n\n\n\n\n\n\n\n\n\n\n\n\n\n\n\n\n\n";

  // Improve it by replacing this with the appropriate calls for your
  // environment. Remember to include the header file after the system.
  // 1. UNIX: #include<stdlib.h>
  //      system("clear");
  // 2. Symantec/Macintosh: #include<console.h>
  //      cgotoxy(1,1,stdout);  // position cursor to upper left
  //      ccleos(stdout);        // clear window to end of screen
  // 3. Borland/Turbo C++ DOS/Windows: #include<conio.h>
  //      clrscr();
}
```

Most systems allow void main functions so you might see other programs where main is written as a void function. In this case, the return statement is not needed:

```cpp
void main()
{
  // This function executes first...
  //
  // return statements cannot appear in void functions
}
```

We now see how a function name encountered as a statement represents all the statements of the function. It gives one name for an entire process.

4.1.1 Modular Control

C++ programs use a large number of functions, often stored in several files. There may even be several functions in the same program file. So to bring order to where the program is to begin, the convention is that it begin with function `main`. If a program contains more than one programmer-defined function, `main` is executed first even if it is not physically located as the first function in a program. For example, the following program produces output indicating that function `main` is called first, and when function `geometry` is called, the statements in `geometry` are executed. When the statements of `geometry` are complete, control transfers back to the caller, which in this case was function `main`.

```
// This program contains two programmer-defined
// functions: void geometry() and int main()
#include <iostream.h>
#include <ourstuff.h>
#include <math.h>

const double pi = 3.1415926535898;

void geometry()
{
  cout << endl;
  cout << "In geometry,  show some geometric equations----" << endl;

  double radius = 1.0;
  double height = 2.0;
  double area = pi * radius * radius;
  decimals(cout, 2);
  cout << "           radius: " << radius << endl;
  cout << "           height: " << height << endl;
  cout << "  area of a circle: " << area   << endl;
  cout << "  area of cylinder: "
       << 2 * pi * area * height << endl;
  cout << "volume of cylinder: "
       << pi * pow(area, 2.0) * height << endl;
  cout << "      area of cone: "
       << pi * area * sqrt(pow(area, 2) + pow(height, 2.0)) << endl;
  cout << "    volume of cone: "
       << 1.0 / 3.0 * pi * pow(area, 2.0) * height << endl;

  cout << "End of geometry,  go back to caller (main)----" << endl;
  cout << endl;
}
```

```
int main()
{
  cout << "****In main, this statement executes first****" << endl;
  geometry(); // <-Execute the statements contained in function geometry
  cout << "****Back in main, about to execute return 0****" << endl;
  return 0;
}
```

--- **Output** ---

```
****In main, this statement executes first****

In geometry, show some geometric equations----
            radius: 1.00
            height: 2.00
   area of a circle: 3.14
   area of cylinder: 39.48
 volume of cylinder: 62.01
       area of cone: 36.76
     volume of cone: 20.67
End of geometry, go back to caller (main)----

****Back in main, about to execute return 0****
```

At the point of a function call, control transfers to the called function. After the function has executed its statements, control returns to the expression following the call. Because a function is a *module*—a repeatedly used component—and function calls transfer *control* to a function, the term *modular control* describes programs executing primarily as a series of function calls. The following program illustrates modular control with the order of statement execution written in comments.

```
// Modular control demonstrated with three functions.
// 1 (in comments) indicates the first statement
// executed and 12 indicates the last statement.
#include "iostream.h"

void one()
{
  cout << endl;                   // Statements 2 and 10
  cout << "In function one()";    // Statements 3 and 11
  cout << endl;                   // Statements 4 and 12
}

void two()
{
  cout << '\n' << "*********";     // Statement 6
  cout << '\n' << "*two two*";     // Statement 7
```

```
    cout << '\n' << "*********" << endl;     // Statement 8
}

int main()
{
  one();                                      // Statement 1
  two();                                      // Statement 5
  one();                                      // Statement 9
  return 0;
}
```

────────── **Output** ──────────

```
  In function one()

  *********
  *two two*
  *********

  In function one()
```

Since there are three functions in this program (main, one, and two), some convention is needed to determine which function is executed first. After all, a program cannot begin execution from three different locations. Typically, the first statement in main is the logical starting point of execution. Therefore, the first statement executed in this program is a call to the previously declared programmer-defined function one. At this time, control transfers to the first statement in function one, and its block is executed (marked statements 2, 3, and 4 in comments). After function one has finished executing, control returns to the statement following the original function call, or in this program, function two. The three statements in function two are then executed before control returns to function main. Again, function one is encountered as a statement. The statements in function one's block are executed again (statements 10, 11, and 12), after which control is transferred back to function main. Since there are no more statements in the main function, the program terminates normally.

Programming Tip ──────────

It is easy to forget the parentheses in a function call. To call a void function f1 declared as:

```
void f1()
{ ...
}
```

we must include the parentheses in the call. Failure to do so results in an error, or the function call may simply be ignored:

```
// Remember to include () after the function name.
// This may generate an error or it may simply be ignored.
f1;
// The correct function call is
f1();
```

4.1.2 Example: Function explainProgram

Function explainProgram is a more useful example of a programmer-defined function. It may be included whenever some sort of explanation is required to explain the program's purpose. Because explainProgram is written as a function, some of the complexity is moved out of the main function. The code has a solitary purpose as well: to communicate instructions to the user.

```
// This program demonstrates a runtime error that can occur
// when entering an invalid format for a numeric value
#include <iostream.h>

void explainProgram()
{ // POST: An explanation is displayed
  cout << "This program illustrates how an input error"  << endl
       << "can occur. Run this program once and enter 5" << endl
       << "at the prompt. Run this program again using"  << endl
       << "'X' as input to see what happens.          "  << endl
                                                          << endl;
}

int main()
{
  int j = 0;

  // Call a function with zero arguments
  explainProgram();
  cout << "Enter an int: ";
  cin >> j;
  cout << "The int object j = " << j << endl;
  return 0;
}
```

─────────────── Dialogue ───────────────
```
This program illustrates how an input error
can occur. Run this program once and enter 5
at the prompt. Run this program again using
'X' as input to see what happens.

Enter an int: X

The int object j = 0
```

4.1.3 Example: Function causeApause

We now look at another void function that causes a pause so users have the chance to read program output. The statements that cause a pause are gathered as a programmer-defined function. The function can be called to allow users to read output that otherwise would scroll off the screen. Before showing function causeApause, it is necessary to introduce a member function of the istream class: function ignore.

```
istream::ignore(int n, char delimiter);
// POST: Skips up to n characters in the input stream.
//       If the delimiter is encountered, the skipping stops
//       and the delimiter is removed from the input stream.
//       The state of the istream is returned, but can be ignored.
```

For example, up to 100 characters are consumed from the input stream until the newline character is encountered with this call:

```
cin.ignore(100, '\n');
```

We take advantage of this to pause program execution until the user presses the Enter key, which generates a newline.

```
#include <iostream.h>  // for cin and iostream::ignore(int, char)

void causeApause()
{
  cout << '\n' << "Press Enter to continue . . . " ;
  cin.ignore(100, '\n');
}

int main()
{
  cout << "\nATTENTION!..." << endl;
  causeApause();
  cout << "\nContinue processing..." << endl;
  return 0;
}
```

───────────────────── **Output** ─────────────────────
```
ATTENTION!...

Press Enter to continue . . . ↵

Continue processing...
```

A programmer-defined function, such as function causeApause shown above, may be called from any point after its declaration. This means that a function can be called from other functions such as main or other programmer-defined programs.

```
// After a programmer-defined function is
// declared, it may be called by other functions
#include <iostream.h>

void causeApause()
{
  cout << '\n' << "Press Enter to continue . . . " ;
  cin.ignore(100, '\n');
}

void explainProgram()
{
  cout << "Any explanation"  << endl;
  causeApause();
}

int main()
{
  explainProgram();
  return 0;
}
```

Self-Check

1. Write the general form (outline) for programmer-defined functions.
2. What does void mean when used as the return type?
3. How many statements may be written in a block delimited by { }?
4. Conceptually, which function is called first when a C++ program executes?
5. What happens when we attempt to call a function that has not yet been physically declared?
6. May a function be called more than once?
7. Is function main a programmer-defined function?
8. What happens if we forget to use the parentheses after the function name in a function call?
9. Write a programmer-defined function that displays your name when the function call myName() is encountered.
10. Is myName a legal call to the function you just wrote?

Answers

1. *return-type function name (parameters)* { ...*statements...* }
2. The function does not return any value and an activation of that function may exist as a stand-alone statement.
3. From zero to many.

4. Function `main`
5. This is system dependent: A compiletime error may be generated. Other compilers may make assumptions about what was intended and issue a warning when a different use is encountered.
6. Yes
7. Yes
8. A compiletime error is generated or the code is ignored (system dependent). Parentheses are required in every function call even if no parameters are specified in the function.
9.
```
void myName()
{
    cout << "Joan Doe";
}
```
10. No, the parentheses must be added.

4.2 Parameters

Many library functions require data in the form of arguments. This will also be true for many of our own functions. Functions receive such data through *argument/parameter associations*. A *parameter* consists of a class name and one identifier enclosed within the parentheses of the function heading. Multiple parameters are allowed when separated by commas:

return-type function-name (type identifier-1, type identifier-2, ... , type identifier-n)

For example, the function prototype:

```
double sqrt(double x);
```

has one `double` parameter named x. Other library functions have a prespecified number of parameters. The number of parameters required for our own functions becomes part of a design decision. First we need to recognize the need for a function. Then we must decide what the function requires. You may be provided with this information. When designing functions as some later point, you will have to determine what parameters a function requires. This is similar to determining the input a program requires. Here is one example of a function prototype that indicates that two `int`s are required by the function:

```
int maximum(int j, int k);
```

This function prototype indicates that two `int`s are required when called from other points in a program:

```
cout << maximum(97, 86);
```

The arguments (97 and 86 in this example) are associated to the function's parameters (j and k in this example) by relative position. In general, the first argument in a function call is associated with the first parameter listed in the function's parameter list, the second argument with the second parameter, and so on.

```
int maximum(int j, int k)

cout << maximum(97,86)
```

The next example shows the complete implementation of a void function that computes and displays the distance between two points. The main function illustrates various ways to match arguments to parameters.

First, we should recognize that four floats are required to compute the distance between two points (x_1, y_1) and (x_2, y_2) using this formula:

$$\text{Distance} = \sqrt{(x_1 - x_2)^2 + (y_1 - y_2)^2}$$

where

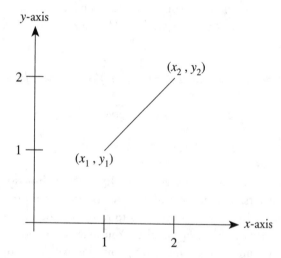

So when we design a function that displays the computed distance, we should be able to write function calls like this:

```
distance(1.0, 1.0, 2.0, 2.0);
```

The four arguments are made available to the function by copying the value of each argument to its associated parameter. This mode of argument/parameter association is named *pass by value* because we are passing a value to a function. Control then transfers to the block of function distance, where the distance is computed and displayed. This complete program calls the programmer-defined function distance a total of four times:

```
// An example of pass by value argument/parameter associations
#include <iostream.h>
#include <math.h>

void distance(float x1, float y1, float x2, float y2)
{
  cout << sqrt(pow((x1 - x2), 2) + pow((y1 - y2), 2)) << endl;
}

int main()
{
  distance(0.0, 0.0, 3.0, 4.0);     // 1. float constants
  distance(0, 0, 3, 4);             // 2. int constants okay
  float x1=0, y1=0, x2=3, y2=4;
  distance(x1, y1, x2, y2);         // 3. float objects okay
  distance(-1.0, y1-1, 2*x2, 3.5);  // 4. expressions with
  return 0;                         //    operators are also okay
}
```

—————————— Output ——————————
```
5
5
5
8.321658
```

The following function evaluation shows values of the parameters after function distance is called. Notice that the arguments are copied to the parameters using relative positions in the list. For example, the first argument is associated with the first parameter (0.0 is copied to x1), and the third argument is associated with the third parameter (3.0 is copied to x2).

```
void distance(x1,  y1,  x2,  y2)
              ↑    ↑    ↑    ↑
     distance(0.0, 0.0, 3.0, 4.0)
```

Passing arguments to parameters is like an assignment—the argument expression is evaluated and the value is moved to the parameter. The parameter can then be used in the function like an object initialized via the function call. The parameters are used to compute the distance between the two points represented by those arguments. Here is the step-by-step computation:

```
sqrt(pow((x1 - x2), 2) + pow((y1 - y2), 2))
sqrt(pow((0.0-3.0), 2) + pow((0.0-4.0), 2))
sqrt(pow(( -3.0  ), 2) + pow(( -4.0  ), 2))
sqrt(           9.0     +          16.0   )
sqrt(                25.0                  )
                  5.0
```

In addition to objects, arguments to a function could also be numeric constants or expressions with parameters, distance(-1.0, y2-1, 2*x2, 3.5);, for example. In a fashion similar to implicit type conversions, arguments do not have to be the same type as the associated parameter. Automatic type conversion takes place whenever possible. Although the arguments should be the same class as the associated parameters, the arguments could be a different class and still produce predictable and correct results. The following table reflects the similarity of argument/parameter association and the familiar assignment operations when it comes to the "acceptable" classes.

Parameter Class	Some "Acceptable" Argument Classes
int	← int
char	← char
float	← int, float
double	← int, float, double
long int	← int, long int

Although it is desirable always to have the argument class match the parameter class, the "acceptable" argument classes shown above are implicitly converted to the proper value. On the other hand, sending a float argument to an int parameter may result in truncation (similar to truncation on assignment of a float to an int). If the acceptable types are ignored, some rather strange events can occur. Consider the following function with one int parameter:

```
void f(int j)  // The parameter's class is int
{
   cout << j << endl;
}
```

If care is not taken, the original value of an argument may be converted to an unexpected value. Hopefully, a warning, an overflow error, or a runtime error occurs. This alert helps avoid the more difficult-to-detect intent errors. Using two different C++ compilers with the following function calls often caused different events to occur:

Function Call	Results with One C++ Compiler	Results with Another C++ Compiler
f(999.999)	Truncates 999.999 to int 999	Same but with a warning
f(999999999)	Incorrectly converted to an int with a garbage value; this is an overflow error	int class had greater range (2,147,483,647) so this was perfectly OK
f("ab")	Since the argument is string rather than int, a "type mismatch" compiletime error occurs	Looks like the address (location in memory) of the string, so the passed value is meaningless
f('a')	'a' is converted to the ordinal value of 'a', which on some systems is 97	Same
f(999e999)	Results in an undetected overflow; the argument j has a garbage value but we are not notified	Real constant out of range for conversion to int

Again, with such potential for error, try to use arguments of the same or acceptable class as the associated parameter.

4.2.1 The return Statement

Many functions are often used to return values, for example, the expression ceil(4.1) returns 5. These non-void functions must contain a *return statement* to specify the returned value. Values are returned to the point of the function call by using a return type such as int or float rather than void, and the C++ return statement:

```
return expression ;
```

When return is encountered, the expression replaces the function call and the program continues to execute from the point of the function call—an exit from the function occurs. In the next example, we see that the function serviceCharge has been declared with the return type float. The call to serviceCharge is replaced by a floating-point value that is dependent upon the values of the arguments.

```
// Call serviceCharge to determine an additional bank debit
#include <iostream.h>

float serviceCharge(int checks, int atms)
{ // Return a float.
  return 0.25 * checks + 0.10 * atms;
}

int main()
{
  int checks, ATMs;
  cout << " Enter checks: ";
  cin >> checks;
  cout << "  Enter ATMs: ";
  cin >> ATMs;
  cout << "serviceCharge: " << serviceCharge(checks, ATMs) << endl;
  return 0;
}
```

Dialogue
```
    Enter checks: 17
      Enter ATMs: 9
  serviceCharge: 5.15
```

When serviceCharge is called, the expression following the keyword return is evaluated and sent back to the point from where it was called—in the cout statement of function main. The type of value returned is specified as the first element of a function heading. In this case, serviceCharge returns a float. Had void been used instead of float, an error would occur at the return statement—void indicates no value is to be returned.

4.2.2 Altering Objects Through References

Although the parameters of functions are usually used for input, output parameters are sometimes used when we wish to return more than one value. Since only one value is returned through a return statement, we need a means of returning more than one value. This is accomplished through the use of a *reference* to the argument in the function call. More specifically, the special symbol & is used before the parameter in the function heading to specify that the parameter is a reference to the associated argument in the function call. Instead of receiving a copy of the argument, the function receives the *address* of the argument. (*Note:* On some systems only objects of the proper class may be associated with reference parameters.) When a change is made to a reference parameter, the argument, if it is an object, is also changed. For example, the function swap alters the arguments aArg and bArg because of the presence of the reference operator & before each parameter. Changes occur because the references in front of aParm and bParm generate another name for the arguments. They are aliases. For example, aArg is also know as aParm.

```
// Notice the reference symbol & is in front of aParm and bParm.
// Now a change to aParm or bParm alters the associated object argument.
#include <iostream.h>

void swap(int & aParm, int & bParm) // & means that any change to the
{                                   // parameter alters the argument
  int temp;
  temp = aParm;
  aParm = bParm;   // Change the argument aArg down in function main
  bParm = temp;    // Change the argument bArg down in function main
}

int main()
{                                          // aArg   bArg
  int aArg = 89, bArg = 76;                //  89     76
  cout << aArg << "  " << bArg << endl;    //   "      "
  swap(aArg, bArg);                        //  76     89
  cout << aArg << "  " << bArg << endl;    //   "      "
  return 0;
}
```

──── **Output** ────
```
89 76
76 89
```

If the reference operators & are removed from the program above, no change is made to the arguments. In this case, the values of aArg and bArg would be passed by value, not by reference. Without the reference &, the values of aParm and bParm are changed locally (within the function only) and the values of the associated arguments are unaffected.

Since functions return either zero values (void functions) or one value (with return), references are used when we need to return more than one value from a function. The following example calls getData, which obtains and converts values input from the keyboard. Two values are returned through reference parameters:

```
// Use references to return more than one value
#include <iostream.h>
#include "ourstr.h"

void getData(string & name, int & age)       // Output parameters
{ // POST: Returns a person's converted name
  //       and age upon her or his next birthday
```

```
      string first, middle, last;

      cout << "Enter your first name: ";
      cin >> first;
      cout << "  your middle initial: ";
      cin >> middle;
      cout << "   and your last name: ";
      cin >> last;
      name = last + ", " + first + " " + middle + ".";
      name.toUpper();

      cout << "       Enter your age: ";
      cin >> age;
   }

int main()
{
   string name;
   int age;
   getData(name, age);
   cout << name << " will be " << age + 1 << endl;
   return 0;
}
```

—————————————————————— **Dialogue** ——————————————————————

```
   Enter your first name: Jody
      your middle initial: m
        and your last name: Manwiller
            Enter your age: 16
   MANWILLER, JODY M. will be 17
```

Self-Check

1. Write the output generated by the following program:

```
   #include <iostream.h>
   void one(int j, float x, char ch)
   {
      cout << " | " << ch << " " << j * x;
   }
   int main()
   {
      one(2, 2.3, 'A');
      one(24 % 10, 1.0 / 3.0, 'B');
      return 0;
   }
```

2. Write the output generated by the following program:

```
#include <iostream.h>
#include <math.h>
float f(float x)
{
  return sqrt(x) + 1.5;
}
int main()
{
  cout << f(4.0) << "  " << f(25);
  return 0;
}
```

3. Write a programmer-defined function `diff` that returns the positive difference between two numeric values. The statements shown below should produce the output shown on the right. *Hint:* Use function `fabs` of `math.h`, which returns the absolute value of its `int` or `float` argument: `fabs(2 - 8.5)` returns +6.5.

```
                              //  Test Oracle
cout << diff(1, 4) << endl;   //  3
cout << diff(4, 1) << endl;   //  3
cout << diff(10.5, -2.3) << endl;  //  12.8
cout << diff(-2.3, 10.5) << endl;  //  12.8
```

4. What are the values of `arg1` and `arg2` after this program runs when the two `int`s 77 and 88 are entered? The dialogue would appear exactly like this:

```
Enter two ints: 77   88
```

a.
```
#include <iostream.h>
void getData(int a, int b)
{
  cout << "Enter two ints: ";
  cin >> a >> b;
}
int main()
{
  int arg1 = 0, arg2 = 0;
  getData(arg1, arg2);
  return 0;
}
// arg1 ____    arg2 ____
```

b.
```
#include <iostream.h>
void getData(int & a, int b)
{
  cout << "Enter two ints: ";
  cin >> a >> b;
}
int main()
{
  int arg1 = 0, arg2 = 0;
  getData(arg1, arg2);
  return 0;
}
// arg1 ____    arg2 ____
```

c.
```
#include <iostream.h>
void getData(int & a, int & b)
{
  cout << "Enter two ints: ";
  cin >> a >> b;
}
int main()
{
  int arg1 = 0, arg2 = 0;
  getData(arg1, arg2);
  return 0;
}
// arg1 ____    arg2 ____
```

d.
```
#include <iostream.h>
void getData(int & a, int & b)
{
  int one, two;
  a = a + 1;
  b = 2;
  cout << "Enter two ints: ";
  cin >> one >> two;
}
int main()
{
  int arg1 = 0, arg2 = 0;
  getData(arg1, arg2);
  return 0;
}
// arg1 ____    arg2 ____
```

Answers
1. ¦ A 4.6 ¦ B 1.333333
2. 3.5   6.5
3. float diff(float x, float y) { return fabs(x - y); }
4. a. arg1 = 0, arg2 = 0   b. arg1 = 77, arg2 = 0   c. arg1 = 77, arg2 = 88   d. arg1 = 1, arg2 = 2

4.3   Scope of Identifiers

The *scope* of an identifier is the part of a program from which an identifier can be referenced. The scope of an identifier extends from the point of the identifier's declaration to the end of the block in which it is declared (recall that a block is delimited by the left and right braces: { and }). For example, the scope of j in the following program is function one. This int j cannot be referenced from main.

```
// Illustrate the scope of an object
#include <iostream.h>

const int currentYear = 1995;

void one()
{                                        // The scope of
  int j = 0;                             // j is limited
  j = j + 1;                             // to this
  // currentYear is a global identifier  // block, i.e.,
  cout << currentYear;                   // function one()
}
```

```
int main()
{
  j = 5; // <- This is an error; j is an unknown identifier
  cout << currentYear << endl;
  return 0;
}
```

When an object is declared outside of a block—as in the case of currentYear—its scope begins at the point of declaration and extends to the end of the source file. Objects declared in a block can be referenced only from within that block. These are *local objects*. Identifiers declared outside of a block (such as currentYear) are said to be global. *Global objects* may be referenced from any subsequent part of the program, unless that identifier is declared again (redeclared) within another block. In this case, the object that was declared first becomes hidden from the block in which it is redeclared. Since many blocks exist within one program, determining the scope of an object can be somewhat complicated. For example, try to predict the output of the following program, which includes four different declarations of the int object j:

```
// This program is a tedious test of your ability to
// determine which of the four int objects identified
// as j is being referenced at any given point.
#include <iostream.h>

int j = 0;              // Global object j

void one()
{
  cout << j;            // This is a reference to the global j
}

void two()
{
  int j = 1;            // This j is local to two()
  cout << j;
}

int main()
{
  int j = 2;            // This j is local to main()
  one();
  two();
  tre();
  cout << j;
  return 0;
}
```

When function one is called, the global j initialized as 0 is referenced. This global object j can be referenced from within any function that does not declare another identifier named j. Therefore, the j that was declared first and initialized to 0 is known (can be referenced) from function one even though it was not declared inside one. But when a reference is made to j in function two, the "global" j is hidden due to the "local" definition of j. To this point in program execution, function one has caused the output 0, and function two caused 1 to be displayed. The final statement in function main references the j local to main—this j is initialized as 2. Therefore the output would be 0, 1, and 2.

We often have functions that need objects to accomplish their tasks. We have seen this already in function main. Typically, a function will have one or more objects declared at the beginning of the block. These objects are said to be local to the function because they may be referenced only from within the function. The same protection applies to the parameters of a function, which are local to the function in which they are declared. The restriction on access provides safekeeping for the local objects so they are not accidentally altered from some other portion of a program.

```
void f1(float x)
{
  int j;
  // Error attempting to reference main's local object ch
  ch = 'A';
  ...
}

int main()
{
  char ch;
  x = 5.0; // Error attempting to reference f1's local object x
  j = 1;   // Error attempting to reference f1's local object j
  ...
  return 0;
}
```

Self-Check

1. Name two things that may be declared local to a function.
2. If an object is declared outside of a function, from where may it be referenced?
3. Use the partial program shown below to determine the functions from which each of the following identifiers may be referenced.

```
      cout    b    cin    MAX    c    f1    a    d    f2
```

```
#include <iostream.h>
const float MAX = 99999.9;
void f1(int a)
```

```
    {
      int b;
      ...
    }

    void f2(float c)
    {
      float d;
      ...
    }

    int main()
    {
      char e;
      ...
    }
```

Answers
1. Parameters between () and objects declared between {}
2. From any point in the file after the declaration
3. cout: everywhere   b: f1 only   cin: everywhere   MAX: f1, f2, main   c: f2 only
   f1: f1, f2, main   a: f1 only   d: f2 only   f2: f2, main

Exercises

1. Which of the following represent valid function prototypes?

   a. `int large(int a, int b);`   **d.** `int f(a, int b);`

   b. `double(double a, double b);`   **e.** `float f();`

   c. `large_int(int a; int b;);`   **f.** `char c(int a);`

2. Write the output generated by the following program:

```
#include <iostream.h>
double f(double x, double y)
{
  return 2 * x - y;
}

int main()
{
  cout << f(1, 2.5) << endl;
  cout << f(-4.5, -3) << endl;
  cout << f(5, -2) << endl;
  return 0;
}
```

3. Write the output generated by the following program:

```cpp
#include <iostream.h>
void one(int j, int k)
{
  cout << "\n  In one: " << j << "  " << k << endl;
}
int main()
{
  int j = 4, k = 6;
  cout << "\n In main: " << j << "  " << k << endl;
  one(j, k);
  one(-123, -456);
  return 0;
}
```

4. Write a function named showSum that *displays* (not returns) the sum of two integers.
5. Write a valid call to function showSum.
6. Write the output generated by the following function:

```cpp
#include <iostream.h>
#include <math.h>

double mystery(double p)
{
  return pow(p, 3) - 1;
}

int main()
{
  double a = 3.0;
  cout << mystery(  a) << endl;
  cout << mystery(4.0) << endl;
  cout << mystery( -2) << endl;
  return 0;
}
```

7. Write a function named returnSum that *returns* (not displays) the sum of two integers.
8. Write a valid call to function returnSum.
9. Which parameters, when altered within function f, also alter the associated argument?

```cpp
void f(int a, char & b, float c, double & d)
```

10. Write the output from the following program:

```cpp
// Use return and & to pass values back to function main
#include <iostream.h>
float monthlyFeeOne(int checks, int atms)
{
  return(checks * 0.25 + atms * 0.10);
}
void monthlyFeeTwo(int checks, int atms, float & charge)
{
  charge = checks * 0.25 + atms * 0.10 + 5.00;
}
int main()
{
  cout << "monthly fee: " << monthlyFeeOne(20, 10) << endl;
  float charge;
  monthlyFeeTwo(10, 5, charge);
  cout << "monthly fee: " << charge << endl;
  return 0;
}
```

11. Detect the intent error in the following program in which function inc is to increment the argument by the amount specified in the second argument. The output from main should be 1.5.

```cpp
#include <iostream.h>

void inc(double x, int increment)
{
  x = x + increment;
}

int main()
{
  float y = 1.0;
  inc(y, 0.5);
  cout << y << endl;
  return 0;
}
```

Lab Projects

4A   Using Objects

Read the following program and try to predict the output. If you cannot determine the value of intParm, write a question mark. Then copy, compile, link, and run the following program and write the actual output to the right of your prediction. Explain the reason for the change, if any, to the value that has been passed to function f.

```cpp
#include <iostream.h>

void f(int intParm)
{
  cout << intParm << endl;
}

int main()
{
  long int j = 2147483647;
  f(j+1);
  f(123);
  f('A');
  f(9.99);
  return 0;
}
```

4B   Using Objects

Write a function named round that will round any float or double argument to the number of decimal places specified as the second argument. To allow the maximum number of digits, return a double value. *Hint:* You will have to multiply the first argument by 10^n where n is the number of decimals (the second argument to round) before applying a ceil or floor function. Then divide the result by 10^n [use pow(10,n)]. *Note:* When rounding 1.25 to the nearest tenth, you may end up with either 1.2 or 1.3 depending on whether you use floor or ceil to round.

```cpp
#include <iostream.h>

// Implement double round(double x, int n) here

int main()
{                                          // Test oracle:
  cout << round(-2.9, 0)    << endl;  // -3
  cout << round(-2.59, 1)   << endl;  // -2.6
  cout << round(0.0059, 2)  << endl;  // 0.01
```

```
    cout << round(1.23467, 3)    << endl;    // 1.235
    cout << round(9.999999, 4)  << endl;    // 10
    return 0;
}
```

4C   Using Objects

Write a function called dec with one parameter which decrements the associated argument by 1. Use this main function to test dec:

```
int main()
{
  int j = 10;
  cout << j << endl;         // Test oracle:
  dec(j);                    // 10
  cout << j << endl;         // 9
  dec(j);                    // 8
  cout << j << endl;         // 7
  dec(j);
  cout << j << endl;
  return 0;
}
```

4D   Using Objects

Write function range with two parameters identified as theta (angle in radians) and velocity (in meters per second) that returns the range (in meters) of a projectile. The formula is:

$$range = \sin(2 \times theta) \times velocity^2 \ / \ gravity$$

where

theta = the angle of the projectile's path (in radians)
velocity = the initial velocity of the projectile (in meters/second)
gravity = 9.8 meters/second^2

Use the program shown below to test function range. *Note:* The takeoff angle (45°) is expressed in degrees, so you must convert this angle to its radian equivalent. This is necessary because the trigonometric functions cos(x) and sin(x) assume the argument (x) is an angle expressed in radians. An angle in degrees can be converted to radians by multiplying the number of degrees by π / 180 where π = 3.14159. For example, 45° = 45 * 3.14159 / 180, or 0.7853975 radians. Perform the conversion locally in your programmer-defined function range.

```
#include <iostream.h>
#include <math.h>
#include "ourstuff.h"   // for decimals(cout,3)
```

```
// Implement function range here. Remember to
// convert the angle from degrees to radians. Do it locally!

int main()
{   // Without ourstuff.h and the call to decimals,
    // output will differ.
    decimals(cout,3);
                                          // Test oracle:
    cout << range(45.0, 100.0) << endl;   // 1020.408
    cout << range(45.0, 200.0) << endl;   // 4081.633
    cout << range(45.0, 300.0) << endl;   // 9183.673
    cout << range(22.5, 300.0) << endl;   // 6493.833
    return 0;
}
```

4E   Using Objects

The monthly payment on a loan is a function of the amount borrowed, the duration of the loan, and the interest rate. Write a program that reads the necessary data and then calls the programmer-defined function payment to return the monthly loan payment. The first task consists of obtaining values for the amount borrowed, the length of the loan in years, and the annual interest rate. Pass these three values as arguments to the function payment. For example, the function call:

```
cout << payment(106000.00, 11.5, 30);
```

must display 1049.71. Therefore, return the value only after it has been rounded to two decimals with the round function in ourstuff.h. Your dialogue should look exactly like this:

```
      Amount Borrowed: 106000
Rate (1 to 35 percent): 11.5
Length (1 to 35 years): 30

      Monthly Payment: 1049.71
```

The formula used to calculate monthly payments on a loan given the Amount, Rate, and the number of Months can be written as:

$$Payment = Amount \times Rate \times \frac{(Rate+1)^{Months}}{(Rate+1)^{Months}-1}$$

Note: Make sure the function payment converts the annual interest rate and the years into the equivalent monthly interest rate (divide Rate [11.5 above] by 1200) and number of months (multiply Years [30 above] by 12), respectively. You will need the function pow, which is declared in the header file math.h, and the function round, which is declared in ourstuff.h.

4F   Using Objects

Write a program containing the function slope that returns the slope of a line given any two points (x_1, y_1) and (x_2, y_2) to define the line. One formula for the slope (m) of a line is:

$$\frac{y_2 - y_1}{x_2 - x_1}$$

Test your function with this data:

```
 x1    y1    x2    y2
----------------------------
  0     0     1     1
  0     0    -1     1
 1.5   3.7   8.6   -34.5
 6.0   5.2   6.0   -13.5
```

using a program that looks something like this:

```
int main()
{
  double x1 = 0, y1 = 0, x2 = 1, y2 = 1;
  cout << slope(x1, y1, x2, y2) << endl;
  cout << slope(0, 0, -1, 1) << endl;
  return 0;
}
```

What type of error occurs with the fourth (final) set of arguments represented by this function call:

```
slope(6.0, 5.2, 6.0, -13.5);
```

4G   Using Objects

Write a function that calculates and displays the distance and height of a golf ball at any given moment in flight. The height and distance after a golf ball is struck by a golf club are given as:

$$distance = (velocity \times \cos(angle)) \times seconds$$

$$height = -0.5 \times gravity \times seconds^2 + (velocity \times \sin(angle)) \times seconds$$

where `velocity` is the initial velocity of the golf club at impact, `angle` is the angle from the level ground that the path of the ball initially takes, `gravity` is the acceleration due to gravity, and `seconds` is the number of seconds that the golf ball is in the air. The following steps may help:

- Open a new file and include the appropriate header files for input, output, and the math functions `sin`, `cos`, and `pow`.
- Define the constant objects `gravity` (9.8) and `pi` (3.1415926). Pick the class wisely (`int` or `float`).
- Write the function `show` with one `float` parameter named `seconds`.
- Implement the function `show` to calculate and display the height followed by distance.
- Retype the following `main` program:

```
int main()
{
  cout << "  Height    Distance" << endl;
  show(0.0);
  show(0.5);
  return 0;
}
```

- Compile, link, and run the program.
- Verify with a calculator that your function works correctly.
- Add enough `show` statements to track the golf ball for at least eight moments before it hits the ground.
- Compile, link, and run the program until the tracking goes from positive to negative.

4.4   ATM Objects

In the second part of this chapter, we will learn how to use objects by reading the declaration of the class. We will see that a class declaration is a combination of object and function declarations wrapped up in a block where the function prototypes represent the operations of the class. Now that we know how to read function prototypes, preconditions, and postconditions, class declarations will provide the necessary documentation to construct and use objects of a class. The first example studied is a class named `ATM`, an acronym for automated teller machine. Before looking at the general form of class declarations and the entire `ATM` class declaration, we will study some small programs that call `ATM` member functions to get a flavor of `ATM` object behavior.

An automated teller machine is a device that allows bank customers to initiate banking transactions such as deposits, withdrawals, transfers, balance queries, credit card payments, and cash advances. An ATM dispenses cash, accepts deposits, and gives receipts. The ATM class we are about to explore simulates some of these transactions. It will become part of an object-oriented bank control program extending over the next several chapters. An ATM object allows us to obtain data and transactions from bank customers with an interface similar in appearance to automated teller machines you may have seen.

ATM objects are capable of simulating a small subset of the many functions normally performed by a human bank teller. These three transactions usually handled in person are part of the automated teller machine:

1. Query the account balance.
2. Make withdrawals in increments of 5.00.
3. Make deposits.

With nonsimulated ATMs, customers insert a card before keying a personal identification number (PIN). Because our computers do not have a magnetic card reader device, our bank customers will enter a name from the keyboard before the PIN is keyed. The substitute for an ATM card is keyboard entry of a character string that looks like a person's last name. Since it is even more unlikely that your computer is equipped to give you cash or accept deposits, these operations are also simulated.

4.4.1   Some ATM Member Functions

The first ATM member function is identified as ATM::getNameAndPIN (recall that :: is the scope resolution operator which means here that getNameAndPIN is in the scope of class ATM). The getNameAndPIN function is a void function that first displays an ATM logo and then prompts for a name and a personal identification number. This input data becomes part of the object's state and is used later to determine if the customer has entered a valid PIN, to determine the account to which withdrawal and deposit adjustments are made, and to determine the proper account for balance queries.

Two member functions that query the state of ATM objects are ATM::name and ATM::PIN. These return the stored name and PIN, respectively. We may query this data any time without asking the customer to reenter the data. The following program uses these three member functions along with a fourth named ATM::message, which takes a string argument and displays it to the ATM screen with a pause. (*Note:* The ATM class is declared in the file ouratm.h.)

```
// Declare an ATM object named moneyMachine
// and use these four member functions:
//    1. void ATM::getNameAndPIN()
//    2. void ATM::message(string aMessage)
//    3. string ATM::name()
//    4. string ATM::PIN()

#include "ouratm.h" // class ATM is declared in the file: ouratm.h

int main()
{
  ATM moneyMachine;
  moneyMachine.getNameAndPIN();
  moneyMachine.message("Welcome " + moneyMachine.name());
  moneyMachine.message("Is your PIN really "
                     + moneyMachine.PIN()
                     + "?");
  return 0;
}
```

─────────────── **Screen 1, Dialogue** ───────────────

```
          AA  TTTTTTTTTT          MM      MM
         AAAA      TT           MMMM  MMMM
        ====Automated Teller Machine=====
       AAAAAAAA     TT       MM    MM    MM
     AA      AA     TT     MM            MM
   AA        AA     TT  MM               MM


         Enter Name: Anyname

          Enter PIN: 1234
```

─────────────── **Screen 2, Output** ───────────────

(*Note:* ATM::message calls the causeApause function shown earlier):

```
ATM------------------------------------
                Welcome ANYNAME

Press Enter to continue . . .
```

─────────────── **Screen 3, Output** ───────────────
```
ATM------------------------------------
              Is your PIN really 1234?

Press Enter to continue . . .
```

After the call to getNameAndPIN, part of the object's state becomes "ANYNAME" for the name, and the four digits entered by a bank customer for the PIN ("1234"). This state of an object does not remain fixed. It is changed by calling the member function(s) intended to alter the state, in this case, getNameAndPIN.

We now demonstrate one other ATM member function. Here is the prototype for ATM::getDeposit complete with its postcondition:

```
void ATM::getDeposit(double & amount);
// POST: Returns any valid numeric input as the amount of
//       money the customer wishes to deposit at an ATM.
//       If the customer enters an invalid input such as a negative
//       number or an invalid number, amount is returned as 0.00
```

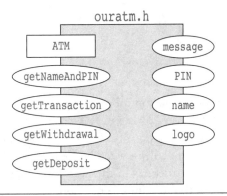

Figure 4.1　Interface diagram for module ouratm.h

The following program attempts to get a deposit amount from the user. The user is expected to enter a valid positive numeric value, in which case amount is changed to the input amount. If an invalid or negative float is input, getDeposit changes amount to 0.00.

```
// Demonstrate getDeposit with a good and bad withdrawal amount
#include "ouratm.h"   // Class ATM is stored in the file: ouratm.h

int main()
{
  ATM moneyMachine;
  double amount;
  moneyMachine.getDeposit(amount);
  cout << "You requested a deposit of: " << amount << endl;
  return 0;
}
```

Entering a valid numeric value will produce a dialogue such as this:

```
─────────────────────────── Dialogue 1 ───────────────
    ATM -------------------------------------
         Enter deposit amount: 123.45
    You requested a deposit of 123.45
```

Entering a invalid value will produce a dialogue such as this:

```
─────────────────────────── Dialogue 2 ───────────────
    ATM -------------------------------------
         Enter deposit amount: BAD 100


    ATM -------------------------------------
                   Invalid currency input

    . . . Press enter to continue . . .
    You requested a deposit of 0.00
```

ATM is part of a bank control program example extended over several chapters. This is done in part because ATMs are "real world" objects most of us have encountered in our daily lives. The behavior of an ATM object should be familiar to anyone who has interacted with a bank teller—whether the teller is a human being or a machine. As we learn other control structures in the next two chapters, the bank control program will provide opportunities to reinforce new topics.

Self-Check

1. List the five ATM member functions introduced in this chapter.
2. When ATM::getDeposit(amount) is called, and the user enters -123.45, what is amount changed to?
3. Will the following program compile and run?

```cpp
#include "ouratm.h"
int main()
{
  ATM moneyMachine;
  moneyMachine.message("Welcome to the Money Machine");
  moneyMachine.getNameAndPIN();
  moneyMachine.message("Name: "
                  + moneyMachine.name()
                  + ",    PIN: "
                  + moneyMachine.PIN());
  return 0;
}
```

4.   If you enter a `name` of `"lastname"` and a `PIN` of `"5555"`, what is the value of the argument sent to `message` at the second call to `ATM::message`?

Answers
1. `getNameAndPIN`, `getDeposit`, `name`, `PIN`, and `message`
2. 0.00
3. Yes
4. `Name: LASTNAME,    PIN: 5555`

4.5   Class Declarations

A C++ *class declaration* combines member functions and data members for objects of the class. The member-function-prototypes are listed after the keyword *public:* and data-members after *private:*

```
class  name {
public:
     member-function-prototypes
private:
     data-members
} ;
```

The *member-function-prototypes* are similar to prototypes we have seen. The *data-members* are similar to object declarations. When we arrive at the point where we implement classes, the class declaration will have to be coded from scratch, but this activity is delayed until we have used and modified a few existing classes. However, once we learn to read class declarations, we can get a sense of the behavior of any object of the class. By perusing the class declarations of this textbook, we see the names of each member function, the number and class of the arguments required, and, through the postconditions, we learn what each does. With this in mind, we look at the `ATM` class declaration, which lists all member functions available to all `ATM` objects (there are some new ones that will be explained later):

```
// The declaration of the ATM class from the file ouratm.h:
//
class ATM {
public:
  // The member functions:

  void ATM::getNameAndPIN();
  //  PRE: The user enters any two strings at the prompt.
  //  POST: The data members of any ATM object are reset.
```

```
void ATM::getTransaction(char & transaction);
// PRE: The user enters one of these letters: w, d, b, or q.
// POST: A menu of ATM options is displayed and transaction becomes
//       one of these four chars 'W', 'D', 'B', or 'Q' is returned.
//       The uppercase char represents one of these transactions:
//             W)ithdraw D)eposit B)alance Q)uit

void ATM::getWithdrawal(double & amount);
// PRE: The user enters something.
// POST: Returns a valid numeric input in an increment of 5.00
//       as the amount a customer wishes to withdraw from an ATM.
//       If the customer enters an invalid input such as a negative
//       number, an invalid number, or a valid numeric input that
//       is not an increment of 5.00, amount is returned as 0.00.

void ATM::getDeposit(double & amount);
// PRE: The user enters something.
// POST: Returns any valid numeric input as the amount of
//       money the customer wishes to deposit at an ATM.
//       If the customer enters an invalid input such as a negative
//       number or an invalid number, amount is returned as 0.00.

void ATM::showBalance(double amount);
// POST: amount is displayed on the ATM screen with a
//       heading and a pause for the customer to read it.

void ATM::message(string aMessage);
// POST: aMessage is displayed on the ATM screen.
//       A pause occurs to allow customer to read the message.

string ATM::PIN();
// PRE: The getNameAndPIN function has been called.
// POST: Returns the current customer PIN.

string ATM::name();
// PRE: The getNameAndPIN function has been called.
// POST: Returns the current customer name.

void ATM::logo();
// POST: The ATM logo is displayed on a cleared screen.

private:
  // The data members:

  string userName;
  string userPIN;
};
```

Note: The complete implementation of class ATM is stored in the file name ouratm.cpp. In general, each class declaration is stored in a dot h file. The implementation is stored in a dot cpp file with the same name.

By reading class declarations such as bankAccounts, we are able to determine information such as the following:

- The class name.
- The name of all member functions.
- The return type of any non-void function.
- The number and type of arguments required in any member function call.
- The action of each member function through postconditions.

And, most important, we can learn how to use the class. With a class that has no constructor function (such as ATM), we can always begin with a declaration of this general form:

class-name object-name ;

For example:

```
ATM anotherMoneyMachine;
```

Now the object name "anotherMoneyMachine" may prepend ATM member functions so long as the correct number and class of arguments are used.

Programming Tip

Unless a class specifically declares a constructor function (a member function with the same name as the class and no return type), the C++ compiler supplies a *default constructor*—a constructor with no arguments. In the case of class ATM, the constructor would look like this:

```
class ATM {
public:
  ATM::ATM();
  // ...
```

Since there is no constructor in this class, the default constructor is generated automatically. The default constructor is called during a declaration like this:

```
ATM moneyMachine;
```

4.5.1 Member Function Implementations: A Preview

The complete implementation of a member function contains the function heading as it exists within the class declaration. Each member function is prepended with the class name and :: (the scope resolution operator). Also, the ; is removed. This modified prototype is followed by the block (statements enclosed in { and }) of the function. For example, the getNameAndPIN member function could start as:

```
void ATM::getWithdrawal(double & amount)
{
  // ... The block for the getWithdrawal member function ...
}
```

Although you will not be implementing classes for some time, revealing some details now proves fruitful for the time when you will. This discussion also will help you complete lab projects that ask you to modify existing classes. Additionally, we use member function implementations to reinforce some things we have already learned. For example, when you look at some of the implementations below, you will notice that ATM::name and ATM::PIN are examples of programmer-defined functions returning string values; ATM::message has one string parameter, and the ATM::getNameAndPIN member function uses input and output streams to initialize the data members of the class.

```
void ATM::getNameAndPIN()
{
  clearScreen();
  logo();
  // Generate three blank lines
  cout << "\n\n\n";
  cout.width(20);
  // Get the name that represents the account number
  cout << "Enter Name: ";
  cin >> userName;
  userName.toUpper();
  // Get the four digit PIN
  cout << endl;
  cout.width(20);
  cout << " Enter PIN: ";
  cin >> userPIN;
}

string ATM::name()
{
  return userName;
}
```

```
string ATM::PIN()
{
  return userPIN;
}

void ATM::message(string aMessage)
{
  clearScreen();
  cout << "\n\n";
  cout << " ATM --------------------------------------" << endl;
  cout.width(40);
  cout << aMessage << endl;
  causeApause();
}

void ATM::logo()
{
  cout << '\n';
  cout << "            AA    TTTTTTTTTT           MM    MM " << endl;
  cout << "           AAAA       TT             MMMM MMMM " << endl;
  cout << "         ======Automated Teller Machine====== " << endl;
  cout << "        AAAAAAAA      TT        MM    MM    MM " << endl;
  cout << " AA       AA      TT        MM            MM " << endl;
  cout << "AA         AA      TT    MM                MM " << endl;
}
```

Data members are part of a class, so any member function can reference them. For example, userName and userPIN exist as valid string expressions for the return statements of ATM::name and ATM::PIN, respectively. In other words, the scope of all data members extends to all member functions of the class. Also, note that the data members are altered though keyboard input during a getNameAndPIN call. However, the data members of the ATM class—userName and userPIN—are not directly available to users of the class—they are private to the class. We need functions like ATM::name and ATM::PIN to access, and ATM::getNameAndPIN to query or alter the state of any ATM object. Because private data members are known only to the member functions, these attempts to directly alter private data are illegal:

```
ATM moneyMachine;
moneyMachine.userName = "Another Name";    // ERROR
moneyMachine.userPIN = "Another PIN";      // ERROR
```

As it currently exists, we must use getNameAndPIN to alter the private data of an ATM object. If we need to access the values of the private data members, we must use the accessor functions name and PIN. In fact, member functions often exist to examine or alter their associated data members.

Programming Tip ─────────────────────────────

For the sake of consistency, member function prototypes in this textbook are the only declarations in the public section of a class. Also, data members are the only declarations in the private section. This rule of thumb reduces some of the complexity of reading and implementing classes. The state of an object is inspected or altered exclusively through associated members functions.

4.5.2   Other ATM Member Functions

As noted earlier, we can better understand class use by viewing programs that call member functions, so we now use the remaining member functions in the context of several C++ statements. The member function ATM::getTransaction displays a menu and returns one char value. The precondition is not satisfied until a lower- or uppercase 'W', 'D', 'B', or 'Q' is typed. The following statements set the char object option to one of the four chars used to later select the requested banking operation:

```
ATM moneyMachine;
char transaction;
moneyMachine.getTransaction(transaction);
cout << "You entered transaction code: '" << transaction
     << "'" << endl;
```

───────────────────────── **Dialogue** ─────────

```
    ATM  -------------------------------------
                    Withdraw [W]
                     Deposit [D]
                     Balance [B]
                        Quit [Q]

                Select [W,D,B,Q]: x
                Select [W,D,B,Q]: 1
                Select [W,D,B,Q]: w
    You entered transaction code: 'W'
```

The preceding dialogue shows that after the user entered 'x', '1', the final input of lowercase 'w' was converted to uppercase and accepted as a valid transaction code. The return value of uppercase 'W' could now be used as code to indicate that the bank customer wishes to complete a withdrawal transaction.

ATM::showBalance(double amount) is another member function that displays the numeric argument in a currency format on the screen. For example, this call:

```
moneyMachine.showBalance(123);
```

generates the following output on a cleared screen:

```
ATM  -------------------------------------
                 Balance: 123.00
```

The final ATM member function, getWithdrawal, is similar to getDeposit. The major difference arises from the ATM's inability to dispense bills that are not in increments of 5.00. We get a valid withdrawal amount from the bank customer as follows:

```
moneyMachine.getWithdrawal(amount);
cout << "You requested a withdrawal of: " << amount << endl;
```

—————————————————————— **Dialogue 1** ——————————————————————
```
ATM  -------------------------------------
              Enter withdrawal amount: 20.00
   You requested a withdrawal of: 20.00
```

Amount is changed to 0.0 whenever one of the following inputs are encountered:

- A negative withdrawal amount.
- An invalid numeric value.
- A withdrawal amount that is not an exact increment of 5.00 (5.01, 6, or 21.00 for example).

—————————————————————— **Dialogue 2** ——————————————————————
```
ATM  -------------------------------------
          Enter withdrawal amount: 21.00
   You requested a withdrawal of 0.00
```

Self-Check

1. *True or False:* ATM::getTransaction returns the next character entered.
2. *True or False:* ATM::message requires exactly one string argument.
3. *True or False:* ATM::getWithdrawal(amount) changes amount to the next double value entered at the keyboard.
4. What information can we get from function prototypes in the public section of a class?
5. Write the output from the cout statements only (the value returned for amount) when each of the following inputs have been entered during the getDeposit operation:

   a. 100   d. 500
   b. -100.00   e. bad
   c. 105.01   f. 5x

```
#include "ouratm.h"
#include "ourstuff.h" // for decimals (cout, 2);
#include <iostream.h>
int main()
{
  ATM moneyMachine;
  double amount;
  decimals(cout, 2);
  moneyMachine.getDeposit(amount);
  cout << "amount: " << amount << endl;
  return 0;
}
```

Answers
1. False: Only uppercase W, D, B, or Q
2. True
3. False: The valid `double` must be positive and an increment of 5.00
4. The member functions available to all objects, their names, the return types of the member functions, and the required argument/parameter associations.
5. a. `amount: 100.00`   d. `amount: 500.00`
   b. `amount: 0.00`   e. `amount: 0.00`
   c. `amount: 0.00`   f. `amount: 5.00`

4.6   Case Study: Bank Control Program

In this case study we begin to design a program destined to control a small simulated bank. The interface for bank operations such as deposits, withdrawals, and balance queries will be the automated teller machine just discussed. This bank control program is presented as an extended example for several reasons. First, it is a "real-life" example familiar to many of us. Second, it uses several existing objects that will interact with each other. Third, it provides us a review of concepts covered in this and subsequent chapters. Fourth, we will see the benefits of *encapsulation*—the packaging together of data and the operations that manipulate that data. And finally, we begin to appreciate the benefits of the abstraction provided through class declarations.

The various phases of this bank control program also provide an opportunity to see how different components of the C++ programming language are used to create a larger program. We begin with a brief problem statement that provides an overall picture of the expected final capabilities of this program. Immediately thereafter, we will look at the first of three phases of implementation.

Problem: *Implement a bank control program that allows multiple transactions for multiple customers. Obtain transactions from an automated teller machine. Maintain the balances for all bank customers.*

Figure 4.2 shows the major classes that will be used. The program uses an ATM object to obtain customer input. The bank class, covered later, is a collection of bankAccount objects. The bank object is used to locate customers and maintain the proper balances.

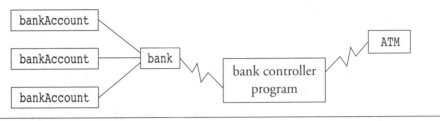

Figure 4.2   Bank control overview and the interacting classes

One of the goals of this case study is to show a program that uses several interacting objects. Another goal is to develop an increasingly complex program through the process of *stepwise enhancement*—a design methodology characterized by the implementation of a program in steps. Programs are implemented incrementally rather than all at once. Each increment, or phase, brings the program closer to the final implementation. Therefore, we must establish intermediate goals (phase one goal is up next). We then strive to achieve these goals to emphasize a strategic approach to the programming process. Along the way, chapter topics are reinforced. In the first phase, we practice using objects and reading a class declaration to understand a new object.

4.6.1   Analysis: Bank Control Program—Phase One

The ultimate goal of this bank control program is to allow multiple customers to perform multiple banking transactions. This requires knowledge of statements not yet covered so we do not see the complete detailed problem specification here. The first phase only establishes the role of interacting classes. One of these classes constructs a bank object to provide account balancing operations. We will be connecting an automated teller machine (designed by an ATM manufacturer) to bank operations (designed by the bank's data processing department).

Problem: *Using an automated teller machine interface, allow one valid bank customer to make one withdrawal, which is recorded at the bank. Verify that the withdrawal is affecting the customer's balance by showing the balance before and after the withdrawal.*

As shown earlier, our bank control program is to reside between an ATM object and a database (collection) of bankAccount objects. The customer must first be found within the bank database. Then we can display the proper balance, subtract from the proper balance during a withdrawal operation, and add to the proper balance during a deposit operation. In short order, we will see how this is done when we explore the other major class of this program: class `bank`.

Drawing on our familiarity with the `ATM` class, input used in this first phase is limited to these items:

Input:
- Name: the customer name (a substitute for bank account data encoded on the ATM card). This can be any set of characters with no spaces.
- PIN: the personal identification number used to uniquely identify a bank customer. A group of four digits, for example, 0000, 0001, . . ., 9998, 9999.
- Withdrawal amount: any valid `int`, `real`, or `double` value that is positive and an increment of 5.00.

The various outputs will be generated mostly by `ATM` member functions and include items such as these:

Output:
- The ATM logo.
- A prompt for the customer's name.
- A prompt for the customer's PIN.
- The balance shown in a currency format.

We have a limited number of customers who have only one chance to correctly identify themselves. This implies that only a few `name`/`PIN` pairs are valid. One is `name = "HALL"` and `PIN = "1234"`. So if we input `"HALL"` and `"1234"`, the correct balance should be shown before and after the one chance to enter a proper withdrawal amount.

4.6.2 Design: Find and Use Existing Objects

To complete the first phase of this stepwise enhancement, we use another design tool that asks us to *find and use existing objects*. In a large software system, finding existing objects follows the discovery that they are needed. This typically requires a careful analysis that goes beyond the scope of this textbook. Much time can be spent identifying and naming the objects of a system. The other important analysis issue involves assigning responsibilities to the proper object, an iterative process that changes the view of a system. This up-front analysis has been done for us.

It should be obvious that we will use an `ATM` object as our bank control interface. It was also discovered that a collaborating class named `bank` would prove useful. You might have already recognized the need for this existing object that is capable of managing a collection of bank customers. It was determined that the `bank` class should have these responsibilities:

- Locate a customer using the name and PIN input.
- Return the balance of any valid bank account.
- Record a withdrawal to the correct bank account.
- Record a deposit to the correct bank account.

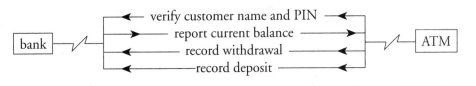

Figure 4.3   *The collaboration of a bank and an ATM object*

The bank class declared in the file "ourbank.h" has already been designed to collaborate with the ATM object of the bank control program.

Programming Tip

One of the more difficult things involving new classes is trying to remember the member functions, the names, number, and classes of the arguments required, and so on. But the new bank class will become more comfortable as you complete bank control lab projects. Also, you need not remember all the details because you may reference the following class declaration anytime you need to remember the names and arguments.

```
class bank {
public:

    // The bank constructor
    bank::bank();
    // POST: The collection of bankAccount objects has been initialized

    void bank::findCustomer(ATM anATM,              // Input
                            int & customerNumber,   // Output
                            int & found);           // Output
    // POST: If the ATM object has obtained a valid name and PIN:
    //       1. customerNumber = the integer used in all bank operations
    //       2. found = 1
    //       If the ATM has obtained an invalid bank customer:
    //       1. customerNumber = -1
    //       2. found = 0

    void bank::recordWithdrawal(double amount,        // Input
                                int customerNumber); // Input
    // POST: The proper bankAccount object is adjusted
    //       to reflect a withdrawal the size of amount.
    //       When customerNumber does not represent a
    //       valid customer, no withdrawal is recorded.
```

```
void bank::recordDeposit(double amount,            // Input
                          int customerNumber);      // Input
// POST: The proper bankAccount object is adjusted
//        to reflect a deposit the size of amount.
//        When customerNumber does not represent a
//        valid customer, no deposit is recorded.

double bank::availableBalance(int customerNumber);
// POST: Return the current balance associated with
//        customerNumber. The value of 0.0 is returned if
//        customerNumber does not represent a valid customer.

private:
    // Customer stores a collection of bankAccount objects. This
    // subscripted object is discussed in detail in Chapter 7.
    bankAccount customer[20]; // Stores up to 20 bankAccount objects
    int size;                  // Stores the number of valid accounts
};
```

Note: The complete implementation of class bank is stored in the file named ourbank.cpp.

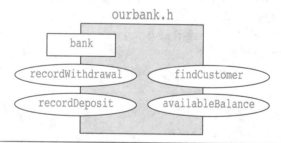

Figure 4.4   Interface diagram for module ourbank.h

We must now become familiar with this new class. In phase one of the bank control program, we will need these three member functions of bank:

1. bank::findCustomer   Given the account name and PIN, return the unique customer number or discover an invalid account number.

2. bank::availableBalance Given the customer number, return the proper account balance.

3. bank::recordWithdrawal Given the customer number and a withdrawal amount, change the proper balance by the withdrawal amount.

The bank::findCustomer function changes the second argument (customerNumber) to a number greater than or equal to zero if the state of ATM represents a valid customer in the collection of bankAccounts. If the name/PIN combination is found, customerNumber is set to the customer's unique number within the database. If the customer is not found, the second argument (customerNumber) is set to -1, a customer number that is never valid. Additionally, bank::findCustomer changes the third argument (found) to 0 if the customer is not found. Otherwise, found is changed to 1. The value of customerNumber is then used for operations such as location of the correct balance in bank::availableBalance and the maintenance of customer balances for each deposit and withdrawal.

As we design a program to meet the specifications set forth in the preceding analysis section, we should recognize that a lot of work has already been done for us. The ATM class provides us with an interface to enter input data such as a name/PIN pair and withdrawal amounts. We use the ATM::getNameAndPIN along with the bank::findCustomer member function to determine if any given customer exists. We can use the same program to verify that nonexistent customers such as "NOTHERE"/"0000" do not exist.

An algorithm is now used to show the steps that will reveal the balance for any legitimate bank customer:

1. Obtain a name and PIN from the bank customer.
2. Find the customer number.
3. Display the balance.

Notice that these steps can be completed with member functions of existing classes. This problem statement of the first phase of this bank control program is complete when these three steps are added to the algorithm:

4. Get the deposit amount from the customer.
5. Record the deposit amount at the bank.
6. Display the updated balance.

These last three steps can also be completed with member functions of the ATM and bank classes.

4.6.3 Implementation: Bank Control Program—Phase One

This implementation of phase one will also be used in a lab project at the end of this chapter. You will be asked to become familiar with the new ATM and bank objects by retyping the implementation. Phase one will form the basis for the continuation into subsequent phases.

The three phases of the bank control program require the modules ourbank.h and ouratm.h. Besides the standard classes (such as double), classes and operations must also be included from iostream.h, ourstr.h, and ouracct.h. But to keep the diagram simple, only the major modules are included in the module diagram of Figure 4.5.

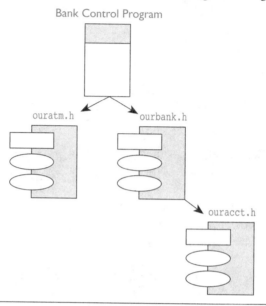

Figure 4.5   *Module diagram for the bank control program*

```
// This program declares an ATM and bank object
// and calls member functions from both
#include "ouratm.h"    // for class ATM
#include "ourbank.h"   // for class bank: a collection of bankAccounts

int main()
{
  ATM moneyMachine;    // The customer interface
  bank firstBank;      // The collection of bankAccounts
  int customerNumber;  // Uniquely identifies a customer
  double amount;       // Represents deposit and withdrawal amounts
  int found;           // Will be 0 if name/PIN match is not found,
                       //   but found is ignored until phase two

  moneyMachine.getNameAndPIN();
  firstBank.findCustomer(moneyMachine, customerNumber, found);

  // Show current balance of the customer
  moneyMachine.showBalance(firstBank.availableBalance(customerNumber));
```

```
// Simulate a withdrawal
moneyMachine.getWithdrawal(amount);
firstBank.recordWithdrawal(amount, customerNumber);
moneyMachine.showBalance(firstBank.availableBalance(customerNumber));
return 0;
}
```

4.6.4 Testing the Implementation

Testing of the bank control program is given as a lab project at the end of this chapter.

Self-Check

1. What design tool is used in this section?
2. What data item is required by `bank::findCustomer`? Which data items are changed?
3. What does it mean if the third argument to `bank::findCustomer` is returned as 1?
4. What does `bank::availableBalance` return? What argument is required?
5. Name all objects that are used by phase one of the bank control program. Conjecture and include any classes that may not be seen.

Answers

1. Find and use existing objects.
2. Required: The name and PIN entered by the customer. They are provided by the `ATM` object.
   Changed: An `int` that uniquely identifies the customer and 0 or 1 for found.
3. The `name` and `PIN` of the `ATM` object were found in the bank's database.
4. Return: The customer's balance using the unique customer number.
   Required: The unique customer number (for instance, 15 is the customer number for "hall"/"1234").
5. `bank`, `ATM`, `string`, `bankAccount`, `ostream`, `istream`, and possibly `ifstream`

Chapter Summary

You now have the ability to build simple abstractions as C++ functions. Each function performs some well-defined service. Two-way communication is possible through argument/parameter associations and the return statement. We supply values as arguments and get values back though the return statement and changes to reference parameters.

There are several new implementation issues related to functions—parameters and scope in particular—that can be somewhat confusing at first. The scope of an object is limited to the function where it is declared. A global object declared outside of any function block can be referenced from many blocks and so may be altered from other functions. Functions are known from the point of declaration throughout the remainder of the file. This implies that the scope of functions declared in an include file are known from the point of the `#include` directive throughout the rest of the file.

Many details should be remembered when using argument/parameter associations. Here are a few:

- The number of arguments used in a function call must match the number of parameters declared in the function prototype.
- The void return type precedes the function name when no value is to be returned.
- When one value is to be returned from a function, the proper return type prepends the function name and the return statement is included in the function block. The expression in the return statement should be the same class as the return type.
- Reference parameters are used when more than one value is to be returned from a function. Pass by reference is accomplished by adding the special symbol & between the class and name of the parameter.
- The argument used in a function call should usually be the same class as its associated parameter. There are exceptions; for example, an int argument may be associated with a float parameter.
- Parameters intended to only receive copies of the argument values (input parameters) should be declared as value parameters without the & symbol.

The following summary shows some differences between reference and value parameters:

Reference (&) Parameters	Value Parameters
& is used in the declaration.	& is not used.
The parameter is the same object as the associated argument; it may have a different name (an alias).	The argument and parameter are different objects; even if they have the same name.
A change to the reference parameter changes the associated argument; the argument should be an object.	A change to the value parameter does not alter the associated argument; the argument may be a constant.

In the second part of this chapter, we learned that reading class declarations of this form:

```
class  name {
public:
    member-function-prototypes
private:
    data-members
} ;
```

allows us to determine information such as the following:

- The class name.
- The name of member functions.
- The return type of any non-void function.
- The number and class of arguments required in any member function call.
- The action of each member function through postconditions.
- How to use objects of the class.

An object-oriented program uses one or more interacting classes. Many of these— ostream, istream, ifstream, string, bankAccount, ATM, and bank—have already been designed and implemented for us. Other important issues include the assignment of responsibilities and the collaborating classes. This up-front work helps reduce the complexity that might otherwise be encountered during program development.

Programming Tip

One of the biggest problems in dealing with the complexity of the bank control program may be remembering the names of the member functions. The interface diagrams for each module are the quickest way to find just the names of the member functions. Appendix E lists all of them with the page numbers they appear on, in case you forget.

Exercises

12. List two member functions available to any ATM object.
13. List all possible values of transaction in the call

    ```
    moneyMachine.getTransaction(transaction);
    ```

14. List two major interacting classes used by the bank control program.
15. Which section of a class contains the member function prototypes?
16. Which section of a class contains data that we cannot alter unless we use a member function?
17. Describe one method for determining the number and type of arguments required by a member function.
18. Write a complete program that displays "Hello World!" to the screen of an ATM object.
19. Given this class declaration:

    ```
    #include "ourstr.h"

    class student {
    public:
      void signup(string initName, string initID);
      // POST: The student object is registered by
      //       initializing the private data members

      string name();
      // POST: Returns the student name

      string ID();
      // POST: Returns the student ID

    private:
      string studentName;
      string studentID;
    };
    ```

    a. Write the class name.
    b. List all member functions.
    c. List all data members.
    d. Write the number and type of arguments required to call student::signup.
    e. Assuming the student class is in the file student.h, write a complete program that declares one student object with your name = "Last name" and ID = "S12345", and then displays the state of the object (use the member functions to inspect these values).

20. Implement the `student` member function `signup` that initializes the private data members `studentName` and `studentID` to `initName` and `initID`, respectively. Remember that all member functions have access to all private data members.
21. Implement the `student` member function `ID` that returns the private data member `studentID`.
22. Implement the `student` member function `name` that returns the private data member `studentName`.

Lab Projects

4H   Using Objects

Copy, compile, and link the following program:

```
// Make four attempts to withdraw some money
#include <iostream.h>
#include "ouratm.h" // The ATM class is stored in the file: ouratm.h
int main()
{
  ATM moneyMachine;
  float amount;

  moneyMachine.getWithdrawal(amount);
  moneyMachine.getWithdrawal(amount);
  moneyMachine.getWithdrawal(amount);
  moneyMachine.getWithdrawal(amount);
  cout << "You requested a withdrawal of " << amount << endl;
  return 0;
}
```

Answer the following questions as you run this program, and enter BAD, 19.56, -5.00, and 20.00 as the four requested withdrawal amounts:

1. What is the message when you enter BAD for the withdrawal amount?
2. What is the message when you enter 19.56 for the withdrawal amount?
3. What is the message when you enter -5.00 for the withdrawal amount?
4. What is the value for amount when you enter 20.00 for the withdrawal amount?

4I   Using Objects

Write a complete program that declares one bankAccount object with input data for all three arguments. Use the ATM interface to display the initial balance. Then process one withdrawal and one deposit and show the ending balance. Make sure the balance sent to the ATM screen is the account balance that is modified with bankAccount member functions. Use class bankAccount—*not* class bank. In other words, use one bankAccount object to store one account balance rather than a bank object to store a collection of account balances. Develop a test oracle that includes some bad deposit and withdrawal amounts. Experiment with these bad values and other legitimate values. One dialogue should look like this, where only valid data is entered:

```
Enter name, pin, and starting balance:  Kay   6543   250.00

ATM ------------------------------------
                        Balance: 250.00

ATM ------------------------------------
            Enter withdrawal amount: 40.00

ATM ------------------------------------
            Enter deposit amount: 123.45

ATM ------------------------------------
                        Balance: 333.45
```

4J   Using Objects

This lab project asks you to become familiar with the ATM and bank classes. It is the implementation of the problem given in the case study. It acts as the first phase of the bank control program that will be continued over the next few chapters.

- Retype, compile, and link phase one of the bank control program:

```
// This program declares an ATM and bank object
// and calls member functions from both
#include "ouratm.h"   // for class ATM
#include "ourbank.h"  // for class bank: a collection of bankAccounts
#include "ourstuff.h" // for causeApause()
#include <iostream.h> // for cout <<

int main()
{
  ATM moneyMachine;   // The customer interface
  bank firstBank;     // The collection of bankAccounts
```

```
int customerNumber;  // Uniquely identifies a customer
double amount;       // Represents deposit and withdrawal amounts
int found;           // Will be 0 if name/PIN match is not found,
                     //    but found is ignored until phase two

moneyMachine.getNameAndPIN();
firstBank.findCustomer(moneyMachine, customerNumber, found);

// Show current balance of the customer
moneyMachine.showBalance(firstBank.availableBalance(customerNumber));

// Simulate a withdrawal
moneyMachine.getWithdrawal(amount);
firstBank.recordWithdrawal(amount, customerNumber);
moneyMachine.showBalance(firstBank.availableBalance(customerNumber));
return 0;
}
```

Run this program using each of the following sets of input data. Answer the numbered questions on a separate piece of paper.

- Enter name = hall and PIN = 1234. You should see an initial balance of 100.00. Make a withdrawal of 25.00.

  1. What is the ending balance?

- Enter hall and 1234. You should see an initial balance of 100.00. Try to make a withdrawal of 27.00.

  2. What message is generated by a withdrawal amount of 27.00?
  3. What is the ending balance?

- Enter hall and 1234. You should see an initial balance of 100.00. Try to make a withdrawal of XYZ.

  4. What message is generated by a withdrawal amount of XYZ?
  5. What is the ending balance?

- Enter hall and 1234. You should see an initial balance of 100.00. Make a withdrawal of 150.00.

  6. What is the ending balance?

4K   Modifying a Class

Modify the `atm::logo` member function such that the logo appears as close as possible to one of the automated teller machine logos in your locale. For example, if the brand name is "Money Access Machine," or MAM for short, the logo might look like this:

```
                WELCOME TO

             MONEY ACCESS MACHINE

       $$    $$   $$$$     $$    $$
      $$$$  $$$  $$ $$    $$$$  $$$
      $$ $$ $$$$ $$ $$   $$ $$ $$$$
     $$  $$$$ $$ $$$$$$$  $$  $$$$ $$
     $$   $$$ $$$$   $$ $$   $$$ $$
    $$$        $$$$    $$$$        $$$
```

You must modify the file `myatm.cpp`. This file contains an exact copy of the ATM class of the associated implementation file. Modifying this copy protects the original ATM class implementation.

- If you do not have both the `myatm.h` and `myatm.cpp` files, you cannot continue with this lab project. They are located on the accompanying disk. If you still can't find these files, ask your instructor or lab assistant for copies.
- Load the file `myatm.cpp` into your editor.
- Go to the end of the file to locate the member function `void atm::logo()`.
- Modify the `cout` statements in `void atm::logo()` to look like a machine you are familiar with or to look like the logo shown above.
- Test your changes with a completely different file. First create a new file and retype this code:

```cpp
#include "myatm.h" // And be sure you modify myatm.cpp, not ouratm.cpp

int main()
{
  ATM moneyMachine;
  moneyMachine.getNameAndPIN();
  return 0;
}
```

- Compile, link, and run this program.
- Verify that the logo has been altered to look like your local ATM or the logo shown above.

5

Selections

We have seen many programs in which every statement was executed. Our attention now turns to programs that execute different sets of statements in response to a variety of conditions. Depending on the values of certain objects, a set of statements may execute one time but not the next. The alternate paths of program execution are made possible though the C++ if, if...else, and switch statements. After studying this chapter you will be able to:

- Use the if statement.
- Use relational and equality operators such as <, <=, == (equal), and != (not equal).
- Create and evaluate logical expressions.
- Use the logical operators ! (logical not), && (logical and), and || (logical or).
- Use the if...else statement.
- Solve problems using nested logic.
- Use the switch statement.
- Use and modify a weeklyEmp class.

5.1   The if Statement

Programs must often anticipate a variety of situations. For example, a program that controls an automated teller machine must serve valid bank customers. It must also reject invalid PINs. Once validated, a customer may wish to perform a balance query, or a cash withdrawal, or a deposit transaction. The code that controls an ATM must permit these different requests. This is impossible given only sequential and modular control. Without the new statements in this chapter, we would have to choose the one single operation every customer would have to perform. For example, forcing all customers to withdraw some money, even those with invalid PINs.

Before any ATM becomes operational, software developers must implement code that anticipates all possible transactions. The code must turn away customers with invalid PINs. The code must prevent invalid transactions such as cash withdrawal amounts that are not in the proper increment (5.00, 10.00, or 20.00 for instance). The code must be able to deal with customers who attempt to withdraw more than they have. To accomplish these tasks, we need a new form of control. We need a statement that permits or prevents execution of certain statements depending on certain inputs. A statement that allows the same program to perform different actions where each action is appropriate to each circumstance. In this chapter, we will examine three control structures to select the actions a program takes. The first selection control structure is the if statement with this general form:

```
if ( logical-expression )
   true-part ;
```

where *logical-expression* is any expression that evaluates to either true or false and the true-part is any valid C++ statement. C++ considers zero to be false. Any other value is considered true. The false and true values are often written as 0 and 1 or zero and nonzero respectively. A few logical expressions are shown as a preview to the more detailed discussion of logical expressions to come (<= is the C++ version of the less than or equal to operator ≤):

Expression	Value
`int hours = 40;`	
`hours > 40`	False
`hours >= 40`	True
`hours < 40`	False
`hours <= 40`	True

When an `if` statement is encountered, the logical expression is evaluated as either a zero (false) or nonzero (true) value. The *true-part* executes only if the logical expression is true.

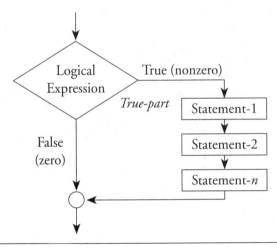

Figure 5.1   The if statement

In the next example, `hours` is unchanged when `hours` is less than or equal to 40, but is modified when `hours` is greater than 40. For example, when `hours` is defined as 42, the logical expression evaluates to true and `hours` becomes 43.0. When `hours > 40` is false, the change to `hours` does not occur.

```
float hours = 40.0;
// Add 1.5 hours for each hour over 40 (overtime)
if(hours > 40)
  hours = 40 + 1.5 * (hours - 40);
```

Here are some other simple examples of the if statement and the generated output. Because the logical expression of the first (j < k) is false, the only true-parts executed are those of the last two if statements.

```
int j = 5,                                    Output:
int k = 3;

if(j < k)
  cout << "j is less than k";      no output

if(j > k)
  cout << "j greater than k";      j greater than k

if(hours > 40)
  cout << "Overtime";              Overtime
```

The next function illustrates how selection alters the flow of control through a group of statements. Each of the three showAwards calls causes different sets of statement execution. The output below shows three different messages appropriate to the three different values of the arguments associated with the parameter unitSales.

```
// This program demonstrates three different execution
// behaviors with different values for the parameter unitSales
#include <iostream.h>
// Note: The long int class is used to allow sales > 32768

void showAwards(long int unitSales)
{ // POST: Display a message appropriate to amount of music sold
/*1*/ cout << endl << endl;
/*2*/ cout << "Sales have reached " << unitSales;
/*3*/ if(unitSales < 500000)
        cout << "--Sorry, no certification yet. Try more concerts.";
/*4*/ if(unitSales >= 500000)
        cout << "--Congrats, your music is certified gold.";
/*5*/ if(unitSales >= 1000000)
        cout << "  It's also gone platinum!";
/*6*/ cout << endl;
}
```

```
int main()
{
  // Call function showAwards three
  // times with three different results
  showAwards( 123456);
  showAwards( 504123);
  showAwards(3402394);
  return 0;
}
```

Function `showAwards` contains a total of six statements, three of which are `if` statements—labeled 3, 4, and 5. Each may or may not generate output. The three `cout` statements—the true-parts of the `if`s—may or may not execute depending on the value of the arguments. This is illustrated by the following output:

```
Sales have reached 123456
--Sorry, no certification yet. Try more concerts.

Sales have reached 504123
--Congrats, your music is certified gold.

Sales have reached 3402394
--Congrats, your music is certified gold. It's also gone platinum!
```

Through the power of `if` statements, the same exact code resulted in three different versions of statement execution. The `if` statement is referred to as a *control structure* because its execution controls the execution of other statements. When the logical expression of this control structure is true, the associated true-part executes. The `if` statement also controls statement execution by disregarding statements when the logical expression is false. In the previous example, the platinum message is disregarded when `unitSales` is less than a million.

5.1.1 Logical Expressions with Relational Operators

We have just seen two new operators, `<` and `>=`, used to test the relationship between the value of `unitSales` and the integer values 500,000 and one million. These are two of the four relational operators, which along with the two equality operators (`==` and `!=`) are available to create simple logical expressions for use with `if` statements.

Relational Operators	Meaning
<	Less than
>	Greater than
<=	Less than or equal to
>=	Greater than or equal to

Equality Operators	Meaning
==	Equal to
!=	Not equal to

We have seen that when an arithmetic operator is applied to two int operands, the result has always been an int. When a relational operator is applied to two int operands, the result is one of two values: zero indicating a false logical expression or nonzero indicating a true logical expression. Here are some examples of simple conditional expressions and their resulting values:

Logical Expression	Result
4 < 5	True (nonzero)
4 > 5	False (zero)
4 <= 5	True
4 == 5	False
4 != 5	True
'A' == 'B'	False
'A' != 'B'	True
1.2 < 10.0	True

Now that == is part of our C++ operator repertoire, it should be noted that the assignment operator = is frequently mistaken for the equality operator ==. This leads to potential intent errors when = replaces ==. For example the following statement is legal:

```
if(option = 'A')   // Warning: = used instead of ==
   addRecord();
```

A warning such as "possibly suspicious assignment" may appear, but chances are the compiler will let this pass. When the program runs, option = 'A' is always true! Therefore addRecord() always executes. In this case, there is no control because option = 'A' always evaluates to true (nonzero). This is due to the fact that in addition to assignment, the = operator also returns the value of the expression being assigned. This allows multiple assignments that look like this:

```
float x, y, z;
x = y = z = 0.0;  // Multiple assignment
```

The assignment operator = groups right to left (most other operators group left to right) so this multiple assignment could also be written with parentheses.

```
(x = (y = (z = -1.0)));  // Equivalent to x = y = z = -1.0;
```

The first action is to assign -1.0 to z. At the same time z = -1.0 returns the assigned value of -1.0 to get this evaluation:

```
( x = (y = (z = -1.0) ) )
              ↓
( x = (y =  -1.0     ) )
        ↓
( x =  -1.0 )
     ↓
  -1.0
```

So the expression shown earlier

```
option = 'A'
```

returns the letter 'A', a nonzero (true) value. The function addRecord() is called every time.

Programming Tip

Remember to use = for assignment and == for equality tests in if statements. If your compiler doesn't catch these errors, and you find this error often, try writing the constant on the left and the object on the right. An accidental omission of an = now results in a compiletime error.

```
if('A' == option) // Okay
if('A' = option)  // Compiletime error
```

Self-Check

1. For the following if statement, which values of logicalExpression cause the true-part to execute?

    ```
    if(logicalExpression)
        cout << "true part" << endl;
    ```

    a. -2   c. 0   e. 2
    b. -1   d. 1   f. 3

2. Which expressions evaluate to true (nonzero) assuming j and k are initialized as follows?

    ```
    int j = 0, k = 4;
    ```

    a. j = 0   c. j >= k   e. j < k
    b. j == 0   d. j != k   f. (j+4) == k

3. Write the output generated by each of the following programs:

a.
```cpp
#include <iostream.h>
int main()
{
    char option = 'z';
    if(option = 'A')
      cout << "addRecord";
    if(option = 'D')
      cout << "deleteRecord";
    return 0;
}
```

d.
```cpp
#include <iostream.h>
int main()
{
    int grade = 45;
    if(grade >= 70)
      cout << "passing" << endl;
    if(grade < 70)
      cout << "dubious" << endl;
    if(grade < 60)
      cout << "failing" << endl;
    return 0;
}
```

b.
```cpp
#include <iostream.h>
int main()
{
    char option = 'D';
    if(option == 'A')
      cout << "addRecord";
    if(option == 'D')
      cout << "deleteRecord";
    return 0;
}
```

e.
```cpp
#include <iostream.h>
int main()
{
    int grade = 65;
    if(grade >= 70)
      cout << "passing" << endl;
    if(grade < 70)
      cout << "dubious" << endl;
    if(grade < 60)
      cout << "failing" << endl;
    return 0;
}
```

c.
```cpp
#include <iostream.h>
int main()
{
    char option = 'z';
    if(option == 'A')
      cout << "addRecord";
    if(option == 'D')
      cout << "deleteRecord";
    return 0;
}
```

f.
```cpp
#include <iostream.h>
int main()
{
    int grade = 75;
    if(grade >= 70)
      cout << "passing" << endl;
    if(grade < 70)
      cout << "dubious" << endl;
    if(grade < 60)
      cout << "failing" << endl;
    return 0;
}
```

Answers

1. every nonzero value (-2, -1, 1, 2, and 3)
2. b, d, e, and f (a is an assignment that returns the assigned value 0, or false)
3. a. addRecord   d. dubious
        deleteRecord   failing
        // = was used, not ==
    b. deleteRecord   e. dubious
    c. No output   f. passing

5.2   The if...else Statement

The C++ if...else statement provides two alternate courses of action. It is written as an if statement with an additional else and a false-part:

if (*logical expression*)
        true-part ;
else
        false-part ;

When an if...else statement is encountered, the logical expression is evaluated to either 0 (false) or to a nonzero (true) value. When the logical expression evaluates to a nonzero value, the true-part is executed and the false-part is disregarded. The *true-part* and *false-part* are any valid C++ statement. When the logical expression evaluates to false, the true-part is disregarded and the false-part executes.

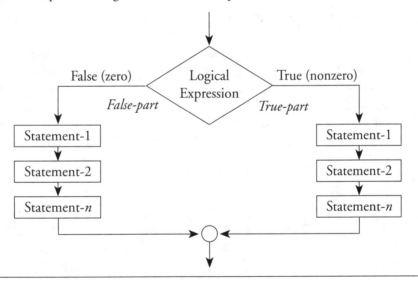

Figure 5.2   The if..else statement

In the next example, when x is initialized with a value less than or equal to zero, the output is FALSE. When x is positive, the true part executes and TRUE is output:

```
float x = 1.234;
if(x > 0.0)
  cout << "TRUE" << endl;  // Output:  TRUE
else
  cout << "FALSE" << endl;
```

Here is another example of an `if...else` statement. Again, the output depends on the value of the logical expression, which in this case is `miles > 24000`.

```
int miles = 30123;
if(miles > 24000)
  cout << "Tune-up " << (miles-24000) << " miles overdue" << endl;
else
  cout << "Tune-up due in " << (24000-miles) << " miles" << endl;
```

When `miles` has the value of `30123`, the output is:

```
Tune-up 6123 miles overdue
```

but when `miles` has the value of `23500`, the false-part executes and the output is:

```
Tune-up due in 500 miles
```

Determine the output when `miles` has the value of `24000`.

The ability to choose an alternative set of statement executions is an important feature of any programming language. The `if...else` statement provides the means to make a program general enough to generate useful information appropriate to a variety of data. For example, an employee's gross pay may be calculated as `hours` times the `rate` when `hours` is less than or equal to `40`. However, certain employers must pay time-and-a-half for any hours worked over `40`. This requires a different calculation, such as:

```
pay = 40 * rate + (hours - 40) * 1.5 * rate;
```

With an `if...else` statement, a program can correctly compute gross pay for a variety of values including less than 40, equal to 40, and more than 40.

```
// A complete if...else statement
float pay, rate = 10.00, hours = 42.0;
if(hours <= 40.0)
  pay = hours * rate;                              // true-part
else
  pay = 40 * rate + (hours - 40) * 1.5 * rate;     // false-part
cout << "pay " << pay << endl;
```

──────────────── **Output** ────────────────

```
pay 430.00
```

5.2.1   The Compound Statement

We have seen { and } delimit the bodies of functions. These two special symbols are also used to delimit (mark the boundaries of) a *compound statement*, also known as a *block:*

```
{
    statement-1 ;
    statement-2 ;   // The compound statement (block)
       ...
    statement-N ;
}
```

The compound statement groups together more than one statement, which can then be treated as one. Required to complete the body of a function, it is also useful for combining more than one statement in a true- or false-part of any if...else statement.

```
// This program uses compound statements for both the
// true- and false-parts. The compound statement makes
// it possible to treat many statements as one.
#include <iostream.h>

int main()
{
  float GPA = 3.7;
  if(GPA >= 3.5)
  {
    // true-part is this compound statement
    cout << "Congratulations, you are on the Dean's List." << endl;
    cout << "You made it by " << (GPA - 3.5) << " points." << endl;
  }
  else
  {
    // false-part is another compound statement
    cout << "Sorry, you are not on the Dean's List." << endl;
    cout << "You missed it by " << (3.5 - GPA) << " points." << endl;
  }
  return 0;
}
```

When the logical expression (GPA >= 3.5) is true, the first compound statement executes. When the logical expression is false, the compound statement after else executes. The compound statement makes it possible to treat more than one statement as one. When GPA = 3.7, this output is generated:

```
Congratulations, you are on the Dean's List.
You made it by 0.2 points.
```

and when GPA = 2.9, this output occurs:

```
Sorry, you are not on the Dean's List.
You missed it by 0.6 points.
```

This alternative execution is provided by the two possible evaluations of the logical expression GPA >= 3.5. If nonzero, the true-part executes; if zero, the false-part executes. Now the false- and true-parts are compound statements.

5.2.2   Common Selection Statement Errors

Neglecting to use the compound statement causes a variety of compiletime and intent errors. Modifying the previous example illustrates what can go wrong if the compound statement is not used when attempting to execute both cout statements.

```
if (GPA >= 3.5)
    // The true-part is the first cout only
    cout << "Congratulations, you are on the Dean's List." << endl;
    cout << "You made it by " << (GPA - 3.5) << " points." << endl;
else    // <- Error
```

With { and } removed there is no compound statement, and this statement:

```
cout << "You made it by " << (GPA-3.5) << " points." << endl;
```

no longer belongs to the preceding if...else even though the indentation might make it appear as such. This is an if statement followed by a cout statement followed by the keyword else. When else is encountered, the C++ compiler complains because there is no statement that begins with the keyword else. Here is another example of what can go wrong when a compound statement is omitted. This time, { and } are omitted after else.

```
else
    cout << "Sorry, you are not on the Dean's List." << endl;
    cout << "You missed it by " << (3.5 - GPA) << " points." << endl;
```

There are no compiletime errors here, but the structure does contain an intent error. The final cout statement always executes. It does not belong to if...else. If GPA >= 3.5 is false, the code executes as one would expect, but when this logical expression is true, the output is not what is intended. The somewhat confusing output is:

```
Congratulations, you are on the Dean's List.
You made it by 0.152 points.
You missed it by -0.152 points.
```

The use of the semicolon before else is also a source of much confusion. A semicolon must not be used after the true-part when it is a compound statement. On the other hand, the semicolon must be placed before else if the true-part is something other than a compound statement.

```
if(j < 0)
  j = j + 1; // <- Semicolon required
else
  j = j - 1;
```

```
if(j < 0)
{
  j = j + 1;
  cout << "j was incremented";
} // <- No Semicolon allowed
else
{
  j = j - 1;
  cout << "j was decremented";
}
```

Even though j = j + 1 and the compound statement are valid true-parts, a semicolon must be placed after j = j + 1, but ; cannot be placed at the end of the compound statement. These missing and extra semicolons are detected at compiletime:

```
if(j < 0)
  j = j + 1 // <- Error, missing ;
else
  j = j - 1;
```

```
if(j < 0)
{
  j = j + 1;
  cout << "j was incremented";
}; // <- Error, extra semicolon
else
{
  j = j - 1;
  cout << "j was decremented";
}; // <- Optional semicolon
```

Programming Tip

Semicolon placement is somewhat confusing at first. If you see an unexplained compiletime error near an if...else statement, look closely at the placement or lack of semicolons.

Self-Check

1. Write the output generated by each of the following programs given these initializations of j and x:

```
int j = 8;
float x = -1.5;
```

a.
```
if(x < -1.0)
    cout << "true" << endl;
else
    cout << "false" << endl;
cout << "after if...else";
```

c.
```
if(x >= j)
    cout << "x is high";
else
    cout << "x is low";
```

b.
```
if(j >= 0)
{
  if(j == 0)
    cout << "zero";
  else
    cout << "pos";
}
else
    cout << "neg";
```

d.
```
if(x <= 0)
{
  if(x < 0)
    cout << "neg";
  else
    cout << "zero";
}
else
    cout << "pos";
```

2. Write an `if...else` statement that displays your name if `option` has the value 1, and displays your school name if `option` has any other value.

Answers

1. a. true
        after if...else

    b. pos

    c. x is low

    d. neg

2.
```
if(option == 1)
    cout << "your name";
else
    cout << "your school";
```

5.3   Logical Operators

C++ has a large number of operators. Three of these, ! (not), | | (or), and && (and), are *logical operators* used to create more complex logical expressions. They typically have logical operands. For example, this logical expression:

```
(test >= 0) && (test <= 100)
```

shows the logical operator "&&" applied to two logical operands. Since C++ uses the value of zero to represent false and any nonzero value to represent true, we use 0 as false and 1 as true in the following tables to show every possible combination of logical values with the three logical operators !, | |, and &&.

! (not)				(or)		&& (and)	
Expression	Result	Expression	Result	Expression	Result
! 0	1	1 || 1	1	1 && 1	1
! 1	0	1 || 0	1	1 && 0	0
		0 || 1	1	0 && 1	0
		0 || 0	0	0 && 0	0

The next logical expression uses the logical operator && (logical and) to test for a range of 0 through 100. The logical expression is true when test has a value greater than or equal to 0 (test >= 0) and at the same time is less than or equal to 100 (test <= 100).

```
if((test >= 0) && (test <= 100))
  cout << "Test in range";
else
  cout << "**Warning--Test out of range";
```

Here is how the if statement evaluates its logical expressions when test has the value 9 and then 977 (to simulate an attempt to enter 97 and accidentally pressing 7 twice):

```
(test >= 0) && (test <= 100)        (test >= 0) && (test <= 100)
( 97  >= 0) && ( 97  <= 100)        (977  >= 0) && (977  <= 100)
      1     &&        1                   1     &&        0
            1                                   0
```

The parentheses used to enclose two smaller logical expressions are not necessary. C++ has precedence rules governing the order in which operators are applied to the operand(s). For example, in the absence of parentheses, the relational operators >= and <= are evaluated before the && operator. The following table lists some (though not all) of the C++ operators in categories of precedence. The :: and () operators are evaluated first, and the assignment operator = is evaluated last. Most operators are evaluated (grouped) in a left-to-right order:

a/b/c/d   is equivalent to   (((a/b)/c)/d)

Recall the one notable exception is the assignment operators that groups in a right-to-left order to allow multiple assignments such as this (*Note:* The expression z = *value* returns *value* that is used as the rValue for y and x):

x = y = z = 0.0   is equivalent to   (x = (y = (z = 0.0)))

Precedence Rules of C++ Operators (Partial List)

Category	Operator	Description	Associativity (Grouping Order)
Highest	::	Scope resolution	Left to right
	( )	Function call	
Unary	!	Logical negation (not)	Right to left
	+	Unary plus	
	−	Unary minus	
Multiplicative	*	Multiplication	Left to right
	/	Division	
	%	Remainder	
Additive	+	Binary plus	Left to right
	−	Binary minus	
Input/Output	>>	Stream extraction	Left to right
	<<	Stream insertion	
Relational	<	Less than	Left to right
	>	Greater than	
	<=	Less than or equal to	
	>=	Greater than or equal to	
Equality	==	Equal	Left to right
	!=	Not equal	
and	&&	Logical and	Left to right
or	!!	Logical or	Left to right
Assignment	=	Assign lValue to rValue	Right to left

The next example illustrates some of the precedence rules of C++ operators.

```
1 + 2 < 3 * 4 && 4 == 5 || !(4 == 5)     Parentheses override precedence sometimes
                              ↓
1 + 2 < 3 * 4 && 4 == 5 || ! false       The unary ! operator has highest precedence
                            ↓
1 + 2 < 3 * 4 && 4 == 5 ||   true        * is next
            ↓
1 + 2 <  12   && 4 == 5 ||   true        + is next
      ↓
   3  <  12   && 4 == 5 ||   true        < is next
      ↓
    true      && 4 == 5 ||   true        == is next
                    ↓
    true      && false  ||   true        && is next
        ↓
        false          ||    true        || is the last operator evaluated
                ↓
                true
```

5.3.1   Short Circuit Evaluation

In the logical expression (E1 && E2), E1 is evaluated first and if it is false, E2 is not evaluated. This is called *short circuit evaluation* and it is satisfactory since false && false and false && true are both false. Evaluating E2 is not necessary. Short circuit evaluation is also possible with the or operator ||. In the expression (E1 || E2), E1 is evaluated first and if E1 is true, E2 is not evaluated. Your compiler should allow you to switch between short circuit and complete evaluation. Complete evaluation generates code that evaluates each expression regardless of the first operand's value. This means the expression:

```
if((x >= 0.0) && (sqrt(x) <= 4.0))
```

is false when x >= 0.0 is false and short circuit evaluation is on. When full circuit evaluation is in effect, the same expression may cause the program to terminate abnormally because the sqrt(x) evaluates even when x is negative.

Self-Check

1. Evaluate the following expressions to true or false:
   a. 0 || 1   d. ! (3 < 4)
   b. 1 && 0   e. ! 0 && ! 1
   c. 1 * 3 == 4 - 1   f. 5 + 2 > 3 * 4 && 11 < 12

2. Write an expression that is true only when the int test is in the range of 1 through 10 inclusive.
3. Write an expression that is true if the int test is greater than 100 or less than 0.

Answers
1. a. True   b. False   c. True   d. False   e. False   f. False
2. (test >= 1) && (test <= 10)
3. (test < 0) || (test > 100)

5.4 Nested Logic

Nested logic refers to a control structure containing another similar control structure, for example, an if...else with a false-part containing another if...else. Here is one such example of nested logic:

```
// Nested selection where exactly one cout statement executes.
// The output is dependent on the input value for GPA.
#include <iostream.h>
int main()
{
  float GPA;
  cout << "Enter your GPA: ";
  cin >> GPA;
  if(GPA < 3.5)
    cout << "Try harder" << endl;
  else                          // <- false-part is another if...else
    if(GPA < 4.0)
      cout << "You made the Dean's List" << endl;
    else
      cout << "You made the President's List" << endl;
  return 0;
}
```

Notice that the false-part of the first if...else statement is another if...else statement. If GPA is less than 3.5, "Try harder" is output and the nested if...else is disregarded. However, if the logical expression is false (when GPA is greater than or equal to 3.5), the second if...else statement is used to determine if GPA is high enough to qualify for either the Dean's List or the President's List.

When using nested logic, it is important to use proper indentation so the code will execute as its written appearance suggests. The readability realized by good indentation habits can save you time during the debugging phase of program implementation. To illustrate the flexibility in formatting, the previous nested logic—written to illustrate that the true- or false-part of an if...else statement may contain another if...else statement—may be rewritten in the following preferred manner to line up the three possible branches through this control structure:

```
if(GPA < 3.5)
  cout << "Try harder" << endl;
```

```
else if(GPA < 4.0)
   cout << "You made the Dean's List" << endl;
else
   cout << "You made the President's list" << endl;
```

5.4.1 Nested Logic with the Bank Control Program

Nested logic will also be part of the second phase of the bank control program (this is given as a lab project). As a preview, consider the short program below that uses nested logic. With superName set to "BOSS," a message operation can be executed to indicate ATM shutdown when "BOSS" is entered. The rest of the program is disregarded. If BOSS is not entered, the customer is searched for in the database of bank customers (findCustomer). If the customer is not found, a message is displayed. Otherwise, one withdrawal operation is permitted.

```
// This program demonstrates the use of several if statements.
// We also see the necessity for the compound statement (block).
#include "ouratm.h"
#include "ourbank.h"

const string superName = "BOSS";

int main()
{
  ATM moneyMachine;
  bank firstBank;
  int customerNumber, found;
  double amount, balance;

  moneyMachine.getNameAndPIN();
  if(moneyMachine.name() == superName)
    moneyMachine.message("Time to shut down ATM for accounting");
  else
  {
    firstBank.findCustomer(moneyMachine, customerNumber, found);
    if(! found)
      moneyMachine.message("Invalid name/PIN combination");
    else
    {
      moneyMachine.getWithdrawal(amount);
      firstBank.recordWithdrawal(amount, customerNumber);
      moneyMachine.message("Here comes a new balance");
      balance = firstBank.availableBalance(customerNumber);
      moneyMachine.showBalance(balance);
    }
  }
  return 0;
}
```

This nested logic selection provides appropriate management of a variety of inputs. The name/PIN pair may be one of three things: a valid customer, an invalid customer, or the superName. Even if the customer is valid, he or she may enter invalid withdrawal amounts such as BAD, or one that is not an increment of 5.00 such as 52.00. When you complete phase two of the bank control program (Lab Project 5G), you will need even more nested logic to process the correct transactions—withdraw, deposit, and balance.

5.4.2 More Nested Logic: Determining Letter Grades

Some instructors use a scale such as the following to determine the proper letter grade to assign to a student. The letter grade is based on a percentage representing a weighted average (to the nearest integer) of all work for the term.

Value of Percentage	Assigned Grade
90 <= percentage	A
80 <= percentage < 90	B
70 <= percentage < 80	C
60 <= percentage < 70	D
percentage < 60	F

We could code the solution with five statements that begin like this:

```
if(percentage >= 90)
  cout << 'A';
if((percentage >= 80) && (percentage < 90)) // Not Necessary
  cout << 'B';
```

or we could code a more efficient solution with less code, which is also less prone to intent errors. The nested logic looks like this:

```
if(percentage >= 90)
  cout << 'A';
else if(percentage >= 80)
  cout << 'B';
else if(percentage >= 70)
  cout << 'C';
else if(percentage >= 60)
  cout << 'D';
else
  cout << 'F';
```

Here, the output depends on the value of percentage. If percentage is greater than or equal to 90, then the statement cout << 'A'; is executed. All other statements after the first else (which contains several other if...elses) are disregarded. If percentage = 50, then all logical expressions are false and the expression after the final else (cout << 'F';) is called.

When percentage has a value between 60 and 89, logical expressions are evaluated until one evaluates to true. Since percentage >= 90 returns false, the opposite logical expression, percentage < 90, must be true. The second logical expression, percentage >= 80, is tested only if the first (percentage < 90) is false. Therefore, we get closer to the desired range each time a logical expression is false. When the first true logical expression is encountered, the very next true-part is executed and the rest of the nested if...else is disregarded.

When all logical expressions are false, the last expression (cout << 'F') is executed and a letter grade of F is output. This is correct since percentage must be less than 60 for all the other logical expressions to be false. The program shown below is written to demonstrate a method for testing a function that displays the letter grade when supplied with various arguments copied to the parameter percentage.

```cpp
// Try several percentages for the nested if...else structure
#include <iostream.h>

void showLetterGrade(int percentage)
{
  cout.width(4);
  cout << percentage << " = ";
  if(percentage >= 90)
    cout << 'A';
  else if(percentage >= 80)
    cout << 'B';
  else if(percentage >= 70)
    cout << 'C';
  else if(percentage >= 60)
    cout << 'D';
  else
    cout << 'F';
  cout << endl;
}

int readInt()
{ // Get an int from the keyboard
  int intObject;
  cout << "Enter a numeric grade: ";
  cin >> intObject;
  return intObject;
}

int main()
{ // Test a function containing nested logic.
  int percentage;
```

```
showLetterGrade(readInt());
showLetterGrade(readInt());
showLetterGrade(readInt());
showLetterGrade(readInt());
return 0;
}
```

─────────────── **Dialogue** ───────────────

```
Enter a numeric grade: 52
  52 = F
Enter a numeric grade: 64
  64 = D
Enter a numeric grade: 76
  76 = C
Enter a numeric grade: 98
  98 = A
```

We can improve this implementation by ensuring that letter grades are displayed only when percentage is within the range of 0 through 100 inclusive. There is a possibility, for example, that someone will enter 777 instead of an intended input of 77. Since 777 >= 90 is true, the input of 777 would improperly display A when C is the correct output. Function showLetterGrade can be modified to contain a test for out-of-range input. This first logical expression checks to see if percentage is either less than 0 or greater than 100.

```
if((percentage < 0) || (percentage > 100))
  cout << "**Error--Percentage is not in range [0..100]";
else if(percentage >= 90)
  cout << 'A';
```

Rather than displaying an incorrect letter grade for percentages less than 0 or greater than 100, this message is displayed instead:

```
777 = **Error--Percentage is not in range [0..100]
```

5.4.3 Branch Coverage Testing

The preceding program demonstrates a method for testing showLetterGrade. To be sure that the nested logic is correct for all possible ints, we could test it with all ints from -999 through +999, for instance. But this takes an unreasonable amount of time, and it is unnecessary. Assuming that no integer outside the range of 0 through 100 is passed to the function containing the nested logic, the test data necessary to perform one test of this function could be limited to the following set of integers:

```
55, 65, 75, 85, 95
```

This set of test data executes every possible branch through the nested if...else. *Branch coverage testing* occurs when we observe what happens when each statement in a nested if...else executes once. To correctly perform branch coverage testing we need to:

- Establish a set of data that satisfies this condition.
- Run the portion of the program containing the nested logic for all selected data values.
- Observe that the program segment behaves correctly for all data values.

5.4.4 Boundary Testing

Looking ahead to the function main below, notice several additional function calls with arguments that check the boundary values of 59, 60, 61, 69, 70, 71, 79, and so on—the borderline values that serve as the cutoffs. *Boundary testing* occurs when we observe what happens for each cutoff value, and for each value that either precedes or succeeds the boundary value. The extra effort could go a long way. For example, we could avoid situations where students with 90 are accidentally shown to have a letter grade of B rather than A. This would occur when the code percentage >= 90 is accidentally written as percentage > 90.

```
int main()
{
  // Branch coverage testing
  showLetterGrade(55);
  showLetterGrade(65);
  showLetterGrade(75);
  showLetterGrade(85);
  showLetterGrade(95);
  // Boundary testing
  showLetterGrade(59);
  showLetterGrade(60);
  showLetterGrade(69);
  showLetterGrade(70);
  showLetterGrade(79);
  showLetterGrade(80);
  showLetterGrade(89);
  showLetterGrade(90);
  return 0;
}
```

---------------------------------- **Output** ----------------------------------

```
55 = F
65 = D
75 = C
85 = B
95 = A
59 = F
60 = D
69 = D
70 = C
79 = C
80 = B
89 = B
90 = A
```

5.4.5 Multiple Returns

The preceding function simply outputs the percentage and the appropriate letter grade. To return the letter grade as a char function, we have two choices. The first assigns the proper letter grade to a local object. This object, named localGrade, becomes the return expression.

```
char letterGrade(int percentage)
{
  char localGrade;
  if(percentage >= 90)
    localGrade = 'A';
  else if(percentage >= 80)
    localGrade = 'B';
  else if(percentage >= 70)
    localGrade = 'C';
  else if(percentage >= 60)
    localGrade = 'D';
  else
    localGrade = 'F';

  return localGrade;
}
```

The other option uses multiple return statements. The first time any return statement is encountered, the function terminates. Therefore, we could also write the same function as follows:

```
// Illustrate a function with multiple returns
#include <iostream.h>
```

```
char letterGrade(int percentage)
{
  if(percentage >= 90)
    return 'A';
  else if(percentage >= 80)
    return 'B';
  else if(percentage >= 70)
    return 'C';
  else if(percentage >= 60)
    return 'D';
  else
    return 'F';
}
```

Self-Check

1. Using the program below, write the output that would occur after the user enters these values when prompted for `temp`:

   a. -40   c. 20   e. -1
   b. 42   d. 15   f. 31

```
#include <iostream.h>
int main()
{
  int temp;
  cout << "Enter current temperature: ";
  cin >> temp;
  if(temp <= -40)
    cout << "extremely frigid";
  else if(temp < 0)
    cout << "below freezing";
  else if(temp < 20)
    cout << "freezing to mild";
  else if(temp < 30)
    cout << "warm";
  else if(temp < 40)
    cout << "very hot";
  else
    cout << "need air-conditioning";
  return 0;
}
```

2. List the entire range of `ints` that would cause the previous program to output warm.

3. Establish a set of data that performs branch coverage testing on the preceding program.

212

Chapter 5   Selections

4. Establish a set of data that could be used to perform boundary testing on the preceding program.

Answers

1. a. extremely frigid   c. warm   e. below freezing
   b. need air-conditioning   d. freezing to mild f. very hot
2. An int in the range of 20 through 29 inclusive
3. There are many possible sets; here's one: -45, -10, 10, 25, 35, and 45
4. -41, -40, -1, 0, 19, 20, 29, 30, 39, 40

5.5   The switch Statement

The C++ *switch* statement is useful for selecting the proper statement(s) based on the value of an object whenever each unique value signifies a different action. The general form of the C++ switch statement is:

```
switch (switch-expression)
{
    case value-1 :
        statement(s)-1
        break ;
    case value-2 :
        statement(s)-2
        break ;
        ...
    case value-N :
        statement(s)-N
        break ;
    default :
        default-statement(s) ;
}
```

The *switch-expression* and each case value must be the same class, usually int or char. When a switch statement is encountered, the *switch-expression* is compared to *value-1*, *value-2*, through *value-N* until a match is found. When the *switch-expression* equals one of these values, the statements following the colon are executed. If no match is made, the default-statement(s), if present, are executed.

The optional *break* statement—seen here for the first time—causes exits from the current control structure. The break statement at the end of each case statement section causes a jump out of the switch statement. This avoids unintentional execution of the remaining portions of the switch statement. When any switch statement executes and no match is found, the optional *default-statement(s)* execute(s). The default needs to be present only if some processing is desired when the switch expression does not match any of the case values. If absent, it is possible that no statements will execute inside the switch statement.

The following code is an example of a switch statement that chooses one of five paths based on the value of option:

```
// Illustrate a switch statement
#include <iostream.h>  //  for cout <<
#include <ctype.h>     //  for toupper(char)

int main()
{
  char option;
  cout << "B)alance  W)ithdraw  D)eposit  Q)uit: ";
  cin >> option;
  option = toupper(option);  // toupper is from <ctype.h>
  // option is in uppercase now

  switch(option)
  {
    case 'B':
      cout << "Balances selected" << endl;
      break;
    case 'W':
      cout << "Withdrawal selected" << endl;
      break;
    case 'D':
      cout << "Deposit selected" << endl;
      break;
    case 'Q':
      cout << "Quit selected" << endl;
      break;
    default:
      cout << "Invalid choice" << endl;
  } // end switch
  return 0;
}
```

Output
(one possible dialogue)
```
B)alance  W)ithdraw  D)eposit  Q)uit: d
Deposit selected
```

If the value extracted for option is 'B', the message "Balances Selected" is output and break is executed to exit the switch control structure. If 'Q' or 'q' is input, "Quit selected" is output and another break is executed. In this example, each case is evaluated until option is matched to one of the four char values following case. If option is any other value, the message "Invalid choice" is displayed.

Programming Tip

Don't forget to include the optional break statements in the case portions of switch. Failure to break out of the switch may cause other case sections to execute inappropriately. For example, if all break statements are removed from the switch statement shown above, every case section executes (including the default) when B is input.

```
B)alance  W)ithdraw  D)eposit  Q)uit: B
Balances selected
Withdrawal selected
Deposit selected
Quit selected
Invalid choice
```

Failure to include breaks at all the proper locations will cause trouble.

Self-Check

1. Write the output produced by the following switch statements:

   a.
   ```
   char option = 'A';
   switch(option)
   {
     case 'A':
       cout << "AAA";
       break;
     case 'B':
       cout << "BBB";
       break;
     default:
       cout << "Invalid";
   }
   ```

   b.
   ```
   float x = 0.65;
   switch (ceil(X))
   {
     case 0:
       cout << "000";
       break;
     case 1:
       cout << "111";
       break;
     default:
       cout << "Neither";
   }
   ```

2. What is the output from Self-Check 1a when option = 'B'?
3. What is the output from Self-Check 1a when option = 'C'?
4. What is the output from Self-Check 1b when option = -0.9?
5. Write a switch statement that displays your favorite music if the int object choice is 1, your favorite food if choice is 2, and your favorite instructor if choice is 3. If the choice is anything else, display Error. Don't forget the break statements.

Answers

1a. AAA   1b. 111   2.   BBB   3.   Invalid 4.   000

5.
```
switch (choice)
{
    case 1:
      cout << "any good music";
      break;
    case 2:
      cout << "any good food";
      break;
    case 3:
      cout << "any good instructor";
      break;
    default:
      cout << "Error";
}
```

Exercises

1. *True or False*: When an `if` statement is encountered, the true-part always executes.

2. *True or False*: When an `if` or `if...else` statement is encountered, valid logical expressions are evaluated to either zero representing true or to some nonzero value representing false.

3. *True or False*: A block used as the true-part of an `if...else` requires a terminating semicolon before `else`.

4. *True or False*: In an `if...else`, a semicolon must terminate the true-part when it is something other than a block.

5. *True or False*: Every `else` is always associated with the `if` that is in the same exact column above.

6. Proper indentation and spacing improves readability. The next code segment is an example of poor indentation; try to predict the output.

   ```
   int j=123;if(j>=0)if(j>0)cout<<"jiszero";else cout
   <<"jispositive";else cout<<"jisnegative";
   ```

7. Write the output from the following code segments:

   a.
   ```
   float x = 4.0;
   if(x == 10.0)
      cout << "is 10";
   else
      cout << "not 10";
   ```

   b.
   ```
   int j = 0, k =1;
   if(j != k) cout << "abc";
   if(j == k) cout << "def";
   if(j <= k) cout << "ghi";
   if(j >= k) cout << "klm";
   ```

c. ```
char ch1 = 'A';
char ch2 = 'B';
if(ch1 == ch2)
  cout << "equal";
if(ch1 != ch2)
  cout << "not";
```

d. ```
float x = -123.4,  y = 999.9;
if(x < y) cout << "less ";
if(x > y) cout << "greater ";
if(x == y) cout << "equal ";
if(x != y) cout << "not eq. ";
```

8. Write the output from the following if...else statements:

a. ```
int t1 = 87, t2 = 76, larger;
if(t1 > t2)
  larger = t1;
else
  larger = t2;
cout << "larger: " << larger;

float x1 = 2.89, x2 = 3.12;
if(abs(x1-x2) < 1)
  cout << "true";
else
  cout << "false";
```

b. ```
string name = "PEREZ";
if(name <= "D")
  cout << "A..D";
else if(name <= "N")
  cout << "E..N";
else if(name <= "T")
  cout << "O..T";
else
  cout << "U..Z";
```

9. Write a statement that displays YES if intObject is positive, NO if intObject is negative, and NEUTRAL if intObject is 0.

10. Write a complete program that reads three distinct ints and displays the largest. Assume the user will never enter ints of the same value; they are always unique.

11. Write all possible sets of test data (*Hint:* There are six sets) for the preceding question and walk through your code for each to ensure that the program works for three unique ints.

12. Which letters represent statements with compiletime errors given int j = 10;?

a. ```
if(j < 10)
  cout << "yes";
```

b. ```
if(j < 10) then
  cout << "Who knows?";
```

c. ```
if(j > 10)
  cout << "yes";
else
  cout << "no";
```

d. ```
if j == 0
  cout << "yes";
```

e. ```
if('a' == 'a') cout << "true";
```

f. ```
if(j != 0)
{
  j = j + 1;
  cout << j;
}
else
  j = j - 1;
```

13. What is the output from the following program fragments, assuming j and k are int objects with the values 25 and 50, respectively?

```
int j = 25;                          int j = 25;
int k = 50;                          int k = 50;
```

a. ```
    if(j == k)
        cout << j;
    cout << k;
    ```

d.  ```
    if(j <= k)
        if(j != k)
            cout << "Five";
        else
            cout << "Six";
    else
        cout << "Seven";
    ```

b. ```
    if(j < k)
        cout << "jjj";
    else
        cout << "kkk";
    ```

e.  ```
    if(j > 0)
        if(j < 50)
            cout << "Eight";
        else
            cout << "Nine";
    ```

c. ```
    if(j < 10)
        cout << j << " One";
    else if(j < 20)
        cout << j << " Two";
    else if(j < 30)
        cout << j << " Three";
    else
        cout << j << " Four";
    ```

f.  ```
    if(k <= 100)
        cout << "Ten ";
    if(k <= 50)
        cout << "Eleven ";
    if(k <= 10)
        cout << "Twelve ";
    else
        cout << "Hmmmm";
    ```

14. Show the output from the previous exercise when j = 30 and k = 10.
15. Show the output from the previous exercise when j = 20 and k = 20.
16. Show the output from the following program:

```
#include <iostream.h>
void whatToDo(int num1, int num2)
{
  cout << num1 << "    " << num2;
}
main ()
{
  int j = 10, k = 35;
  if(j == k)
    whatToDo (j * 3, k + 6);
  else
    whatToDo (k + 6, j * 3);
}
```

17. Write a statement that will add 1 to the int object j only when the int object counter has a value less than the int object n.

18. Write a statement that will display "Hello" if the int object hours has a value less than 8, or "Good-bye" if hours has any other value.

19. Write a program segment that will add 1 to the int object amount if amount is less than 10. In this case, also display "Less than 10". If amount is greater than 10, subtract 1 from amount and display "Greater than 10". If amount is 10, just display "Equal to 10".

20. Write a program fragment that guarantees that the int object amount is even. If amount is odd, increment amount by 1.

21. Write function min that *returns,* not displays, the smaller of two int values. Write three function calls that completely test min (if the ints are equal, return the equal value).

22. Write function largest that *returns,* not displays, the largest of three ints. Write the six function calls that completely test largest. Here are two to get you started:

```
cout << largest(1, 2, 3) << endl;
cout << largest(2, 1, 3) << endl;
```

23. Write the output from the following program when:
    a. option = 0;   b. option = 1;   c. option = 2;   d. option = 3;

```
#include <iostream.h>
int main()
{
  int choice;
  choice = 2;  // This changes
  switch(choice)
  {
    case 1:
      cout << "1 selected" << endl;
      break;
    case 2:
      cout << "2 selected" << endl;
      break;
    case 3:
      cout << "3 selected" << endl;
      break;
    default:
      cout << "Invalid choice" << endl;
  } // end switch
  return 0;
}
```

24. Write a switch statement that displays "Monday" if int day = 0, "Tuesday" if int day = 1, and so on up through "Sunday" if int day = 6.

Lab Projects

5A   Using Objects

Implement function pay that determines a person's pay based on hours worked and hourly rate of pay. Overtime hours over 40 are calculated at 1.5 times the hourly rate. Test your function with the following code after writing down the expected output. The first argument to pay represents the hours worked; the second argument is the hourly rate of pay.

First, create a new file with a main function that begins like this (you don't need to copy the test oracle written in comments, but use it later to verify completion of this lab project):

```
int main()
{
  decimals(cout, 2);              // Test oracle:
  cout << pay(38, 10.00) << endl; // 380.00
  cout << pay(40, 10.00) << endl; // 400.00
  cout << pay(42, 10.00) << endl; // 430.00
  return 0;
}
```

Second, add function pay immediately before int main. *Reminder:* If your output does not have trailing zeros, include "ourstuff.h" and call the decimals function to show two decimal places with trailing zeros:

```
decimals(cout, 2);  // Declared in "ourstuff.h"
```

5B   Using Objects

Implement function salary that returns a salesperson's salary for the month based on this table:

Sales Over	But Not Over	Monthly Salary
0	10,000	Base salary
10,000	20,000	Base salary plus 5% of sales over 10,000
20,000		Base salary plus 500.00 plus 8% of sales over 20,000

The base salary is 1500.00, which means salary returns a value that is never less than 1500.00. When sales are over 10,000, commission is added to the base salary. For example, when sales equals 10001, the monthly salary is 1500.00 + 5% of 1.00 for a total of 1500.05, and when sales is 20001, the monthly salary is 1500.00 + 500.00 +

8% of 1.00 for a total of 2000.08. Include function `salary` that inputs `sales` through a value parameter and returns the monthly salary through a `return` statement. Test your function with the calls shown below where the one argument to `salary` represents `sales`.

First, create a new file with a `main` function that begins like this (you don't need to copy the test oracle written as comments, but use the output later to verify completion of this lab project):

```
int main()
{                                   // Test oracle
  decimals(cout, 2);
  cout << salary(10000.00) << endl; // 1500.00
  cout << salary(10001.00) << endl; // 1500.05
  cout << salary(20001.00) << endl; // 2000.08
  // Note: Your output may not show the trailing zeros ".00"
  return 0;
}
```

Second, immediately before `int main`, declare the function heading for `salary`. Declare one `double` parameter to obtain input from function `main`. Use this `double` parameter to return the appropriate value.

Third, complete the function body to compute and return the values as shown in comments above. Review the salary table given earlier.

Reminder: If your output does not have trailing zeros, include "ourstuff.h" and call the `decimals` function to show two decimal places with trailing zeros.

```
decimals(cout, 2);   // From "ourstuff.h"
```

5C   Using Objects

Implement function `grade(int percentage)` that determines the proper letter grade for a plus/minus system with the following scale:

Percentage	Grade Assigned
93 <= percentage	"A"
90 <= percentage < 93	"A-"
87 <= percentage < 90	"B+"
83 <= percentage < 87	"B"
80 <= percentage < 83	"B-"
77 <= percentage < 80	"C+"
70 <= percentage < 77	"C"
60 <= percentage < 70	"D"
percentage < 60	"F"

After implementing the function, perform boundary and range testing and try a few invalid arguments. In this case, if the argument is a value outside the range of 0 through 100, return "??" as the string letter grade.

First, create a new file with a main function that begins like this (you don't need to copy the output written as comments, but use the output later to verify completion of this lab project):

```
int main()
{                              // Test Oracle
  cout << grade(-1) << endl;   // ??
  cout << grade( 0) << endl;   // F
  cout << grade( 1) << endl;   // F
  cout << grade(59) << endl;   // F
  // ...
```

In the same manner, complete a test set that performs complete branch and boundary testing. The last two lines should look like this:

```
// ...
// Complete test set! Finish up with these two test values:
cout << grade(100) << endl;   // A
cout << grade(101) << endl;   // ??
return 0;
}
```

Verify that your main function performs complete branch and boundary testing. Compare your member function calls to the table above.

5D   Using Objects

Implement a function whichChar that displays an appropriate message indicating whether the char argument is a digit, an uppercase letter, a lowercase letter, or one of these five arithmetic operators:

```
+ - * / %
```

Any other character argument should generate the output "is something else" after the character in question. Use either a nested if...else or a switch statement with a default statement to display "is something else". The selection must be placed within function whichChar. Perform branch coverage testing on the function.

First, create a new file with a main function that looks exactly like this (you don't need to copy the output written as comments, but use the output later to verify completion of this lab project):

```
int main()
{                    // Test Oracle
  whichChar('a');   // a is a lower case letter
  whichChar('A');   // A is an uppercase letter
  whichChar('7');   // 7 is a digit
  whichChar('%');   // % is an arithmetic operator
  whichChar('?');   // ? is something else
  return 0;
}
```

Second, declare the function heading. Declare ch as a char parameter to obtain input from function main.

Third, use the parameter ch in the selection statement to choose the appropriate output, and complete the function body to produce output as shown in comments above.

5E   Using Objects

Implement a function leapYear that displays an appropriate message indicating if any particular year is a leap year. Every year after 1582 (the first year of the Gregorian calendar) that is evenly divisible by 4 is a leap year unless it is the end of a century. In this case (where the year is evenly divisible by 100) it must also be divisible by 400. For example, 1996 and 2000 are leap years but 1900 and 1999 are not leap years. Include function leapYear with one int parameter to display a message indicating whether the year is a leap year or not. Perform branch coverage testing on the function.

First, create a new file with a main function that looks exactly like this (you don't need to copy the output written as comments, but use the output later to verify completion of this lab project):

```
int main()
{                       // Test oracle
  leapYear(1995);      // 1995 not
  leapYear(1996);      // 1996 is a leap year
  leapYear(2000);      // 2000 is a leap year
  leapYear(2100);      // 2100 not
  leapYear(1581);      // 1581 is before leap years existed
  return 0;
}
```

Second, declare the function heading. Declare year as an int parameter to obtain input from function main.

Third, complete the function body to produce output as shown in comments above. Use the int parameter year to select the appropriate output.

5F   Using Objects

Write a function `romanNumeral` that displays the decimal equivalent of an upper- or lowercase Roman numeral. If the input is not a valid Roman numeral, display an appropriate message. Write a program that tests for every possible upper- or lowercase Roman numeral. The complete list of Roman numerals and their decimal equivalents are: I = 1, V = 5, X = 10, L = 50, C = 100, D = 500, and M = 1000. Perform branch coverage testing on the function.

- First, create a new file with a `main` function that begins like this (you don't need to copy the output written as comments, but use the output later to verify completion of this lab project):

```
int main()
{                                   // Test oracle
  cout << romanNumeral('i') << endl;  // 1
  cout << romanNumeral('I') << endl;  // 1
  cout << romanNumeral('v') << endl;  // 5
  //...
```

  After trying all upper- and lowercase Roman numerals, complete function `main` like this:

```
  //...
  cout << romanNumeral('m') << endl;  // 1000
  cout << romanNumeral('M') << endl;  // 1000
  return 0;
}
```

- Next, immediately before `int main`, declare the `romanNumeral` function heading. Make the return type `int` and declare `romanChar` as a `char` parameter to obtain input from function `main`. Use the parameter `romanChar` in the selection statement to choose the appropriate return value.
- Complete the function body to return the values as shown in comments above. Use a local object to temporarily store the `int` until the single `return` statement is encountered. Otherwise, use multiple `return` statements.

5G   Bank Control Program—Phase Two (*Using Objects*)

Implement phase two of the bank control program to allow one customer to make any one of the four valid transactions. Also include appropriate messages to notify the user of any unsuccessful operations. Verify that all proper transactions do modify the balance at the bank. Do this with a function call like this:

```
moneyMachine.showBalance(firstBank.availableBalance(customerNumber));
```

To demonstrate, the following events happen with the given inputs for `name`, `PIN`, `nextTransaction`, and `withdrawal` or `deposit` amount.

───────────────── **Test Oracle** ─────────────────

Name	PIN	Pick	Amount	What Should Happen
xyz	0000	NA	NA	It is your responsibility to display this message: `"Invalid name/PIN combination"`
hall	1234	w	50.00	A successful transaction occurs. The balance is changed by -50.00.
hall	1234	w	200	Everything is okay, except our customer does not have 200.00 to withdraw. Whenever this occurs, it is your responsibility to generate this message: `"Cannot process withdrawal-- Insufficient Funds"`
hall	1234	d	67.89	A successful transaction occurs. The balance is changed by +67.89.
hall	1234	b	NA	This balance is shown: 100.00.
hall	1234	Q	NA	Nothing.

Verify this test oracle. Do not continue phase three (in Chapter 6) until you have completed this phase.

5H   Modify a Class

See Appendix A, "Additional Lab Projects."

5.6 Case Study: U.S. Income Tax

The second part of this chapter is devoted to an exhaustive case study of one particular "real world" problem. It reinforces topics covered in the first part of this chapter, so it may be considered optional if time does not permit covering it. On the other hand, this analysis, design, and implementation of a problem implemented as a member function of a class illustrates the use of nested logic, branch coverage, and boundary testing with a real-world problem that has changed almost annually since 1986. With this case study, we see the need for software maintenance—a topic of great importance. Also, the `weeklyEmp` class introduced during the case study is the topic of a lab project in Appendix A that provides detailed instruction concerning the modification of a class. This gives an opportunity to modify an existing class as a prelude to class implementation.

A payroll program for employees in the United States requires calculation of federal income tax. Many other items such as gross and net pay are easily determined, but the algorithm for computing the federal income tax is more complex. So in this case study, we examine this one tax only. The table below is from the Internal Revenue Service (IRS) publication *Circular E: Employer's Tax Guide*. It is one of several methods used to calculate the amount of income tax to withhold from a weekly paycheck. The cutoffs and percentages are from an older table, which shows that the tax rate goes down from 33% to 28% for adjusted gross incomes over $200,000.00 per year [column (b) MARRIED PERSON]. This was the subject of intense debate during a recent U.S. presidential election campaign.

```
                    Tables for Percentage Method of Withholding
               Table 1—If the Payroll Period with Respect to an Employee Is Weekly

 (a) SINGLE person--including head of household:    (b) MARRIED person--

 If the amount of wages                             If the amount of wages
 (after subtracting        The amount of income tax (after subtracting        The amount of income tax
 withholding allowances) is:  to be withheld shall be withholding allowances) is:  to be withheld shall be

 Not over $23................ 0                      Not over $65................ 0

 Over--  But not over          of excess over--     Over--  But not over          of excess over--
 $23      --$397............ 15%          --$23     $65      --$689............ 15%          --$65
 $397     --$928 ............ $56.10 plus 28% --$397 $689     --$1,573............ $93.60 plus 28%  --$689
 $928     --$2,121........... $204.78 plus 33% --$928 $1,573   --$3,858............ $341.12 plus 33% --$1,573
 $2,121 ..................... $598.47 plus 28% --$2,121 $3,858 ..................... $1,095.17 plus 28% --$3,858
```

5.6.1   Analysis

Problem: *Implement a method as part of class* weeklyEmp *that determines the amount of income tax to withhold from an employee who is paid on a weekly basis. Use the weekly method as specified in the IRS Circular E: Employer's Tax Guide. Make sure the member function* weeklyEmp::incomeTax() *returns a floating-point value rounded to the nearest penny (hundredth).*

At this point, we can refer to the table for the percentage method of withholding for employees paid on a weekly basis (shown above). The two categories—single and married—are referred to as the employee *filing status*. Under each category there are five cutoffs with tax ranging from $0.00 to 15%, 28%, 33%, or back down to 28% of wages (after subtracting withholding allowances). In addition to an employee's gross pay, we need a piece of information called *exemptions* to compute the adjusted wages to make meaning of this:

```
 If the amount of wages
 (after subtracting        The amount of income tax
 withholding allowances) is:  to be withheld shall be
```

Although the input to this function might be:
- Gross pay
- Filing Status
- Exemptions

we simply state that all required data is part of class weeklyEmp (discussed later). All data required to determine the tax is immediately available. The output is the income tax with the additional requirement that the return value is rounded to the nearest penny (hundredth). The input and output are summarized as follows:

Input:

Input data is encapsulated or available through member functions rather than being supplied via argument parameter associations. All weeklyEmp objects have access to their own gross pay, exemptions, and filing status.

Return Value:

The United States federal income tax rounded to the nearest penny (hundredth).

5.6.2 Design: Stepwise Refinement

The algorithm for determining this tax is a bit complicated. To counteract this, we use a design technique called *stepwise refinement*, which starts with an initial statement that is then refined into other more explicit statements. This process of refining steps continues until we have enough detail to implement the algorithm in a programming language such as C++. For example, we might start with this nonspecific statement:

Determine the income tax to withhold from an employee's paycheck

We then refine this initial step. Each refinement should become more detailed, explicit, and closer to the target programming language. For example, if we studied the entire IRS document *Circular E: Employer's Tax Guide*, we would learn that employees don't pay tax on their entire gross pay. Although this may not be immediately obvious in the tables shown above, we must first determine a taxable income—the amount of wages after subtracting withholding allowances. Then we must pick the proper category into which the taxable income falls; there are ten possible categories (five for those filing under the single status and five for married status). With this in mind, we could refine our first step like this:

Determine the income tax to withhold from an employee's paycheck
- Determine taxable income (wages after subtracting withholding allowances).
- Find the range into which taxable income is applied—single or married category.

- Use the formula for the proper range to compute the tax.
- Round the tax to the nearest penny.
- Return the income tax.

Although several of these steps require further refinement because they are not specific enough, we have made significant progress. We now have an outline. Let's look at some of the first steps in more detail.

To find the correct range we must first understand something about the U.S. income tax laws. For each person in a family, a tax deduction may be made from the annual gross pay. This amount, which for many years remained constant at $1,000.00 per person, has been growing. The annual withholding allowance per person increased to $2,050.00 in 1991. For 1993 it was increased to $2,350.00. Using the weekly percentage method summarized in the table above, an employee was entitled to a deduction of $39.42 per week [39.42 per week = `round(2050.00/52, 2)`] for each exemption claimed. For example, the federal income tax to be withheld for a married person with a weekly pay of $900.00 claiming three exemptions (withholding allowances) has an adjusted gross pay as follows:

$$\begin{aligned} \text{taxable income} \;&=\; 900.00 - 3 * 39.42 \\ &=\; 900.00 - 118.26 \\ &=\; 781.74 \end{aligned}$$

This employee must pay tax on $781.74, not the total gross pay of $900.00. Now the first step in the algorithm can be refined as follows:

Determine taxable income (wages after subtracting withholding allowances)
taxable income = gross pay - (exemptions * value of one weekly exemption)

and the second step in our outline could be:

Find the range into which taxable income is applied—single or married category.
- If filing under the single status, select the proper formula from Table 1(a).
- If filing under the married status, select the proper formula from Table 1(b).

Both of these steps could be refined using a similar description of nested logic to find the proper range. Instead, the two columns of the table will be translated directly into the target language as two if statements—one for single filing status, and one for married filing status. Each if statement could then have a true part that is implemented as a nested if...else statement to select the correct range. We should also see that applying the formula is accomplished by consulting the proper table. With the weekly percentage method tax table in hand and this algorithm, we can now compute the tax withheld for any employee.

> *Determine the federal income tax to withhold from an employee's paycheck*
> - taxable income = gross pay - (exemptions * value of one weekly exemption)
> - If filing status is single, select the *proper formula* from Table 1(a).
> - If filing status is married, select the *proper formula* from Table 1(b).
> - Calculate the federal income tax using the *proper formula*.
> - Round the tax to the nearest penny.
> - Return the federal income tax.

Here is an example for an employee filing as single with a gross pay of $1,000.00 and one exemption when the value of one exemption was 39.42:

taxable income = gross pay - (exemptions * one weekly exemption)

$$1000.00 - (\quad 1 \quad * \quad 39.42 \quad)$$
$$1000.00 - \quad\quad 39.42$$
$$960.58$$

Under Table 1(a) SINGLE, we discover the proper formula when we see that 960.58 falls into the range 928 through 2121. The tax is computed as follows:

federal tax = $204.78 + 33% of excess over $928

$$204.78 + 0.33 * (\text{taxable income} - 928)$$
$$204.78 + 0.33 * (960.58 - 928)$$
$$204.78 + 0.33 * (32.58)$$
$$204.78 + 10.7514$$
$$215.5314$$

federal tax =   215.53   *(Rounded to the nearest hundredth)*

Self-Check

1. Determine the taxable income for any weekly paid employee with gross pay = 500.00 and exemptions = 2.
2. Determine the amount of income tax (rounded to the nearest hundredth) for an employee with a married filing status, gross pay = $850.00, and one exemption.

Answers
1. 500 – 2 * 39.42 = 421.16
2. adjusted wages = 850.00 - (1 * 39.42) = 810.58
   tax = 93.60 + 0.28 * (810.58 - 689) = 93.60 + (0.28 * 121.58) = 93.60 + 34.0424 = 127.64

5.6.3   Implementation

One possible implementation to our solution might have been a function that requires three arguments in each call, which might look something like this:

```
fredsFedTax = incomeTax(fredsGrossPay, fredsExemptions, fredsFilingStatus)
```

Instead, incomeTax is a member function of the existing weeklyEmp class declared in the file ouremp.h. Each weeklyEmp object always contains the necessary data members and member functions to store and calculate the taxes. Since the data of each object is always available to any member function of that class, we need not pass any arguments at the function call. The gross pay is returned as a function of class weeklyEmp. Gross pay is determined by referencing the hours worked and the hourly rate of pay. Other data members may include the employee's name, Social Security number, filing status, number of exemptions, retirement contribution, accumulated vacation time, hire date, employer, health-care contribution, year-to-date totals, and so on. The data members of an employee can be quite complicated, especially if the employee works for more than one employer or the company pays some employees an hourly rate weekly or biweekly, and others a salary monthly. For the sake of simplicity, we present a fairly simple employee class with a restricted number of data members:

Data Members of Class weeklyEmp

Data member	Class	Purpose
empName	string	The employee's name—a string of any length
hours	double	The hours worked in the week; hours over 40 are considered overtime and are calculated at 1.5 times the hourly rate of pay
rate	double	The employee's hourly rate of pay
exempts	int	The number of exemptions declared on an employee's W-4 form
status	char	'S' if filing under single status or 'M' for married

weeklyEmp objects are initialized with the constructor and the five arguments in the order shown in the table above and the constructor call below:

```
weeklyEmp anEmployee("Jergen, Fred", 40.00, 15.50, 3, 'M');
```

After the constructor sets the state of a weeklyEmp object, many useful member functions are available. weeklyEmp objects have been designed to make them easy to use within a payroll program, especially a United States payroll program where each employee works for one company. The gross pay, income taxes, and the FICA (Social Security) tax are returned with these member functions:

grossPay   Returns the gross pay using hours and rate supplied in the construc-
                tor (rounded to the nearest hundredth).

incomeTax   Returns the federal income tax using the weekly tables (rounded to
                the nearest hundredth).

FICA   Returns the amount of social security tax to withhold (rounded to
                the nearest hundredth).

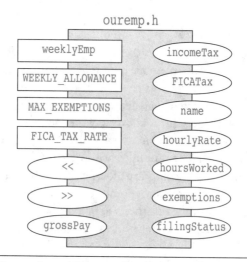

Figure 5.4   Interface diagram for module ouremp.h

The following program initializes a weeklyEmp object and demonstrates all of its
public member functions. Two other private member functions—weeklyEmp::single()
and weeklyEmp::married()—are described below. Both are used within
weeklyEmp::incomeTax.

```
// Demonstrate all public member functions of weeklyEmp.
// weeklyEmp::WeeklyEmp(string, double, double, int, char);
// string weeklyEmp::name();
// double weeklyEmp::grossPay();
// double weeklyEmp::incomeTax();
// double weeklyEmp::FICATax();
#include "ouremp.h"
#include "ourstuff.h"  // for decimals(cout, 2)
// Note: the setw(int n) function can be inserted into output
//       streams to make the next output appear in n columns.
#include <iomanip.h>  // for setw(int n)

int main()
{
  string name = "Jergen, Fred";
  double hoursWorked = 40.0;
```

```
double hourlyRate = 15.50;
int exemp = 3;
char filstat = 'M';
weeklyEmp anEmployee(name, hoursWorked, hourlyRate, exemp, filstat);

cout << anEmployee.name() << endl;
decimals(cout, 2);
cout.fill('*');
cout << "  Gross: " << setw(8) << anEmployee.grossPay()  << endl;
cout << " Income: " << setw(8) << anEmployee.incomeTax() << endl;
cout << "   FICA: " << setw(8) << anEmployee.FICATax()   << endl;
return 0;
}
```

---------------------- **Output** ----------------------

```
JERGEN, FRED
  Gross: **620.00
 Income: ***65.51
   FICA: ***47.43
```

The following code shows the weeklyEmp class declaration as stored in the file ouremp.h. Once again, notice that the public section is a summary of all available member functions. We can peruse this declaration for the names of the member functions, the number of parameters, and the class of parameters. This is especially useful for the constructor function, which has five parameters of four different classes. The public member functions can be referenced from any function that has access to the header file containing the class.

```
// The value of WEEKLY_ALLOWANCE has changed almost every year so
// the named constant must be checked every year for proper maintenance
// Use IRS publication Circular E, Employer's Tax Guide each new year.
const double WEEKLY_ALLOWANCE = 39.42;
const int    MAX_EXEMPTIONS = 99;
const double FICA_TAX_RATE = 0.0765;

class weeklyEmp {
public:
  // Default Constructor:
  weeklyEmp::weeklyEmp();
  // POST: Set weeklyEmp object to defaults

  // Copy Constructor:
  weeklyEmp::weeklyEmp(const weeklyEmp & source);
  // POST: Object is copied during argument/parameter associations
  //       and during a function return. Object is also initialized as
  //       weeklyEmp anotherEmp(anEmp);
```

```
                // Initializer Constructor:
                weeklyEmp::weeklyEmp(string initName,
                                     double initHours,
                                     double initRate,
                                     int    initExemptions,
                                     char   initStatus);
                // POST: Object is initialized using arguments when constructed as
                //       weeklyEmp anEmp("Hall, Rob", 40, 9.75, 3, 'M')

                double weeklyEmp::grossPay();
                // POST: The gross pay is returned with 1.5 * rate for any hours > 40

                double weeklyEmp::incomeTax();
                // POST: The federal income tax is returned

                double weeklyEmp::FICATax();
                // POST: The Social Security Tax is returned

                // Accessor functions:
                string weeklyEmp::name();
                // POST: The empName data member is returned

                double weeklyEmp::hourlyRate();
                // POST: Return rate

                double weeklyEmp::hoursWorked();
                // POST: Return hours

                double weeklyEmp::exemptions();
                // POST: Return exempts

                double weeklyEmp::filingStatus();
                // POST: Return status

            private:
              int single();
              int married();
              string empName;
              double hours, rate;
              int exempts;
              char status;
            };
```

We now look at the implementation of the algorithm just developed through stepwise refinement. The weeklyEmp:: qualification prepended to the function name ensures that this function is a member of weeklyEmp. This ensures access to private data such as exemptions and private member functions such as single(). (*Note:* The named constants in the header file are also accessible to the implementation file so WEEKLY_ALLOWANCE of the following member function implementation is a legal reference to the named constant in the specification file.)

```
double weeklyEmp::incomeTax()
{ // Return the federal income tax rounded to the nearest penny

  // Declare two local objects
  double taxableIncome, tax;

  taxableIncome = grossPay() - exemptions * WEEKLY_ALLOWANCE;
  if(single())
  {
    if(taxableIncome <= 23.00)
      tax = 0.00;
    else if(taxableIncome <= 397.00)
      tax = 0.15 * (taxableIncome - 23.00);
    else if(taxableIncome <= 928.00)
      tax = 56.10 + 0.28 * (taxableIncome - 397.00);
    else if(taxableIncome <= 2121.00)
      tax = 204.78 + 0.33 * (taxableIncome - 928.00);
    else
      tax = 598.47 + 0.28 * (taxableIncome - 2121.00);
  }

  if(married())
  {
    if(taxableIncome <= 65.00)
      tax = 0.00;
    else if(taxableIncome <= 689.00)
      tax = 0.15 * (taxableIncome - 65.00);
    else if(taxableIncome <= 1573.00)
      tax = 93.60 + 0.28 * (taxableIncome - 689.00);
    else if(taxableIncome <= 3858.00)
      tax = 341.12 + 0.33 * (taxableIncome - 1573.00);
    else
      tax = 1095.17 + 0.28 * (taxableIncome - 3858.00);
  }

  return round(tax, 2);
}
```

This member function would have been modified for each of the past several years. Updating this member function to reflect more recent tax laws is left as a lab project in Appendix A: "Additional Lab Projects."

5.6.4 Testing the Implementation

In order to fully test every possible calculation of the federal income tax for each `if` statement (both single and married filing status), we start with a test oracle of six hand-calculated results that can be compared later to program output resulting from associated member function calls that use the same data. This testing process can be simplified by concentrating on one filing status at a time. Federal income tax computed by hand for values that should exercise each branch of code for the single status is as follows:

Federal Income Tax for Six Taxable Incomes: Single Filing Status

Taxable Income	Federal Income Tax	Calculation Based on the Weekly Method
-123.45	0.00	Negative taxable incomes are possible
23.00	0.00	Tax = 0.00 for all adjusted wages <= 23.00
24.00	0.15	0.15 * (24 - 23) = 0.15 * 1
398.00	56.38	53.55 + 0.28 * (398 - 397) = 56.10 + 0.28 * 1
929.00	205.11	195.51 + 0.33 * (929 - 928) = 204.78 + 0.33 * 1
2122.00	598.75	572.70 + 0.28 * (2122 - 2121) = 598.47 + 0.28 * 1

Now that we have known values for given input, we can write calls to `incomeTax` using the same values as those in our hand calculations. Included in this program are additional tests for the married status. The results of running the program should match the hand-calculated results for the single employees, at least. Perusal of the output and the married table verifies that all branches have been executed and are correct.

```
// This program performs branch coverage testing for the
// federal income tax method in weeklyEmp::incomeTax()
#include <iostream.h>
// Note: The setw(int n) function can be inserted into output
//       streams to make the next output appear in n columns.
//       In this particular program, it's easier to insert setws
#include <iomanip.h>  // for setw(int n)
#include "ourstuff.h"
#include "ouremp.h"   // for class weeklyEmp

int main()
{
  weeklyEmp emp1, emp2, emp3, emp4,  emp5,  emp6,
            emp7, emp8, emp9, emp10, emp11, emp12;

  // All weeklyEmps objects have strange names("S_emp, 1") and work 1 hour at
  // outrageous pay rates to make it easier to perform branch coverage testing.
  // First, we initialize 12 weeklyEmp objects using the constructor.
  emp1 = weeklyEmp("S_emp,  1", 1,  23.00, 0, 's');
  emp2 = weeklyEmp("S_emp,  2", 1,  24.00, 0, 'S');
  emp3 = weeklyEmp("S_emp,  3", 1, 398.00, 0, 's');
```

```
emp4 = weeklyEmp("S_emp,  4", 1,  929.00, 0, 'S');
emp5 = weeklyEmp("S_emp,  5", 1, 2122.00, 0, 'S');
emp6 = weeklyEmp("M_emp,  6", 1,   65.00, 0, 'M');
emp7 = weeklyEmp("M_emp,  7", 1,   66.00, 0, 'm');
emp8 = weeklyEmp("M_emp,  8", 1,  690.00, 0, 'M');
emp9 = weeklyEmp("M_emp,  9", 1, 1574.00, 0, 'm');
emp10= weeklyEmp("M_emp, 10", 1, 3859.00, 0, 'm');
// Add 11 & 12 to verify that exemptions are used correctly
emp11= weeklyEmp("S_emp, 11", 1, 24+39.42, 1, 's');
emp12= weeklyEmp("M_emp, 12", 1, 66+39.42, 1, 'm');
decimals(cout, 2);
cout << endl
     << "The single employees: " << endl;

// Note: With #include <iomanip.h>, setw(10) causes the very
// next output item to be displayed in at least 10 columns

cout << emp1.name() << setw(10) << emp1.grossPay()
                    << setw(10) << emp1.incomeTax() << endl;
cout << emp2.name() << setw(10) << emp2.grossPay()
                    << setw(10) << emp2.incomeTax() << endl;
cout << emp3.name() << setw(10) << emp3.grossPay()
                    << setw(10) << emp3.incomeTax() << endl;
cout << emp4.name() << setw(10) << emp4.grossPay()
                    << setw(10) << emp4.incomeTax() << endl;
cout << emp5.name() << setw(10) << emp5.grossPay()
                    << setw(10) << emp5.incomeTax() << endl;

cout << endl
     << "The married employees:" << endl;
cout << emp6.name() << setw(10) << emp6.grossPay()
                    << setw(10) << emp6.incomeTax() << endl;
cout << emp7.name() << setw(10) << emp7.grossPay()
                    << setw(10) << emp7.incomeTax() << endl;
cout << emp8.name() << setw(10) << emp8.grossPay()
                    << setw(10) << emp8.incomeTax() << endl;
cout << emp9.name() << setw(10) << emp9.grossPay()
                    << setw(10) << emp9.incomeTax() << endl;
cout << emp10.name()<< setw(10) << emp10.grossPay()
                    << setw(10) << emp10.incomeTax()<< endl;

cout << endl
     << "The employees with one exemption:" << endl;
cout << emp11.name()<< setw(10) << emp11.grossPay()
                    << setw(10) << emp11.incomeTax() << endl;
cout << emp12.name()<< setw(10) << emp12.grossPay()
                    << setw(10) << emp12.incomeTax()<< endl;
return 0;
}
```

```
─────────────────────────  Output  ─────────────────────────
  The single employees:
  S_EMP,  1     23.00      0.00
  S_EMP,  2     24.00      0.15
  S_EMP,  3    398.00     56.38
  S_EMP,  4    929.00    205.11
  S_EMP,  5   2122.00    598.75

  The married employees:
  M_EMP,  6     65.00      0.00
  M_EMP,  7     66.00      0.15
  M_EMP,  8    690.00     93.88
  M_EMP,  9   1574.00    341.45
  M_EMP, 10   3859.00   1095.45

  The employees with one exemption:
  S_EMP, 11     63.42      0.15
  M_EMP, 12    105.42      0.15
```

Because the first 10 `weeklyEmp` objects (`emp1` through `emp10`) have no exemptions, two other important tests are included to make us feel more confident that the `incomeTax` member function is correct. The first 10 calls of `incomeTax` result in a taxable income that is the same as the gross pay—the amount to subtract is always $0.00 because there are 0 exemptions. We should verify that taxable income is being computed properly for employees with more than 0 exemptions. Note that `emp11` and `emp12` have one exemption and a gross pay that is exactly one exemption ($39.42) larger than the cutoff. The resulting tax should be, and is, $0.15 for both.

Chapter Summary

We have now looked at three C++ control structures that implement selection. The `if`, `if...else`, and `switch` statements manage a variety of input data in a meaningful fashion. The ability to choose alternate paths is made possible through construction of logical expressions that evaluate to zero (false) or nonzero (true). The logical expressions of the `if` and `if...else` statements usually have one or more of the following relational, equality, or logical operators:

```
  <   >   <=   >=   !=   ==   !   ||   &&
```

We saw some logical operations with rules such as `1 && 0 = 0` (true and false is false), and `1 || 0 = 1` (true or false is true). We also saw a compound statement—delimited by `{` and `}`—used as the true- or false-part of a selection statement, that semicolons can be particularly troublesome with selection statements, and that the precedence rules of C++ are quite elaborate.

We saw several examples of nested logic—of if...else statements existing as the true- or false-part of other if...else statements. Nested logic can be applied to a wide variety of problems where we need to find the range into which a value falls, such as finding the correct letter grade when given a percentage. It should be implemented with application of branch and boundary testing. Without this approach, a program may only appear to work when in fact one or more untested branches have some errors.

Exercises

25. Write a complete program that declares topEmployee as a weeklyEmp object. Initialize it using your own name, one exemption, your marital status, and 45 hours worked. Supply your own hourly rate of pay. Also write the code that will display your gross pay and federal income tax.

26. Determine the federal income tax that should be withheld from an employee with a weekly gross pay of $450.00, filing under the single status with two deductions.

27. Determine the federal income tax that should be withheld from an employee with a weekly gross pay of $450.00, filing under the married status with two deductions.

28. *True or False:* A person earning $1,000.00 with three exemptions will have the same tax withheld from his or her paycheck as a person who earns $1,000.00 and claims zero exemptions (assuming that both use the same filing status).

29. *True or False:* Using the weekly method for withholding federal income tax, a single person who earns $739.42 for the week with one exemption will have $140.94 withheld in federal income tax.

To answer the next two questions, use the first statement in weeklyEmp::incomeTax where grossPay is a member function and exemptions is a private data member:

```
taxableIncome = grossPay() - exemptions * WEEKLY_ALLOWANCE;
```

30. To compute taxableIncome, what values are returned or referenced by:
    a. grossPay()
    b. exemptions
    c. WEEKLY_ALLOWANCE

    using this initialization and call to weeklyEmp::incomeTax:

```
weeklyEmp anEmp("Whitbread, Seymour", 42, 10.00, 2, 'M');
cout << anEmp.incomeTax();
```

31. To compute `taxableIncome`, what values are returned or referenced by:
    a. `grossPay()`
    b. `exemptions`
    c. `WEEKLY_ALLOWANCE`

    using this initialization and call to `weeklyEmp::incomeTax`:

    ```
    weeklyEmp anEmp("Cordona, Hilly", 40, 5.00, 1, 'M');
    cout << anEmp.incomeTax();
    ```

Lab Projects

51   Modifying a Class

See Appendix A, "Additional Lab Projects."

6

Repetitions

Looping refers to the repeated execution of a set of statements. Looping is a natural way to express algorithms such as:

- Add the remaining flour ¼ cup at a time, whipping until smooth.
- For every name on the attendance roster, call the next name. Mark 0 if absent or √ if present.

Looping is also a natural way to express algorithms intended for computer implementation:

- Process customers while the ATM is operating.
- Repeat transaction processing until the user wishes to quit.
- While there are more fast food items, sum each item.
- Compute the course grade for every student in a class.
- Microwave the food until either the timer reaches 0, the cancel button is hit, or the door is opened.

In this chapter, we look at the C++ statements that implement these kinds of loops. We begin our study of repetitive control structures with the `while` statement that executes a given set of statements a specified number of times or while certain conditions exist. We also look at the similar `for` and `do while` statements.

After studying this chapter, you will be able to:

- Use the `while` statement.
- Implement counter- and event-controlled loops.
- Use nested loops.
- Use the `for` and `do while` loops.

6.1   Why Iterate?

Many jobs once performed by hand are now accomplished by computers at a much faster rate. Think of a payroll department with the job of producing employee paychecks. With only a few employees, this task could certainly be done by hand. However, with several thousand employees, a large payroll department would be necessary to hand produce that many paychecks. Other situations requiring iteration (repetition) include, but are certainly not limited to: finding an average, searching a list for a particular item, alphabetizing a list of names, and processing records of information in a file. Because the same steps are performed with different data, we need some way to repeat the same process. The repetitive statements of this chapter are one solution. We begin our discussion with some code that could be used to find the average of exactly three numbers without the help of any repetitive control structure:

```
int sum = 0;
cout << "Enter number: ";    // <- Repeat these
cin >> number;               // <- three
sum = sum + number;          // <- statements

cout << "Enter number: ";
cin >> number;
sum = sum + number;

cout << "Enter number: ";
cin >> number;
sum = sum + number;

average = sum / 3.0;
cout << "average = " << average;
```

There is a drawback to this method. Any time a larger or smaller set of integers needs averaging, the program must be modified. Since three statements are repeated for every integer to be averaged, averaging 100 integers would require an additional 97 sets of these three statements. Also, the integer constant 3 in `average = sum / 3.0;` would have to be changed to 100. This situation is improved through a structure that allows a set of statements to be executed a specific number of times. Using the three repeated C++ statements inside this example of a `while` loop provides the following modified solution:

```
// Using this while loop averaging method, the user must know in
// advance, the number of input values that are to be averaged
#include <iostream.h>

int main()
{
  int number;
  // Initialize sum, counter, and n:
  float sum = 0;
  int counter = 1;
  int n;
  cout << "Enter number of entries to be averaged: ";
  cin >> n;
  // While there are more numbers to be averaged
```

```
while(counter <= n)
{
  // Execute this block n times:
  cout << "Enter number: ";  // <-Repeat these
  cin >> number;             // <-   three
  sum = sum + number;        // <-statements

  // counter keeps track of the number of loop repetitions.
  // counter is incremented n times. When counter exceeds n
  // (counter <= n is false), the loop is terminated.

  counter = counter + 1;
}
float average = sum / float(n);
cout << endl
    << "     Average: " << average << endl;
return 0;
}
```

──────────────────── **Dialogue** ────────────────────

```
Enter number of entries to be averaged: 3
Enter number: 70
Enter number: 80
Enter number: 90

    Average: 80
```

The three repeated steps are part of a control structure called the *while statement* in this general form:

```
while ( loop-test )
{
    iterative-part
}
```

The *loop-test* is an expression that often uses relational operators, resulting in either a nonzero value (true) or zero (false). The *iterative-part* may be any C++ statement, but it is usually a compound statement. The iterative part is the set of statements that execute each time the loop-test evaluates to true. When a while loop is encountered, the loop-test is evaluated to true or false. If true, the iterative-part is executed and the loop-test is evaluated again. This process continues until the loop-test is false.

while statements that execute their iterative parts a specific number of times are called *counter-controlled loop*. Those that execute until a particular event occurs to terminate the loop are called *event-controlled loops*. We first look at a few examples of the counter-controlled variety.

6.1.1   Counter-Controlled while Loops

A *counter-controlled loop* uses an `int` object (sometimes called a counter) to track the number of loop repetitions. These are useful when we need to repeat a process a specific number of times. For example, if something needed to be done for each of the 31 days in January, we could use a counter-controlled loop that executed that process 31 times. In this case, the counter could range from 1 through 31 inclusive. If something needed to be done for each of 3,451 inventory items in a database, we could use a counter-controlled loop that repeats that process 3,451 times.

At the start of each loop repetition, the counter is compared to an expression representing the number of times the loop is to execute. Inside the loop body reside the statements to be repeated along with an increment of +1 applied to the counter. In general, the following template could be used whenever we need to execute a set of statements n times:

> n = *Number of intended iterations*
> counter = 1;
> while (counter <= n)
> {
>   ... *statements to be repeated* ...
>   counter = counter + 1;
> }

This outline uses the object n to represent the number of iterations and `counter` to count the number of times the loop executes. Eventually `counter <= n` becomes false and the loop terminates at the proper time.

The behavior of a counter-controlled loop is perhaps best simulated first by displaying the changing value of the `counter`. As shown above, the `counter` is usually an `int` object that starts with the assigned value of 1. It is usually incremented by +1 as the last statement in the loop:

```
#include <iostream.h>
int main()
{
  // Iterate a loop n times
  int n = 4;
  int counter = 1;
  while(counter <= n)
  {
    //
    // The repeated process outputs the changing value of counter:
    cout << "Iteration# " << counter << endl;
    //
```

```
    // The counter is incremented to eventually terminate the loop:
    counter = counter + 1;
  }
  cout << "After loop, counter = " << counter << endl;
  return 0;
}
```

Output

```
  Iteration# 1
  Iteration# 2
  Iteration# 3
  Iteration# 4
  After loop, counter = 5
```

Another counter-controlled while loop is shown below to sum the first n (n=5) positive integers. The answer is the sum of $1 + 2 + 3 + 4 + 5$ [when n is larger, as a test oracle, we could use Gauss's formula for the sum of the first n integers: $(n*(n+1))/2 = 15$]. All five integers—represented by the changing value of counter—are added to accumulator. Since accumulator represents the running sum of all the ints from 1 through n, accumulator must be set to 0 before the loop and incremented for each value of counter. Then, for each iteration, accumulator is incremented by the value of counter as it ranges from 1 through n. The first iteration of the loop changes the accumulator from 0 to 1 (when counter is 1), the second iteration changes accumulator from 1 to 3 (when counter is 2), and so on.

```
  // An example of a counter-controlled while loop
  #include <iostream.h>
  int main()
  {
    // Initialize the objects used in the while loop
    int n = 5;
    int accumulator = 0;
    int counter = 1;
    // The counter controlled while loop
    while(counter <= n)
    {
      accumulator = accumulator + counter;
      counter = counter + 1;
    }
    cout << "Sum of the first " << n << " integers is " << accumulator;
    return 0;
  }
```

┌─────────────────────────── **Output** ───────────────────────────┐
│   │
│   Sum of the first 5 integers is: 15   │
│   │
└──┘

The compound statement executes five times with the `accumulator` changing from 0 to its final value of 15 as `counter` increments from 1 through 5. When `counter` is incremented to 6, the loop-test evaluates to false and the loop finishes executing.

Object Name	State
n	5
accumulator	0, 1, 3, 6, 10, 15
counter	1, 2, 3, 4, 5, 6 After `counter` goes to 6, the loop test is false

After `accumulator` is updated from 10 to 15, `counter` is incremented to 6 and the loop test evaluates to false. At this point, it is said that the *termination condition* has been satisfied. This is the circumstance that must be true to terminate the loop. In this example, the termination condition is `counter > 5`. The termination condition of a `while` loop has the logical negation of the loop-test that must be true before each loop iteration, or in this example, `counter <= 5`.

It should be noted that the iterative-part of a `while` statement is usually a compound statement. It is often necessary to perform some extra action to control the loop, such as tracking the number of repetitions, in addition to repeating the process. So we are usually doing at least two things. For example, in the `while` loop above, it was necessary to update the `accumulator` and to increment the `counter` inside the loop to make the loop test eventually evaluate to false. It should also be noted that `accumulator` and `counter` are initialized before the `while` loop is encountered. Failure to initialize all objects of the `while` loop causes unpredictable results. For example, can you predict the number of times this `while` loop will execute its iterative-part?

```
// How many repetitions occur when counter and n are uninitialized?
while(counter <= n)
{
    counter = counter + 1;  // The statement(s) that need repeating...
}
```

Since neither `counter` nor `n` were given initial values, the iterative part might never execute, or it might execute as many as several billion times. So one proper answer to the question posed is this: "No, I can't predict the number of repetitions."

Programming Tip ─────────────────────────────────

Some programmers prefer to write while loops with the beginning of the loop body, the starting brace {, to the right of the loop test. This stylistic preference leads to code you are likely to encounter in many places. It looks like this:

```
while(counter <= n) {
   // Note: The curly braces { and } are not aligned in the same column
}
```

6.1.2 Infinite Loops

It is possible that a while loop may never execute, not even once. It is also possible that a while loop will never reach its termination condition. The next example shows a while loop that continues to execute until external forces are applied, such as a power failure. It is an example of an *infinite loop*, something that is usually undesirable.

```
// This is an 'infinite' loop:
int counter = 1;
while(counter <= 2)
   cout << "I am repeated endlessly" << endl;
   counter = counter + 1;   // <- this is NOT part of the while loop
```

The loop iterates virtually forever because the loop-test is always true. There is no statement, such as incrementing a counter, that brings us closer to the termination condition. The loop-test is never false. The value of counter never changes; it remains 1.

Even though it may appear that counter should be incremented, no change is made because counter = counter + 1 is not part of the while statement. Immediately after the cout extraction, the loop-test is once again evaluated to true and this process repeats until some intervention occurs. When writing while loops, we should ensure that the loop-test will eventually fail. With counter-controlled loops, this usually means incrementing a counter by 1. To fix this while loop so only two repetitions occur, a compound statement should be used to include counter = counter + 1.

```
int counter = 1;
while(counter <= 2)
{ // Always use a compound statement (block)
   cout << "I am repeated twice" << endl;
   counter = counter + 1;
}
```

Programming Tip

It is recommended that you use the following antibugging technique: Always write a compound statement for the iterative part of a `while` loop even if it is not necessary. This provides a better chance of including any increment statement as part of the loop rather than accidentally leaving `counter = counter + 1` outside the loop. If you do get a program that executes a loop over and over again, the following system-dependent methods can be used to exit the program containing the infinite loop:

UNIX	Enter the interrupt control sequence, usually Ctrl-C.
DOS	1. Enter Ctrl-Break.
	2. Reboot: Ctrl-Alt-Del.
	3. Turn off computer.
MS-Windows	Enter Ctrl-Alt-Del once and then press the Enter key.
MacOS	Enter the key sequence command-period.

Note: Some of these methods for terminating programs with infinite loops may not always work as advertised on your system. In UNIX, Ctrl-C interrupts a process such as a program executing an infinite loop. Methods 2 and 3 for terminating DOS programs are not recommended because you may lose the most recent version of your program. In Microsoft Windows, entering the key sequence Ctrl-Alt-Break informs you that the application is not responding. You can return to where you were before the program break by pressing any key. (*Caution:* In MS-Windows, entering Ctrl-Alt-Del a second time causes a computer to reset. In this case, you will lose your program source code if it was not saved to disk.)

Self-Check

1. Write the output from the following C++ program fragments:

    a.
    ```
    int n = 3;
    int counter = 1;
    while(counter <= n)
    {
        cout << counter << "  ";
        counter - counter + 1;
    }
    ```

    b.
    ```
    int last = 10;
    int j = 2;
    while(j <= last)
    {
        cout << j << "  ";
        j = j + 2;
    }
    ```

2. What modifications to Question 1b are required to generate this output?

    ```
    -4  -2  0  2  4  6  8
    ```

3. Write the number of times each while loop repeats its iterative part. Assume counter, accumulator, and n have been declared as int objects. *Hint:* zero, infinite, and unknown are perfectly valid answers.

a.
```
while(counter <= n)
{
   cout << counter << endl;
}
```

d.
```
n = 5;
counter = 1;
while(counter <= n)
   cout << counter << endl;
   counter = counter + 1;
```

b.
```
counter = 1;
n = 0;
while(counter <= n)
{
   cout << " " << counter;
}
```

e.
```
counter = 1;
sum = 0;
while(counter <= 5)
{
   sum = sum + counter;
   sum = sum + 1;
}
```

c.
```
counter = 1;
n = 5;
while(counter <= n)
{
   counter = counter + 1;
}
```

f.
```
counter = 10;
while(counter >= 0)
{
   counter = counter - 2;
}
```

Answers
1. a. 1 2 3   b. 2 4 6 8 10
2. Let j = -4 and let last = 8
3. a. unknown   d. infinite
   b. zero   e. infinite (counter is not incremented)
   c. five   f. six

6.2   Case Study: Test Range

In this section we use stepwise refinement to design a solution to the problem of finding the range of test scores in a set of known size. Before reading the problem, contemplate how you would find the highest number in a list of thousands of numbers. You will gain the most insight into a computer solution by not thinking of a small list with the highest value clearly visible. Instead, we will need a systematic algorithm to solve this problem for a large list.

6.2.1   Analysis

Problem: *Write a program that determines the range of test scores recorded in a list of test scores. The range is defined as the difference between the highest and lowest values. The user enters the total number of test scores followed by the test scores themselves. The number of test scores input must be stored as an* int. *The user should be allowed to enter tests as* ints *or* floats *for greater flexibility in the type of tests. The output is labeled as* Range *followed by the range of test scores (100-57 = 43 with this dialogue). One dialogue should look like this:*

```
─────────────────────────── Dialogue ───────────────────────────
    Enter number of test scores: 5

    Enter test scores 1 per line
    76.5
    82
    90.5
    100
    57
    Range:   43
```

Note: The highest and lowest are not to be computed separately, instead both are computed at the same time, within a loop, so data is entered only once.

6.2.2   Design

We start with an IPO algorithm that captures the three major steps of one solution. But now the process step is more complex since repetition is involved.

I) Obtain the number of test scores (the size of the list).
P) Determine the range.
O) Display the range.

The first and third steps are easily accomplished through insertion and extraction with cout and cin. However, determining the range (the second task) is more involved. To help design a solution, we use the design technique called *stepwise refinement* that involves clarification of one step into two or more other steps that bring us closer to a more specific solution. The refined steps are more easily translated into a programming language. Stepwise refinement allows us to identify the tasks that can be easily translated into a language and other steps that need further clarification. We now refine the second step: determine the range.

The range of test scores is the difference between the highest and lowest test in the list. Therefore we must first find the highest and lowest. Here is the first refinement of the second step:

Determine the range
- Find the highest
- Find the lowest
- Let range = highest - lowest

If we were to find the range of tests without the aid of a computer (easier with a small collection of tests), we might glance at each test in a list of test scores and simply keep track of the highest test and lowest test as we scan from top to bottom:

Tests	Highest	Lowest
80	80	80
82	82	"
71	"	71
95	95	"
82	"	"

Range = Highest - Lowest = 95 - 71 = 24

For a large list of tests—an approach more suited to a computer—we implement an algorithm that mimics this noncomputer-based solution. We can start by inputting the first test score and making it the highest so far and also the lowest so far.

Algorithm	C++ Code
Obtain the number of test scores (the size of the list)	`cin >> testsToCheck ;`
<u>Determine the range</u>	`// Determine highest test`
Input the first test	`cin >> test;`
Record the first test as the highest test input so far	`highestTest = test;`
Record the first test as the lowest test input so far	`lowestTest = test;`
...	`. . .`

We finish the second step of the original algorithm using our knowledge of repetitive and selective control structures. Each remaining test is input and compared to the highest test and to the lowest test, making changes to the highest and lowest wherever appropriate.

Algorithm	C++ Code
<u>Determine the range</u>	
Input the first test	`cin >> test;`
Record the first test as the highest test input so far	`highestTest = test;`
Record the first test as the lowest test input so far	`lowestTest = test;`
while there are more tests to check	*while there are more tests to check*
	`{`
Input test	`cin >> test;`
If test is greater than highest,	`if(test > highestTest)`
store it as the highest	`highestTest = test;`
If test is less than highest,	`if(test < lowestTest)`
store it as the lowest	`lowestTest = test;`
	`}`
range = highest - lowest	`range = highest - lowest;`

The algorithmic statement in the right column above, *while there are more tests to check*, will be replaced with appropriate C++ code for counter-controlled loops in the implementation section.

6.2.3   Implementation

Since the problem stated that we are to be supplied with the number of tests (`cin >> testToCheck;`), we are able to determine the exact number of repetitions before the repeated steps are to occur. Therefore, we should consider the counter-controller loop template. The counter can be compared to `testsToCheck` like this (`testsToCheck` is used here in place of n):

```
while(counter <= testsToCheck)
```

To bring the counter-controlled loop closer to loop termination the `counter` must be incremented inside the loop like this:

```
counter = counter + 1;
```

But since the first test is input and assigned to `highestTest` and `lowestTest` before the loop, we should start the `counter` at 2 instead of 1:

```
int counter = 2;
```

The following program implements the algorithm shown above along with the counter-controlled loop. Notice that we need not input the same tests twice—the checks are made for both the highest and the lowest within one `while` loop.

```cpp
// Determine the range of test scores in a set of known size
#include <iostream.h>

int main()
{
  int test, highestTest, lowestTest;
  int testsToCheck;
  cout << "Enter number of test scores: ";
  cin >> testsToCheck;
  cout << endl << "Enter test scores 1 per line" << endl;

  // Input first test to record it as highest and lowest
  cin >> test;
  highestTest = test;
  lowestTest = test;

  // We have processed one check, so start counter at 2.
  int counter = 2;
  while(counter <= testsToCheck)
  {
    cin >> test;
    if(test > highestTest)
      highestTest = test;
    if(test < lowestTest)
      lowestTest = test;
    counter = counter + 1;
  }

  int range = highestTest - lowestTest;
  cout << "Range: " << range;
  return 0;
}
```

6.2.4 Test the Implementation

Testing could be performed by finding the range of many lists and comparing them with hand-checked results. For example, values that are all the same should show a range of zero. With two tests to check, the range should be computed as the positive difference between those two values. We should try to input one value and verify the range is also zero. We should also try a set of values where the size of the set is greater than 2. This leads to many possible tests, especially if the same numbers are input in all possible orders. Three inputs have 6 orders, four inputs have 24 orders, and in general n inputs have n! orders (n * (n–1) * (n–2) *,..., * 3 * 2 * 1). Such exhaustive testing is not only impractical, it is also unnecessary. We do gain some confidence in the algorithm by picking an arbitrary number of tests as shown here:

```
Enter number of test scores: 5

Enter test scores 1 per line.
76
82
97
61
88
Range:  36
```

We glance at the list, and find the difference between the highest and lowest (97–61) to determine the range as 36. Looking at the dialogue and seeing the range is 36 leads us to believe that the algorithm and implementation are correct. However, all we can be sure of is this: when these particular five tests are entered, the correct range is displayed. The data used in this previous test of our algorithm seems to indicate that everything is okay, but to paraphrase E.W. Dijkstra, such tests can only reveal the presence of errors, not the absence of errors. If the range were shown as obviously incorrect answers such as 0 or -36, we might spot the presence of the error. In this case, it is useful to display the key high and low values for each loop iteration. In general, a good loop debugging tool involves output of key values for each loop iteration. A few cout insertions can be very revealing.

We should also consider what happens if the user enters 0 or a negative number when prompted for the number of tests to check. The implementation shown above does not gracefully handle these unusual—yet certainly possible—extractions for testsToCheck. This implementation could be made more robust with the addition of an if...else statement that notifies the user of invalid entry when the number of inputs is less than 1.

```
cout << "Enter number of test scores: ";
cin >> testsToCheck;
if(testToCheck < 1)
  cout << "Input error for number of test scores" << endl;
else
{
  cout << endl << "Enter test scores 1 per line" << endl;
// ...
```

Further still, consider input of a bad numeric value. This puts the input stream in a bad state—subsequent input is ignored. This could happen during any cin extraction. Later in this chapter we will see how to fix cin after its state is reset to BAD due to invalid numeric input.

Self-Check

The following questions refer to the implementation of the range problem in Section 6.2.3.

1. What would happen if we initialize counter to 1 before the loop rather than 2 as shown?
2. What would happen if we forget to increment counter inside the loop?
3. What would happen if we forget to obtain the number of testsToCheck?
4. Some programmers implement a solution as shown below. Trace through the program using the same input as shown above (76, 82, 97, 61, 88) and predict the value stored in range. Is it correct?

```cpp
#include <iostream.h>
int main()
{
  //PRE:  Works only for values in the range [-999, 999]
  int testsToCheck;
  cout << "Enter number of test scores: ";
  cin >> testsToCheck;
  int highestTest = -999;
  int lowestTest  =  999;
  int test;
  cout << endl << "Enter test scores 1 per line" << endl;
  while(testsToCheck > 0)
  {
    cin >> test;
    if(test > highestTest)
      highestTest = test;
    else if(test < lowestTest)
      lowestTest = test;
    testsToCheck = testsToCheck - 1;
  }
  int range = highestTest - lowestTest;
  cout << "Range: " << range;
  return 0;
}
```

5. Testing the program above should indicate it worked for the given test set, but trace through the program with these test scores and determine the value stored in range. Enter 5 for the number of test scores.

```
100
90
80
70
60
```

Is the range correct?

6. Testing the program above indicates it appears to works. But trace through the program with these same test scores extracted in *reverse* order. Predict the value stored in range. Enter 5 for the number of test scores.

```
60
70
80
90
100
```

Is the range correct?

7. After the detection of a bug, we have to locate the source. Carefully trace the code again and write the values for the lowestTest and highestTest. Which one is incorrect?

8. When is range incorrectly computed?
   a.   When the input is in descending order.
   b.   When the input is in ascending order.
   c.   When the input is in neither ascending or descending order.

9. What must be done to correct the error?

Answers

1. We would have to enter an extra test that is not part of the set to terminate the loop.
2. We have an infinite loop.
3. We have a loop that iterates an unknown number of times (0, 12, 5000, or whatever).
4. 36. Yes, this is the correct range for the data supplied.
5. 40. Yes.
6. -899. No.
7. lowestTest is incorrect. It is still -999.
8. When the input is in ascending order.
9. *Answer intentionally omitted.*

6.3   Event-Controlled Loops

An *event-controlled loop* repeats its iterative part until some event occurs to terminate the loop. Whereas the number of repetitions for counter-controlled loops is known before the while statement begins to execute, event-controlled loops use other methods for loop termination. With event-controlled loops, it is not necessary to know the number of repetitions that should occur before the while loop begins to execute.

Sometimes we need to write code that will execute a set of statements an unspecified number of times, for example, when processing report cards for every student in a school, where the number of students changes from year to year and even during the year. We cannot depend on prior knowledge of the exact number of repetitions. It is more convenient to think in terms of "process a report card for all students" rather than "process a report card for 892 students." An event-controlled loop is one that depends on the occurrence of some particular event to terminate the loop, such as a sentinel value.

6.3.1   Sentinel Loops

A *sentinel* is a specific predetermined value used to terminate one type of event-controlled loop. The sentinel is the same type as the other extracted data. However it is not a valid part of that input data. It is a special value used only to terminate the event-controlled loop. For example, the int constant -1 can be used as a sentinel when all valid data must be greater than or equal to zero. A message is usually displayed to the user so he or she will know how to indicate the end of data input. The user must be informed that a sentinel is being used and what that sentinel value must be. For example, the following program sums integers while the input is not the sentinel value of -1.

```cpp
// Use a sentinel of -1 to terminate a loop. A sentinel is a value
// that cannot be within the range of valid data. It is the final
// input indicating there is no more data. The extraction of this
// sentinel value is the event that terminates the loop.

#include <iostream.h>

int main()
{
  // PRE:  The user enters at least one valid int != -1
  const int sentinel = -1;
  int testScore;
  float accumulator = 0;
  int n = 0;   // Incremented for every input != -1
```

```
// Display a prompt
cout << "Enter test scores or " << sentinel
     << " to quit" << endl;
// This next statement is used to obtain a value for the loop-test
cin >> testScore;
while(testScore != sentinel)
{
  accumulator = accumulator
               + testScore;   // Update the accumulator
   n = n + 1;                  // Update total inputs
   cin >> testScore;          // Input next test or the sentinel
}
cout << endl
     << "Average of " << n << " tests = "
     << (accumulator / n)
     << endl;
  return 0;
}
```

────────────────────── **Dialogue** ──────────────────────

```
Enter test scores or -1 to quit
70
80
90
-1

Average of 3 tests = 80
```

6.3.2 Priming Extraction

There are two cin statements in the preceding program, both used to obtain keyboard input. The first cin extraction occurs immediately before the while loop. The second cin extraction is the last statement in the iterative part. In both cases, cin >> testscore executes immediately before the loop test. The first cin is required to initialize the object testScore before it is used in the loop-test (testScore!=sentinel). This is called a *priming extraction*. If the first input is -1, the loop-test evaluates to false, the iterative part never executes, and sum correctly remains 0. Any other positive integer or zero causes the loop body to execute. The first cin extraction is called a priming extraction because it exists only to initialize objects used in the loop test for the first repetition—it gets the loop going. If a priming extraction is not used in a sentinel loop, unpredictable errors may occur.

The placement of both cin statements in sentinel loops is also important. Consider the following modification to this sentinel loop using the same input:

```
cout << "Enter test scores or -1 to quit" << endl;
cin >> testScore;
while(testScore != sentinel)
{
  cin >> testScore;              // Input a test or the sentinel
  accumulator =  accumulator
               + testScore;  // Update the accumulator
}
cout << "Sum: " << accumulator;
```

────────────────── **Dialogue** ──────────────────

```
Enter test scores or -1 to quit
2
4
6
8
-1
Sum: 17
```

Although 2 + 4 + 6 + 8 is 20, the sum has been incorrectly computed here as 17. The reason: This modified loop places cin >> testScore at an incorrect location. A new testScore is entered as input immediately after the loop test is evaluated rather than immediately before. Even though the first integer is 2, this intended input is overwritten by the second cin extraction before it is added to the accumulator. But then shouldn't the output be 18? Verify that the sum is 17 by stepping through the code. You should find that in addition to the loss of the first int, the sentinel of -1 is improperly added to the sum.

Programming Tip ──

When using a priming extraction for a sentinel loop, it is most common to have the other cin extraction placed at the end of the loop. Here is a rule of thumb that helps avoid intent errors: place both cin statements immediately before the loop-test is evaluated. The priming cin that extracts the first value must immediately precede the while loop. Place the cin statement extracts at the end of the iterative part. This prevents loss of the first input and the improper processing of the sentinel.

```
cin >> testScore;   // Priming extraction
while(testScore != sentinel)
{
  accumulator = accumulator
              + testScore;    // Update the accumulator
  n = n + 1;                  // Update number of inputs
  cin >> testScore;           // Input remaining tests or sentinel
}
```

6.3.3   Using the Extraction Event for Loop Termination

Up to this point we have often used the insertion operator >> for input but ignored the fact that the state of the input stream is returned at the same time. Nonzero (true) is returned if the input operation found a constant of the proper type. If the input operation was not successful, zero (false) is returned. This means that an extraction itself may exist as a test expression in an if...else or while statement:

```
if(cin >> intObject)    or    while(cin >> intObject)
```

Both tests return true (nonzero) when cin successfully extracts a valid int. However, both tests return false (zero) if an invalid int is encountered.

> **Programming Tip**
>
> Many C++ programmers use the shortcut expression for the if and while statements just shown. When the cin operation (cin >> intObject) is successful, the state of the input stream is returned as nonzero or true. When unsuccessful, the input stream state is 0, so false is returned. The expressions used in if and while statements are also written using this more readable longhand form as follows:
>
> ```
> if((cin >> intObject) != 0)    /*or*/    while((cin >> intObject) != 0)
> ```

With this new information we can simplify sentinel loops by moving the cin extraction into the loop test. In this case only one cin statement is necessary.

```
// The priming extraction is now part of the loop test
while( ((cin >> testScore)!=0) && (testScore != sentinel) )
{
  accumulator = accumulator
              + testScore;  // Update the accumulator
  n = n + 1;                // Update total inputs
}
```

Now the entire loop test is evaluated before the iterative part executes. The first expression, cin >> testscore, is true (nonzero) if a valid integer value is input. Next we see testScore compared to the sentinel. The loop test is evaluated in the following order, assuming 95 is input:

```
// Testscore is input as 95
while( ((cin >> testScore)!=0) && (testScore != sentinel) )
               true        && (  95   !=   -1  )
               true        &&         true
                    true
```

After applying `&&` to the two expressions, we obtain a true loop-test. When the sentinel of -1 is entered, the loop test is false—the termination condition is reached. Because the `testScore` is compared to the `sentinel` before the iterative part executes, improper processing of the `sentinel` is avoided.

```
// Testscore is input as -1
while( ((cin >> testScore)!=0) && (testScore != sentinel) )
                true        && (  -1    !=   -1  )
                true        &&              false
                        false
```

6.3.4 Clearing Input Streams

After the state of the `cin` is reset from good to bad because of invalid numeric input, we can no longer extract input from that input stream—all subsequent extractions attempts will fail. To make our programs more robust the input stream must be fixed when the user enters bad data. This may be done with the `flush` function declared in `ourstuff.h`. Here is its prototype:

```
void flush(istream & is);
// POST: Resets an istream object (cin, for example) to a good state
//       while clearing any extraneous characters from the stream
```

The implementation uses some features that we have not covered, so it is not supplied here (you can view the implementation of the `flush` function in `ourstuff.cpp` if you wish). Instead, the function is used in the following bit of code to clear the input stream `cin` after BAD is encountered:

```
// Demonstrate what happens when an input stream is in an error state
#include <iostream.h>
#include "ourstuff.h"  // for flush(cin)

int main()
{
  double testScore;
  double sum = 0;
  double n = 0;

  cout << "Enter test scores or -1 to quit" << endl;
  while( ((cin >> testScore)!= 0) && (testScore != -1) )
  {
    sum = sum + testScore;
    n = n + 1;
  }
  cout << "Ave: " << (sum / n) << endl;
```

```
// Demonstrate flush(cin) to allow further input
// ...
flush(cin);
cout << "Enter another testScore: ";
cin >> testScore;
cout << "testScore: " << testScore << endl;
cout << "and one more: ";
cin >> testScore;
cout << "testScore: " << testScore << endl;
return 0;
}
```

---------------------------------- **Dialogue** ----------------------------------

```
Enter test scores or -1 to quit
98
94
BAD
Ave: 96
Enter another testScore: 88
testScore: 88
and one more: 77
testScore: 77
```

The dialogue indicates that the two cin extractions (88 and 77) performed successfully. But if the function call flush(cin) is not included, the attempt to input BAD as a valid double sets cin to a bad state. In this case, the user notices that no further extractions are performed. This is indicated by the following dialogue:

---------------------------------- **Dialogue** ----------------------------------

```
Enter test scores or -1 to quit
98
94
BAD
Ave: 96
Enter another testScore: testScore: 94
and one more: testScore: 94
```

On two occasions, cin >> testScore fails to cause a pause and extract a numeric value.

Event-controlled loops take on many different forms. Shortly, we will see an event-controlled loop that shuts down a specific ATM. We will also see another event-controlled loop that terminates when the user chooses the quit option from the ATM menu system.

6.3.5 Using the End of File Event for Loop Termination

The eof function—available to ifstream and istream objects—returns true when the end of file event has been encountered on the input stream. At other times, the eof function returns false. For example, if the file input.dat is successfully opened with this constructor call:

```
ifstream inFile("input.dat");  // or   inFile = "input.dat";
```

then the value returned by eof can be shown with this statement:

```
cout << inFile.eof();     // Output: 0
```

If there is data in the file named input.dat, inFile.eof() returns false. The eof function returns true when there is no more data in the file (or the file was not found) after extracting all the ints from a file of integer data, or all the strings from a file of text data, for example.

This eof function is an event that can be used to implement a useful type of event-controlled loop. We can use it to process all data in a file without knowing the amount of data in that file. This is shown in the following program where the eof function is part of the loop test. When eof returns false, we have an input stream object with more data (! false is true). When eof returns true, there is no more input data to process (! true is false).

```
! inFile.eof() // True while end of file is not reached on inFile
```

This loop-test will be true as long as there is more string data to extract. When the end of file is reached through repeated extraction of the strings, the loop-test fails and the loop is terminated. The loop-test is false when the end of the input stream has been reached. As long as there is one more string in the file, the loop-test is true and a string is successfully extracted. In order to visualize this loop action, each successfully extracted string object is converted to its uppercase equivalent and then displayed on its own line.

```
#include <fstream.h>
#include <iostream.h>
#include "ourstr.h"

int main()
{
  ifstream inFile("input.dat");
  cout << "Before loop, eof = " << inFile.eof() << endl;
  string s;
```

```
while(! inFile.eof())
{
  inFile >> s;
  s.toUpper();
  cout << "s = " << s << endl;
}
cout << " After loop, eof = " << inFile.eof() << endl;
return 0;
}
```

When the file named "input.dat" contains this data:

```
Several strings
on two lines.
```

the output indicates the state of the ifstream object before and after the extractions:

```
──────────── Output ────────────
Before loop, eof = 0
s = SEVERAL
s = STRINGS
s = ON
s = TWO
s = LINES.
 After loop, eof = 1
```

6.3.6 (*Optional*) Using eof() with cin

To use the same type of logic to extract keyboard input with cin, we have to know something about the operating system. The end of file sequence is entered from the keyboard using Ctrl-Z with DOS or (usually) Ctrl-D in UNIX. So we could also process keyboard input until end of file.

```
// Use the eof function with keyboard input
#include <iostream.h>

int main()
{
  double x, sum = 0.0;
  cout << "Enter doubles, Ctrl-D (UNIX), or Ctrl-Z (DOS), to quit"
       << endl;
  while((! cin.eof()) && cin >> x)
  {
    sum = sum + x;
  }
  cout << "Sum: " << sum << endl;
  return 0;
}
```

Dialogue

```
Enter doubles, Ctrl-D (UNIX), or Ctrl-Z (DOS), to quit
1.2
3.4
^Z
Sum: 4.6
```

Programming Tip

The end of file event may be entered from the keyboard. This allows `cin.eof()` to return a meaningful value for end of file loops where data is entered from the keyboard. The actual key sequence varies between operating systems. In UNIX, end of file is usually indicated with the key sequence Ctrl-D (appears as `^D`). But it may be set to something different. Use the `stty` (or `stty -a` or `stty all`) command to verify what is used as the end of file key sequence on your UNIX system. In DOS and MS-Windows, Ctrl-Z (appears as `^Z`) may be used as the end of file key sequence that makes `cin.eof()` return `true`. A word of warning: The end of file event sets the state of the input stream such that subsequent keyboard input is ignored unless some extra work is performed such as calling `flush(cin)`.

6.3.7 (*Optional*) Another eof Loop with Disk File Input

If we know exactly how data is stored in a file, we can write event-controlled loops to read and process a line of data where each line contains a large number of data fields. This process continues until the end of file is reached and there is no more data to process. These end of file loops are capable of processing an unspecified number of inputs with data that need not be entered from the keyboard. Another advantage of disk file input with the end of file event as the termination condition is this: The number of iterations depends on the size of the file. We can write code that effectively processes all the employees in a file whether there are 0, 1, 2, or many employees. For example, if the file `employee.dat` contains the following data:

```
Demlow Mary        40    8.88  1 S
Barrister Harvey   42    7.77  2 M
Manuala Ho          0   10.00  3 M
Kline Sue          38    9.99  0 S
```

an `eof` controlled loop should process exactly four employees. The same code should also work with files of different sizes (different numbers of employees). This is an advantage over counter-controlled loops that require that the number of iterations be known before the `while` loop begins to execute. Another advantage of using the end of file event with disk files is the time gained from not typing in all the data.

The next program implements an event-controlled loop using the end of file event as the termination condition. Inside the loop, a weeklyEmp object is extracted from inFile. At that point, a few weeklyEmp member functions show the gross pay and name of each employee on file. This algorithm provides an outline of the execution:

Algorithm

Process All Employees
  While there is more employee data in the file, do the following:
    Input all data from one line in the file. This data represents one employee.
    Store data as the state of one weeklyEmp object.
    Use two weeklyEmp member functions: grossPay() and name().

```cpp
// This program reads data from an input file to alter one weeklyEmp
// object just long enough to produce a simple payroll report
// of the gross pay and the name of each employee in the disk file.

#include <fstream.h>    // class ifstream
#include <iostream.h>   // class ostream and cout
#include "ouremp.h"     // class weeklyEmp
#include "ourstuff.h"   // decimals(cout, 2);

int main()
{
  weeklyEmp emp;

  // Initialize an input stream with a disk file as the source
  ifstream inFile("payroll.dat");

  // Show error if the file "payroll.dat" is not found on the disk
  if(! inFile)
    cout << "**Error opening file 'payroll.dat'" << endl;

  // Set output format
  cout.fill('*');
  decimals(cout, 2);
  cout << "Gross Pay   Name" << endl << endl;

  // Process data until end of file
  while(! inFile.eof())
  {
    // Extract data from inFile to initialize one weeklyEmp object
    inFile >> emp;
    // Show return values of two weeklyEmp member functions
    cout.width(9);
    cout << emp.grossPay() << "    " << emp.name() << endl;
  }
  return 0;
}
```

```
┌──────────────────────── Output ────────────────────────┐
│                                                         │
│   Gross Pay   Name                                      │
│                                                         │
│   ***355.20   DEMLOW, MARY                              │
│   ***334.11   BARRISTER, HARVEY                         │
│   *****0.00   MANUALA, HO                               │
│   ***379.62   KLINE, SUE                                │
│                                                         │
└─────────────────────────────────────────────────────────┘
```

Notice the output shows exactly four employees were processed. Had the disk file contained a different number of employees, a different size report would have been generated without any change to the program or the need to count the number of lines in the file.

Programming Tip

Use the ! operator with the `ifstream` object to detect if there was an error trying to find and/or open the file. The ! operator is overloaded to return `true` if the file object was not opened. There are many reasons for this: a path may be specified incorrectly, a disk may be bad, there may be an improper match of upper- and lowercase letters (in UNIX), or the file simply may not exist as supplied by the argument to the `ifstream` constructor. For example, if the file was not successfully opened in the previous program we would have seen this message:

```
**Error opening file 'payroll.dat'
```

6.3.8 Loop Termination with break

The keyword `break` is used to jump out of `switch` statements and terminate loops. For sentinel loops, the `break` statement improves on the priming extraction approach shown earlier. With those, two extractions were required along with a loop continuation test— the logical negation of the termination condition. This complicates the implementation of event-controlled loops.

When `break` exists as the true part of an `if` statement inside the loop, only one extraction is required. To make things even simpler, the logical expression is the termination condition! Negating the terminating condition logic is not necessary. This simplifies the implementation of event-controlled loops.

The following program has a loop that terminates if the end of file or a negative integer is encountered during a stream extraction. In either case, the logical expression is true, `break` executes, and the `while` loop control structure terminates. Without `break`, we have an infinite loop because the loop-test 1 is a constant value that can never become false.

```
// Demonstrate break for loop termination
#include <iostream.h>

int main ()
{
  int test;
  int n = 0;
  cout << "Enter tests. Use a negative int or end of file to quit."
       << endl;
  while(1)
  { // Without break; this is an infinite loop, 1 is always true
    cin >> test;
    if(cin.eof() || test < 0)  // Terminate loop on either event
      break;
    n = n + 1;
  }
  cout << "Number of tests = " << n << endl;

  return 0;
}
```

──────────────────── **Dialogue** ────────────────────

```
Enter tests. Use a negative int or end of file to quit.
85
95
91
-1
Number of tests = 3
```

Notice that the loop termination conditions are coded directly in the if statement.

```
if(cin.eof() || test < 0)  // Terminate loop on either event
  break;
```

Once inside the loop and immediately after the input of any test, the if statement checks to see if either one of the two terminating events occurred:

1. A negative int was input.
2. The end of file key sequence was entered from the keyboard.

The break statement simplifies loop termination, especially with nested loops like the one in the final phase of the bank control program (see Section 6.5).

Self-Check

1. Write the output of the following program assuming the data stored in the file in.dat is

   a. 1 2 3

   b. 1 2 3 4 5.789

   c. 1 2 3 BAD

```
#include <fstream.h>    // for class ifstream
#include <iostream.h>   // for cout
int main()
{
   ifstream inFile("in.dat");
   int sum = 0;
   int intObject;
   while( (inFile >> intObject) != 0 )
   {
      sum = sum + intObject;
   }
   cout << sum << endl;
   return 0;
}
```

2. Write a statement that will inform us the file in.dat was not opened correctly.

3. Write the expression that returns true if end of file has been reached on inFile.

4. Write the expression that returns true if end of file has *not* been reached on inFile.

5. Associate the identifier empFile with the file employee.dat of the working (current) directory.

6. List two events that may terminate an event-controlled loop.

7. Write a complete program that displays the average of the floats in the file called float.dat. This file is known in UNIX as /user/magulla and in DOS as c:\magulla. The average should be correct even when the same program reads the same file with different data.

8. Write the complete dialogue of the following program when the user enters 1, 2, 3, and 4 on separate lines.

```
#include <iostream.h>
int main()
{
   int test;
   int sum = 0;
   cout << "Enter tests or -1 to quit: " << endl;
```

```
    while(1)
    {
      cin >> test;
      if(test == -1)
        break;
      sum = sum + test;
    }
    cout << "Sum: " << sum;
  }
```

Answers

1. a. 6   b. 15 (.789 causes loop termination)   c. 6 (BAD causes loop termination)
2. `if (!inFile) cout << "Not found";`
3. `inFile.eof();`
4. `! inFile.eof()`
5. `ifstream empFile("employee.dat");  or  ifstream empfile = "employee.dat"`
6. Extraction of a sentinel value, end of file, bad numeric data, an external interrupt such as Ctrl-C
7.
```
#include <fstream.h>
#include <iostream.h>
int main()
{
  float x;
  float sum = 0;
  int n = 0;
  // In UNIX:
  ifstream inFile("/user/magulla/float.dat");
  // In DOS:
  // ifstream inFile("c:\\magulla\\float.dat");
  if(! inFile) cout << "**Error** float.dat not open" << endl;
  while((inFile >> x) != 0)
  {
    sum = sum + x;
    n = n + 1;
  }
  cout << "Average: " << (sum / n) << endl;
  return 0;
}
```
8.
```
Enter tests or -1 to quit:
1
2
3
4
-1
Sum: 10
```

6.4   More Nested Logic

As previously discussed in Chapter 5, nested logic refers to the use of one control structure nested inside another similar control structure. Specifically, nested logic refers to the occurrence of a selection control structure containing another selection control structure—an `if...else` embedded in another `if...else`, for example. Nested logic also refers to a repetitive control structure embedded within another repetitive control structure—a `while` loop nested within another `while` loop, for example. This form of logic is found in algorithms encountered in the study of computer science. Consider the following program segment, which has an outer `while` loop that repeats three times. The number of inner loop iterations changes from one to two to three as the inner loops are encountered on three separate executions.

```
// This code illustrates nested logic with while loops
int inner, outer;

// Begin an outer loop that executes the iterative part three times.
// Notice outer=outer+1 occurs as the last statement of the outer loop.
outer = 1;
while(outer <= 3)
{
  cout << endl << endl
       << "Outer loop repetition #" << outer << endl;
  // Begin nested loop that repeats once, then twice, then thrice

  inner = 1;
  while(inner <= outer)
  {
    cout << outer << "  " << inner << endl;
    // Increment the inner loop counter
    inner = inner + 1;
  } // The end of the nested loop

  // Increment the outer loop counter
  outer = outer + 1;
} // The end of the outer loop
```

───────────────── **Output** ─────────────────

```
Outer loop repetition #1
1  1

Outer loop repetition #2
2  1
2  2
```

```
Outer loop repetition #3
3  1
3  2
3  3
```

A form of nested while loops will be used in the next case study to allow multiple bank customers to perform multiple transactions.

Self-Check

1. Write the output produced by these nested while loops:

a.
```
int j, k;
j = 1;
while(j <= 2)
{
  k = 1;
  while(k <= 3)
  {
    cout << j << "  " << k
        << endl;
    k = k + 1;
  }
  j = j + 1;
}
```

c.
```
int j, k;
j = 1;
while(j < 5)
{
  k = 7;
  while(k > 1)
  {
    cout << j << "  "
        << k << endl;
    k = k - 3;
  }
  j = j + 2;
}
```

b.
```
int inner, outer;
outer = 1;
while(outer <= 3)
{
  inner = 1;
  while(inner <= outer)
  {
    cout << inner << "  "
        << outer << endl;
    inner = inner + 1;
  }
  outer = outer + 1;
}
```

d.
```
#include <iostream.h>
int main()
{
  int j = 0;
  while(1)
  {
    if(j > 5 )
      break;
    cout << "  " << j;
    j = j + 1;
  }
}
```

Answers

1.	a.		b.		c.		d.						
	1 1		1 1		1 7		0 1 2 3 4 5					
	1 2		1 2		1 4						
	1 3		2 2		3 7						
	2 1		1 3		3 4						
	2 2		2 3							
	2 3		3 3							

6.5 Case Study: Bank Control, Final Phase

In this case study, nested `while` loops help implement the final phase of the bank control program.

6.5.1 Analysis

Problem: *Allow ATM customers to perform as many banking transactions as desired. Let the ATM run virtually forever. The transactions are limited to the withdrawal, deposit, and balance query operations that are available through interacting bank and ATM class member functions.*

6.5.2 Design

This first stab at an algorithm:

> *while there are more customers*
> *   process one customer*

indicates nested logic is necessary because processing one customer requires another loop to allow for multiple transactions:

> *while there are more customers*
> *   while there are more transactions*
> *   process the transaction requested by the user*

The problem specification states that the ATM should stay running forever (virtually). The following outer loop allows an unlimited number of customers. This loop never terminates because the constant 1 is the loop-test and 1 is always nonzero, or true.

> *// Process multiple customers with an infinite loop*
> *while(1)*
> *{*
> *   get the next customer*
> *   if the customer is not found*
> *   notify customer of invalid name/PIN entry*
> *   else*
> *   while there are more transactions*
> *   process the transaction requested by the user*
> *}*

After customer verification, the inner loop should allow the customer to process as many automated transactions as desired. These two nested `while` loops allow many customers to process many transactions.

It should be noted that the only events that would terminate the outer loop include turning the computer off or terminating the program with Ctrl-C or Ctrl-Break. But this situation improves with a more graceful way to shut down the ATM (see Lab Project 6E).

6.5.3   Implementation

To allow multiple transaction requests, we could use a sentinel as the inner loop. A call to the `ATM::nextTransaction` member function requests the next transaction from the user, setting transaction to either a `'W'`, `'D'`, `'B'` or `'Q'`. To use `'Q'` as the sentinel to quit processing, we need a priming extraction and another `getTransaction` extraction at the bottom of the loop.

```
// Inner Loop: Process multiple transactions
moneyMachine.getTransaction(transaction);    // Priming extraction
while(option != 'Q')
{
  // Process a valid transaction
  // ...

  moneyMachine.getTransaction(transaction); // For the next iteration
}
```

Or we could use the `break` statement to simplify this `while` loop implementation. In this case, `getTransaction` need only be called once, as one of the first statements inside another infinite loop. The difference now is this: the `break` statement inside the loop body is executed when the customer enters `'Q'`. This effectively terminates the otherwise infinite loop. If `transaction` is one of the other codes, the loop continues to execute the remainder of its compound statement to process the appropriate transaction.

```
// This is the final implementation of the bank control program
#include "ouratm.h"    // for class ATM
#include "ourbank.h"   // for class bank

int main()
{
  ATM  moneyMachine;    // Customer interface for getting transactions
  bank firstBank;       // Collection of bankAccount objects
  int customerNumber;   // Set to the customer number if valid
```

```
    // An infinite loop to process virtually unlimited customers
    while(1) // Begin outer while loop
    {
      moneyMachine.getNameAndPIN();
      int found;
      firstBank.findCustomer(moneyMachine, customerNumber, found);
      if(! found)
        moneyMachine.message("Invalid name/pin combination");
      else
      {
        while(1) // Begin inner while loop
        {
          char transaction;
          moneyMachine.getTransaction(transaction);

          // Terminate inner loop if transaction is changed to 'Q'
          if(transaction == 'Q')
            break;

          // Otherwise, process the valid transaction
          // ...
        } // End inner while loop
      } // End else
    } // End outer while loop

    return 0;
} // End of function main()
```

Although this algorithm could be assigned to the bank or ATM class as a member function, the entire implementation was given as a main function that uses the bank and ATM classes. It acts as the adhesive for these two collaborating classes.

6.5.4 Test the Implementation

Testing the implementation is specified as Lab Project 6E.

Exercises

1. How many times will "Hello" be displayed using the following program segments, assuming j is an int with an unassigned value?

a.
```
while(j <= 10)
    cout << "Hello";
```

b.
```
j = 7;
while(j <= 1)
{
    cout << "Hello";
}
```

c. ```
    j = 1;
    while(j <= 7)
    {
      cout << "Hello";
      j = j + 2;
    }
    ```

d.  ```
    j = 1;
    while(j <= 5)
      cout << "Hello";
      j = j + 1;
    ```

2. Write the output from the following program.

```
#include <iostream.h>
int main()
{
  int j = 0;
  while(j < 5)
  {
    cout << "  " << j;
    j = j + 1;
  }
  return 0;
}
```

3. Write a while loop that produces this output:

```
   -4  -3  -2  -1  0  1  2  3  4  5  6
```

4. Write a while loop that sums all the integers between start and stop inclusive that are input from the keyboard. You may assume start is always less than or equal to stop. If the input were 5 for start and 10 for stop, the sum would be 5 + 6 + 7 + 8 + 9 + 10 (45).

5. Write an event-controlled loop that counts the number of words contained in the file named eng15.doc. A word is any collection of characters separated by spaces, tabs, or newlines. For example, there are six words in the following sentence:

```
        Here's a word, another,
      and another.
```

Recall that string constants are separated in input streams by blanks and newlines.

6. Write a while loop that displays 100, 95, ..., 5, 0 on separate lines.

7. Write a sentinel event-controlled loop that counts the number of 100s entered from the keyboard. Make sure the user understands how to terminate the loop.

8. Write an eof event-controlled loop that counts the number of 100s entered from the keyboard.

Lab Projects

6A   Using Objects

Write a program that determines the lowest, highest, and average of a set of wind speed readings. Prompt the user for the number of wind speed readings in the set. Use a counter-controlled `while` loop.

```
Enter number of wind speed readings: 4
3
6
1
4

    N: 4
High: 6
 Low: 1
 Ave: 3.5
```

6B   Using Objects

Write a program that determines the lowest, highest, and average of a set of wind speed readings, which are all positive or zero. Terminate the loop with a sentinel of -1. Be sure you notify the user how to terminate data entry. The following is a sample dialogue. The user is told to enter -1 to quit:

```
Enter wind speed readings or -1 to quit:
3
6
1
4
-1

    N: 4
High: 6
 Low: 1
 Ave: 3.5
```

6C   Using Objects

Write a program that determines the lowest, highest, and average of a set of wind speed readings from a file. The number of readings is not known in advance. First create a file in your working (current) directory as `wind.dat` and use the `ifstream` constructor to open the file for input as follows:

```
ifstream inFile("wind.dat");  // Call ifstream constructor
```

The program should work for all files containing only ints so any number of inputs should produce correct results. Run your program with the following file called wind.dat. Verify that the output is correct by producing results by hand and comparing your output. Use an event-controlled eof while loop.

```
 2  6  1  2  5
 5  4  3 12 16
10 11 12 13 14
```

Once you have verified the program with the test oracle started above, delete the third line and run the program again to verify the hand-checked results match program output.

6D   Using Objects

In this lab project you are asked to use an existing class as the basis for a payroll program that processes many employees. The input data to be processed is stored in an external file with the following format:

Field Name	Columns	Description
firstName, lastName	1-20	The employee's first and last names (*Note:* Two objects are required as all input is separated by blanks. The names may be concatenated.)
hoursWorked	21-24	Number of hours the employee worked in a week.
hourlyRate	26-30	Pay in U.S. dollars for each hour worked.
exemptions	32-33	Number of exemptions claimed on the employee's W-4 form.
filingStatus	35	The IRS filing status where 'S' means single or head of household filing status and 'M' means married filing status.

Example input file:

```
Ross Greene        38.0 10.45  4 M
Mary Kristner      42.0 12.00  0 S
Mellisa Nicholson  30.5  9.99  1 S
Samuel Woodley     40.0 11.57  1 S
```

Create a report saved in a DOS file that looks like the following (with ? replaced by the correct answers, of course). Also show all totals for every category except the total pay rate.

Employee Name	Hours Worked	Pay Rate	Gross Pay	Income Tax	FICA Tax	Net Pay
====================	=====	=====	======	======	=====	=========
Greene, Ross	38.0	10.45	397.10	14.60	30.38	352.12
Kristner, Mary	42.0	?	?	?	?	?
Nicholson, Mellisa	30.5	?	?	?	?	?
Woodley, Samuel	40.0	?	?	?	?	?
Totals	140.5		??????.??	????.??	????.??	??????.??

Either write all code from scratch or use the weeklyEmp class declared in ouremp.h and discussed in Section 5.6: "Case Study: U. S. Income Tax." Recall that a weeklyEmp object is constructed as follows:

```
weeklyEmp emp1("Len Fourth", 40, 9.50, 4, 'm');
```

where the arguments represent these values: name, hours worked, pay rate, exemptions, and filing status, respectively. You can also use an infile >> emp operation.

6E   Bank Control Program—Phase Three

Note: Before starting this lab project, complete the second phase of the bank control program, Lab Project 5G. Verify that your implementation satisfies the test oracle given there.

Using the problem specification of Section 6.5, "Case Study: Bank Control, Final Phase," implement the final phase of the bank control program—a program that allows multiple customers to conclude multiple banking transactions with an ATM interface. Add these specifications to the problem statement:

1. Let the program terminate normally, effectively shutting done the ATM, when the user enters BOSS as the name (let the PIN be anything).
2. Don't allow customers to withdraw more than their balance. If the request is made, display the message: "Cannot process withdrawal--Insufficient Funds". In order to prevent withdrawals greater than the customer balance, you will have to call bank::availableBalance.

First complete the following test oracle to predict what should happen at each turn. Recall that the balance of customer Hall always starts at 100.00.

━━━━━━━━━━━━━ Test Oracle ━━━━━━━━━━━━━

Name	PIN	Transaction	Amount	What Should Happen
xyz	0000	NA	NA	
hall	1234	w	bad	
		w	50.00	
		d	12.34	
		w	200	
		b	NA	
		Q	NA	
Austen	2222	B	NA	
Hall	1234	B	NA	
Robber	$$$$	NA	NA	
boss	0000	NA	NA	

Hint: Because of the heavy nesting of control structures, consider writing a void function called processOneCustomer that completely processes all customers except BOSS. This simplifies the main function to an infinite while loop which "breaks" when BOSS is entered. Under all other circumstances, the function processOneCustomer is called. You may have to do some cut and paste editing commands, but the additional procedure should simplify the implementation. The outline of your program might look like this:

```
#include "ouratm.h"  // for class ATM
#include "ourbank.h" // for class bank

// Don't forget & after bank, otherwise, balances are not changed!
void processOneCustomer(const ATM & moneyMachine, bank & firstBank)
{ //   PRE: moneyMachine has the current name and PIN
  // POST: All transactions have been properly recorded at the bank

  int customerNumber, found;
  // ...Either say name/PIN are invalid or allow one valid
  // ...customer to perform as many transactions as desired
}

int main()
{ // POST: An undetermined number of customers are processed
  ATM moneyMachine;
  bank firstBank;
  while(1)
  {
    // ...Either break or call processOneCustomer...
  }
}
```

To ensure your bank control program handles all possible inputs, run the program and enter each set of data to compare with your predictions in the test oracle. To terminate the program, enter BOSS for the name followed by any PIN.

6F   Using Objects

See Appendix A, "Additional Lab Projects."

6G   Using Objects

See Appendix A, "Additional Lab Projects."

6.6   The for Statement

The while statement is general enough to implement many forms of repetition. In fact, it is the only repetition statement we need. On the other hand, the C++ *for statement*, a specialized form of the while loop, is often used in counter-controlled loop situations. It has this more compact and convenient form:

```
for (counter = initial-expression ;  loop-test ;  repeated-statement )
{
    iterative-part
}
```

When a *for* loop is encountered, the *initial-expression* is assigned to the *counter* and the *loop-test* is evaluated. If *loop-test* results in a zero (false) value, the for loop is terminated. If *loop-test* is nonzero (true), the *iterative-part* is executed and the *repeated-statement* is executed. The repeated-statement is the step that brings us closer to a termination condition such as an increment or decrement to the counter. Here is an example:

```
int counter;
for(counter = 1;  counter <= 3;  counter = counter + 1)
    cout << counter << "  ";
```

--------- Output ---------
```
1  2  3
```

Here, the counter is assigned the value of the initial expression (1). Since the loop-test (counter <= 3) is true, the iterative-part of the for loop (a single cout extraction here) is executed and the value of the counter is displayed. Immediately after each iterative-part executes, the repeated-statement (counter = counter+1) brings us one step closer to loop termination. After two more iterations, counter is incremented from 3 to 4 and the loop-test (counter<=3) is false. The for loop terminates.

If we were to use a counter-controlled while loop to perform the same function (to execute the iterative-part three times), the int object counter would have to be initialized before the loop and incremented within the iterative-part:

```cpp
// An equivalent while loop
int counter = 1;
while(counter <= 3)
{
  cout << counter << "  ";
  counter = counter + 1;
}
```

The for loop includes the initialization and increment of the counter as part of the for loop itself. This has an advantage over the while loop in that we are more likely to include these statements in the parentheses after for. This makes for loops less prone to errors than an equivalent counter-controlled while loop.

The counter of a for loop could be other types such as float. And the counter can be declared and initialized as part of the for statement:

```cpp
// Declare and use a float for the counter of a for loop
#include <iostream.h>
#include <math.h>
#include "ourstuff.h"

float f(float x)
{
  return  x - cos(x);
}

int main()
{
  cout << endl << "   x   |   f(x) ";
  cout << endl << "------+--------" << endl;
  decimals(cout, 2);
  for(float x = 0;  x <= 2; x = x + 0.5)
  {
    cout.width(6);
    decimals(cout, 1);
    cout << x << " |";
    cout.width(7);
    decimals(cout, 4);
    cout << f(x) << endl;
  }
  return 0;
}
```

```
──────────────────────── Output ────────────────────────
    for Loop 3:
       x   |   f(x)
    -------+--------
      0.0 |-1.0000
      0.5 |-0.3776
      1.0 | 0.4597
      1.5 | 1.4293
      2.0 | 2.4161
```

The previous for loops used a single statement as the iterative part, but we will often be required to use a compound statement. For example, a for loop that produces an average of a set of numbers needs to repeat more than one statement. This is shown in the next program that calls function produceAverage to average any set of floats entered from the terminal. The for loop requires a compound statement to input each number while maintaining a running sum of the values input. Also, the for loop is made more general by using the loop-test control <= n. Different-size sets of data can be processed as long as the number of inputs is known in advance.

```cpp
// Call produceAverage to illustrate for loops need to know the
// number of repetitions before they are encountered in the program.

#include <iostream.h>

void produceAverage(int n)   // In: Number of floats to be averaged
{
  //  PRE: n > 0 and no bad input is encountered in cin
  // POST: n floats are entered from the keyboard and averaged
  float ave;               // Average of n floats.
  float value, sum;        // value: the input; sum: the running sum.

  // Initialize sum to 0 to ensure the correct average
  sum = 0;
  for(int counter = 1; counter <= n; counter = counter + 1)
  {
    cout << "Enter number: ";
    cin >> value;
    sum = sum + value;
  }

  // Compute and display the average
  ave = sum / n;
  cout << "Average: " << ave;
}
```

```
int main()
{
  produceAverage(3);
  return 0;
}
```

```
─────────────────── Dialogue ───────────────────
  Enter number: 85.0
  Enter number: 95.0
  Enter number: 90.0
  Average: 90
```

6.6.1   Other Incrementing Operators

Assignment operations alter computer memory even when the lValue itself is involved in the rValue expression. For example, the int object n is updated by +1 with this assignment operation:

```
n = n + 1;    // lValue n is also on the right of =
```

This type of update—incrementing an object—is used so frequently that C++ offers several other increment operators. Two of these are ++ and --, which increment and decrement an object by 1, respectively. For example, the expression n++; adds 1 to the value of n, and the expression x-- reduces x by 1. These two new operators alter the numeric object that they follow:

```
int n;      n:
n = 0;       0
n++;         1
n++;         2
n--;         1
```

Within the context of a for loop, the repeated-statement can be written as counter++ rather than counter = counter + 1:

```
for(int counter = 1; counter <= n; counter = counter + 1)
```

now becomes this equivalent loop with the ++ operator used in the repeated-statement

```
for(int counter = 1; counter <= n; counter++)
```

These new assignment operators are shown because they provide a convenient method for accomplishing incrementing and decrementing operations in the for loop. Another reason has to do with the fact that most C and C++ code you will see uses the ++ operator in for loops.

Note: Early versions of the C++ programming language were known as "C with classes." In 1983, the name C++ was coined to signify that the language was an extension of the popular C language. The current name is based on this ++ new increment operator.

Self-Check

1. *True or False:* In the first iteration of a `for` loop, the repeated-statement is executed before the loop-test.
2. *True or False:* A `for` loop can only increment its counter by +1.
3. *True or False:* A `for` loop will always execute the iterative part at least once.
4. Write the output from the following program segments, assuming `j` and `n` are `int` objects:

   a.
   ```
   n = 5;
   for(j=1; j<=n; j++)
     cout << j << " ";
   ```

   c.
   ```
   for(j=5; j >= 1; j--)
     cout << j << " ";
   ```

   b.
   ```
   for(j = -3; j <= 3; j = j + 2)
   {
     cout << j << " ";
   }
   ```

   d.
   ```
   for(j=5; j <= 1; j++)
     cout << j << " ";
   cout << "done";
   ```

Answers

1. False: The repeated-statement is executed after the iterative part executes.
2. False: The counter may be incremented or decremented by any int or float value.
3. False: The test expression may be false before the iterative part can be executed.
4. a. 1 2 3 4 5   c. 5 4 3 2 1
   b. -3 -1 1 3   d. done

6.7 The do while Statement

The `do while` statement is similar to the `while` loop. Both allow a set of statements to be repeated while an expression is true. But the primary difference is the time at which the loop-test is evaluated. The `while` loop-test is evaluated at the *beginning* of each iteration; the `do while` statement evaluates the loop-test at the *end* of each iteration. This means that the `do while` loop always executes its iterative part at least once. The general form of the `do while` loop is given as:

```
do {
    iterative-part
} while (loop-test) ;
```

When a `do while` statement is encountered, all expressions are executed down to the associated `while`. The test expression is evaluated at the end of the loop (not at the beginning). If the result is nonzero, the iterative part executes again. If the test expression is zero, the loop terminates. Although the braces are not always needed with while and for loops, a compound statement must always exist between the do and the while. Here is an example of the do while loop that displays the counter to simulate its execution:

```
int counter = 1, n = 4;
cout << endl << "Before loop..." << endl;
do {
   cout << "Loop #" << counter << endl;
   counter++;
} while (counter <= n);
cout << "...After loop" << endl;
```

```
───────────── Output ─────────────
   Before Loop...
   Loop #1
   Loop #2
   Loop #3
   Loop #4
   ...After Loop
```

Although an equivalent *pretest* while loop can be written like this:

```
int counter = 1, n = 4;
cout << endl << "Before Loop..." << endl;
while(counter <= n)
{
   cout << "Loop #" << counter;
   counter++;
}
cout << "...After loop" << endl;
```

there are times when a *posttest* loop is better. Although this while loop produces the same exact output as its do while counterpart when n is greater than or equal to counter, a difference can be seen when the statement n = 1 is replaced with n = 0. The while loop does not execute its iterative-part but the do while loop does execute the iterative part once, even when n is 0:

```
   Before Loop...
   Loop #1
   ...After Loop
```

This example indicates that the while loop (or a for loop) may be the better choice for counter-controlled loops, even when it has been predetermined that the loop should repeat zero times. However, the do while loop is a good choice for repetition whenever a set of statements must be executed at least once to initialize objects in the loop-test. For example, the do while loop is useful when asking the user of the program to enter options from a menu. A *menu* is a screen containing a list of options.

For example, when the ATM::getTransaction menu is active, it acts as a prompt for any of these characters: W, w, D, d, B, b, Q, q.

```
ATM  ----------------------------------------
                       Withdraw [W]
                        Deposit [D]
                        Balance [B]
                           Quit [Q]


        Select [W,D,B,Q]: _
```

Here is one possible algorithm that could be used to return any of the valid transactions in uppercase. The algorithm is designed to allow any number of entries until one of the correct choices is entered. The function is designed not to return any char other than one of the valid transaction codes in uppercase.

> *do*
>> *Extract a character from the keyboard for the char object transaction*
>> *Convert transaction to its uppercase equivalent*
> *while transaction is not one of these characters: 'W', 'D', 'B', or 'Q'*

Because we know we must try to obtain at least one character from the keyboard before the test expression evaluates, we can use a do while loop instead of a while loop. We know the loop must iterate at least once. The advantage of do while over while is that the do while loop eliminates the need for a priming extraction. Without the do while, we would need something like the following, where the input and conversion to uppercase must be done twice rather than once:

> <u>*getTransaction*</u>: *the long version without a do while loop*
>> *Extract a character from the keyboard for the int object transaction*
>> *Convert transaction to its uppercase equivalent*
>> *while transaction is not 'W', 'D', 'B', or 'Q'*
>>> *Extract a character from the keyboard for the int object transaction*
>>> *Convert transaction to its uppercase equivalent*

The actual implementation of the ATM::getTransaction function uses the shorter do while version:

```
void ATM::getTransaction(char & transaction)
{
  clearScreen();
  cout << "\n\n";
  cout << " ATM --------------------------------------" << endl;
  cout << setw(32) << "Withdraw [W]";
  cout << "\n";
  cout << setw(32) << " Deposit [D]";
  cout << "\n";
  cout << setw(32) << " Balance [B]";
  cout << "\n";
  cout << setw(32) << "    Quit [Q]";
  cout << "\n\n";

  // Currently any letter pressed will be returned
  // as its uppercase equivalent.  Only four choices
  // should be returned: w/W, d/D, b/B, and q/Q to quit

  do {
    cout << setw(30) << "Select [W,D,B,Q]: ";
    cin >> transaction;
    transaction = toupper(transaction);
  } while((transaction != 'W') &&
          (transaction != 'D') &&
          (transaction != 'B') &&
          (transaction != 'Q'));
}
```

Once called, the user is prompted until one of the four upper or lowercase choices have been entered.

Self-Check

1. Write the output produced by the following code:

   a.
   ```
   int j = 1;
   do {
     cout << j << endl;
     j++;
   } while(j <= 3);
   ```

   b.
   ```
   float x = -1.0;
   do {
     cout << x << endl;
     x = x + 0.5;
   } while(x <= 1.0);
   ```

2. Write a do while loop that prompts for and inputs any number of ints until the int is in the range of 1 through 10 inclusive.

Answers

1. a.   1   b.   -1   2.   int pick;
        2   -0.5   do {
        3   0.0   cout << "Enter an int in the range of 1 through 10: ";
                     0.5   cin >> pick;
                     1.0   } while(pick < 1 || pick > 10);

6.8   Loop Selection and Design

For some people, loops are easy to implement, even at first. For others, infinite loops and intent errors are more common. In either case, the following outline is offered to help you choose and design loops in a wide variety of situations:

1.   Write the statements to be repeated.
2.   Determine which type of loop to use.
3.   Determine the loop-test.
4.   Bring the loop one step closer to termination.
5.   Initialize objects if necessary.

6.8.1   Write the Statements to be Repeated

This is why the loop is being written in the first place. Some common tasks include summing a set of numbers or keeping track of a high or low value. Other tasks that will be seen later include searching for a name in a list, or repeatedly comparing all string elements of a list in order to alphabetize it.

6.8.2   Determine Which Type of Loop to Use

If the number of repetitions is known in advance or read as input, use the specialized version of a for loop. Counter-controlled while loops could also be used, but then you must remember to include the initialization and increment steps. If you wish to stop the loop when some event occurs during execution of the loop, determine if an event-controlled loop, such as a sentinel loop, is appropriate. If the loop must always execute once, consider using a do while loop, for example, when input data must be checked for its validity (an integer value that must be in the range of 0 through 100, for example). A do while loop is also a good choice for menu-driven programs that repeatedly request options until the menu choice for quit is entered.

6.8.3   Determine the Loop-Test

If the loop-test is not obvious, try writing the conditions that must be true for the loop to terminate. For example, if we are processing file input, we usually terminate the loop when the end of file is reached. If the expression is:

```
inFile.eof()  // Termination condition
```

the opposite logic (with ! applied) can be used directly as the loop-test of a while loop:

```
while(!inFile.eof()) // ! inFile.eof() is opposite of term. cond.
{
    Body of loop
}
```

Here are some other examples of the termination conditions and the opposite loop-tests for while loops:

Termination Condition	Opposite Logic is the while Loop-Test
counter > 10	counter <= 10
intObject == -1	intObject != -1
inFile.eof() || (counter > max)	! inFile.eof && (counter <= max)

6.8.4   Bring the Loop One Step Closer to Termination

To avoid an infinite loop, there should be at least one action in the loop body that brings it closer to termination. In a counter-controlled loop this might mean incrementing or decrementing a counter by some specific value. The istream >> operator function is one method that brings some event-controlled loops closer to termination—we must keep inputting values until the sentinel is extracted from the input stream. In a for loop, the repeated-statement should be designed to bring the loop closer to termination. In general, the loop test should contain at least one object that is altered during each iteration of the loop.

6.8.5   Initialize Objects If Necessary

Check to see if any objects used in either the body of the loop or the loop-test need to be initialized. Doing this usually ensures that the objects of the loop and the objects used in the iterative-part have been initialized. For example, consider this loop:

```
while(j <= n)
{
    sum = sum + j;
    j++;
}
```

Assuming j, n, and sum are declared as int objects, we cannot be sure what the value of sum will be since j may be greater than n already and sum may start at -1234 or 999. We should consider each object in the loop test and the iterative-part as potential candidates for initialization. Assuming the initializations j=1, n=4, and sum=0, we easily predict the value of sum is 1+ 2 + 3 + 4 or 10.

Self-Check

1. Which loop best accomplishes these tasks?
    a. Sum the first 5 integers (1 + 2 + 3 + 4 + 5).
    b. Find the average value for a set of numbers when the size of the set is known.
    c. Find the average value for a set of numbers when we don't know the size of the set until we finish entering data.
    d. Obtain a character from the user that must be an uppercase 'F', 'S', or 'Q'.

2. For a sentinel-controlled loop that is to process inputs called `value`, and where the sentinel is -1,
    a. write a termination condition.
    b. write the loop-test for a `while` loop.
    c. could we use a `for` loop as a sentinel-controlled loop with a priming extraction?

3. For each loop, which objects are not initialized but should be? (*Note:* "..." represents a set of statements.)

    a.
    ```
    while(j <= n)
    {
        // ... ;
    }
    ```
    c.
    ```
    for(int j = 1; j <= n; j = j + inc)
    {
        // ... ;
    }
    ```

    b.
    ```
    do {
        cin >> intObject;
        // ... ;
    } while(intObject != -1);
    ```
    d.
    ```
    while(!cin.eof())
    {
        cin >> intObject;
        sum = sum + intObject;
        n++;
    }
    ```

Answers

1. a. A counter-controlled loop, preferably a For loop.
   b. A counter-controlled loop, preferably a For loop.
   c. Sentinel-controlled while loop (if we are guaranteed that one input will always occur, a do while loop could be used)
   d. do while
2. a. value == -1
   b. value != -1
   c. Yes, it might look like this: for (cin >> j; j != -1; cin >> j)
3. a. j and n   c. n and inc
   b. none   d. sum and n should be set to 0

Chapter Summary

Repetition is an important method of program control for programming languages. C++ is no exception. Typically, the body of a loop has statements that may change the state of one or more objects during each loop iteration.

The while loop covered in the first part of this chapter can be used to implement both counter- and event-controlled loops. Counter-controlled loops require that we determine the number of iterations before it is encountered. They rely on a properly initialized and incremented counter to count the iterations. This counter is compared to the known number of iterations for the termination condition.

Event-controlled loops rely on some external event for their termination. The terminating event may occur at any time. We use events when we are unable and/or unwilling to predict the number of times these loops iterate. The termination condition is met through events such as sentinels extracted from the input stream (-1 as a test or 'Q' as an ATM transaction request), and the end of file event (keyboard input of Ctrl-Z in DOS or Ctrl-D in UNIX). These types of loops provide the ability to process all the data in a file no matter its size, allow any number of ATM bank customers to make any number of transactions, or repeatedly prompt a user for input.

Although the while loop is the only repetitive statement we would need, the for and do while loops are more convenient under certain circumstances. The for loop requests that we take care of the initialization, loop-test, and repeated statement all at once. It provides a more compact and less error-prone counter-controlled-loop. The do while loop has the loop-test at the end and is useful for obtaining user input that must meet certain specifications.

Exercises

9. How many times will the following loops execute cout << "Hello ";? (Zero, unknown, and infinite are perfectly legitimate answers.)

a.
```
n = 5;
for(int j = 1; j <= n; j++)
  cout << "Hello  ";
```

b.
```
j = 1;
n = 10;
do {
  cout << "Hello  ";
} while (j > n);
```

c.
```
for(int j = 5; j >= 0; j--)
  cout << "Hello  ";
```

d.
```
j = -1;
do {
  cout << "Hello  ";
} while (j != j)
```

10. Write the output generated by the following program:

```cpp
#include <iostream.h>
int main()
{
  int j = -2;
  do {
    cout << "    " << j;
    j--;
  } while(j > -6);
  return 0;
}
```

11. Write the output generated by the following loops:

a.
```cpp
n = 1;
for(int j=1; j<=n; j++)
{
  cout << "    " << j;
}
```

c.
```cpp
j = 1;
n = 5;
do {
  cout << j << endl;
  j++;
} while (j < n);
```

b.
```cpp
for(j = 5; j >= 0; j--)
  cout << "    " << j;
```

d.
```cpp
j = 3;
do {
  cout << j << endl;
  j--;
} while (j > 0)
```

12. Convert the following code to its for loop counterpart:

```cpp
cout << "Enter number of ints to be summed: ";
cin >> n;
counter = 1;
sum = 0;
while(counter <= n)
{
  cin >> intObject;
  sum = sum + intObject;
  counter++;
}
cout << sum;
```

13. Write the output produced by these `for` loops:

```
for(counter = 1; counter <= 5; counter++)
   cout << "  " << counter;
   cout << "Loop One"; // Incorrectly indented to confuse

for (counter = 10; counter >= 1; counter--)
   cout << "  " << counter;
cout << "Blast Off";  // Correctly indented to avoid confusion
```

14. Convert the following code to its `do while` counterpart:

```
char option;
cout << "Enter option A, B or Q: ";
cin >> option;
option = toupper(option);
while((option != 'A') && (option != 'B') && (option != 'Q'))
{
   cout << "Enter option A, B or Q: ";
   cin >> option;
   option = toupper(option);
}
```

15. Write a `for` loop that produces this output:

```
10  9  8  7  6  5  4  3  2  1  0
```

16. Write a function named `option` that prompts for and returns an uppercase S, A, M, or Q only. The return type of function `option` must be `char`. Return `'S'`, `'A'`, `'M'`, or `'Q'` through the function name, not as a reference. The following code must assign one of the only four allowed letters to `choice`:

```
char choice = option();
cout << choice;  // Output must be either S, A, M, or Q only!
```

17. Rewrite the following `do while` loop as a pretest `while` loop (loop-test first before the body):

```
int counter = 0;
do {
   cout << counter;
   counter = counter + 1;
} while(counter <= 100);
```

18. Write nested `for` loops that generate the following output:

```
1
2  3
3  4  5
4  5  6  7
5  6  7  8  9
```

19. Write a program to display a triangle of size 3 (number of characters in the middle row) to look like this:

```
  #
 ##
###
 ##
  #
```

a. Write a `do while` loop that repeatedly prompts for and reads an `int` named `size` that is both odd and within the range of 1 through 77 inclusive. If the input is even, output is "`**Error** Size must be odd`". If the input is out of range, output is "`**Error** Size must be > 1 and <= 77`". Display both messages for sizes such as -2 and 77.

b. Write at least four `int`s you should use to test an answer to the previous question.

c. Using the `int` object `size`, write C++ code to display the middle row in the triangle for any value of `size` that is odd and in the range of 1 through 77.

d. Using the `int` object `size`, write C++ code to display the top portion of the triangle for any value of `size` that is odd and in the range of 1 through 77.

e. Using the `int` object `size`, write C++ code to display the bottom portion of the triangle for any value of `size` that is odd and in the range of 1 through 77.

Lab Projects

6H   Using Objects

Write a function that returns N! ("N factorial") where N! is the product of all the positive integers from 1 to N. For example, 5! = 1 x 2 x 3 x 4 x 5 = 120; 4! = 4 x 3 x 2 x 1 = 24; and 0!=1 (by definition). Test your function with these arguments: 0, 1, 2, and 7.

6I   Using Objects

Write a program that displays a table which shows exponents of 2. The exponent range must be 0..30. (*Note:* $2^0=1$). Input should include the first and last exponent of 2 to be displayed. Make sure that both high and low powers are in the range of 0..30 and that the low power is less than or equal to the high power. Ensure that both powers are in the correct ranges.

```
Enter low exponent from  0  to 30: -1
                    Try again

Enter low exponent from  0  to 30: 31
                    Try again

Enter low exponent from  0  to 30: 4

Enter high exponent from  4 to 30: 2
                    Try again

Enter high exponent from  4 to 30: 10

     X      2^X
     ==     =====
      4       16
      5       32
      6       64
      7      128
      8      256
      9      512
     10     1024
```

6J   Using Objects

This program requires the use of random numbers. The file `stdlib.h` declares two functions that generate seemingly random numbers. First call the function `randomize`:

```
void randomize();  // from stdlib.h
// POST: Initializes the random number generator

int rand();  // from stdlib.h;
// POST: Returns an integer in the range of 0 through RAND_MAX
//       where RAND_MAX is a large integer defined in stdlib.h
```

The following program generates 10 random numbers like those shown in the column to the right. The expression `rand() % 10 + 1` always results in an integer in the range of 1 through 10. If `randomize` is not called first, the same 10 numbers will be generated.

```
#include <iostream.h>
#include <stdlib.h>
int main()
{
  randomize();
  for(int j = 1; j <= 10; j++)
    cout << rand() % 10 + 1 << endl;
  return 0;
}
```

```
─────────────── Output ───────────────
    2
    9
    10
    1
    5
    6
    9
    2
    5
    8
```

Write a complete C++ program that implements a guessing game. Ask the user for a number in the range of 1 through 100 inclusive. If the guess is larger than the random number you generated in the range of 1 through 100, inform the user that the guess was too high. If the guess is too low, say so, and when the guess matches the random number, say so. Also show the user how many guesses were required. Here is a sample dialogue:

```
Pick a number from 1..100: 25
25 is too low
Pick a number from 1..100: 75
75 is too high
Pick a number from 1..100: 40
40 is too low
Pick a number from 1..100: 60
60 is too high
Pick a number from 1..100: 49
49 matches the random number
Number of guesses: 5
```

6K   Using Objects

The square of an integer value ±n can be found by adding the first n positive odd integers. For example, both 4 squared and -4 squared are the sum of the first four positive odd integers (1+3+5+7=16). Write a function that displays the square of an integer

using your own function. Do not use the built-in function pow or the multiplication (*)
operator. Complete your function named showSquareOf. Test it with this main function:

```
int main()
{                      // Test Oracle:
  showSquareOf(0);     // The square of 0 is 0
  showSquareOf(-1);    // The square of -1 is 1
  showSquareOf(1);     // The square of 1 is 1
  showSquareOf(5);     // The square of 5 is 25
  showSquareOf(-8);    // The square of -8 is 64
  return 0;
}
```

6L   Using Objects

Calculate the amount of money that will be in a savings account after one year when the
interest is compounded on an annual, monthly, and daily basis. Input must consist of
the annual interest rate and principal, which is the single amount deposited on the first
day. You are to calculate the interest in two ways: using for loops and this formula:

$$futureValue = presentValue * (1 + rate)^n$$

where presentValue is the amount invested today, rate is the interest rate the investment is to earn for each period, and n is the number of periods the investment is to
earn interest. You will need the math.h pow function for the exponentiation of this
formula. The for loop method involves applying the appropriate interest rate to the
principal the correct number of times. For example, to determine the futureValue of
a principal amount that is to be compounded on a monthly basis, the monthly interest
rate must be applied 12 times where the principal is updated (monthly interest added)
for each month (period). Since you are to determine the future value over a one-year
period, no for loop is required to determine the futureValue of an amount that is
compounded annually. Format your output as follows:

```
            Enter principal: 1000
Enter annual interest rate [0..15]: 6

                    Annual    Monthly    Daily
    Formula method:  1060.00   1061.68   1061.83
    For loop method: 1060.00   1061.68   1061.83
```

6M   Using Objects

Write a program that creates triangles of different sizes. It should generate the following output when `size` is entered as 4:

```
*
**
***
****
***
**
*
```

The `size` (4 here) refers to the number of columns contained in the middle row of the triangle. The user should be prompted for `size` within the range of 1 through 77 (the `int` may be even or odd). Notice that each row has one more or one less character than the row above or below, respectively.

6N   Using Objects

See Appendix A, "Additional Lab Projects."

7

Arrays

Some classes, such as int and float, store exactly one value per object. Others classes, such as string and bankAccount, store several values for each object. We now turn our attention to the C++ array—an object that manages a collection of objects under one name. After studying this chapter, you will be able to:

- Distinguish simple and structured classes.
- Declare and use arrays with one subscript to reference many values with one name.
- Perform a variety of array-processing applications.
- Use a sequential search algorithm to locate a specific array element.
- Manage a simple list with display, add, and remove operations.
- Sort arrays into ascending or descending order.
- Read or implement the binary search algorithm.

7.1   Arrays

A class is the set of values that an object may store during program execution along with the operations that define the behavior of those objects. For example, the int class is the collection of integers within a specific range combined with operations that manipulate that data, such as =, ==, <, +, -, *, %, /, <<, and >>. Classes fall into these three categories: simple, structured, and pointer:

1. *Simple classes* such as int, float, and char create objects that store exactly one value. For example, precisely one integer is represented as one int object and precisely one floating point number is represented as one float object.
2. *Structured classes* create objects that store many values under the same name. Individual elements of structured objects are referenced with a variety of methods. For example, the bankAccount class is structured because each bankAccount object stores three objects referenced with the member functions name, PIN, and balance. The string class can also be considered structured because many individual char values and a length are stored. The primitive C++ array introduced in this chapter is another structured type. Arrays store many simple or structured objects as a collection of elements under the same name. Arrays are used to create other structures such as lists, stacks, queues, and binary trees.
3. The *pointer class* creates objects that store addresses of other objects. Pointer objects (covered in Chapter 9) allow the programmer to access specific memory locations through addresses rather than names. Pointer objects allow us to manipulate addresses and to create other classes such as lists, stacks, queues, and binary trees.

An *array* is a fixed-size collection of elements that are of the same class. Arrays are *homogeneous* in that they store collections of like objects. The objects in the collection may be declared as one of the fundamental classes char, int, float, long, or double. The objects may also be declared as one of the programmer-defined classes such as string or bankAccount.

The general form used to declare array objects is as follows:

class-name   array-name [*int-expression*] ;

where *class-name* specifies the type of objects stored under the *array-name*, and the *int-expression* specifies the maximum number of elements in the collection of objects. For example, the array object shown next stores a maximum of five float objects (floatArray is used over the next several pages to illustrate subscript use and array processing):

```
float floatArray[5];
```

Individual array elements are referenced through subscripts of this form:

array-name [*int-expression*]

The subscript range of a C++ array is an integer value in the range of 0 through *int-expression* -1. Therefore, the individual objects of floatArray are referenced using the int-expression 0, 1, 2, 3, and 4. Because C++ starts counting at zero, the first array element is referenced with subscript 0 or floatArray[0] and the fifth element with subscript 4 or floatArray[4]. This subscript notation allows us to insert individual array elements into output streams, extract values for them from input streams, reference them in computations, and store values into them with assignment operations. In fact, we can do anything to an array element that can be done to an object of the same class. For example, values are stored into array elements with assignment operations like this

```
floatArray[0] = 12.6;
floatArray[1] = 5.7;
```

The same assignment rules apply to array elements. For example, since we cannot assign a string constant to a float object, we cannot store a string constant into an array element that was declared to store floating-point values.

```
floatArray[2] = "Wrong type of constant";  // ERROR
```

And because we can add any two float objects with +, we can also use subscripted array elements in an arithmetic expression like this:

```
floatArray[2] = floatArray[0] + floatArray[1];    // Store 18.3
```

Also, as with all float objects, keyboard input can be used to set the state of array elements like this:

```
cout << "Enter two float values: ";
cin >> floatArray[3] >> floatArray[4];
```

Dialogue
```
Enter two float values: 9.99 15.0
```

After user input of *9.99 15.0* and the previous assignments, all elements of floatArray would have these defined states.

Subscripted Array Element	Current Value
floatArray[0]	12.6
floatArray[1]	5.7
floatArray[2]	18.3
floatArray[3]	9.99
floatArray[4]	15.0

Programming Tip

Remember that C++ starts counting at 0 so the first element is referenced with subscript [0] and the last with [*int-expression*-1] (one less than the value of the integer expression in the declaration). Referencing x[10] when x is declared as int x[10]; causes major problems. The proper subscript range of x begins at 0 and ends at 9.

Also remember that all elements of an array are of the same class. More specifically, floatArray stores only float objects. We cannot store other classes of data into floatArray.

7.1.1 Processing Arrays with the for Loop

Programmers must frequently reference many consecutive array elements. The simplest case might be to display all the elements of an array, for example. The for loop provides a convenient way to do this:

```
int j;
decimals(cout, 2);
cout << "All 5 Elements of floatArray: " << endl;
for(j = 0; j < 5; j++)
    cout << j << ':' << setw(6) << floatArray[j] << endl;
```

──────────────── **Output** ────────────────

```
All 5 Elements of floatArray:
0:  12.60
1:   5.70
2:  18.30
3:   9.99
4:  15.00
```

All elements of floatArray are easily referenced by altering the int object that acts both as the counter in the for loop and as the subscript in the subscripted array expressions inside the for loop. With j serving both roles—as shown in the code above—the specific array element referenced as intArray[j] will depend on the value of j. For example, when j = 0, intArray[j] is a reference to the first element in intArray; when j = 4, floatArray[j] is a reference to the fifth element of floatArray. Here is another example of a for loop used to inspect array elements to find the largest floating-point value.

```
// Let the first element be the largest
float largest = floatArray[0];
// Now compare the other array elements
for(j = 1; j < 5; j++)
{
    if(floatArray[j] > largest)
        largest = floatArray[j];
}
cout << "The largest floatArray element = " << largest;
```

──────────────── **Output** ────────────────

```
The largest floatArray element = 18.30
```

for loops are frequently chosen to perform array processing, which is the inspection of, or reference to, a selected number of array elements. Examples of array processing in this chapter include:

- Displaying some or all elements of an array.
- Initializing some or all of the array elements.
- Finding the sum, or average, or highest of all array elements.

- Arranging elements in a certain order (largest to smallest or alphabetizing an array of strings).
- Searching for a given value in the array.

7.1.2 Out-of-Range Subscripts

C++ does not check to ensure each subscript is within the proper range. So we must be careful to avoid subscripts that are not in the range specified at declaration. Unfortunately, the following changes to memory do *not* generate errors at compiletime:

```
floatArray[-2] = 4.56;  // Careful: These are not caught by the
floatArray[5]  = 7.89;  // compiler, you could crash your system
```

Instead, some other portion of memory, such as an object, is destroyed, resulting in unpredictable errors and even a system crash. The precondition could be stated like this: The subscript must be in the proper range of 0 through the maximum size minus 1. In the case of floatArray, all subscript references must be in the range of 0 through 4. Any reference to an array element outside of the range is undefined.

Programming Tip

As C++ programmers, we must ensure that the integer used as a subscript is within the range specified by the declaration. If an out-of-range value is used as a subscript, an area of memory may be unintentionally altered, creating difficult-to-detect bugs. More dramatically, your computer may "hang" or "crash."

Self-Check

1. A simple class stores how many values per object?
2. A structured class stores how many values per object?
3. Name one simple class.
4. Name one structured class.
5. How do we reference individual elements of an array?

Use this declaration to answer the questions that follow:

```
int x[4];
```

6. How many ints are properly stored in x?
7. Which integer is used as the subscript to reference the first element in x?
8. Which integer is used as the subscript to reference the last element in x?
9. Write code that stores 89 into the first element in x.
10. Write a for loop that stores 0 into the second through last elements of x.
11. Write code that sums all elements of x.

Answers

1.	One	5.	Through subscripts "[int]"
2.	Zero to many	6.	4
3.	int (or float, or char, or long)	7.	0
4.	array (or string, or bankAccount)	8.	3

9. x[0]=89
10. for(int j = 0; j < 4; j++)
       x[j] = 0;
11. int sum = 0;
    for(int j = 0; j < 4; j++)
       sum = sum + x[j];

7.2   Calling Member Functions with Arrays

The class of objects that may be stored in an array includes all the fundamental ones such as char, int, and as previously shown by example, float. We can also declare and manage arrays of other objects using programmer-defined classes such as string and bankAccount. In fact, each bank object contains an array data member that is a collection of bankAccount objects. This array of bankAccount objects comprises the majority of the database of customers. An array of bankAccounts is also used in several examples that follow. In the following program, an array of bankAccount objects is declared, given meaningful values, and then displayed. In it, the constructor call is used three times to create bankAccount objects, which in turn are assigned to the array. We also see what a call to a member function looks like when the object belongs to an array.

```
// This program illustrates arrays of programmer defined objects.

#include <iostream.h>
#include "ouracct.h"   // for class bankAccount

int main()
{
  int j;
  // Declare an array of bankAccount objects
  bankAccount customer[3];
  customer[0] = bankAccount("Hall", "1234", 100);
  customer[1] = bankAccount("Small", "4321", 0);
  customer[2] = bankAccount("Ewall", "1082", 10000.00);

  cout << "Show the three elements of customer: " << endl;
  for(j = 0; j < 3; j ++)
    cout << "customer[" << j << "]: " << customer[j] << endl;

  return 0;
}
```

```
──────────────── Output ────────────────
Show the three elements of customer:
customer[0]: { bankAccount: HALL, 1234, 100.00 }
customer[1]: { bankAccount: SMALL, 4321, 0.00 }
customer[2]: { bankAccount: EWALL, 1082, 10000.00 }
```

If `customer` were a `bankAccount` object rather than an array of `bankAccount` objects, it could be inserted as `cout << customer;`. But since `customer` is an array, it must be subscripted to show each individual element of the array like this:

```
cout << customer[0];  // Display the first bankAccount object
```

Since `customer` accommodates a collection of objects, the subscript notation must also be used to call member functions for individual objects. This is shown in the following code fragment where the name of each `bankAccount` object is displayed:

```
for(j = 0; j < 3; j++)
  cout << customer[j].name() << endl;
```

```
──────────────── Output ────────────────
   HALL
   SMALL
   EWALL
```

Here, the array name is accompanied by a subscript to specify the particular element in the array. This general form

array-name [*subscript*] . *member-function-call*

is required to call a member function for a particular array element. The subscript distinguishes which object the operation is to be applied to. For example, the PIN of SMALL is referenced with this expression:

```
customer[1].PIN();
```

An expression such as `customer.PIN()` would not be legal because it represents an attempt to find the PIN of the entire array of `bankAccounts`. This is not a defined operation for the C++ array. The next example of array processing shows how to find the total balance of all bank customers:

```
float sum = 0.0;
for(j = 0; j < 3; j++)
  sum = sum + customer[j].balance();
cout << "The total balance is: " << sum << endl;
```

─── **Output** ───

```
The total balance is: 10100.00
```

7.2.1   Initializing an Array of Objects with File Input

The bank object of the bank control program maintains an array of bankAccounts. The bank constructor—called during declaration bank firstBank;—initializes an array of bankAccount objects with 16 assignment operations. Once the array is set, it can supply account balances, allow updates with deposit and withdrawal operations, and be searched to confirm a customer and PIN.

However, the array of bankAccounts could also have been initialized using input from a disk file. To demonstrate, imagine the following is part of the input data file named bank.dat and that it is associated with the ifstream object (there are a total of 16 customers on 16 lines in this file) :

```
Cust0        0000 000.00
YourLastName ANY4 111.11
Austen       2222 222.22
Chelsea      3333 333.33
Kieran       4444 444.44
```

... Note: Nine customers are omitted ...

```
Cust14       1414 1414.14
Hall         1234 100.00
```

An array of bankAccount objects can be initialized one account at a time with these steps:

1. Extract three pieces of data per line.
2. Initialize a bankAccount object and add it into the next available array location.
3. Increase the number of customers by 1.

But first, some declarations and initializations are necessary. If the array is declared of maximum size 20 like this:

```
const int MAX_CUSTOMERS = 20;
bankAccount customer[MAX_CUSTOMERS];
```

then the first bankAccount object can be stored in customer[0]. The largest allowable array subscript is MAX_CUSTOMERS-1. So an object named numberOfCustomers starts at 0:

```
int numberOfCustomers = 0;
```

To avoid subscripts beyond the customer's boundaries of 0 through MAX_CUSTOMERS-1 (19), and to avoid extractions beyond the end of file, the following while loop expression should be true before a bankAccount object can be added at the end of the array:

```
while((numberOfCustomers < MAX_CUSTOMERS) && (! inFile.eof()))
```

When there is room for another bankAccount object in the array and there is more data in the file, the loop body will execute. Inside the loop, three values are extracted from the file with this statement:

```
inFile >> name >> PIN >> balance;
```

These three objects (name, PIN, and balance) are passed on to the bankAccount constructor to create one bankAccount object. The bankAccount object is stored into the next consecutive array position with this statement:

```
customer[numberOfCustomers] = bankAccount(name, PIN, balance);
```

This initialization and assignment occur *before* numberOfCustomers is incremented from 0 to 1 during the first iteration of the loop:

```
numberOfCustomers++;
```

Now numberOfCustomers accurately indicates the number of customers processed so far and the first bankAccount object is stored into customer[0]. For each customer on file, numberOfCustomers is incremented by +1. For each loop iteration, numberOfCustomers represents not only the total customers stored in the array, but also the next available array subscript into which the next bankAccount object can be stored. When the end of file is encountered, numberOfCustomers will have the correct value—it is one greater than the subscript storing the last customer.

This processing is shown in the context of a complete program, which also displays the number of initialized array elements and each of the bank customers stored in the array object named customer.

```
// Initialize an array of bankAccount objects through file input. The
// file stores sixteen (16) customers. The first bankAccount object
// is stored in customer[0] and the 16th is stored as customer[15].

#include <fstream.h>  // for class ifstream
#include "ouracct.h"  // for class bankAccount
```

```
int main()
{ //  PRE: The input file 'bank.dat' is in the proper directory,
  //       has valid format, and has no extraneous lines at the end
  // POST: An array of bankAccount objects and the number of
  //       customers stored in the file bank.dat are set

  ifstream inFile("bank.dat");
  if(! inFile)
    cout << "**Error** The file 'bank.dat' was not opened" << endl;
  else
  {
    const int MAX_CUSTOMERS = 20;
    bankAccount customer[MAX_CUSTOMERS];
    string name, PIN;
    float balance;
    int numberOfCustomers = 0;

    while( (numberOfCustomers < MAX_CUSTOMERS) && (!inFile.eof()) )
    {
      inFile >> name >> PIN >> balance;
      // Go to next line or make eof true
      inFile.ignore(80, '\n');
      customer[numberOfCustomers] = bankAccount(name, PIN, balance);
      numberOfCustomers++;
    }

    // Antibugging tip:
    // It is good practice to verify an array is properly initialized!
    // The numberOfCustomers is very important as is the data stored
    // at each array element. So first output numberOfCustomers.
    // Then display # each bankAccount object with cout <<.
    cout << "Number of customers on file: " << numberOfCustomers << endl;
    cout << endl;
    cout << "               The customers"         << endl;
    cout << "   ===============================" << endl;
    for(int j = 0; j < numberOfCustomers; j++)
      cout << j << ". " << customer[j] << endl;
  } // end else
  return 0;
}
```

```
───────────────────── Output ─────────────────────
  Number of customers on file: 16

           The customers
  ===================================
  0. { bankAccount: CUST0, 0000, 000.00 }
  1. { bankAccount: YOURLASTNAME, ANY4, 111.11 }
  2. { bankAccount: AUSTEN, 2222, 222.22 }
  3. { bankAccount: CHELSEA, 3333, 333.33 }
  4. { bankAccount: KIERAN, 4444, 444.44 }
  5. { bankAccount: CUST5, 5555, 555.55 }
  6. { bankAccount: CUST6, 6666, 666.66 }
  7. { bankAccount: CUST7, 7777, 777.77 }
  8. { bankAccount: CUST8, 8888, 888.88 }
  9. { bankAccount: CUST9, 9999, 999.99 }
  10. { bankAccount: CUST10, 1010, 1010.10 }
  11. { bankAccount: CUST11, 1111, 1111.11 }
  12. { bankAccount: CUST12, 1212, 1212.12 }
  13. { bankAccount: CUST13, 1313, 1313.13 }
  14. { bankAccount: CUST14, 1414, 1414.14 }
  15. { bankAccount: HALL, 1234, 100.00 }
```

Now we have a database of bank customers with two important pieces of data: the number of customers (16) and the initialized singly subscripted array (the collection of bankAccount objects). This array of bankAccounts was used in the bank control program. It was:

1. Searched by the bank::findCustomer member function.
2. Queried during balance transactions.
3. Modified during withdraw and deposit transactions.

Programming Tip ──────────────────────────────────

When working with arrays, output the initialized array elements and the object representing the number of initialized elements. This antibugging technique saves time and avoids frustration by preventing the bugs that arise when an incorrectly initialized array is assumed to be set up properly. This antibugging effort requires only a few minutes and signals success up to that point in program development. Remember this adage: *Code a little, test a lot.*

Also, remember that an extra iteration may occur with end of file loops unless care is taken. If this were the case in the preceding example, we might get a 17th bankAccount object with unknown state. When this was tried with the above code, the extra blank line in the file resulted with this extra object and a garbage state:

```
  16. { bankAccount: , , 100.00 }
```

One way to avoid this is to execute the `ignore` function for each line inside the loop:

```
inFile.ignore(80, '\n');  // Go to next line or make eof true
```

Or the extraction statement can be used as the loop test instead of using `eof`:

```
while( (numberOfCustomers < MAX_CUSTOMERS) &&
       (inFile >> name >> PIN >> balance )   )
```

With only newlines left in the file, the extraction fails (returns 0) and the loop is terminated before an extraneous iteration occurs.

Self-Check

Use this declaration to answer the questions that follow:

```
bankAccount account[5];
```

1. How many `bankAccount` objects are properly stored with the array `account`?
2. Which integer is used as the subscript to reference the first element in `account`?
3. Which integer is used as the subscript to reference the last element in `account`?
4. Write code that initializes the first element of `account` to a bank account with the name `"Dedre"`, a PIN of `"5555"`, and an initial balance of `500.00`.
5. Write a `for` loop that sums the balances of all five `bankAccount` objects.
6. Write two assignment statements that initialize the second and 16th elements in the array of `bankAccounts` (`customer[1]` and `customer[15]`). Use the data as shown in the input file `bank.dat`.
7. What would happen if the input file `bank.dat` had contained 21 lines, each line representing one account (remember, `MAX_CUSTOMERS = 20`)?
8. Write code to initialize an array of `int`s from a file named `int.dat`. Assume the file never has more than 20 `int` values.
9. Which object in your code of question 8 represents the number of initialized elements?
10. Write code that verifies proper initialization of the array discussed in questions 8 and 9.

Answers
1. 5
2. 0
3. 4
4. `account[0] = bankAccount("Dedre", "5555", 500.00);`
5. ```
   int sum = 0;
   for(int j = 0; j < 5; j++)
     sum = sum + account[j].balance();
   ```
   ```

6. `customer[1]  = bankAccount("YourLastName", "ANY4", 111.11);`
   `customer[15] = bankAccount("Hall", "1234", 100.00);`

7. The 21st account on the 21st line of the file would not become part of the customer database. The array size would not be big enough and the loop would terminate because `numberOfCustomers < MAX_CUSTOMERS` would be false.

8.
```
#include <iostream.h>
#include <fstream.h>
int main()
{
  const int MAX = 20;
  int intArray[MAX];
  // File name will do if it is in the working directory
  ifstream inFile("int.dat");
  int n = 0;
  int el;
  while( (n < MAX) && (inFile >> el) && (!inFile.eof()) )
  {
    intArray[n] = el;
    n++;
  }
  return 0;
}
```

9. `n`

10.
```
cout << endl << "Total ints in intArray: " << n << endl;
for(int j = 0; j < n; j++)
  cout << j << ".   " << intArray[j] << endl;
```

7.3 Sequential Search

Another common array processing operation involves searching for the existence of some element in that collection of elements. Examples include, but are certainly not limited to, searching for a student name in the registrar's database, looking up the price of an item in an inventory, or obtaining information about a bank customer given the customer's name and PIN. One such algorithm used to "look up" an array element is called *a linear* or *sequential* search, a searching algorithm that attempts to locate a given element via comparison with every object in a one-after-the-other (sequential) fashion. A sequential search continues until the search value is found in the array and we have obtained the subscript value for use in subsequent operations. If the search value is not found in the array, we have still learned something important—the search value was not in the array! The sequential search algorithm is presented here within the context of the `bank::findCustomer` function. Then in the next section, the sequential search becomes part of a `stringList::remove` function that searches for a string in an array of `string` objects—to remove the object if found or to display a message if not found. This algorithm is also employed by one of the member functions we have already encountered.

For the bank control program to work correctly, we must locate the correct bankAccount object in the array base of bank customers. Once the proper bankAccount element is located, we can get the balance or PIN, or update the balance through withdrawal and deposit operations. We also prevent noncustomers from accessing the withdrawal transactions of an ATM. To do this, a search is made through the array of bank accounts comprising the bank object's data store. This database of bank customers is implemented like the array of bank accounts shown in the previous section.

The function call that searches for the customer number in the bank controller program is coded as follows:

```
firstBank.findCustomer(moneyMachine, customerNumber, found);
```

After a successful search (found is true), the array *index*—a pointer to the array element that stores the valid customer—is returned as customerNumber. The value of customerNumber may then be used for subsequent deposit, withdrawal, and balance transactions. For example, the following code uses the bank::findCustomer member function to determine if a customer is not found or to display the current balance if the ATM user enters a valid name/PIN pair:

```
moneyMachine.getNameAndPIN();
firstBank.findCustomer(moneyMachine, customerNumber, found);
if(! found)
    moneyMachine.message("Invalid name/PIN combination");
else
    moneyMachine.showBalance(firstBank.availableBalance(customerNumber));
```

We can now look at the search algorithm of findCustomer.

Before a search begins, the name and PIN are obtained from the customer (through ATM::getNameAndPIN). The ATM object with this data is then passed as an argument during the call to the bank::findCustomer member function.

bank::findCustomer sets found to either true or false to indicate the presence or absence of the customer in the array of bankAccount: 1 when the customer is found and 0 when the search fails. The bank::findCustomer function also returns the valid customerNumber (or -1 when the search fails) through an argument/parameter association. If found is returned as true, the user should be allowed to conclude unlimited ATM transactions using the customerNumber. With a successful search and the data stored in the file bank.dat, the int object customerNumber ranges from 0 through 15—the last customer. This index (customerNumber) is essential to procure the correct balance. The customerNumber object is also used during a balance operation, to debit the correct bankAccount object during withdrawal operations, and to credit the correct bankAccount object during a deposit operation.

The search begins by creating a temporary bankAccount object to compare to the bankAccount objects in the array. The == operator has been defined for bankAccount object equality tests. Two bankAccount objects are equal if the name of one equals the name of the other and the PIN of one equals the PIN of the other. For example, the expression temp == customer[0] is true if and only if temp.name() == customer[0].name() and temp.PIN() == customer[0].PIN(). Or in the code below, when the test-expression comparing two entire objects is true,

```
if(temp == customer[customerNumber])
```

a flag named found is set to true to terminate a successful search. If there is no match, customerNumber is incremented by 1 to compare the next bankAccount object in the array to the customer being searched for. This process is repeated until the search bankAccount matches a bankAccount in the array or until all bankAccounts have been compared. Since the search loop should terminate when either of these two events occur, the event-controlled loop has two logical expressions.

```
while((! found) && (customerNumber < numberOfCustomers))
```

Loop termination occurs when the bankAccount being searched for is found or there are no more array elements to compare.

```
void bank::findCustomer(ATM moneyMachine,     // In
                        int & customerNumber, // Out
                        int & found)          // Out
{
  // The temporary bankAccount object temp is compared to array
  // elements with the overloaded == bankAccount operation.
  // Two bankAccount objects are equal if the name and PIN match.
  // The balance is not compared and so is arbitrarily set to 0.00.
  bankAccount temp(moneyMachine.name(), moneyMachine.PIN(), 0.00);

  // Presume the account has not been found yet:
  found = 0;

  // Begin a sequential search:
  customerNumber = 0;
  while((! found) && (customerNumber < numberOfCustomers))
  {
    if(temp == customer[customerNumber])
      found = 1;            // Found a match, so terminate loop
    else
      customerNumber++;  // Prepare for next comparison
  }
```

```
// If not found, return a customerNumber that can not exist (-1)
if(! found)
   customerNumber = -1;
}
```

There are three possible outcomes of a sequential search.

First is the rarest case when there are no customers in the array; there are no comparisons to make because the array is empty (numberOfCustomers == 0). The loop test customerNumber < numberOfCustomers (0 < 0) fails. The loop is terminated immediately and found retains its initial value of 0. At the end of the function, customerNumber is set to -1. Otherwise, the loop iterates at least once.

In the second scenario, a temporary bankAccount object (temp) is constructed with information gathered at the ATM. This will be compared to bankAccount objects in the array with the overloaded bankAccount operator ==. One bankAccount object is equal to another if the name and PIN match exactly. When the size of the array is at least 1, the search is on. The loop object customerNumber is incremented from 0 to 1, from 1 to 2, from 2 to 3, and so on until temp matches an array element or there are no more elements in the array to compare. Assuming we are using sixteen bankAccount objects shown earlier (here are the first four),

```
0. { bankAccount: CUST0, 0000, 000.00 }
1. { bankAccount: YOURLASTNAME, 1111, 111.11 }
2. { bankAccount: AUSTEN, 2222, 222.22 }
3. { bankAccount: CHELSEA, 3333, 333.33 }
```

When the name is "CHELSEA" and the PIN is "3333", the loop stops as when customerNumber changes from 2 to 3. At that point, found is reset to true (1). The reference parameter customerNumber changes the associated argument to 3, which is the array subscript of the found customer.

Example: In searching for CHELSEA/3333, findCustomer sets found to 1 and customerNumber to 3:

Identifier	Values of Objects before loop	After Iteration #1	#2	#3	After Loop Terminates
searchAcct.name()	CHELSEA	same	same	same	same
searchAcct.PIN()	3333	same	same	same	same
numberOfCustomers	16	same	same	same	same
found	0	same	same	same	same
customerNumber	0	1	2	3	same (3)

The third possible situation takes place when the customer name/PIN combination is not part of the array. In this case, customerNumber increments to 16 and the loop test (16 < 16) fails. Since found is still false, customerNumber is changed from 16 to -1 and 0 is returned to announce to the caller that the name and PIN entered at the ATM do not represent a valid bank account.

Example: In searching for ANDERS/5555, findCustomer sets found to 0 and customerNumber to -1:

Identifier	Values of Objects before loop	After Iteration #1	#2	...	#15	#16	After Loop Terminates
search.name()	ANDERS	same	same	...	same	same	same
search.PIN()	5555	same	same	...	same	same	same
numberOfCustomers	16	same	same	...	same	same	same
found	0	same	same	...	same	same (0)	same (0)
customerNumber	0	1	2	...	15	16	-1

Self-Check

1. How many comparisons (iterations of the search loop) are necessary when the search element matches customer[0]?
2. How many comparisons are necessary when the search element matches customer[15]?
3. How many comparisons are necessary when the search element is not found in the array?
4. Beginning with this code

```
// Declare and initialize an array of ints
int intArray[500];
intArray[0] = 8879;
intArray[1] = 9018;
intArray[2] = 7653;
// ...
intArray[498] = 4043;
intArray[499] = 1789;
int n = 500;

int searchInt;
cout << "Enter the int to be searched for: ";
cin >> searchInt;

int index, found;
```

write the remaining code that properly implements a sequential search for the `int` object `searchInt`. If the user enters a value for `searchInt` that is not in the array, assign -1 to the `int` object `index` and make sure `found` is 0. If the user enters a value for `searchInt` that is in the array, make sure `index` is the proper index in the array and that `found` is 1. You may assume all elements of `intArray` are unique.

Answers
1. 1
2. 16
3. 16   (`customerNumber < numberOfCustomers` is false immediately after the 16th iteration)
4.
```
found = 0;
index = 0;
while(! found && index < n)
{
  if(intArray[index] == searchInt)
    found = 1;
  else
    index++;
}
  if(! found)
    index = -1;
```

7.4   Case Study: A List of Strings

As you continue your study of computing, you will likely spend a good deal of time exploring ways to manage collections of data. The array is one such mechanism. It is likely that you will encounter classes that manage collections of objects with higher-level operations such as add, remove, and search. As a preview, we now look at a simple *list* class that uses an array to store the collection of `string` objects. The `stringList` class of this section manages from zero to many `string` objects with a limited set of member functions: `init`, `add`, and `display`. Data members that store the relevant data include an array of `string` objects and the current size of the list, which is the number of added elements.

7.4.1   Analysis

Problem: Write a program that manages a simple list of strings. The list operations consist of the ability to add a string and to display the list of strings. With an interactive menu-driven program left as a lab project (7F), for now the main function must be able to call these functions of a stringList class (a stringList constructor will be implemented in Chapter 8, making the need for stringList::init unnecessary):

`stringList::init();`	Creates an empty list of `strings` by making the size zero (0).
`stringList::add(string);`	Add a `string` to the end of the list (as the last element in the array).
`stringList::display();`	Show the number of `strings` that have been added followed by each individual `string` on its own line. If the list is empty (no `strings` have been added), the number of `strings` in the list is shown as 0 and no `strings` are displayed.

For now, there is no input. However, there is a lot of output, mostly in the form of messages, the size of the list, and the strings that have been added to the list during calls to `stringList::display()`.

init   When `stringList::init()` is called, the size of the list is set to zero and this message is displayed:

```
An empty list has been constructed (size is 0)
```

display   If no `strings` have been added, a call to `stringList::display()` generates this message:

```
Number of strings in this stringList object is 0
```

If the size of the list is greater than 0 and each `string` is displayed on its own line.

add   If an attempt is made to add a `string` object to the `stringList` object, and there is no more room in the array, we should see this message:

```
stringList is full! 'Kim Stahl' could not be added
```

The required outputs are summarized in the following program. The program calls all three member functions. To quickly demonstrate what happens in an attempt to add to a full list, the maximum number of `strings` has been limited to three at this time:

```cpp
// Maximum number of strings limited to 3 for testing
#include "ourstrli.h"

int main()
{
  stringList names;
```

```
    names.init();
    names.display();
    names.add("Sally Small");
    names.add("Linda Ewall");
    names.add("Larry Westphall");
    names.add("Kim Stahl");
    names.display();
    return 0;
}
```

—————————————————————— **Output** ——————————————————————

```
An empty list has been constructed (size is 0)

Number of strings in this stringList object is 0

stringList is full! 'Kim Stahl' could not be added

Number of strings in this stringList object is 3
0. Sally Small
1. Linda Ewall
2. Larry Westphall
```

7.4.2 Design: Encapsulating Data and Functions Within a Class

In the design phase of this case study, we use a class declaration to summarize and describe the member functions. We also see an array used as the major data member of this class. The data members listed after private are accessible from any member function. They are str (an array of string objects) and size (the number of strings that have been added). This allows us to concentrate on the array processing. Just remember this rule as you look at each algorithm within the context of a member function:

—————————————————————— **Rule** ——————————————————————
Data members are directly accessible to all member functions.

The following stringList class declaration provides a summary of list operations, the structure to encapsulate the array, and size data members with the operations (member functions) that manage this data.

```
// ----------------------------------------------------------------
// SPECIFICATION FILE
//
// File Name: ourstrli.h
// Declares: class stringList
//
// ----------------------------------------------------------------
```

```
// The maximum size of the array is intentionally kept small here to
// make testing easier--we get a full list after only three (3) adds
const int MAX = 3;

class stringList {
public:
  void stringList::init();
  // POST: The size of the list is initialized to 0

  void stringList::add(string newString);
  // POST: The string is added at the end of the array
  //       and the size of the list is increased by 1.
  //       If the array is full, a message is displayed.

  void stringList::display();
  // POST: All string objects currently stored in the array are
  //       displayed after a heading indicating the size of the list.
  //       If no strings have been added, no strings are displayed.

private:
  string str[MAX]; // Store up to MAX string objects and also store
  int size;        // exactly how many string objects have been added
};

#include "ourstrli.cpp"  // Add member function implementations
```

7.4.3   Implementation

With the postconditions to describe each member function, we now look at how the array helps manage a list of string objects. The init function establishes an empty list by setting the size data member to zero (all member functions are stored in ourstrli.cpp):

```
void stringList::init()
{ // Create an empty list
  cout << "An empty list has been constructed (size is 0)" << endl;
  size = 0;
}
```

After this code executes:

```
stringList names;
names.init();
```

the data store of the names object is represented as the size (currently 0) along with the array of string objects, which currently has zero initialized elements. These undefined array positions are marked with '?':

size	0
str[0]	?
str[1]	?
str[2]	?

Once the `stringList` object is initialized, the other `stringList` functions—display and add—may be called. For example, the following function calls add three names to the list, which become output with `names.display()` :

```
names.add("Kieran");
names.add("Mellisa");
names.add("Cody");
names.display();
```

When adding a `string` to a list of size 0, the argument is stored at the first array position, `str[0]`. When the size of the list is 1, the new `string` is stored at the second array position, `str[1]`. If the size of the list is 2, a third `string` is stored at the third array position, `str[2]`. The values of the `stringList` object now look like this after the three adds:

```
size   3
str[0] "Kieran"
str[1] "Mellisa"
str[2] "Cody"
```

Let's now look at how the `stringList::add` function is implemented.

To add a `string` at the end—or first available location—of the array, we must have access to both the size of the list (`size`) and the array that stores individual `string` objects (`str`). From within any member function of class `stringList`, we do have this access. The processing can now be summarized by this two-step algorithm:

Add a string
str[size] = the new name passed as an argument to the add function
increment size of the list by +1

First the new `string` is stored into the proper array location using `size` as the subscript. Then the size of the list is incremented in response to this change. This second step also conveniently sets up a situation where the next `string` will be added at the proper location.

The implementation of `stringList::add()` also includes a message to indicate a full list—one in which all array locations are used up. This is achieved by comparing the current list size to `MAX-1` before adding any `string`. Recall that the array was declared with the constant object `MAX` temporarily set to 3:

```
// Declared at the top of the file:
const int MAX = 3;

// Declared as a data member of class stringList:
private:
  string str[MAX];
```

Using this information we see the range of subscripts is limited to 0 through 2, or 0 through MAX-1. We should not attempt to store a string into str[MAX]. The if...else statement does and at the same time prevents destruction of memory values that are not part of the array. If size is greater than or equal to MAX, there are no more array elements available to store any more string objects.

```
void stringList::add(string newString)
{
  // Remember, str[MAX] should not be altered!
  // That memory does not belong to the array!
  if(size >= MAX)
    cout << endl << "stringList is full! '" << newString
                 << "' could not be added" << endl;
  else {
    // Store the argument into the array of string objects...
    str[size] = newString;
    // ...and make sure the size is always increased by +1:
    size++;
  }
}
```

Because any stringList object keeps track of its own size and its own array of strings at all times, stringList::display can be implemented with a for loop that traverses the entire array from subscript 0 through size-1 (remember, the first string is stored at str[0] and the last string at str[size-1]):

```
void stringList::display()
{
  cout << endl;
  cout << "Number of strings in this stringList object is " << size << endl;

  // Output all strings. No iterations occur when size == 0
  for(int j = 0; j < size; j++)
    cout << j << ". " << str[j] << endl;
}
```

7.4.4   Test the Implementation

We can test the array processing part of this class with a main function that declares a strList object and sets it to empty by calling the init member function. We can verify that no strings have been added with a call to display(); the size should be 0. Strings can then be added until the list is full, using a small value for MAX, which allows the program to reach a full state quickly. It is also important to see what happens at an attempt to add to a full list. An attempt to add a fourth string object results in a message indicating there is no room to store a new string. Therefore, no change is made to the list. Any of these states can be observed by calling stringList::display. The main function that performed these steps was shown earlier in the analysis section.

Self-Check

1. Write the code that places "Bob" at the end of a stringList object declared as stringList myFriends;. Assume the list is not full.
2. What change(s) must be made to store a list of 100 names, addresses, and telephone numbers, each of which is treated as one string?
3. What change(s) need to be made to the stringList class to manage a simple list of bankAccount objects?
4. Using the bankAccountList of question 3, write the minimum main function code that creates a list of two bankAccount objects (use any names, PINs, and balances you desire).

Answers

1. names.add("Bob");
2. Change MAX=3; to MAX=100; and add arguments like this: add("Bob Hardy, Laurel Hall, 555-1234")
3. Replace every occurrence of string with bankAccount
4.
```
int main()
{
    bankAccountList accounts;
    account.init();
    // Use this form to add a bankAccount object
    bankAccount anAcct("Second", "5432", 11230.00);
    accounts.add(anAcct);
    // or use this more compact explicit conversion as an argument to add
    accounts.add(bankAccount("Hall", "1234", 100.00));
    // ...
    return 0;
}
```

7.5 Another List Operation: stringList::remove

As another example of array processing, consider a function that removes a string from a stringList object. In order to concentrate on the remove algorithm, assume str (an array of strings) and size (the number of strings in the array) are always available. This is accomplished by implementing remove as a member of the stringList class. Here is the prototype:

```
void stringList::remove(string searchString);
// POST: If searchString is found, the string is removed from list.
//       If searchString is not found, a message is displayed.
// NOTE: The array of strings (str) and the number of string elements
//       added (size) are accessible from this member function.
```

Once it is implemented, we should be able to call stringList::remove anytime after stringList::init has been called. The argument, if found, is removed and the size of the list is reduced by one. The effect of remove on the list is illustrated in the following program in which five names are added and three are removed (assume MAX has been increased to 20). Notice that an attempt to remove a string that is not part of the stringList object results in a message indicating that no changes were made.

```
// When this program executed, the maximum number
// of string objects in the list was set to 20
#include "ourstrli.h"

int main()
{
  stringList names;

  names.init();
  names.add("Sally Small");
  names.add("Linda Ewall");
  names.add("Larry Westphall");
  names.add("Doris Hall");
  names.add("Kim Stahl");
  names.display();
  names.remove("Linda Ewall");
  names.remove("Sally Small");
  names.remove("Kim Stahl");
  names.remove("Not There");   // <- This string is not in the list
  names.remove("Hoang Dinh");  // <- This string is not in the list

  names.display();
  return 0;
}
```

—— **Output** ——
```
An empty list has been constructed (size is 0)

Current number of strings in this stringList object is 5
0. Sally Small
1. Linda Ewall
2. Larry Westphall
3. Doris Hall
4. Kim Stahl

Removing 'Linda Ewall' from this stringList object

Removing 'Sally Small' from this stringList object

'Not There' not found in this stringList object-no changes made

Removing 'Kim Stahl' from this stringList object

Current number of strings in this stringList object is 2
0. Doris Hall
1. Larry Westphall
```

The remove operation, which need not maintain the list in order, first searches for the string argument to remove. For example, in this call:

```
names.remove("Larry Westphall");
```

the string argument "Larry Westphall" is passed as the name to remove from the list. The remove algorithm begins with a sequential search:

```
void stringList::remove(string searchString)
{
  int location = 0;
  int found = 0;
  while((location < size) && (! found))
  {
    if(searchString == str[location])
      found = 1;
    else
      location++;
  }

  // Either display a message or alter the array by removing searchString.
  // The choice depends on the value of found.
  // ...
  // ...  The stringList::remove function is continued below
  // ...
```

After the sequential search loop terminates, the flag named found indicates whether or not the string argument has been located in the list. When found is true, location represents the subscript storing searchString. When found is false, the searchString was not previously stored in the stringList object—the value of location is meaningless. So for the times when searchString is not found, processing is easy. This message is displayed:

```
// found is false (0) if searchString was not found in the list
if(! found)
{
  cout << endl
       << "'" << searchString
       << "' not found in this stringList object."
       << "  No changes made." << endl;
}
```

But to remove a found string from a stringList object, adjustments must be made to the array. First, let's examine the values of all objects (str and size) and the values of the objects that are local to remove when trying to take out the string "Larry Westphall":

Objects local to remove	Value
searchString	"Larry Westphall"
location	2
found	1

Data members of stringList	Value
str[0]	"Sally Small"
str[1]	"Linda Ewall"
str[2]	"Larry Westphall"
str[3]	"Doris Hall"
str[4]	"Kim Stahl"
str[5]	"??"
str[6]	"??"
...	
size	5

We must somehow remove str[location] from the array, which is currently str[2] or "Larry Westphall". The simple way to do this is to move the last string into the location of the removed string. Or in this case, overwrite str[2] with str[size-1], which is the last string in the array, to have the state of list look like this:

Data members of stringList	Value
str[0]	"Sally Small"
str[1]	"Linda Ewall"
str[2]	**"Kim Stahl"** ← Notice "Larry Westphall" is removed
str[3]	"Doris Hall"
str[4]	"~~Kim Stahl~~"
str[5]	"??"
str[6]	"??"
...	
size	4

Although the strings are not in the same order (this was not a precondition), we have the same strings as before with the requested removal in effect. Because the last string was moved we need to decrease the size of the list by size--.

```
// found is 1 if searchString was found in the list
if(found)
{ // Remove searchString from the array:
  // First, move the last string to where the remove string was found
  str[location] = str[size-1];
  // and then decrease size by 1
  size--;
}
} // end of member function stringList::remove(string searchString);
```

The same code works even when the last string in the list is to be removed. With the code shown above, the assignment is still done even though it is not necessary. Merely decreasing size by 1 effectively eliminates the last string.

Self-Check

1. What is supposed to happen when an attempt is made to remove a string that is not part of the list?
2. Using the implementation of remove just given, what happens when an attempt is made to remove a string from an empty list?
3. Write a complete, yet minimal, main function that adds and then removes your name from a stringList object.
4. What is the value of size after your program of question 3 executes?
5. Does a remove operation always maintain the list of strings in the same order as the added strings?

Answers
1. The argument should precede this message: "not found in this stringList object. No changes made".
2. Since the sequential search loop-test (location < size) is false immediately, we should see the argument precede the message "not found in this stringList object. No changes made".

```
3.  int main()
    {
      stringList names;
      names.init();
      names.add("Your Name");
      names.remove("Your Name");
      return 0;
    }
4.  Zero
5.  No, not always. The last element may be moved to the first array position, or the second, or somewhere else.
```

Exercises

Use this declaration to answer questions 1 through 7:

```
double x[20];
```

1. How many doubles may be referenced by subscripting x?
2. Which integer is used as the subscript to reference the first double in the array object x?
3. Which integer is used as the subscript to reference the last double in the array object x?
4. Write code that stores 123.45 into the second element of x.
5. Write code that initializes all elements of x to 0.0.
6. Write the code that displays all elements of x from the first to the last, each element on its own line.
7. Write the code that increments every element of x by +1.0.
8. Show the output of the following program:

```
#include <iostream.h>
int main()
{
  const int MAX = 10;
  int x[MAX];
  int j;
  for(j = 0; j < 3; j++)
    x[j] = j * 2;
  for(j = 3; j < MAX; j++)
    x[j] = x[j-1] + x[j-2];
  for(j = 0; j < MAX; j++)
    cout << j << ". " << x[j] << endl;
  return 0;
}
```

9. How many elements must be given meaningful values for an array with 100 elements?

10. Declare a C++ array called `intArray` that can manage 10 `ints` with subscripts 0 through 9.

11. Write the code that determines the largest value of the following array, assuming all 75 values are initialized:

```
double y[75];
```

12. Write the code that determines the average element of the following array, assuming only the first 43 elements are initialized:

```
double z[100];
```

13. Write the output from the following program:

```cpp
#include <iostream.h>

const int MAX = 20;

class charList {
public:
   void charList::init();
   void charList::display();
   char charList::huh();
   void charList::mixup();
private:
   char c[20];
   int size;
};

void charList::init()
{
   c[0] = 'c';
   c[1] = 'b';
   c[2] = 'e';
   c[3] = 'd';
   c[4] = 'a';
   size = 5;
}
```

```
void charList::display()
{
   cout << endl;
   cout << "Array of chars:  ";
   for(int j = 0; j < size; j++)
     cout << c[j] << "  ";
   cout << endl;
}

char charList::huh()
{
   char tempHuh;
   tempHuh = c[0];
   for(int j = 1; j < size; j++)
   if(c[j] < tempHuh)
     tempHuh = c[j];
   return tempHuh;
}

void charList::mixup()
{
   char ch;
   ch = c[2];
   c[0] = 'x';
   c[5] = ch;
   c[2] = 'y';
   c[4] = 'z';
}

int main()
{
   charList characters;
   characters.init();
   characters.display();
   cout << "huh: " << characters.huh() << endl;
   characters.mixup();
   characters.display();
   cout << "huh: " << characters.huh() << endl;
   return 0;
}
```

14. Write a complete program that declares and interactively initializes an array of 10 strings. Your dialogue should look like this:

```
Enter string
#0 First
#1 Second
...
#9 Tenth
```

15. Write the code that sets found to 1 if a given string is found in the following array. If a string is not in the array, let found equal 0. Assume only the first size array elements are initialized.

```
string s[200];
```

16. How many comparisons does a sequential search make when the search element is stored in the first array element and there are 1000 elements in the array?

17. How many comparisons does a sequential search make when the search element does not match any array element and there are 1000 elements in the array?

18. Assuming a large number of searches are made on an array, and it is just as likely that an element is found in the first as the last position, approximate the average number of comparisons after 1000 searches when there are 1000 elements in the array.

19. Write the values stored in the array of the stringList object after function main executes. Assume the maximum size is 20.

```
int main()
{
    stringList courses;            str[0]:
    courses.init();                str[1]:
    courses.add("CmpSc 101");      str[2]:
    courses.add("Art 1");          str[3]:
    courses.add("Soc 150");        str[4]:
    courses.remove("Art 1");       str[5]:
    courses.add("Math 140");       str[6]:
    courses.remove("Math 141");    ...
    return 0;                      size:
}
```

Lab Projects

7A   Using Objects

Write a complete C++ program that extracts an undetermined number of ints (maximum of 100) and displays them in reverse order. The user may not supply the number of elements, so a sentinel loop must be used. Here is one sample dialogue:

```
Enter up to 100 ints using -1 to quit:
70
75
90
60
80
-1
Reversed:  80  60  90  75  70
```

7B   Using Objects

Write a complete program that inputs an undetermined number of positive numeric values, determines the average, and displays every value that is greater than or equal to the average. The user may not supply the number of elements, so a sentinel loop must be used. Here is one sample dialogue:

```
Enter numbers or -1 to quit
70
75
90
60
80
-1
Average: 75
Inputs >= average:  75  90  80
```

7C   Using Objects

A palindrome is a set of characters that reads the same backward as forward. Write a program that extracts an array of characters from the keyboard and determines whether or not the resulting string is a palindrome. Some examples of palindromes are: 'YASISAY', 'racecar', '1234321', 'ABBA', 'level', and 'MADAMIMADAM'. Here are two sample dialogues (Note: Do not use any blank characters!):

```
Enter string: MADAMIMADAM          Enter string: RACINGCAR
     Reversed: MADAMIMADAM               Reversed: RACGNICAR
   Palindrome: Yes                     Palindrome: No
```

7D   Using Objects

Write a program like the previous lab project, but this time allow the user to enter a mix of upper-or lowercase letters. Also allow input of blanks and punctuation marks. Your program should be able to determine if the string is a palindrome. For example, "A man, a plan, a canal, Panama" should be recognized as a palindrome even though the blanks and commas don't match in reverse and there is only one uppercase 'A'. Hint: Consider creating a new string with the help of function isalpha() declared in <ctype.h> to strip all characters that are not letters (or make up your own function isAlpha):

```
char isalpha(char ch);  // from ctype.h
// POST: Returns true if ch is a letter 'a'..'z' or 'A'..'Z'
//       and false (0) when ch is not a alphabetic letter.
```

Then use string::toUpper to convert all letters of this new string to uppercase. At this point all nonletters such as blanks and commas are ignored. Also, you shouldn't find any difference between 'A' and 'a' since all letters are in uppercase.

7E   Using Objects

The Fibonacci numbers start as 1, 1, 2, 3, 5, 8, 13, 21 such that the first two are 1 and any successive Fibonacci number is the sum of the preceding two. Write an entire program that properly initializes an array identified as `fib` representing the first 20 Fibonacci numbers. Do not use 20 assignment statements to do this; three should suffice.

7F   Using Objects

Write a menu-driven program that allows the user to add as many `strings` as desired and to see the list at any time. Use the following dialogue to establish the prompts and choices (you may clear the screen at appropriate times and/or change the appearance of the prompt):

```
An empty list has been constructed (size is 0)
Enter option: A)dd  D)isplay Q)uit: d
Number of strings in this stringList object is 0
Enter option: A)dd  D)isplay Q)uit: a
Enter string: First
Enter option: A)dd  D)isplay Q)uit: a
Enter string: Second
Enter option: A)dd  D)isplay Q)uit: d
Number of strings in this stringList object is 2
0. First
1. Second
Enter option: A)dd  D)isplay Q)uit: q
```

7G   Modifying a Class

In this lab, you are asked to add the `remove` operation to class `myStringList`. It is declared in the file "`mystrli.h`" and implemented in the file "`mystrli.cpp`." Class `myStringList` is similar in function to `stringList` except that the `remove` function is not a member.

First, edit the file "`mystrli.h`" and add the following prototype to the class declaration after `void myStringList::display()` (near line 28):

```
void myStringList::remove(string searchString);
// POST: If searchString is found, the string is removed from list.
//       If searchString is not found, a message is displayed.
// NOTE: The array (str) and the number of string elements
//       added (size) are accessible from all member functions.
```

Save the specification file, then edit the implementation file named "`mystrli.cpp`." At the very end of the file, after the implementation of `void myStringList::display` (near line 72), implement the `remove` member function as shown below. It does nothing other than indicate that the function has been called (you'll change this later). A function like this is called a *test stub*—an incomplete function that displays the value(s) of the argument(s) passed to it.

```
void myStringList::remove(string searchString)
{
    cout << "remove under construction: " << searchString << endl;
}
```

Save the implementation file, create a new file, and enter the following main function:

```
#include "mystrli.h"
int main()
{
    myStringList friends;
    friends.init();
    friends.add("June");
    friends.add("Chris");
    friends.add("Devon");
    friends.remove("Chris");
    friends.display();
}
```

Run this program. During the call to the remove function, you should see this message:

```
remove under construction: Chris
```

Replace the message "myStringList::remove" with code that properly implements the remove function according to the postconditions given in the class declaration. Run your program and verify that its behavior matches that of the stringList class discussed earlier. Modify the main function with code that:
- adds at least five names;
- removes the first name;
- removes the last name;
- displays the list (recall that the list may not show names in the same order as they were added).

7H   Using Objects

Write a program that extracts an undetermined number of annual salaries from an input file stream. After this, display all salaries and the percentage of salaries above the average. The average salary is determined by summing all salaries and dividing that sum by the number of salaries on file. Use the eof function to detect the end of the input file. If the input file contains this data:

```
30000
24000
35000
32000
25000
```

your output should look like this:

```
Average salary = 29200
Above average salaries:
$30000
$35000
$32000
60% of reported salaries were above average
```

71   Using Objects

Write a complete C++ program that creates an unknown number of bankAccount objects and stores them into an array. The input should come from an external file that looks like the following, but may contain 1, 2, 3, or up to exactly 20 lines (each line represents all data necessary to create one bankAccount object):

```
Hall       1234    100.00
Salvador   1111     53.45
Kirstein   2222    999.99
   ...
Pantone    6666   8790.56
Brendle    7777      0.00
Kentish    8888   1234.45
```

After initializing the array and determining the number of bankAccount objects, display every object that has a balance greater than or equal to 1,000.00. Then display each object with a balance less then 100.00. Your output should look like this:

```
Balance >= 1000.00
{ bankAccount: PANTONE, 8790.56 }
{ bankAccount: KENTISH, 1234.56 }

Balance < 100.00:
{ bankAccount: SALVADOR, 53.45 }
{ bankAccount: BRENDLE, 0.00 }
```

7.6 Sorting

The elements of an array are often arranged into either an ascending or descending order—a process known as *sorting*. For example, an array of test scores are sorted into descending order by rearranging the numeric values in a highest to lowest order. An array of string objects sorted in ascending order establishes an alphabetized list (As before Bs, Bs before Cs). To sort an array, we must be able to compare elements with either a < or > relationship. If one object can be less than or greater than another object of the same class, then arrays of those objects are *sortable*. For example, 79 < 85 and "A" < "B" are valid expressions. Arrays of string objects are also sortable. (*Note:* C++ allows operators such as < for classes that do not already have this operator defined. For example, an employee class may be made sortable using a hire date member).

The following code declares and initializes part of an array used to demonstrate a sort on an array of ints. It also sets n as the number of initialized elements.

```
int n, test[10];
test[0] = 76;
test[1] = 74;
test[2] = 100;
test[3] = 62;
test[4] = 89;
n = 5;
```

There are many sorting algorithms. Even though some are more efficient, we will use the relatively simple *selection sort*. Our goal is to arrange this array of five int elements into descending order.

Object Name	Start: Unsorted Array	Goal: Sorted Array
test[0]	76	100
test[1]	74	89
test[2]	100	76
test[3]	62	74
test[4]	89	62
n	5	5

With the selection sort algorithm, the largest test int must end up in test[0] and the lowest in test[4]. In general, an array x of size n is sorted in descending order if $x[j] >= x[j+1]$ for j = 0 to n-2.

The selection sort begins by locating the largest element in the array from the first (test[0]) through the last (test[4]). The largest element, test[2] in this array, is swapped with the top element, test[0]. Once this is done, the array is sorted at least through the first element.

		Before:	*After:*	
top →	test[0]	76	100	← Sorted through test[1]
	test[1]	74	74	
	test[2]	100	76 ←	
	test[3]	62	62	
	test[4]	89	89	

The subtask of finding the largest element is accomplished by examining all array elements and keeping track of the subscript that is the index of the largest int. After this, the largest element found is swapped with test[0]. Here is an algorithm that accomplishes these two subtasks:

// *Use selection sort to sort the list through the first element*

(a)   top = 0

// *At first, assume that the first element is the largest*

(b)   largestIndex = top

// *Check the rest of the list (test[top+1] through test[n-1])*

for j ranging from top+1 through n - 1

(c)   if test[j] > test[largestIndex]

(c1)   largestIndex = j

// *Place largest element into the first position and also place*
// *the first element into the position where the largest was located*

(d)   swap test[largestIndex] with test[top]

The following trace results show how the array is sorted through the first element with the largest test stored at test[0]. Notice that largestIndex changes only when an array element is encountered that is larger than the one stored in test[largestIndex].

Step	top	largestIndex	j	test[0]	test[1]	test[2]	test[3]	test[4]	n
	?	?	?	76	74	100	62	89	5
(a)	0	"	"	"	"	"	"	"	"
(b)	"	0	"	"	"	"	"	"	"
(c)	"	"	1	"	"	"	"	"	"
(c1)	"	1	"	"	"	"	"	"	"
(c)	"	"	2	"	"	"	"	"	"
(c1)	"	2	"	"	"	"	"	"	"
(c)	"	"	3	"	"	"	"	"	"
(c1)	"	"	"	"	"	"	"	"	"
(c)	"	"	4	"	"	"	"	"	"
(c1)	"	"	"	"	"	"	"	"	"
(c)	"	"	5	"	"	"	"	"	"
(d)	"	"	"	100	74	76	62	89	"

This trace shows largestIndex changing three times to represent the index of the largest value in the array. After traversing the entire array, the largest element is swapped with the top array element. In our example, the preceding algorithm swaps the values of the first and third array elements so 100 is stored in test[0] and 76 is stored in test[2].

The array is now sorted through the first element. The same algorithm can be used to place the second largest element into test[1]. But the second traversal must begin at a new false "top" of the array—index 1 rather than 0. This is accomplished by incrementing top from 0 to 1. Now a second traversal of the array begins at the second element rather than the first. The largest element in the unsorted portion of the array is to be swapped with the second element. A second traversal of the array ensures the first two elements are in order. In this example array, test[4] is swapped with test[1] and the array is sorted through the first two elements:

```
         test[0]    100      Sorted through test[0]
top →    test[1]     89   ←  Sorted through test[1]
         test[2]     76
         test[3]     62
         test[4]     74   ←
```

This process repeats a total of n-1 times—for all the elements in the list except the last. This nth element must be the smallest (or equal to the smallest) since the array preceding the last element is already sorted. So an outer loop is employed to change top from 0 through n-2.

Selection Sort

```
{
    for top ranging from 0 through n - 2
      largestIndex = top
      for each element in the remaining list
          for j ranging from top + 1 through n - 1
        if test[ j ] > test[ largestIndex ] then
            largestIndex = j
        swap  test[largestIndex] with test[top]
}
```

```
         test[0]    100      Sorted through test[0]
         test[1]     89      Sorted through test[1]
         test[2]     76      Sorted through test[2]
top →    test[3]     74   ←  Sorted through test[3] and
         test[4]     62   ←  Sorted through test[4] since this is <= smallest array element
```

One implementation of the selection sort algorithm is shown next as a member function of class intList. The init member function initializes the first five elements of the array—named data here—and sets the number of assigned elements (n) to 5. The display member function is called to show the first through nth elements of the array on separate lines. Finally, selection sort is implemented as intList::sort from which the private swap member function is called to switch any two ints.

```cpp
// The main function is a test driver program that initializes an array
// of five tests, displays all 5 array elements when not sorted, sorts
// the array in descending order, and then displays the sorted array
#include <iostream.h>

class intList {
public:
  void intList::init();
  void intList::display();
  void intList::sort();
private:
  int n;
  int test[10];
  void swap(int & a, int & b);
};

void intList::init()
{ // Constructor initializes the first five elements
  n = 5;
  test[0] = 76;
  test[1] = 74;
  test[2] = 100;
  test[3] = 62;
  test[4] = 89;
  // Not used: test[5], test[7], test[8], test[9], and test[9]
}

void intList::display()
{ // Output element from first through the nth
  for(int j = 0; j < n; j++)
    cout << "test[" << j << "]: " << test[j] << endl;
}

void intList::sort()
{ // Selection sort is used to arrange an array of ints into descending order
  int j, top, largestIndex;

  for(top = 0; top < n-1; top++)
  {
    // Presume the first element in the array is the largest
    largestIndex = top;
```

```
    // Search the remainder of the array for the largest element
    for(j = top + 1; j < n; j++)
      if(test[j] > test[largestIndex])
        largestIndex = j;

    // Then place the largest at the beginning of the sublist
    swap(test[largestIndex], test[top]);
  }
}

void intList::swap(int & a, int & b)
{ // The two argument values are interchanged
  int temporary = a;
  a = b;
  b = temporary;
}

int main()
{
  intList ourTests;
  ourTests.init();

  cout << endl << "tests before sorting " << endl;
  ourTests.display();
  ourTests.sort();
  cout << endl << "tests after sorting " << endl;
  ourTests.display();
  return 0;
}
```

─────────── **Output** ───────────

```
    tests before sorting
    test[0]: 76
    test[1]: 74
    test[2]: 100
    test[3]: 62
    test[4]: 89

    tests after sorting
    test[0]: 100
    test[1]: 89
    test[2]: 76
    test[3]: 74
    test[4]: 62
```

In general, the private swap member function exchanges the values of the two objects: test[largestIndex] with test[top]. Consider what would happen if `top == largestIndex`? An array element is switched with itself, leaving the array unchanged, but nonetheless in the proper order to that point. Although these occasional swaps may seem unnecessary, avoiding them would require code like this:

```
if(top != largestIndex)
  swap(test[largestIndex], test[top]);
```

The selection sort arranged an array of `ints` into descending numeric order. However, the same sorting algorithm arranges any class of data that has < or > defined (such is the case with `float` or `string`, for example). Also, with just one change, data of any class may be arranged into ascending order. For example, a list of names could be arranged in ascending (alphabetical) order by changing the relational operator from > to < in the selection sort `if` statement.

```
if(data[j] > data[largestIndex])   // Descending order
```

becomes

```
if(data[j] < data[smallestIndex]   // Ascending order
```

Since operators may be overloaded, any class object can be sortable by defining < or >. For example, `bankAccounts` could be sorted by name and PIN, which means both data members must be compared. An `employee` class may be sorted by hire date, a student class by grade point average, and so on.

7.6.1   (*Optional*) Array Argument/Parameter Associations

The preceding sort demonstration was enclosed within a class so the array and the number of meaningful assigned elements were accessible from the four functions that managed the data. However, sometimes it may be necessary to pass an array through argument/parameter association. This requires a different syntax in the parameter list—empty square brackets [ ]. The general form of a function prototype with exactly one array parameter is as follows:

return-type function-name (*class-name   array-name* [ ])

This example prototype is used to pass an array of `doubles` (named x) to and back from a `void` function named `init` along with the number of assigned elements n:

```
void init( double x [ ], int & n ); // Output parameters
```

The main function may now use a function call like this:

```
int main()
{
  double test[100];
  int n;
  // Initialize test and n
  init(test, n);  // test and n are passed to reference parameters
  // Use test and n ...
```

The empty square brackets indicating an array parameter also have another significance: The associated argument will be passed by reference even without &. Whereas the & is required in front of n, placing & in front of x is an error. This is because arrays are automatically passed by reference. Part of the reason for this is efficiency (the program may execute more quickly) and better memory utilization. Instead of creating memory for 100 double values and copying all values from the main function to another function—as is the case in pass by value— the address of the array is automatically passed instead. This means that a change to the parameter (x) inside will also change the argument (test)—the same situation as if a reference parameter had been used. The array name is actually the address of the first array element (more on this in Chapter 9).

In the case of a function that initializes the main function array (test), passing by reference (with [ ] rather than &) is not only preferable for efficiency's sake, it is required. However, if you want to prevent changes to the parameter from affecting the argument, const can be applied to the parameter. With a *const parameter*, an attempt to change the parameter inside the function body generates an error at compiletime:

```
void display(const int test[], const int n)
{
  n++;       // <- Compiletime error:
  test[0]++; // <- Compiletime error:
  // System dependent compiletime error messages include:
  // 1. increment of constant
  // 2. increment of read-only location
  // 3. Cannot modify a const object
}
```

Passing arrays as const parameters and by reference through [ ] is illustrated in the following program, which is equivalent to the preceding intList class and program sorting example. Recall that function prototypes can be compiled and called upon before the complete definition of the function, which is given below after the main function:

```
// This program initializes an array of five ints, displays it, sorts
// the array in descending order, and displays the sorted array. The
// difference between this and the program in sort.cpp is this:
//
//      Rather than being encapsulated along with member functions
//      of a class, the array and its number of assigned elements
//      are passed through argument parameter associations among
//      the four nonmember functions init, display, sort, and swap

#include <iostream.h>

//--------------------------------------------------------------------
// 1. The declaration of the function prototypes with array parameters
//--------------------------------------------------------------------

void init(int test[], int & n);  // Both are Output parameters

void display(const int test[], const int n); // Input parameters

void sort(int test[], const int n); // test is Output, n is Input

void swap(int & a, int & b); // Both are Input/Output parameters

//--------------------------------------------------------------------
// 2. The main function with array arguments
//--------------------------------------------------------------------

int main()
{
  int ourTests[10];
  int n;
  init(ourTests, n);
  cout << endl << "tests before sorting " << endl;
  display(ourTests, n);
  sort(ourTests, n);
  cout << endl << "tests after sorting " << endl;
  display(ourTests, n);
  return 0;
}

//--------------------------------------------------------------------
// 3. The implementation of function prototypes given earlier
//--------------------------------------------------------------------

void init(int test[], int & n)
{
  n = 5;
  test[0] = 76;
```

```
    test[1] = 74;
    test[2] = 100;
    test[3] = 62;
    test[4] = 89;
    // Not used: test[5], test[7], test[8], and test[9]
}

void display(const int test [], const int n)
{ // Output the first through nth arguments
  for(int j = 0; j < n; j++)
    cout << "test[" << j << "]: " << test[j] << endl;
}

void sort(int test[], const int n)
{ // Selection sort is used to arrange an
  // array of ints into descending order
  int j, top, largestIndex;

  for(top = 0; top < n-1; top++)
  {
    // Presume the first element in the sublist is the largest
    largestIndex = top;

    // Search the remainder of the array for the largest test
    for(j = top+1; j < n; j++)
      if(test[j] > test[largestIndex])
        largestIndex = j;

    // Then place the largest at the beginning of the sublist
    swap(test[largestIndex], test[top]);
  }
}

void swap(int & a, int & b)
{ // The two argument values are interchanged
  int temporary = a;
  a = b;
  b = temporary;
}
```

Programming Tip

Array parameters and nonmember (free) functions have been covered here only for the sake of completeness, that is, for the time when you or your instructor feel the need to pass arrays and the number of defined elements among nonmember functions. But you should consider encapsulating the data, such as the array and its current size, along with the functions that manage that data. We will be able to do this better after formally studying the C++ class in the next chapter and reviewing the `stringList` and `intList` classes. As shown several times already, encapsulation—one of the key concepts of object-oriented programming—is implemented though a C++ class, its collection of member functions, and its collection of data members that are accessible from all member functions. This reduces the number of argument/parameter associations.

Self-Check

1. Alphabetizing an array of `strings` ("A" is less than "B" and "Z" > "Y") requires a sort in which order, ascending or descending?

2. If the largest element in an array already exists as the first, what happens when the `swap` function is called for the first time (when `top = 0`)?

3. Write code that searches for and stores the largest `int` element of array `x` into the `int` object largest. Assume that all elements from `x[0]` through `x[n-1]` have been given meaningful values.

4. (*optional*) Write the output of the following program:

```cpp
#include <iostream.h>

void one(int data[]);

int main()
{
  int x[2];
  x[0] = -3;
  x[1] = 9;
  cout << x[0] << "  " << x[1] << endl;
  one(x);
  cout << x[0] << "  " << x[1] << endl;
  return 0;
}

void one(int data [])
{
  data[0]++;
  data[1]++;
}
```

5. (*optional*) Conjecture what would happen if in the preceding program, the function prototype and implementation both declare `data` as a `const` parameter.

```cpp
void one(const int data[]);
```

Answers
1. Ascending
2. The first element swaps with itself leaving the array virtually unchanged.
3. ```
   largest = x[0];
   for(int j = 1; j < n; j++)
     if(x[j] > largest)
       largest = x[j];
   ```
4. *Note:* The array x is changed.

   ```
   -3  9
   -2  10
   ```
5. Both attempts to increment the parameter data result in compiletime errors on most systems. `data[0]++;` and `data[1]++;` are flagged as an attempts to modify a `const` object.

7.7   Binary Search

We have already used sequential search to locate one bank customer in an array of `bankAccount` objects and to search for a `string` array element during the `stringList::remove` operation. We now look at the *binary search* algorithm that accomplishes the same search task with the precondition that the array is sorted. The advantage of binary search is efficiency. It is faster than a sequential search, especially when the array is large. By contrast, the slower sequential search does not require the array to be sorted and the algorithm is simpler.

In general, binary search works like this. If an array of `string` objects representing names is sorted in alphabetical (ascending) order, half the search range is eliminated from the search field each time a comparison is made. This is summarized in the following algorithm that searches for any string:

> *while the string element (such as a name) is not found and it still may be in the array*
> {
>> *Determine the position of the string in the middle of the array.*
>> *If the name in the middle is not the string being searched for,*
>>> *eliminate the half of the array that cannot contain the string being searched for.*
>
> }

Each time the search element is compared to one array element, the binary search effectively eliminates half the array elements from the search field. In contrast, the sequential search only eliminates one name from the search field for each comparison. Assuming an array is sorted in alphabetic order, to sequentially search for `"AAA"`, we would not have to go too far since `"AAA"` is likely to be located as one of the first array elements. But searching for `"Zevon"` sequentially would take much more time because we would first have to search through all names beginning with A through Y before even arriving at the Zs. Binary search gets to `"Zevon"` much more quickly.
   ```

Before we begin a binary search, these preconditions must be satisfied:

1. The array must be sorted.
2. The subscripts that reference the first and last elements must represent the entire range of initialized elements.

The element in the middle of the array is accessed by computing the array index that is halfway between the first and last positions of the array. This is the average of the indexes. These become indexes in the search and will be referred to as first, mid, and last. The binary search algorithm is preceded with several assignments:

```
searchString = "The string being searched for"
first = index of the first assigned array element
last =  index of the last assigned array element
mid = (first + last) / 2
```

At this point, one of three things can happen:

1. The element in the middle of the array matches the search name—the search is complete.
2. The search element precedes the middle element. The second half of the array can be eliminated from the search field.
3. The search element follows the middle element. The first half of the array can be eliminated from the search field.

This is written algorithmically as:

```
if searchString = str[ mid ] then
    searchString is found
else
    if searchString < str[ mid ]
        eliminate mid..last elements
    else
        eliminate first..mid elements
```

The binary search algorithm is implemented here as if it were a member of the stringList class shown earlier; that is, size and str are initialized and are accessible.

Trace of Binary Search Algorithm

```
// PRE: The array named str is sorted in ascending order.
//      str[0] through str[6] are defined array elements.
int first = 0;
```

```
int last = size - 1;            // last = 6;
int found = 0;
string searchString = "LISA";

while( (! found) && (first <= last) )
{
  mid = (first + last) / 2;     // (0+6)/2 = 3
  if(searchString == str[mid]) // Check the three possibilities
    found = 1;                  // 1. searchString is found in str
  else                          //    so indicate it's been found.
    if(searchString < str[mid])// 2. searchString is in first half
      last = mid - 1;           //    of str so eliminate second half.
    else                        // 3. searchString is in second half
      first= mid + 1;           //    of str so eliminate first half.
}
```

Objects before comparing searchString ("LISA") **to** str[mid] ("LAU"):

```
str
[0]    "ABE"         ←first= 0
[1]    "CLAY"
[2]    "KIM"
[3]    "LAU"         ←mid=3
[4]    "LISA"
[5]    "PELE"
[6]    "ROE"         ←last=6
```

After comparing searchString **to** str[mid], first **is increased and a new** mid **is computed:**

```
str
[0]    "ABE"     Because "LISA" is greater than str[mid],
[1]    "CLAY"    the objects str[0] through str[3] no longer
[2]    "KIM"     need to be searched and can now be
[3]    "LAU"     eliminated from subsequent search.
[4]    "LISA"    ←first=4
[5]    "PELE"    ←mid=5
[6]    "ROE"     ←last=6
```

searchString ("LISA") < str[mid] ("PELE"), **so** last **is decreased and a new** mid **is computed**

```
str
[0]    "ABE"
[1]    "CLAY"
[2]    "KIM"
[3]    "LAU"
[4]    "LISA"    ←first=5    ←last=5    ←mid=5
[5]    "PELE"    Because "LISA" is less than str[mid], eliminate str[5]
[6]    "ROE"     through str[6] from the search field.
```

Now str[mid] does equal searchString so found is set to true. Let's review this particular binary search.

The first iteration compared "LISA" to "LAU". Since these two values are unequal, searchStr was compared to see if it was greater than or less than str[mid]. Because "LISA" < str[mid] was false, the first half of the array was effectively eliminated from further search by setting first to mid+1 (4). Then "LISA" < str[mid] was true so last was moved before mid with the assignment last = mid-1 (5). The third iteration of the loop found "Lisa" == str[mid] so found was set to true and loop termination was achieved. This binary search algorithm can be more efficient than the sequential search that eliminates only *one* element from further search for each iteration. Binary search eliminates *half* the elements. For example, when n = 1024, a binary search eliminates 512 elements from further search for each comparison.

In a moment, we will see a program that searches for every name in the array. But first we should consider the possibility that the data being searched for is not in the array. For example, if "CARLA" were the searchString, the values of first, mid, and last progress as follows:

Iteration	first	mid	last	Comment
#1	0	3	6	Compare "CARLA" to "LAU"
#2	0	1	2	Compare "CARLA" to "CLAY"
#3	0	0	0	Compare "CARLA" to "ABE"
#4	1	0	0	first <= last is false—the loop is terminated

Objects when searchString ("CARLA") is not stored in the array

```
str
[0]    "ABE"      ←last=0    ←mid=0
[1]    "CLAY"     ←first=1
[2]    "KIM"
[3]    "LAU"
[4]    "LISA"
[5]    "PELE"
[6]    "ROE"
```

After searchString ("CARLA") is compared to str[1] ("ABE"), no further comparisons are necessary. The binary search also stops when first becomes greater than last, as shown above. This is the second of two conditions that terminate the loop. Since first is no longer less than or equal to last, searchString is not in the array. In summary, the binary search, which is implemented below, has the following two preconditions:

1. The array is sorted in ascending order.
2. The first array subscript is 0. The last initialized element has a subscript of size-1.

These preconditions are guaranteed by implementing search as a member of the stringList class with all names carefully added in alphabetical order. You will see some code has been added after the binary search to indicate the outcome of the search (a string is either found or not found). The following member function indicates access to size and the array named str, which are data members of the stringList class:

```
void stringList::search(string searchString)
{ // Search an array that must be in ascending (alphabetical) order
  int first, last, mid, found;

  first = 0;      // Presume 1 is the first subscript of the array
  last  = size-1; // Presume size is the last initialized array element
  found = 0;      // We haven't found it yet

  while(! found && first <= last)
  {
    mid = (first + last) / 2;
    if(searchString == str[mid])  // Check the three possibilities
      found = 1;                   // 1. searchString is found in str
    else                           //    so indicate it's been found.
      if(searchString < str[mid])  // 2. searchString is in first half
        last = mid - 1;            //    of str so eliminate second half.
      else                         // 3. searchString is in second half
        first= mid + 1;            //    of str so eliminate first half.
  }

  // Indicate success or failure as part of stringList::search()
  // to reduce the amount of code in the main function test driver.
  cout.width(6);
  cout << searchString;
  if(found)
    cout << " found as str[" << mid << "]" << endl;
  else
    cout << " not found" << endl;
}
```

Now, if names are carefully added to ensure they are in alphabetical order—so no sort is necessary—the following program uses the binary search algorithm to locate the following items:

1. Every name in the stringList object.
2. The name "KARL" that could have been in the first half, but is not.
3. The name "RUTH" that could have been in the second half, but is not.
4. A name that precedes the first name alphabetically ("AAA").
5. A name that follows the last name alphabetically ("ZZZ").

```
int main()
{
  stringList names;
  names.init();

  // The names must be added in alphabetic order
  names.add("ABE");
  names.add("CLAY");
  names.add("KIM");
  names.add("LAU");
  names.add("LISA");
  names.add("PELE");
  names.add("ROE");

  // Search for every name and four that are not there
  cout << endl;
  names.search( "ABE");
  names.search("CLAY");
  names.search( "KIM");
  names.search( "LAU");
  names.search("LISA");
  names.search("PELE");
  names.search( "ROE");
  names.search("CARL");   // Not there
  names.search("RUTH");   // Not there
  names.search( "AAA");   // Not there
  names.search( "ZZZ");   // Not there
  return 0;
}
```

—————————————————— **Output** ——————————————————

```
 ABE found as name[0]
CLAY found as name[1]
 KIM found as name[2]
 LAU found as name[3]
LISA found as name[4]
PELE found as name[5]
 ROE found as name[6]
CARL not found
RUTH not found
 AAA not found
 ZZZ not found
```

The binary search can also be utilized to search through an array of any class that has been sorted in descending order (largest first). The modification simply requires a reverse of the relational operator from < to >:

```
      else                          //    so indicate it's been found.
        if(searchData > data[mid])  // 2. searchData is in first half
          last = mid - 1;           //    of data so eliminate second half.
        else                        // 3. searchData is in second half
          first = mid + 1;          //    of data so eliminate first half.
```

Self-Check

1. Write at least one precondition for a successful binary search.
2. What is the maximum number of comparisons (approximately) performed on a list of 1024 elements during a binary search? (Hint: After one comparison, only 512 array elements need be searched; after two searches, only 256 elements need be searched, and so on.)
3. During a binary search, what condition signals that the search element does not exist in an array?

Answers
1. The array must be sorted.   2. Approximately 10   3. `first > last`

Chapter Summary

We have now studied many simple and structured classes. Fundamental types such as char and double are called simple types since they store one value per object. The C++ class and array create structured objects since they store many values. Whereas objects may store data of many different types at the same time (a string, a float, and even several arrays, for example), arrays usually store collections of the same class (an array of char, int, string, or bankAccount, for example).

Individual array elements are referenced with subscripts. With a C++ array, the int-expression of a subscript reference should be in the range of 0 through the declared size minus 1. For example, the valid subscript range of the array double x[100] is 0 through 99 inclusive. Out-of-range subscripts are not detected at compiletime and may cause system crashes, destruction of other objects, or some other system-specific problems. As programmers, we must guard against these potential hazards. For management of collections of values, the stringList class offered the following improvements:

- The stringList class won't allow additions to a "full" list. This avoids out-of-range subscripts.
- The size of the list is managed through higher-level abstractions like init, add, and remove. An int object named n or size is an important piece of data that is not part of any primitive C++ array. But the C++ class allows us to encapsulate the number of initialized elements within the stringList class. The size data member was required in order to add a string, to search for an element during a

remove operation, and to display the assigned elements of the array. This and the array itself are accessible from all member functions.

The selection sort algorithm was used to arrange array elements into descending order. Any object with < or > operations may also be sorted with the selection sort algorithm. Arrays may also be sorted in ascending order, which is more appropriate sometimes, especially with string elements where ascending order means alphabetical order. We studied the binary search algorithm that more efficiently accomplishes the same task as the sequential search as long as the array is sorted.

Exercises

20. Write the output generated by the program segment below using the initialized array of string objects.

```
#include <iostream.h>
#include "ourstr.h"
int main()
{
  string x[10];
  int n = 5;
  x[0] = "Michael";
  x[1] = "Rochelle";
  x[2] = "Joshua";
  x[3] = "Adam";
  x[4] = "Judy";
  for(int top = 0; top < n-1; top++)
  {
    int index = top;
    for(int j = top+1; j <= n-1; j++)
      if(x[j] < x[index])
        index = j;
    string temp = x[index];
    x[index] = x[top];
    x[top] = temp;
  }
  for(int j = 0; j <= n-1; j++)
    cout << x[j] << endl;
  return 0;
}
```

21. Write the output of the program segment below using this initialized array of strings:

```
str
[0]   "ABE"
[1]   "CLAY"
[2]   "KIM"
[3]   "LAU"
[4]   "LISA"
[5]   "PELE"
[6]   "ROE"
[7]   "SAM"
[8]   "TRUDY"

  int first = 0;
  int last = 8;
  int found = 0;
  string searchString = "CLAY";
  cout << "First Mid Last" << endl;
  while( (! found) && (first <= last) )
  {
    int mid = (first + last) / 2;
    cout << first << "      " << mid << "      " << last << endl;
    if(searchString == str[mid])
      found = 1;
    else
      if(searchString < str[mid])
        last = mid - 1;
      else
        first= mid + 1;
  }
  if(found)
    cout << searchString << " was found " << endl;
  else
    cout << searchString << " was not found " << endl;
```

22. Write the output generated by the preceding program segment when searchString is assigned each of the following values:

    a. searchString = "LISA"   d. searchString = "ABLE"
    b. searchString = "TRUDY"   e. searchString = "KIM"
    c. searchString = "ROE"   f. searchString = "ZEVON"

23. List at least one condition that must be true before a successful binary search can be implemented.

24. What is the maximum number of comparisons (approximately) that will be performed on a list of 256 elements? (*Hint:* After one comparison, only 128 array elements need be searched, after two searches, only 64 elements need be searched, and so on.)

Lab Projects

7J   Modify a Class

Currently, the `intList::init` function always sets the number of tests to 5 and uses the same test values. Rather than accepting this rigid data each time, modify the `intList::init()` method to extract interactive input of up to 20 test scores of your choosing. Make sure you notify the user how to terminate the input loop. Either retype the class and main function test driver from the example shown earlier, or modify `intList::init()` as it is included in the file `myintli.cpp` (**my integer list**). A call to `intList::init` should cause a dialogue like this:

```
Enter tests or -1 to quit:
80 70 90 100 65 78 98 100 45 87 76 92 71 -1
```

If the user attempts to enter more than 20 tests, display an appropriate message and stop the interactive input.

Hint: A `while` loop will process `cin` extractions no matter how many integers are on a line. You could also enter your data on separate lines.

7K   Using Objects

The pseudocode that follows is a simplified version of the notorious *bubble sort*. Translate this algorithm into C++ code that sorts an array into descending order.

```
done = false
while not done do the following
{
    done = true
    for j = 1 through n-1
    if x[j] < x[j+1]
    {
        // The two array elements are out of order
        done = false
        swap x[j] with x[j+1]
    }
}
```

First declare an array named x that may store up to 20 `ints`. Test this procedure with the following unsorted array of integers: 3, 8, 9, 6, 6, 5, 1, 2, 4, where 3 is stored in x[1] and 4 in x[n], where n=9;.

7L   Using Objects

Write a complete C++ program that inputs a collection of floating-point numbers from an input file. Even though you must create your own input file, your program does not know how many numbers will be on file. The program code may only presume that there will never be more than 100 numeric values stored in the input file. Sort the array of numeric values into descending order and display the following:

1. Every array element in descending order, each `double` on its own separate line
2. The average
3. The highest
4. The lowest
5. The mode (The value with as many values above as below the middle element of a sorted array)

7M   Modifying a Class: An Ordered List

See Appendix A, "Additional Lab Projects."

7N   Using Objects

See Appendix A, "Additional Lab Projects."

8

Class Design and Implementation

The class is a major feature of the C++ language and of object-oriented programming in general. Up to this point we have used objects, looked at some class implementations, and modified other classes. We now turn to the design of classes and details of class implementation so we can design and build our own software abstractions. After studying this chapter, you will be able to:

- Declare and implement C++ classes.
- Understand the role of constructors and use multiple constructors.
- Design and implement simple classes and classes with array data members.

8.1   The C++ Class Revisited

Data abstraction refers to the practice of understanding and using a class without full knowledge of the implementation details. The characteristics of the data and the operations that manage that data are important. For example, the int class can be understood by examining the characteristics of integers along with some of the operators used to manipulate the integer data—operators and functions such as +, -, /, *, %, <<, >>, abs, sqrt, pow, and so on. By now, we should realize that it is possible to understand and use int objects without knowing all the details of the internal representation of the int class and how the operations are actually implemented in the hardware and software. We can consider the int class at the more abstract level of operations and data characteristics, or at a lower level of abstraction by looking at the bits and bytes and the different coding schemes used to implement the int class. We can also view classes such as string, bankAccount, ATM, and bank from a higher level of abstraction simply by understanding the available operations—the functions and operators that can be applied to any object of the class.

We have been using data abstraction since the beginning of this text, typically perusing a class with the member function prototypes and pre- and postconditions. We have used classes to simplify some complex algorithms, especially those dealing with array processing. Our preference has been to *use* or to *modify* these classes rather than to *implement* them. In this chapter, abstraction finally yields to formal coverage of class design and implementation.

8.1.1   Class Declarations

A C++ class declaration consists of any number of member functions, data members (objects), and access modes (private and public are two of C++'s three access modes). The following general form is the one consistently used for all the programmer-defined class declarations in this textbook:

```
class class-name {
public:
    member-function-prototypes
private:
    data-members
} ;
```

The *member-function-prototypes* after the access mode public represent the operations. The *data-members* after access mode private are the objects that store the state. The familiar bankAccount class declaration is shown again. Operations include withdraw. State includes accountBalance.

```
//------------------------------------------------------------------
// SPECIFICATION FILE: ouracct.h
//
//   Declares: class bankAccount
//------------------------------------------------------------------
#include "ourstr.h"

class bankAccount {
public:
    bankAccount::bankAccount(string initName,        // Constructor
                             string initPIN,
                             double initBalance);
    // POST: Object is initialized using 3 arguments when initialized as
    //       bankAccount anotherAcct("Jones", "4321", 457.75);

    void bankAccount::deposit(double amount);
    // POST: amount is added to current balance of the object

    void bankAccount::withdraw(double amount);
    // POST: amount is deducted from the current balance of the object

    double bankAccount::balance();
    // POST: The current balance of any object is returned

    string bankAccount::name();
    // POST: The name attribute of any object is returned

    string bankAccount::PIN();
    // POST: The PIN attribute of any object is returned

private:
    double accountBalance;
    string accountName;
    string accountPIN;
};
```

As shown in the comment, the `bankAccount` class declaration, documented with pre-and postconditions, is stored in the file `ouracct.h`. It provides an interface to the class—an abstract view of how to initialize `bankAccount` objects and how to apply operations to those objects. The `bankAccount` member functions, completed in the accompanying implementation file named `ouracct.cpp`, will be examined shortly, but first we will scrutinize some of the decisions that went into the design of this `bankAccount` class.

Programming Tip ⎯⎯⎯⎯⎯⎯⎯⎯⎯⎯⎯⎯⎯⎯⎯⎯⎯⎯⎯⎯⎯⎯

Improper use of semicolons causes many different compiletime errors. Some are difficult to detect. One example is forgetting to place the semicolon at the end of the class declaration. Remember to always place a semicolon at the end of each class declaration after the closing brace.

8.1.2   Design of Class bankAccount

From the `bankAccount` declaration shown above, we see six public member functions (names shown in boldface). There could have been more, or there could have been less. Deciding which functions belong to a class is a design decision. Assuming there is a need for bank account objects, we must decide which operations best represent suitable behaviors of those objects. The member functions shown above were chosen with the following goals in mind:

1. To suit the needs of the bank control program
2. To keep the class simple
3. To provide a collection of operations that are relatively easy to relate to

One could argue for a different set of member functions, and in a different setting, the class might have had a different behavior. There is no single "right" way. The design of classes is an iterative process that evolves with time. The design is influenced by personal opinion, evolving research, setting, and a variety of other influences.

We must also select the data members that represent the all-important state for each object of the class. With `bankAccount`, it was decided that a name like `"Hall"` would be easier to use rather than a more realistic account number such as `"104268212C"`. It was also decided to have a PIN for each object because it served the bank control program well. Another object that stores the account balance is an obvious data member for any `bankAccount` class, but a real-world bank account may have two balances—a ledger balance and an available balance. For the sake of simplicity, only one balance was included in the `bankAccount` class, so each object has only one `balance` data member.

Another consideration in the design of any class is placement of member functions and data members under the most appropriate access mode—public or private. The public members of a class have different scope than the private members of the same class. The private data members of a class are only accessible to other members of the class. For example, the bankAccount data member named accountBalance has scope that extends only to the members of the class (bankAccount::bankAccount, bankAccount::withdraw, bankAccount::deposit, and so on). On the other hand, any member declared in the public section of a class has scope that extends to the entire class and then to any block in which an object of that class is declared.

Access Mode	Scope
private:	Only the members of the class.
public:	The members of the class and any block in which an object of the class is declared.

Most C++ classes typically have one or more public member functions available to users of the class. For example, the public member functions of bankAccount include the constructor bankAccount and the other member functions deposit, withdraw, balance, name, and PIN. These are located in the public section so users can manipulate objects of the class from anywhere the object is declared—from int main(), for example.

The data members represent the state of an object. Because they are declared private, they are altered through *modifying functions* and inspected by *accessor functions*. Modifying functions of the bankAccount class include bankAccount::deposit, bankAccount::withdraw, and bankAccount::bankAccount (the constructor that will be shown to initialize the private data members). Accessor functions include bankAccount::name, bankAccount::PIN, and bankAccount::balance, which return the state of the private data members that otherwise would be inaccessible.

Although data members could have been declared under the bankAccount class' public access mode, the convention used in this text is to have all data members of all classes declared private. There are several reasons besides the consistency this practice provides. First, this should help simplify some of the design decisions in the classes you will write.

But more importantly, when data members are declared private, they can only be altered or inspected through a member function. This prevents users of the class from indiscriminately changing certain data such as his or her account balance. The state of an object is protected from accidental or improper alteration. For example, when the data members are private, the state of any object can only be altered through the member functions of the class. It becomes impossible to accidentally make a credit like this:

```
bankAccount myAcct("Mine", "8765", 100.00);
// A compiletime error occurs at this attempt to modify private data
myAcct.accountBalance = myAcct.accountBalance + 100000.00;
```

or a debit like this:

```
// A compiletime error occurs at this attempt to modify private data
myAcct.accountBalance = myAcct.accountBalance - 100.00;
```

Having made accountBalance private, users of the class are forced to apply deposit and withdraw operations instead. With member functions to alter the state of an object and data members declared as private, all credits and debits must "go through the proper channels," and this might be quite complex. For example, each bank transaction may be recorded onto a transaction file to help prepare monthly statements for each bankAccount. The withdraw and deposit operations may have additional processing to prevent unauthorized credits and debits. Part of the hidden red tape might include manual verification of a deposit, or a check clearing operation at the host bank; there may be some sort of human or computer intervention before any credit is actually made. Such additional processing and protection within the deposit and withdrawal operations help make bankAccount a "safer" class. However, all hidden processing and protection is easily circumvented when data members are declared public. It is the designer's responsibility to enforce proper object use and protection by declaring data members private.

Other benefits are derived from forcing public member function usage. An operation (member function implementation) may change internally while the interface remains the same. For example, even if the bank decides to change its credit verification procedures, the program may remain the same. Perhaps the bank administration decides that each transaction is so critical that it is henceforth to be recorded in two separate files, on separate systems in different buildings. So a fire in one building, accidental erasure from one disk, a communications failure, or a hardware failure on one system will not affect the integrity of the duplicate recorded transaction. This modification need not affect programs that use the class. Whereas the implementation file might be changed, the class declaration in the specification file remains the same.

Another benefit derived from a well-defined class interface is this: Users are not required to know the implementation details of the class. For example, bank::findCustomer locates a customer or informs the user that the customer does not exist. We don't know the particular search routine used—sequential or binary—or the manner in which the database of customers is stored—in an array, a list, or a file. And the algorithms may change. Just as an automobile engine might be modified to run more efficiently and cleanly, the implementation might be altered. Just as the interface to the automobile engine (the gas pedal and tachometer) can remain unchanged, the interface to a class (the member functions) can remain unchanged. Users of a class need not know the name of the object that stores the balance. It shouldn't matter to a user that the name is exactly accountBalance rather than BALANCE, acctBalance, acct_balance, or whatever. Changes can be made to the class to improve efficiency, to adapt to other changes, or to correct bugs detected in the life cycle of the software. Many of these changes may be made without affecting the interface.

8.1.3 (*Optional*) Alternate Class Declarations

Class declarations can be quite complex. C++ offers a variety of methods for their completion. For example, because public and private access modes can be given in any order, there are two or three accepted conventions for placing these sections in class declarations. The convention used in this text is to have one public section followed by one private section. This consistently places the class interface—the member functions we use—at the beginning of each class declaration. The private data members are at the end. Other programmers prefer other arrangements. Because you are likely to encounter a variety of class declaration options in other sources, a few options and shortcuts are highlighted in an equivalent bankAccount class declaration given below:

Textbook Convention	*Option or Shortcut Seen Elsewhere*
1. The public and private access modes are always provided for the sake of clarity.	1. Some programmers do not write private: in the class declaration because the default access mode is private.
2. Parameter names are always written in the function prototypes of the class declaration. This helps document the class interface.	2. Only the class of a parameter is required in a function prototype. Parameter names are sometimes omitted from class declarations.
3. The qualification of member functions with "class-name::" is added inside the class declaration. Although redundant, this practice is legal and employed in this text to reduce confusion.	3. Member functions need not be qualified with class-name:: when enclosed inside the class declaration. This is the most common approach.
4. Member functions are implemented outside of the class declarations, usually in a separate file. This is done for the sake of consistency even though a shortcut is available.	4. Member functions are sometimes completely implemented within the class. Therefore { } may be seen in class declarations (this inconsistency has the benefit of improving efficiency).

These four optional shortcuts are highlighted in the following declaration, which is equivalent to the class bankAccount declaration shown in ouracct.h:

```
#include "ourstr.h"

class bankAccount {

    // 1. Some C++ programmers put members first without private:
    double accountBalance;
    string accountName;
    string accountPIN;

public:

    // 2. Parameter names need not be supplied in the class declaration
    bankAccount::bankAccount(string, string, double);
    void bankAccount::deposit(double);

    // 3. The class-name:: qualification is rarely used
    void withdraw(double);

    // 4. Some programmers implement member functions in the declaration.
    double balance() { return accountBalance; };
    string name() { return accountName; };
    string PIN() { return accountPIN; };
};
```

8.1.4 Implementing Member Functions

The full implementation of member functions typically includes the following items:

1. The member function's declared return type.
2. The class name.
3. The C++ scope resolution operator :: (two consecutive colons).
4. The member function name.
5. The parameters between (and).
6. A block that delimits the statements of the member function.

Because the function prototypes in the declaration are qualified and parameter names are given, the first five items are copied directly from the class declaration (with ; removed). Thus the general form for most member functions could be presented like this:

> *member-function-prototype*   // Note: ; must be removed
> *block*

or in more detail, as follows:

return-type   class-name :: *member-function-name* (*parameter-list*)
{
  ... declarations
  ... statements
}

The example member function implementations are given as the implementation file of the bankAccount class. This simplified version of the file, ouracct.cpp, and ouracct.h comprise the entire bankAccount module.

```
//------------------------------------------------------------
// IMPLEMENTATION FILE: ouracct.cpp
//
//  Implements: class bankAccount
//------------------------------------------------------------
#include "ourstr.h"

bankAccount::bankAccount(string initName,
                         string initPIN,
                         double initBalance)
{ // The initializer constructor called with 3 arguments
  accountName = initName;
  accountName.toUpper();
  accountPIN = initPIN;
  accountBalance = initBalance;
}

void bankAccount::deposit(double amount)
{
  accountBalance = accountBalance + amount;
}

void bankAccount::withdraw(double amount)
{
  accountBalance = accountBalance - amount;
}

string bankAccount::name()
{
  return accountName;
}

string bankAccount::PIN()
{
  return accountPIN;
}
```

```
double bankAccount::balance()
{
  return accountBalance;
}
```

8.1.5   Whose Data Member Is It?

You may have noticed that data members are freely referenced and altered within almost every member function implementation shown in this textbook. Because one class is used to construct many objects, you may have wondered how C++ determines which object's data to reference. For example, using only this code:

```
void bankAccount::withdraw(double amount)
{
  accountBalance = accountBalance - amount;
}
```

it is impossible to determine the value of accountBalance, the private data member that is part of every bankAccount object. So how does C++ determine which particular accountBalance to alter during any given call to bankAccount::withdraw? This information is provided by the particular object name that must precede the call to the member function. For example, the accountBalance affected by the following call is the double value that belongs to the object named Pat:

```
Pat.withdraw(50.00);
```

When we see balance() preceded by Pat., we get back Pat's balance, not that of Chris or Bob.

```
cout << Pat.balance();
```

So when bankAccount is initialized like this:

```
bankAccount Rob("Hall", "1234", 100.00);
```

we should understand that this function call

```
Rob.withdraw(50.00);
```

adds 50.00 to Rob's accountBalance for an updated value of 150.00.

Here are some other examples:

```
Pat.deposit(133.33)    // Change Pat's balance, not Chris's
Chris.withdraw(250.00) // Change Chris's balance, not Pat's
str1.length()          // Return the length of str1, not str2
myATM.getNameAndPIN()  // Alter the data for myATM, not MoneyMachine
```

Self-Check

1. List two access modes of the C++ class.
2. Can we reference private data members from the `main` function?
3. Can we reference public member functions from the `main` function?
4. For both class `one` and class `two` declared below, list:
   a. The data members.
   b. The member functions.
   c. Any data members and/or member functions accessible from nonmember functions.
   d. Any data members that may only be referenced from member functions of the class.
   e. The parameters that have their scope limited to the function in which they are declared.

```
class one {                      class two {
public:                          public:
  void one::init(int J,            void two::init(double X,
               int K);                         double Y);
  int one::f1();                   double two::f2();
private:                         private:
  int j, k;                        double x, y;
};                               };
```

5. Implement `int one::f1()` that returns the sum of the private data `j+k`.
6. Using the class declaration for class `two`, write the output generated by these function implementations and the `main` function:

```
#include <iostream.h>
two::init(double X, double Y)
{
  x = X;
  y = Y;
}

double two::f2()
{
  return x * y;
}
```

```
int main()
{
  two a, b;
  a.init(4.5, 2.3);
  b.init(5.6, 7.8);
  cout << a.f2() << "  " << b.f2() << endl;
     return 0;
}
```

7. For each of the following, explain the syntax error(s) in the class declaration.

```
class one                          class two {
public:                            public
  one::one(int J,                    two::two(float X,
           int K);                            float Y);
  int one::f1();                     float two::f2();
private:                           private
  j, k;                              float x, y;
};                                 }
```

Answers
1. Public and private.
2. No, private data may only be referenced from the member functions of the class.
3. Only if an object of the class has been declared in the body of main.
4. class one {   class two {
   a. j and k   a. x and y (not X and Y)
   b. init() and f1()   b. init() and f2()
   c. init() and f1()   c. init() and f2()
   d. j and k   d. x and y
   e. J and K (not j and k)   e. X and Y (not x and y)
5. int one::f1()
   {
     return j + k;
   }
6. 10.35   43.68
7. one: two:
   a. Missing { after one   a. Missing : after public and private
   b. Missing class name before j, k   b. Missing semicolon ; after }
```

# 8.2 Constructors

Constructors are special member functions that may perform behind-the-scenes initialization such as assignment of values to some or all private data members. Constructors can guarantee all necessary steps are automatically performed during an object initialization because the constructor is called when we bring a new object name into existence. Constructors provide the ability to guarantee that object initialization is automatic. They
```

remove some of the complexity that would otherwise be imposed on users of our classes (and we may be the ones using our own classes). To accomplish these tasks, constructor functions must be declared and implemented using a general form that varies slightly from other member functions:

```
class  class-name {
public:
    class-name::class-name ( parameters ) ;
```

The following restrictions concern constructor implementation:

- Constructors are usually declared in the public section of a class.
- Constructors must be given the same name as the class.
- Constructors cannot be given a return type, not even void.

Example:

```
class bankAccount {
public:
    bankAccount::bankAccount(string initName,      // In
                             string initPIN,       // In
                             double initBalance);  // In
```

Using this constructor prototype as an example, we note that this constructor must be called with three arguments. The following are illegal constructor calls detected at compiletime:

```
//  Three compiletime errors:
bankAccount one("Hall");                    // missing arguments
bankAccount two("Hall", 1234, 100.00);      // 1234 is not a string
bankAccount three(100.00, "1234", "Hall"); // class mismatch
```

This particular bankAccount constructor requires three arguments of the correct type: a string, a string, and a numeric. The following is a valid call to the bankAccount constructor:

```
bankAccount one("Hall", "1234", 100.00);
```

The major difference between constructors and other member functions is this: Constructors are called at the point of an object's initialization. Therefore, the calling syntax does not require the usual dotting. Instead, the constructor is called with the familiar object initialization.

The general form of constructor implementation varies slightly from the form used for other member function implementations:

class-name :: *class-name* (*parameter-list*)
{
  ... *statements*
}

Notice that there is no return type and the member-function-name must be the class-name. Other than these differences, constructor functions behave like other functions. The following implementation of the bankAccount constructor function differs from other member function implementations in that there is no return type and the function name is the same as the class.

```
bankAccount::bankAccount(string initName,     // In: "Hall"
                         string initPIN,      // In: "1234"
                         double initBalance)  // In: 100.00
{
    accountName = initName;
    accountName.toUpper();  // Convert string to uppercase
    accountPin = initPIN;
    accountBalance = initBalance;
}
```

This implementation also shows how data passed as arguments to the constructor affect the state of all objects of the bankAccount class. The argument values are first passed to the associated parameters (initName="Hall", initPIN="1234", and initBalance=100.00). These values are then copied into the private data members (accountName, accountPIN, and accountBalance) through the three assignment statements in the constructor function body. Constructors may also impose some additional behind-the-scenes processing. For example, all bankAccount names are converted to uppercase. At the time of the specific initialization shown above, the private data members will obtain the following state:

Private Data Member	State after initialization
accountName	"HALL"
accountPin	"1234"
accountBalance	100.00

The three parameter bankAccount constructors guarantee initialization of all bankAccount objects constructed with three arguments and ensure that account names are always converted to uppercase—a requirement for proper searching during a call to bank::findCustomer.

Constructors may also be designed with no parameters. As another example of how constructors can prove themselves useful, consider what happens if in a program with a stringList object (from the case study in Chapter 7): we forget to call the init function. Recall that stringList::init() established the list size at 0.

```
// Forget to call stringList::init()
#include "ourstrli.h"  // class stringList is now declared in this file

int main()
{
  stringList friends;
  friends.add("Carlos Sempres, 147 Lembke Hall, 555-5432");
  friends.display();
  return 0;
}
```

The result is system dependent and may vary from one program execution to the next:

1. *On one DOS system, this intent error occurred:*
   At least 568 strings of garbage values were dumped to the screen. After watching the contents of memory fly by, Ctrl-Break was entered to terminate the program.
2. *On one Windows PC system, this runtime error occurred:*
   The message "Program has violated system integrity" appeared with a suggestion to save all work and reboot the computer. This advice was followed.
3. *On one UNIX system, this runtime error occurred:*
   Segmentation fault (the program was terminated abnormally).
4. *On another UNIX system, there was no error!*
   The program ran as advertised. The size data member probably had the garbage value of zero. This is probably the most dangerous consequence—the program appeared to work during testing. There is a good chance it will fail later.

These problems are caused whenever the user of the stringList forgets to make this function call to initialize size to 0:

```
friends.init();
```

If init is not called, unpredictable errors like those above are the result. Because new strings are added to the array named str like this:

```
str[size] = newString;
```

we might very well be writing a string into some memory that is not part of the underlying array that stores strings. We might be attempting to store the string argument into str[-1234] or str[9142]. This could happen because we can never be sure of the value of size. And imagine what happens when friend.display() is called with size as 9142. There is an attempt to display 9,142 string elements, all of which are garbage, many of which may be 0 length or hundreds of characters long. This is what happened on one system (see 1. in the table above). We shouldn't have to worry about these types of errors. But to make a point, the stringList class was designed so users must always remember to call init immediately after the object is declared, which performs no initialization. This situation can be improved.

If the initialization of size were part of a stringList constructor function, guaranteed initialization occurs at object declaration. Potential hazards are eliminated! And if stringList::init() is removed, we prevent the possibility of calling init a second time. This is potentially more disastrous because setting size back to 0 could effectively eliminate a collection of important data—sales orders or reservations, for example. The improved situation is accomplished by adding the following stringList constructor to the declaration in ourstrli.h and deleting stringList::init from the class. Here is the new and improved version of stringList:

```
#include "ourstr.h"
#include <iostream.h>

const int MAX = 20;

class stringList {
public:
    stringList::stringList();        // Add this constructor function.
    // POST: The list is empty (size=0) and ready to add strings

    void stringList::add(string newString);
    // POST: The string is added at the end of the array
    //       and the size of the list is increased by 1.
    //       If the array is full, a message is displayed.

    void stringList::display();
    // POST: All string objects currently stored in the array are dis-
    //       played after a heading indicating the size of the list.
    //       If no strings have been added, no strings are displayed.

    private:
    string str[MAX];   // Store up to MAX string objects and also
    int size;          // store exactly how many have been added
};
```

The following constructor implementation must then be added to the implementation file `ourstrli.cpp`:

```
stringList::stringList()
{
  size = 0;
}
```

Now objects can be initialized with the zero parameter constructor function like this:

```
stringList friends;
```

and we are guaranteed that every `string` is stored into the proper array position and the size is always correct. The object is protected because it cannot be redeclared. This error would be caught at compiletime:

```
stringList friends; // Object names must be unique in the same scope
stringList friends; // <- Compiletime error redeclaring friends
```

Constructors can also perform a variety of tasks that we might otherwise have to do ourselves. For example, the `bank` constructor sets up a small database of `bankAccount` objects. With this one simple call to the `bank` constructor:

```
bank firstBank;
```

`bank::bank()` automatically creates a collection of 16 `bankAccount` objects. The private data member `numberOfCustomers` is set to 16. The first 16 elements of the private array data member named `customer` are also initialized with calls to the `bankAccount` constructor:

```
bank::bank()
{
  numberOfCustomers = 16;
  customer[0] = bankAccount("CUST0", "0000", 000.00);
  customer[1] = bankAccount("CUST1", "1111", 111.11);
  // ... 12 assignments deleted
  customer[14] = bankAccount("CUST14", "1414", 1414.14);
  customer[15] = bankAccount("HALL", "1234", 100.00);
}
```

The declaration of a `bank` object guarantees an initialized array of 16 `bankAccount` objects with the number of customers properly set to 16. The constructor hides these details. Such behind-the-scenes automatic initializations are performed simply and automatically.

Now, consider what would happen if the private data (customer and numberOfCustomers) of the object firstBank had not been initialized as shown above. Either we would have zero customers or some random number of garbage array elements. In either case, using the bank object would have been useless.

The code of bank::bank allowed us to use a bank object in Chapter 4, before arrays were covered. If the constructor did not do this for us we would have had to study arrays before Chapter 4 and then with tedious precision add customers at the keyboard every time a program runs with a bank object. Both requirements were assessed as unworkable. Hopefully you can now appreciate the usefulness of constructors: automatic, guaranteed, and proper object initialization.

Programming Tip

Whenever possible, the data members should not be altered or inspected directly. Instead, it is recommended that:

1. Constructors be designed to initialize private data members.
2. Modifying functions be designed to modify data (bankAccount::withdraw, for example).
3. Accessor functions be designed to query private data members (bankAccount::balance, for example).

Self-Check

1. What name do we give to a constructor function?
2. What return type(s) may be returned from a constructor function?
3. Use the class declaration below to determine the following:
   a. The class name.
   b. The number and class of arguments that must be used at declaration.
   c. Data that can be referenced only from the member functions.
   d. The member functions that may reference initX.
   e. The functions that may be referenced from the main function.

```
class doNothing {
public:
    doNothing::doNothing(int initX);
    void doNothing::display();
    void doNothing::doubleIt();
private:
    int x;
};
```

4. Given the following implementation of class doNothing, write the output generated by function main:

```
doNothing::doNothing(int initX)
{
  x = initX;
}

void doNothing::doubleIt()
{
  x = 2 * x;
}

void doNothing::display()
{
  cout << "{ doNothing: " << x << " }" << endl;
}

int main()
{
  doNothing a(4);
  doNothing b(3);
  a.doubleIt();
  a.doubleIt();
  b.doubleIt();
  a.display();
  b.display();
  return 0;
}
```

Answers
1. The class name
2. None: Constructors cannot have a return type, not even void.
3. a. doNothing
   b. One int argument
   c. x
   d. initX may only be referenced from within the constructor (doNothing::doNothing) because the scope of any parameter is limited to the function in which it is declared.
   e. doNothing (the constructor called at declaration), display, and doubleIt
4. { doNothing: 16 }
   { doNothing: 6 }

8.3   Multiple Constructors

We have observed the + operator perform several different operations. In each case, the meaning of + is determined by the operands. With two ints, integer addition is performed; with two doubles, floating-point addition is performed; and with two string operands, + executes a concatenation operation. We have also seen the << operator display chars, ints, floats, strings, and bankAccount objects. This flexibility of having one operator mean different things with different operands is called *operator overloading*.

The concept of overloading also applies to function names. In both cases new meanings are given to operations whether they are recognized as overloaded operators such as + and << or as identifiers such as init, display, or bankAccount.

Recall that bankAccount objects have sometimes been declared with zero arguments like this:

```
bankAccount one, two, three;
```

To allow for these different object initializations (with zero arguments), a constructor with zero parameters must be declared and implemented.

8.3.1   Function Overloading

The existence of multiple constructors for the same class, one with three parameters and another with zero parameters, is made possible though the process known as *function overloading*. C++ allows more than one function with the same name as long as the parameters are substantially different in number and/or type, or the functions are members of different classes. For example, an init and display operation could be added to any class. Also, because of the different types of parameters in these function prototypes,

```
void show(double x);
void show(string s);
void show(bankAccount b);
```

all three may reside within the same scope. These three different functions have the same name; what makes them different is their *distinguishable* parameters. The C++ compiler easily discerns the difference between the double, string, and bankAccount classes.

Overloaded functions are also possible by using a different number of parameters for each function. The compiler clearly distinguishes functions with zero, one, two, or three arguments even if those functions have the same name. Consider the two functions named round as declared in ourstuff.h and implemented in ourstuff.cpp. When round is called with one argument, the nearest integer is returned. When a second argument is supplied, the double returned is rounded to that many decimal places.

```
// Function overloading with a different number of parameters
#include <math.h>
#include <iostream.h>

// Nonmember function prototypes as declared in ourstuff.h
double round(double x);
// POST: Returns x rounded to the nearest integer
```

```
double round(double x, int n);
// PRE: n >= 0
// POST: Returns x rounded to n decimals if n > 0.
//        If n is 0, the integer nearest to x is returned.

int main()
{
  cout << round(1.49999)    << endl;
  cout << round(1.50001, 1) << endl;
  cout << round(4.56789, 2) << endl;
  cout << round(4.56789)    << endl;
  return 0;
}
```

Output

```
1
1.5
4.57
5
```

And here are the function implementations as declared in ourstuff.cpp.

```
double round(double x)
{
  return ceil(x - 0.5);
}

double round(double x, int n)
{
  if (n < 0)
    return x;
  else
  {
    double factor = pow(10.0, n);
    return ceil(x * factor - 0.5) / factor;
  }
}
```

8.3.2 Default Constructors

Unless the programmer specifies a constructor, the compiler provides every C++ class with a *default constructor*, a do-nothing constructor with zero parameters. For example, even this simple class has a default constructor, which is shown to be called from function main to declare an array of doNothing objects:

```
class doNothing {
};

int main()
{
  doNothing aDoNothingObject[20]; // Uses the default constructor
  return 0;
}
```

Therefore, the class declaration above is equivalent to the following code, which we could have written ourselves:

```
class doNothing {
public:
  doNothing::doNothing();
};

doNothing::doNothing()
{
  // A default constructor like this is generated by the compiler when no
  // other constructor is declared for the class. There are no statements.
}
```

However, default constructors are generated by the compiler only if no other constructors are present. Thus if you write a class with any constructor that has one or more parameters, C++ demands that you also add the default constructor in order to

1. Initialize objects with zero arguments.
2. Allow for an array of objects.

The main motivation for a default constructor is to allow the class name to be used in array declarations. For example, default constructors were added to the string and bankAccount classes (both of which have several constructors).

```
#include "ourstr.h"
#include "bankAccount.h"
int main()
{
  string a;          // Call string::string()
  string b[100];     // Call string::string()
  string c(a);       // Call string::string(const string & source)

  // Call bankAccount::bankAccount(string, string, double)
  bankAccount e("Hall", "1234", 100.00);
  bankAccount d;     // Call bankAccount::bankAccount()
```

```
bankAccount f(e);  // Call bankAccount(const bankAccount & source)
// ...
```

Function overloading can also be used to obtain *multiple constructors* as long as the number and/or class of parameters are distinguishable. Using only the simplified bankAccount declaration shown earlier in this chapter, we could not declare bankAccount objects like this:

```
bankAccount anAcct;  // Need a constructor with zero parameters
```

Instead, we could only initialize bankAccount objects with three arguments (string, string, float) that call the *initializer constructor*. The default constructor is unavailable because C++ does not generate the default constructor if any other constructor is made to be part of a class. Because a constructor with zero parameters is clearly distinguishable from a constructor with three parameters, the default constructor is added to the bankAccount class declaration like this:

```
// Use function overloading to create two constructors
class bankAccount {
public:
  bankAccount::bankAccount();              // 1. Default
  bankAccount::bankAccount(string initName, // 2. Initializer
                           string initPIN,
                           double initBalance);
  //...
```

After implementing the default constructor, bankAccount objects may be declared in two different ways:

```
int main()
{
  bankAccount a;                   // Call default constructor
  bankAccount b("Hall","1234",100); // Call initializer constructor
  return 0;
}
```

If the default constructor had not been added, we could not have had any banks because a bank object has an array of bankAccount data members. Instead, these types of errors would occur at compiletime:

Turbo C++ for DOS, and Borland C++ for Windows:
```
Cannot find default constructor to initialize array element of type 'bankAccount'
```

UNIX / Sun C++:

```
array of class bankAccount that does not have a constructor taking no arguments
```

UNIX / GNU g++:

```
too few arguments for constructor 'bankAccount'
in base initialization for class 'bankAccount'
```

Not only does the default constructor allow arrays of objects, the default constructor also allows us to declare an object that cannot be immediately initialized. For example, to construct a bankAccount object using keyboard input of the name and PIN, two string objects must be declared before the input occurs. In this case, the string objects are declared with the default constructor of the string class:

```
// Call default constructors for string and bankAccount
#include "ouracct.h"
#include "ourstr.h"
#include <iostream.h>

int main()
{
  string name, PIN;   // Call string's default constructor twice
  bankAccount anAcct; // Call bankAccount's default constructor
  float startBalance;

  cout << "Enter name, PIN, and starting balance: ";
  // The string objects can now be initialized thanks
  // to the default constructor of the string class
  cin >> name >> PIN >> startBalance;
  // Now call bankAccount's initializer constructor
  anAcct = bankAccount(name, PIN, startBalance);
  cout << anAcct << endl;
  return 0;
}
```

--- **Dialogue** ---
```
Enter name, PIN, and starting balance: Voorhies 5432 4256.78
{ bankAccount: VOORHIES, 5432 4256.78 }
```

8.3.3 Implementing Default Constructors

At first look, it might appear odd that default constructors need not have any statements within the function body. Witness the actual implementation of default constructors for the string and bankAccount classes. There are no statements in either function:

```
string::string()
{ // Default constructor for the string class
}


bankAccount::bankAccount()
{ // Default constructor for the bankAccount class
}
```

Object declarations with zero arguments are acceptable because initialization may occur at some other point in the program, just like the char, int, or float objects declared at the beginning of a block and initialized later with input, assignment, or after a loop executes.

Default constructors serve other purposes such as initialization of objects with default values of our own choosing. Specifically, the default string constructor sets objects to a default null string of length 0. As another example of default assignments, the bankAccount class default constructor could be made to look something like this:

```
bankAccount::bankAccount()
{ // Allow for an array (more than one) of bankAccount
  // objects and give an object our own default values
  accountName = "?name?";
  accountPIN = "?PIN?";
  balance = 0.00;
}
```

Now an object declaration with zero arguments calls the default constructor and the arbitrary default values of question marks and 0.00 are given to the private data members.

```
// Use the default constructor to establish a default object state
#include "ouracct.h"
#include <iostream.h>

int main()
{
  bankAccount acct3;
  cout << acct3 << endl;
  return 0;
}
```

——————————————— **Output** ———————————————
```
{ bankAccount: ?name?, ?PIN?, 0.00 }
```

Self-Check

1. How many constructors are implied by each of the following class declarations:

```
class one {                          class three {
public:                              public:
   one::a();                            three::three()
private:                             private:
   string name[100];                    bankAccount acct[20];
};                                   };


class two {                          class four {
public:                              public:
  two::two(int initSize);              four::four();
private:                               four::four(int initMin,
  int size;                                       int initMax);
  int x[20];                         private:
};                                     int min, max;
                                     };
```

2. Implement the default constructor for class four such that min is always set to 0 and max is always set to 20.

3. Implement the initializer constructor for class four such that min is set to 1 and max is set to 100 with the following initialization of anObject:

```
four anObject(1, 100);
```

Answers

1. one: 1   two: 1   three: 1   four: 2
2. ```
   four::four()
   {
      min = 0;
      max = 20;
   }
   ```
3. ```
   four::four(int initMin, int initMax)
   {
      min = initMin;
      max = initMax;
   }
   ```

Exercises

1. Take a first stab at defining some potential operations for a useful transcript class. Each transcript object should be capable of managing a collection of courses that represents the history of all courses taken by one particular student at one particular school. *Note:* With this very loose specification, many different answers are possible.

2. Define some potential data members that represent the state of a transcript object.

3. Using class abc, predict the output from each main function given below.

```
#include <iostream.h>

class abc {
public:
  abc::abc();
  abc::abc(int initMax);
  int last();
private:
  int max;
};

abc::abc()
{
  max = 10;
}

abc::abc(int initMax)
{
  max = initMax;
}

int abc::last()
{
  return max;
}
```

a.
```
int main()
{
  abc x;
  cout << x.last();
  return 0;
}
```

b.
```
int main()
{
  abc y(99);
  cout << y.last();
  return 0;
}
```

c.
```
int main()
{
  abc a;
  abc b(1234);
  cout << a.last()
       << " "
       << b.last();
  return 0;
}
```

4. Assuming class abc of exercise 1 is available, which of the following are legal statements? Explain the reason for any illegal statement. Assume the following declaration of x:

```
abc x(2);
```

a. cout << x.max;

b. cout << x.last();

c. cout << last();

d. x.max = 2 + x.max;

5. Write the output generated by the following program:

```cpp
#include <iostream.h>

class tic {
public:
  tic::tic(char one, char two, char three);
  void tic::show();
private:
  char a1, a2, a3;
};

tic::tic(char one, char two, char three)
{
  a1 = one;
  a2 = two;
  a3 = three;
}

void tic::show()
{
  cout << a1 << '¦' << a2 << '¦' << a3 << endl;
}

int main()
{
  tic first ('X', ' ', 'O');
  tic second('O', 'X', 'O');
  tic third ('O', ' ', 'X');
  first.show();
  second.show();
  third.show();
  return 0;
}
```

6. Implement class hiThere that automatically displays Hello on a separate line when an object of the class is declared. The constructor has no arguments and there is no private data. This main function declares two hiThere objects to produce the output shown in comments.

```
int main()
{                        // Output:
  hiThere one, two;      // Hello
  return 0;              // Hello
}
```

7. Implement two void functions named show. One version of show must be declared
    with a string parameter. The associated string argument is to be displayed after "{
    string:" and before "}". The second version of show must be declared with a double
    parameter. The associated int, long, float, or double argument must be displayed
    after "{ numeric: " and before "}". For example, these calls

```
show("Any old string");
show(10.0 / 3.0);
```

    should produce output like this:

```
{ string: Any old string }
{ numeric: 3.33333 }
```

Lab Projects

8A   Implementing a Class

Implement a four-function expression class that returns the sum, difference, product,
and quotient of the arguments used at initialization. Your class should allow this main
function to generate the output exactly as shown. This class acts as a review of introduc-
tory class implementation details. We will not be using it as the class in an array so there
is no need to declare a default constructor.

```
#include <iostream.h>

// Declare class expression here
// ...

// Implement the member functions here
// ...

int main()
{
  double left = 25.0;
  double right = 3.2;
  expression exp(left, right);
```

```
    cout << "left+right: " << exp.sum()        << endl;
    cout << "left-right: " << exp.difference() << endl;
    cout << "left*right: " << exp.product()    << endl;
    cout << "left/right: " << exp.quotient()   << endl;
    return 0;
}
```

———————— **Output** ————————
```
left+right: 28.2
left-right: 21.8
left*right: 80
left/right: 7.8125
```

8B   Implementing a Class

Use the following steps to implement class `student` with a `display` function and a `standing` function that returns the grade point average and the current class standing, respectively:

- Declare class `student` with a constructor that takes these three arguments:

    1. Student's name (a `string`)
    2. Total grade points earned (a `float`)
    3. Total credits earned (a `float`)

- In the same file, implement the constructor function to initialize three appropriately named private data members. Make sure the data members are declared in the private section of class `student`.
- Let the constructor convert the `name` data member to uppercase with void `string::toUpper()`.
- Add a public member function to class `student` named `display()` so it displays the class name, the student's name, and the grade point average (GPA) to three decimal places. The GPA is calculated as the total number of grade points divided by the total number of credits. If credits = 0.0, compute GPA as 0.000.

Your class should now be only partially implemented, but complete enough to construct an object.

- In the same file, retype this `main` function:

```
int main()
{
  student aStudent("Nguyen", 123.5, 36.5);
  student anotherStudent("Stella", 0, 0);
  aStudent.display();
  anotherStudent.display();
  return 0;
}
```

- Run your program and verify that your output looks exactly like this:

```
{ student: NGUYEN:   GPA = 3.384 }
{ student: STELLA:   GPA = 0.000 }
```

If your program caused a runtime error (division by 0), fix it. Before proceeding, make sure your output looks exactly like that shown above. The names must be converted to uppercase (use `void string::toUpper()` in `student::student`). A GPA of 0 should be shown as 0.000, not as 0. Use `decimals(cout,3);`.

- Add the public member function `string student::standing()` that returns the following values for the credits shown:

Return this string:	for credits in this range:
"Freshman"	0 <= credits <= 30
"Sophomore"	30 < credits <= 60
"Junior"	60 < credits <= 90
"Senior"	90 < credits

The function call `aStudent.standing()` should now return the `string` object `"Senior"`. In other words, the following statement generates the output shown in the comment:

```
cout << aStudent.standing() << endl;   // Output: Senior
```

- Use the table above to perform branch coverage testing on the code in `student::standing`. Construct enough objects in function `main` such that each of the four standings is returned to `main`.

8C   Implementing a Class

Implement class `elevator` with a constructor that places an elevator at a selected floor. The constructor requires exactly one argument to represent the starting floor. Include a `select` operation that allows floors to be selected. For every floor, the message "going up" or "going down" should be displayed before the current floor of the elevator. Here is one sample output to give you an idea of what simulated elevators will look like on your screen:

```
start on floor 1
going up to 2
going up to 3
going up to 4
Open at 4
```

Start by implementing and testing the constructor such that the following code declares an elevator and sets the current floor to 7:

```
elevator b(7);
```

Using the following steps, begin the implementation of elevator with only one initializer constructor:

- Open a new file.
- You will be using cout <<, so include iostream.h.
- Begin the class declaration using elevator as the class name.
- Under the public section, write the function prototype for the constructor with one int parameter named initFloor. Recall that constructors must have the same name as the class and no return type.
- Add a private section with one int data member currentFloor.
- Add the closing (right) brace and the semicolon that terminates the class declaration.
- Implement the constructor such that the private data member currentFloor is assigned the value of the constructor's parameter initFloor. The constructor should also display the initial value of currentFloor as shown in the output:

```
int main()
{
  elevator b(7);
  return 0;
}
```

─────────────────── **Output** ───────────────────

```
start on floor 7
```

- Test your class with the previous main function as shown above. Correct any errors.
- To the class declaration, add a void function prototype named select that can be called as follows:

```
int main()
{
  elevator a(7);
  a.select(11);
  a.select(9);
  return 0;
}
```

- Implement the `select` member function such that each floor passed produces the output `"going up to"` or `"going down to"` followed by the appropriate floor number. When the selected floor has been reached, display the message `"Open at "` followed by the selected floor. For example, the preceding `main` function should generate this output exactly:

```
start on floor 7
going up to 8
going up to 9
going up to 10
going up to 11
open at 11
going down to 10
going down to 9
open at 9
```

8D   Implementing a Class

Declare and implement a `doubleList` class in a file named `numlist.h` to manage a collection of numeric elements. Use the default constructor to initialize the array from a disk file. The file may contain from 0 to 100 numbers, so keep track of how many are on file. We are interested in arranging and displaying the numeric values in descending order, so include these member functions:

```
numberList::numberList();
// PRE: The file named numberList.dat is in the working directory
//       and it contains no more than 100 valid numbers.
// POST: The array and size data members are initialized

numberList::display();
// POST: All assigned array elements are displayed after a heading

numberList::sort();
// POST: The assigned array elements are in descending numeric order
```

Completely declare and implement the class in the same file (`numlist.h`) as its declaration (not the ideal situation, but it will do for now). Create another file containing the `main` function shown below to test the `numberList` class (don't forget to `#in-clude` the file with class `numberList`). If the input file has these numbers:

```
98   88.5   79  66.5  76
85   91.5  100  62.0  74.0
```

the following `main` function should generate the output on the right after `sort` is called:

```
#include "numlist.h"              numberList:
                                      98.0
int main()                            88.5
{                                     79.0
  doubleList test;                    66.5
  test.display();                     76.0
  test.sort()                         85.0
  test.display();                     91.5
  return 0;                          100.0
}                                     62.0
                                      74.0
                                  numberList:
                                     100.0
                                      98.0
                                      91.5
                                      88.5
                                      85.0
                                      79.0
                                      76.0
                                      74.0
                                      66.5
                                      62.0
```

8.4 Case Study: Online Telephone Book

Program development follows the three-phase method of analysis, design, and implementation. The analysis phase involves reading the problem specification, understanding the requirements, and identifying input and output. In the design phase a solution is developed. The implementation phase involves writing code, testing the computer program, and other implementation issues such as fixing compiletime, runtime, linktime, and intent errors.

Some of the problem solutions in previous case studies were designed with simple IPO algorithms. Some steps needed further refinement. Whenever there was a need for selection and repetition, the design concentrated on the steps that were required, the steps that should be executed next (sequence and selection), and the number of times a set of steps should execute (repetition). Another design, the bank control program of Chapter 4, concentrated on finding and using existing objects. This *object-oriented design* tool concentrated on the objects found in a problem statement and the operations that were associated with those objects. But all the objects that were needed already existed, and all operations were already assigned to the proper object. A bank object was available for managing a collection of bankAccount objects. The bankAccount objects were constructed from the existing bankAccount class. We already had an ATM object to act as the customer interface to the bank. Finally, string, char, and floating-point objects already existed along with their associated arithmetic, input, and output operations. However, in most software developments of significant scale, all required objects do not exist in the software. They must be purchased or constructed from new classes that become part of the program development process. It is not always easy to recognize the objects while designing a solution, even when we are looking for them.

In the case study that follows, we delve into *object-oriented analysis*. The focus is on recognition of objects and identification and assignment of operations to the proper object. This brief excursion into object-oriented analysis differs from most other case studies—the analysis phase focuses on recognizing the objects and operations provided by the problem specification. We will look at the important nouns in the problem statement and consider them as potential objects. We will also look at the verbs in the problem statement and consider them as potential operations.

An Object-Oriented Analysis Strategy

1. Find the objects by considering each major noun in the problem statement.
2. Find the operations by considering each major verb in the problem statement.
3. Use existing objects, find a class to construct them, or design and implement new classes.
4. Write an algorithm to manage flow of control.

8.4.1   Analysis

Problem: Implement a menu-driven program to allow the following operations for an on-line telephone book.

1. *Lookup:* The user enters a last name. All telephone listings matching the last name are shown.
2. *Display:* Displays all phone book listings.
3. *Add:* The user is prompted for a last name, first name, and phone number to be added to the phone book.
4. *Remove:* The user is prompted for a last name and a first name. The phone book listing is removed from the phone book.

5. *Quit:* Shuts down the phone book program and updates the file that stores the phone listings. Any added phone listings are written to the file; removed phone listings are not.

The input and output considerations should allow users to make selections from a menu (L for Lookup, A for Add, and so on). User-supplied input consists of letters indicating the menu selection (L, D, A, R, or Q), the numbers of new listings, the names to be removed, and responses to other prompts such as Y to verify adding a new telephone listing to the collection of telephone numbers (details included in the implementation section). Other input consists of the names and phone numbers stored in a file named phone.dat. There are three fields:

1. First Name
2. Last Name
3. Phone Number

This file could be very large and could change because of new listings and deletions. Part of the input file to be used might look like this:

```
Abrahams Sue         555-1111
Bellsharp Bob        555-2222
Callarusso Bella     555-3333
Depford Lee          555-4444
Ellios Michel        555-5555
Feinstein Linda      555-6666
Gabriel Francessa    555-7777
...      ...         ...
Whitman Jo           555-9999
Zevon Warren         555-0000
```

8.4.1.1   Find the Objects and Operations

As is often the case in software development, we reduce the problem's complexity by discovering objects that model real-world entities. Our limited version of object-oriented analysis begins here with the identification of objects. One technique for recognizing required objects is to consider the main noun clauses in the problem statement.

8.4.1.2   Consider Nouns as Potential Objects

The following nouns are written only once and in the order they were found in the analysis section:

Major Noun Clauses of Problem Statement

menu-driven program	last name	file
operations	first name	menu selection
on-line telephone book	telephone listings	letters
user	phone number	prompts

Each of these can be considered an object, but not all of them will pass through to the design. We try to distinguish the nouns that represent objects that help design a solution from other nouns that are superfluous to our design. This is not an easy task.

For example, should the noun phrase *menu-driven program* be considered an object that is useful to us? This may depend on your programming environment and the level of sophistication, which is not specified in the problem statement. If you have a windowed environment, you probably have access to the same objects used to model the windows you see on your screen. Window objects are useful and they are used in most modern applications of substance. Also, if we are to provide the conveniences of a mouse, the noun *mouse* becomes an ideal candidate for a useful object we might want to use. Many of these software/hardware objects already exist. We only need to learn how to use them or modify them to fit our application. However, a windowed environment was not specified, so we eliminate menu-driven program as a potential class.

The noun *operations* is only a clue to potential operations and is eliminated as a useful design object.

Online telephone book—a noun clause with specified operations—should be considered a beneficial object. The fact that we have not encountered a phone book object yet should not eliminate consideration of a phoneBook object. We can design one later.

Through experience with the bank class—an object that managed a collection of bankAccount objects—we might see an online telephone book object as a collection of *telephone listing* objects—another one of the noun clauses repeatedly encountered in the problem statement. The primary data members of a telephone book object could be the collection of objects (phone listings in this case) and the size of that collection. Therefore, telephone listing and telephone book should be considered as potential objects.

The noun *file* could also prove helpful in our implementation. If we view a file as an object—as we have done in the past—our picture could be an object that stores names and numbers while the computer is turned off. We can use this file object to help initialize a telephone book object. We could also use the file object immediately before the program is terminated to store updated (after adds and removes) phone listing objects—an example of *persistence* in which the data outlives the program.

We also see nouns such as last name, first name, and phone number. These are best represented as string objects. So we have found other useful objects that can be constructed from an existing class. From the problem definition we see that users must input keyboard data and view screen output. Thus there must be input and output. For this we can use two other familiar objects: cin and cout. Other nouns such as *menu selection* and *letters* could be considered as char objects.

8.4.1.3   Consider Verbs as Potential Operations

After recognizing object candidates, we can now look at the major verbs in the problem statement and consider them as potentially useful operations. Objects have assigned responsibilities that include input with the cin object, output with the cout object, string management with string objects, and input from a file object. What other responsibilities are there, and to which object do we assign them? We look to the major verbs of the problem statement for useful operations.

Major Verbs of Problem Statement

provide	enters	added
giving	matching	Remove
listed	Display	Quit
implement	Add	Updates
lookup	prompted	stored

Some verbs do little toward analysis and may even get in the way. Such is the case of the first four verbs shown above. They are included here, but major verbs are better recognized as potential operations when read in the context of the problem statement. For example, lookup was specified as one of the menu options, so lookup should be considered an operation. In fact, the five menu selection verbs *lookup, display, add, remove,* and *quit,* are potential member functions of some class. The verbs *enters* and *matching* imply operations such as input and comparison with ==. The verb *prompted* implies input and *stored* implies output to a file. This first attempt to recognize objects and operations from the nouns and verbs of the problem statement are summarized in the following table.

Object	Data Characteristics	Operations
First Name Last Name Phone Number	Strings	Extract input with >> Insert output with <<
File	Extract input data stored on file	Extract file input with >> Update file with new data

Phone Listing	All information stored for one listing: last name, first name, and phone number	Compare with == Output
Phone Book	A collection of phone listing objects and its current size	Initialize, Lookup, Display, Add, Remove, Quit
Menu Selection	Chars: L, D, A, R, Q	Input, Output

This object-oriented analysis strategy (nouns = objects, verbs = operations) might lead other designers to different conclusions. And any first analysis is certainly subject to modification and refinement.

8.4.2 Design

The line between object-oriented analysis and design are not always clear. However, in the analysis phase we have attempted to model the problem by identifying objects and operations provided by the problem statement itself. We used an easygoing approach of concentrating on the vocabulary of the problem. The design phase concentrates more on finding existing software abstractions and the design of new ones. With C++, this means the class mechanism.

8.4.2.1   Which Objects and Operations Already Exist?

At this point we can examine the list of objects in terms of objects that already exist. The names and the phone numbers are recognized as string objects and menu selection as a char object. The operations are already defined. Strings can be input, output, and compared, for example. A file object can be constructed from the ifstream class, as we have seen. We will also see that data can be saved (inserted) to an output file stream object.

Let's summarize this design so far. We use the nouns to recognize objects to help design a solution. We use the verbs to recognize operations. We have observed that some of these objects already exist. string and char objects can be constructed from the string and char classes, respectively, and the input file from istream. There may be other classes to construct some of these objects. They may be part of an existing library. For example, the ofstream class (not covered yet) is used to create an output file stream object. It is available with the same include directive for the ifstream class #include <fstream.h>.

For the other objects, we can look for add-on software from a variety of sources such as computer retail stores or software catalogues. In fact, there may be an electronic phone book class waiting to be bought. Assuming the class does not exist as canned software, we still have the ability to design our own. The only objects we don't have are the phone book and phone listing objects. So we can create our own C++ class to model these real-world objects. Here is a preview of what these classes might look like in terms of data members and member functions:

Class	Data Members	Member Functions
Phone Listing	Last name, first name, phone number	Compare, Output
Phone Book	An array of phone listing objects and its size	Initialize, LookUp, Display, Add, Remove, Quit

8.4.2.2   Design the Main Algorithm

We can now begin to design an algorithm that exemplifies the online phone book specified in the problem statement. If the high-level algorithm assumes the phone book and phone listing classes already exist, the resulting algorithm can be quite simple—a selection statement inside a do while loop.

```
// Initialize a phone book object
do the following {
    Get menu selection option:  L)ookup, D)isplay, A)dd , R)emove, or Q)uit
    if option is  L)ookup
       call the phoneBook::lookup member function
    else if option is D)isplay
       call the phoneBook::display member function
    else if option is A)dd
       call the phoneBook::add member function
    else if option is R)emove
       call the phoneBook::remove member function
    else if option is Q)uit
       call the phoneBook::quit member function
} while the user has not chosen Q)uit
```

Here the emphasis shifts from past efforts that used existing objects. We now see an approach that demands certain operations even though the class is still in the design phase. In other words, we have selected the responsibilities of a potential phoneBook class.

Responsibilities of a phoneBook Class	*Data Members*
1. Constructor to initialize a phone book object 2. lookup 3. display 4. add 5. remove 6. quit	1. An array of telephone listing objects 2. The size of the collection

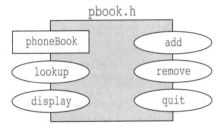

pbook.h

phoneBook   add

lookup   remove

display   quit

Figure 8.1   Interface diagram for module pbook.h

The phoneBook class has been described as a set of member functions encapsulated with a collection of telephone listings. Now we must consider phoneListing as a class to determine the operations and data members of each phoneListing object. All phoneListing objects must be constructed to store a last name, a first name, and a telephone number. This leads us to believe that we need one constructor member function and three data members (two names and a phone number) as a minimum. We should also be able to search for names in the collection of phone listings, so we must have access to the name portion of each object. And since phoneBook objects must be able to display phone numbers, we should provide access to the phone number portion of each object. This is accomplished with one accessor function for each data member. In summary, each phoneBook object should contain two names and the phone number. We should also be able to initialize and reference this data.

This leads to a first design of a phoneListing class:

Member Functions of Class phoneListing	*Data Members*
1. Constructor to initialize one object 2. Access to the firstName 3. Access to the lastName 4. Access to the phone number 5. Display a phoneListing object	1. First Name 2. Last Name 3. Phone Number

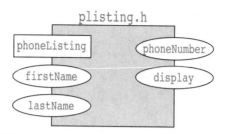

Figure 8.2   Interface diagram for module plisting.h

8.4.3 Implementation

Even without an existing phoneBook class, we have identified member functions such as lookup and add to allow for an implementation of a simple menu-driven program (the class declarations and implementation of individual operations follow). Assume nextChoice will be implemented as a global function after function main and that it displays a menu and returns one of the option choices (this responsibility could also be assigned to the phoneBook class). The main function can be reduced to this:

```
// The top-level algorithm to manage an on-line telephone
// book implemented as a simple menu-driven program
#include "pbook.h"  // Allegedly contains class phoneBook

char nextChoice();

int main()
{
  phoneBook myFriends;
  char option;
  do {
    option = nextChoice();    // POST: option is 'L', 'D', 'A', or 'Q'
    if(option == 'L' )
      myFriends.lookup();
    else if(option == 'D')
      myFriends.display();
    else if(option == 'A')
      myFriends.add();
    else if(option == 'R')
      myFriends.remove();
    else
      myFriends.quit();
  } while(option != 'Q');
  return 0;
}
```

All input and output operations will be contained in the member functions of these two classes. For example, the phoneBook constructor inputs data from an external file to initialize an array of phoneBook objects and the number of listings on file. The prompts, pauses, clear screens, blank lines, and formatting are encapsulated within this class.

These two new modules, named pbook.h and plisting.h are required by the main function and pbook.h module, respectively. These relationships are shown in Figure 8.3.

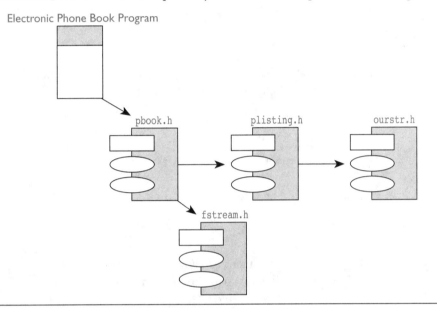

Figure 8.3   Module Diagram for the Electronic Phone Book Program

8.4.3.1   Declare and Implement the phoneListing class

Because the major data store of a phoneBook object will be an array of phoneListing objects, the phoneListing class is implemented first, before the phoneBook class. The three data members (fn, ln, pn) and the member functions are listed next in the specification of class phoneListing:

Specification for class phoneListing

`phoneListing();`	A constructor for phoneListing list[20];

`phoneListing(string initLast,`
`          string initFirst,`
`          string initNumber);`
	A constructor that converts the two names to uppercase and initializes the three data members of phoneListing:
	`     string fn;   // First name`
	`     string ln;   // Last name`
	`     string pn;   // Phone Number`

```
void phoneListing::display();          Displays one phoneListing object.
string phoneListing::firstName();      Returns fn
string phoneListing::lastName();       Returns ln
string phoneListing::phoneNumber();    Returns pn
```

Because we will need an array of phoneListing objects for the phoneBook class, we will use the default constructor (listed first above) to allow for declarations like this:

```
phoneListing list[20];
```

And to initialize each phoneListing object, we need an initializer constructor to which we may pass these three string arguments:

1. Last Name
2. First Name
3. Phone Number

in a constructor call like this:

```
list[0] = phoneListing("Browne", "Steve", "555-1232");
```

The other member functions allow us to inspect the state of any phoneListing object. Display will show the entire state of the object and members like phoneListing::firstName() and phoneListing::lastName() can be used in comparisons for searching and/or sorting.

Class declarations are typically stored in a file ending with ".h". The member functions are typically implemented in a separate file ending with ".cpp", ".cc", or ".c" (".cpp" is the convention used for the classes of this textbook). So we begin by declaring class phoneListing in a file named ourphone.h. The following class declaration is added to any program containing the directive #include "plisting.h".

```
//------------------------------------------------------------------
// SPECIFICATION FILE: plisting.h
//
//   Declares: class phoneListing
//------------------------------------------------------------------
#ifndef PLISTING_H   // Avoid duplicate compilations
#define PLISTING_H
#include "ourstr.h" // for class string
```

```
class phoneListing {
public:
  phoneListing::phoneListing();
  // POST: A phonelisting object is constructed without setting state

  phoneListing::phoneListing(string initLast,
                             string initFirst,
                             string initNumber);
  // POST: A phoneListing object is completely initialized. Example:
  //       phoneListing oneListing("Gavon", "Harold", "555-1234");

  void phoneListing::display()
  // POST: The complete phoneListing object is displayed

  string phoneListing::lastName()
  // POST: The last name is returned

  string phoneListing::firstName()
  // POST: The first name is returned

  string phoneListing::phoneNumber()
  // POST: The phone number is returned

private:
  string ln, fn, pn;
};

#include "plisting.cpp"  // Include member function implementations

#endif  // #ifndef PLISTING_H
```

Because class declarations are separated from their implementation at the file level, we must have some technique for combining the two separate files during compilation and linking. There are several techniques to do this. Some are awkward and require extra steps for each compilation. The convention used in this text is to "include" the implementation from each header file. This simplifies program development because this compiler directive

```
#include "plisting.cpp"  // Add member implementations automatically
```

located at the end of the header file automatically includes this implementation of the phoneListing member functions stored in the file "plisting.cpp":

```
//--------------------------------------------------------------
// IMPLEMENTATION FILE plisting.cpp
//
// Implements: class phoneListing
//--------------------------------------------------------------


phoneListing::phoneListing()
{ // Default constructor
}

phoneListing::phoneListing(string initLast,
                           string initFirst,
                           string initNumber)
{ // Make sure all names are in upper case
  ln = initLast;
  ln.toUpper();
  fn = initFirst;
  fn.toUpper();
  pn = initNumber;
}

string phoneListing::lastName()
{
  return ln;
}

string phoneListing::firstName()
{
  return fn;
}

string phoneListing::phoneNumber()
{
  return pn;
}

void phoneListing::display()
{
  cout.width(15);
  cout << firstName() << ' ' << lastName();
  cout.width(20 - lastName().length());
  cout << ' ' << phoneNumber() << endl;
}
```

Class phoneListing is now complete. To demonstrate, consider the following program which declares a small array of phoneListing objects along with the output that it
generates:

```
#include "plisting.h"  // for class phoneListing

int main()
{
  phoneListing list[3];
  list[0] = phoneListing("Hall", "Rob", "555-1234");
  list[1] = phoneListing("Esterly", "Anna", "555-9999");
  list[2] = phoneListing("Melinowski", "June", "555-8888");

  cout << list[0].firstName()   << endl;
  cout << list[1].lastName()    << endl;
  cout << list[2].phoneNumber() << endl;

  for(int j = 0;  j < 3;  j++)
    list[j].display;
  return 0;
}
```

```
────────────────────────────── Output ──────────────────────────────
ROB
ESTERLY
555-8888
        ROB HALL            555-1234
        ANNA ESTERLY        555-9999
        JUNE MELINOWSKI     555-8888
```

This test driver for the `phoneListing` class calls every member function.

8.4.3.2   Declare and Implement the phoneBook class

The following specification of the new `phoneBook` class is declared and implemented below (the `remove` member function will be declared but its implementation is left as a lab project):

Specification for class phoneBook

`phoneBook::phoneBook();`	A constructor that initializes an array of listings and sets n as the number of initialized elements. In other words, this single constructor initializes all private data members.
	```\nprivate:\n // The data members of phoneBook\n phoneListing list[MAX_PHONE_LISTINGS];\n int n; // total # of objects\n};\n```
`void phoneBook::lookup();`	Displays all listings with the search name.

```
void phoneBook::display();        Show all listings with the same last name.
void phoneBook::add();            Add a phoneListing to the collection.
void phoneBook::remove();         Remove a phoneListing object from the phoneBook.
void phoneBook::quit();           Updates the input file if necessary and desired.
```

The class declaration is in the header file named "pbook.h" shown next. Because the major data store of phoneBook is an array of phoneListing objects, "pbook.h" must #include the phoneListing class to allow for the declaration of the array of phoneListings data members.

```
//------------------------------------------------------------------
// SPECIFICATION FILE pbook.h
//
// Declares: class phoneBook
//------------------------------------------------------------------
#ifndef PBOOK_H
#define PBOOK_H
#include "plisting.h"  // for class phoneListing
#include "ourstr.h"    // for class string

const int MAX_PHONE_LISTINGS = 20;
const string fileName = "phone.dat";

class phoneBook {
public:
  phoneBook::phoneBook();
  //  PRE: No more than MAX_PHONE_LISTINGS are in the file
  //       associated with fileName
  // POST: The array of phoneListing objects (list) is initialized
  //       with file input from the file known as fileName

  void phoneBook::lookup();
  // POST: All phoneListings matching the input name are displayed

  void phoneBook::add();
  //  PRE: The user enters all information and confirms the add
  // POST: A new phoneListing is added to the phoneBook

  void phoneBook::remove();
  // POST: The phoneListing object is removed from the phoneBook

  void phoneBook::display();
  // POST: The entire list of phonebook objects is displayed

  void phoneBook::quit();
  // POST: If the user verifies updates, the phoneBook listings are
  //       saved to disk reflecting any new adds or removals
```

```
private:
  phoneListing list[MAX_PHONE_LISTINGS]; // array of phoneListings
  int n;           // Number of listings on file
  int updatesMade; // If > 0, user will be asked to update file
};


#include "pbook.cpp"   // Include member function implementations

#endif
```

Before looking at the complete implementation of the phoneBook member functions, some input/output details and behavior of operations are previewed. The constructor is implemented to input data from a file. After the phoneBook is initialized with this constructor call:

```
phoneBook myFriends;  // Initialize a phoneBook object
```

a call to phoneBook::display() generates output that looks like this:

```
Current Phone Book Listings
============================================
        MARY ESTERLY              555-2222
     SYLVIA MAJEWSKI              555-9999
    CHANDRA SHRESTRA              555-8888
    JACKSON SUMNER               555-0000
  SYLVESTER PALINDRUBALLITANIO    555-8764
         SUE KIM                  555-7464
     KIERAN STEWART               555-1234

. . . Press Enter to continue . . .  _
```

The main function that drives the phoneBook object was given earlier. It is also stored on disk as "testphon.cpp". You will see the global nextChoice function implemented there. It prompts for one of the five options and returns either an uppercase L, D, A, R, or Q. The prompt looks like this on a cleared screen:

```
              —My Little Phone Book—

   L)ookup  D)isplay  A)dd  R)emove  Q)uit: d
```

The phoneBook::lookup(); operation prompts for a last name and shows all phone listings with that last name—and there may be none. Two sample dialogues are shown next:

```
────────────────── Dialogue 1 ──────────────────
  Enter LAST name: SUMNER
  ------------------------------------------------
  All names matching 'SUMNER':
          JACKSON SUMNER              555-0000
  ------------------------------------------------
```

```
────────────────── Dialogue 2 ──────────────────
  Enter LAST name: NotHere
  ------------------------------------------------
  All names matching 'NOTHERE':
  ------------------------------------------------
```

The phoneBook::remove is currently implemented as a *test stub*—an incomplete operation that can be called. Currently this message is displayed (completion of phoneBook::remove is left as a lab project):

```
    phonebook::remove() is under construction
```

The phoneBook::add() operation prompts for a first name, a last name, and a phone number. Before adding a new phoneListing object, the user verifies the addition of the new phoneListing. Here is a sample dialogue:

```
────────────────── Dialogue ──────────────────
    First Name: Margaret
     Last Name: Gemmel
  Phone Number: 555-1040

        MARGARET GEMMEL              555-1040
  Do you wish to add this new listing? Y)es N)o y
```

Before the program terminates during the quit operation, the user is asked to update the file that stores the phoneListing objects until the next program run—but only if an add operation has occured. At this point, the user will see this prompt:

```
  Do you wish to store the 3 updates? Y)es N)o  y
```

If the user enters N, the updates will not occur. With Y, the input file is destroyed and replaced with the phoneListing objects as they currently exist in the phoneBook object. The new object required for this update is constructed from class ofstream (output file stream) declared in the file "fstream.h." An ofstream object is similar to an ostream object. Data is inserted with <<. It is initialized like ifstream objects. In phoneBook::quit() the same file name associated with inFile is associated with outFile.

```
ofstream outFile(fileName.chars());
for(int j = 0; j < n; j++)
{ // Save all phoneListing objects to disk
  outFile << list[j].lastName() << ' '
          << list[j].firstName() << endl
          << list[j].phoneNumber() << endl;
}
```

The for loop creates a file reflecting the current state of the phoneBook object that will be available during the next program run. This provides a form of persistence and more accurately reflects the maintenance of a phone book. Here is the implementation of all phoneBook class member functions as stored in the implementation file "pbook.cpp":

```
//-------------------------------------------------------------
// IMPLEMENTATION FILE: pbook.cpp
//
// Implements: class phoneBook
//-------------------------------------------------------------
#include <fstream.h>
#include <stdlib.h>
#include "ourstuff.h"

/***********************************************
   Implement class phoneBook member Functions
***********************************************/

phoneBook::phoneBook()
{
  updatesMade = 0;
  // string::chars returns the part of string objects accepted by
  // the ifstream constructor (a char * object covered in Chapter 9)
  ifstream inFile(fileName.chars());
  if(! inFile)
  {
    cout << endl << "**Error** File '" << fileName << "' not opened";
    cout << "\nChange path or file name at top of file 'pbook.h'"
         << endl;
    cout << "**Program terminated**" << endl;
    exit(0);
  }
  else
  {
    n = 0;
    string last, first, number;
    while( (! inFile.eof()    ) &&
           (n < MAX_PHONE_LISTINGS) &&
           (inFile >> last >> first >> number) )
    {
      list[n] = phoneListing(last, first, number);
```

```
        n++;
      }
    inFile.close(); // The disk file associated with inFile can now
                    // be reopened later for output (insertions)
  }
}

void phoneBook::lookup()
{
  string searchName;
  cout << endl << endl << "Enter LAST name: ";
  cin >> searchName;
  searchName.toUpper();
  cout << "--------------------------------------------";
  cout << endl << "All names matching '" << searchName << "': " << endl;
  for(int j = 0; j < n; j++)
    if(searchName == list[j].lastName())
      list[j].display();
  cout << "--------------------------------------------";
  cout << endl;
}

void phoneBook::add()
{
  if(n >= MAX_PHONE_LISTINGS)
    cout << "**Array is full** Cannot add any more phone listings"
         << endl;
  else
  {
    string last, first, number;
    cout << "   LAST name: ";  cin >> last;
    cout << "  First name: ";  cin >> first;
    cout << "Phone Number: ";  cin >> number;
    phoneListing temp(last, first, number);
    temp.display();
    cout << "Do you wish to add this new listing? Y)es N)o ";
    char ch;
    cin >> ch;
    if(ch == 'y' || ch == 'Y')
    {
      list[n] = temp;
      n++;
      // The save prompt in phoneBook::quit appears when upDatesMade
      // is nonzero. The number of updates is shown there also
      updatesMade++;
      cout << temp.lastName() << " added" << endl;
    }
    else
      cout << temp.lastName() << " not added" << endl;
```

```
    }
}

void phoneBook::remove()
{
  cout << endl << "phoneBook::remove is under construction" << endl;
  causeApause();
}

void phoneBook::display()
{
  cout << endl << endl
       << "Current Phone Book Listings \n";
  cout << "=========================================" << endl;
  for(int j = 0; j < n; j++) {
    // Pause at every 12 listings unless there are no more.
    list[j].display();
    if( ((j+1) % 12 == 0) && (j != n))
      causeApause();
  }
  causeApause();
}

void phoneBook::quit()
{
  if(updatesMade)
  {
    cout << "Do you wish to store the " << updatesMade
         << " updates? Y)es N)o ";
    char ch;
    cin >> ch;
    if(ch == 'y' || ch == 'Y')
    {
      cout << endl << endl
           << "Updating file '" << fileName
           << "' to store updates" << endl;
      // string::chars returns the part of string objects accepted by
      // the ofstream constructor (a char * object covered in Chapter 9)
      ofstream outFile(fileName.chars());
      for(int j = 0; j < n; j++)
      {
    outFile << list[j].lastName() << ' '
                << list[j].firstName() << endl
                << list[j].phoneNumber() << endl;
      }
    }
  }
}

/****** End class phoneBook member function implementations *******/
```

Chapter Summary

After using classes through data abstraction for some time, we formally covered the implementation of C++ classes. A C++ class usually has a public section for member functions, a private section for data members, and one or more objects to represent the state of any object of the class. The simplified implementation of C++ classes used in this text prevents direct access to the data members (they are declared private in this text) so we use member functions to initialize, reset, or access the state of objects:

```
class class-name {
public:
    function-prototypes ;
private:
    data-members
} ;
```

We also talked about some of the issues that went into the design of the bankAccount class.

Constructor functions have the same name as the class, may not have a return type, and are called at declaration. They are a convenient method for guaranteeing initialization of every object's state. Many classes have more than one constructor through function overloading—many functions with the same name—and default arguments, which allow any single constructor function to take a varying number of arguments. Member functions are implemented after the class declaration with this general form (*Note:* constructors do not use *return-type*):

```
return-type  class-name :: function-heading
{
... statements
}
```

In the case study, we saw an example of object-oriented analysis and design. The problem statement was probed for nouns that suggested potential objects. Responsibilities were recognized by examining verbs of the problem statement and then assigning them to the objects. Many operations were assigned to the phoneBook class.

Exercises

Given this problem statement:

Problem: *Implement an on-line library checkout system. The software should manage all books in the library by allowing check-in and check-out. To simplify things, assume there are no due dates or late fines. Make these operations available to the user (a librarian):*
*   1. *CheckOut: The book's call number is entered and the book becomes unavailable if it is not already checked out. If it is unavailable, display an appropriate message.*
*   2. *Return: The librarian enters the book's call number and the book becomes available.*

8. Identify any existing objects such as `strings`, `chars`, `ints`, or `floats`.
9. Identify at least one class that should help simplify the problem.
10. Write a `main` function algorithm that allows a librarian to check in and check out library books for an undetermined period of time.

Lab Projects

8E   Modifying a class

In this lab, you will be completing the `remove` operation and adding a `sort` operation to the `phoneBook` class.

*   Edit the file `"pbook.cpp."`
*   Modify the `phoneBook::remove` member function to prompt for a first name and a last name. If the names match a `phoneListing` object, remove it from the phone book. One dialogue should go like this:

```
First Name: Paula
 Last Name: Gebhart
phoneListing object not in directory—No changes made

First Name: Mary
 Last Name: Esterly
phoneListing object has been removed from phone book
```

- Implement void phoneBook::sort() to arrange the listings in alphabetical order by the last name. If you removed Mary Esterly and updated the file at the prompt, the list of phoneBook objects should look like this after a call to sort (your names may differ):

```
Current Phone Book Listings
==============================================
         SUE KIM                    555-7464
     SYLVIA MAJEWSKI                555-9999
  SYLVESTER PALINDRUBALLITANIO      555-8764
     CHANDRA SHRESTRA               555-8888
      KIERAN STEWART                555-1234
     JACKSON SUMNER                 555-0000


. . . Press Enter to continue . . .  _
```

- Change the code in the driver program stored in "testphon.cpp" to allow the user to sort the phoneBook listings any time it is desired.
- Run this program with a series of adds, deletes, displays, and sorts to verify that your program and the phoneBook class are properly maintaining a collection of phoneListing objects.

8F   Implementing a Class

Implement a golfList class that initializes a collection of golfer objects using data from an external file. The first line contains an int representing par for the course. The remaining lines contains a first name (string), last name (string), and final golf score (int). The constructor golfList::golfList should initialize the collection of golfer objects and sort them in ascending order based on the score data member. A display member function should display all golfers and the score in relation to par (shown below as 216). The names of golfers precede the number of strokes over or under par. The word "even" should be displayed if the player is at even par. The list should show the best performances to the worst (ascending order).

If the file contains this input data: *The output should look like this:*
```
216
Arnie Plummer   218          Gary Players    -7
Steve Bally     214          Steve Bally     -2
Gary Players    209          Fonzy Cellar    even
Fonzy Cellar    216          Arnie Plummer   +2
Mick Waldo      218          Mick Waldo      +2
```

9

Pointers

We have seen how arrays can be useful data members of a class. In this chapter we look at a related class of data known as pointers that provide additional advantages. C++ pointers store addresses of other objects. Pointers are used in combination with memory management operations that allocate memory when it is needed and release that memory when it is no longer needed—like string objects that may grow or shrink in length while the program is executing. After looking at some of the details of pointer initializations and other operations, we will study memory management operations that allocate and deallocate computer memory. The string class provides a context to show how these operations are used advantageously to manage computer memory. We will also see that classes with pointer objects need two additional types of member functions for proper memory management—a copy constructor and a class destructor function. First, however, we will spend some time getting used to manipulation of pointer objects that store addresses of other objects. We will see, for instance, that array names are actually pointers—the value stored in an array name is the address of the zeroth element of that array.

After studying this chapter, you will be able to:

- Use several methods for pointer initialization.
- Manipulate pointers to a collection of chars (char* objects).
- Use the new and delete operators for memory management.
- Recognize and use pointer objects within classes.
- Implement destructor functions.
- Understand how the size of an object may grow and/or shrink at runtime, particularly string objects.
- Implement destructors and copy constructors.

9.1 Pointer Objects

Object initializations such as this:

```
int able = 123;
int baker = 987;
```

satisfy the four characteristics of an object:

1. Name
2. Class
3. State
4. Address

An object's name is used within a program to inspect or alter the state value. The class attribute describes the characteristics of the object, the operations defined for the object, and how the object is viewed by the rest of the program. The state attribute is altered through initialization, assignment, and stream extraction, and inspected through stream insertion or an appearance in an expression. These are the attributes we are familiar with. However, the address of an object is the one that we have not directly manipulated. Until now, we have relied on the runtime system to manage addresses. However, C++ allows us to manipulate those addresses directly.

We reference an object through its name. The runtime system references the same object through its address. Each object resides in a specific memory location—one or more bytes of computer memory addressed as the first byte. For example, here is a machine-level view of objects showing able stored at address 63,000 and baker at address 63,004 (the addresses shown are arbitrary and infer that ints are stored in four bytes of memory):

Name	Class	State	Address
able	int	123	63000
baker	int	987	63004

The object able is shown to reside in the bytes 63000, 63001, 63002, and 63003. The address of able is 63000. We do not always need to know the exact addresses of objects. However, the concept of objects that store addresses eventually becomes important in the study of computing fundamentals.

The memory allocated for many objects is determined at compiletime. char objects require one byte of memory. int and float objects require a specific and predictable number of bytes, and, as we are about to learn, *dynamic objects* consume chunks of memory at runtime. The major benefit is that memory is allocated on an as-needed basis and then deallocated (returned) to the system when it is no longer needed. Dynamic objects manage collections that may shrink and grow in size. The size is limited only by available memory so programmers can more effectively control computer resources. For example, the string class uses some behind-the-scenes memory allocation that permits runtime sizing of string objects. Since we usually do not know how many characters will be entered by the user, the string class was designed to allocate exactly the number of bytes needed during a cin >> operation:

```
string name;
cout << "Enter your name: ";
cin >> name;
```

The class also allows programmers to assign strings of varying length:

```
string a, b;
a = "The string object a should have its own space";
b = "The string object b should also";
```

On assignment, memory used by the object is returned to the system before the new value is stored.

The alternative would be to allocate an array of chars of arbitrary size for every string object during the call to the constructor. But what size should we use? We could pick a size large enough to accommodate most strings, but this would waste large amounts of memory. Imagine an array of 1000 strings where each string is 128 or 200 bytes long. Without the pointers we are about to study, we might be forced into this alternative.

Pointer objects store the addresses of other objects—they *point to* other objects. Data objects are stored or retrieved through pointers objects if declared with * between the class-name and the identifier:

*class-name * identifier ;*

The value placed into a pointer object is the first of potentially many bytes of memory that store the object. For example, after this declaration:

```
int *intPtr;
```

the pointer object named intPtr may store the address of any int object. Currently, this pointer object intPtr has not been assigned a value.

Programming Tip

The asterisk in a pointer declaration may be written anywhere between the class name and identifier. The * may even "touch" one, the other, or both:

```
int* intPtr;     float  *floatPtr        char*charPtr;
```

Take care to include * for each pointer object. For example, the following does *not* declare two pointers, as it might appear:

```
int *p, q; // Equivalent to int *p; int q;   q is an int, not a pointer
```

A pointer object may have or may obtain one of these values:

1. It may be undefined (garbage).
2. It may contain the special pointer value 0, an address signifying a pointer to nothing.
3. It may point to some object.

Currently, `intPtr` has not been assigned a value, and any attempt to use it results in undefined system behavior. One way to set the state of `intPtr` is to assign it the special pointer constant 0 that means the pointer does not point to anything.

```
intPtr = 0;  // intPtr points to nothing
```

9.1.1 Initializing Pointer Objects with & (the Address Of Operator)

Because pointer objects store addresses, their values become visually more meaningful when written in a box with an arrow pointing to the object. So these three statements

```
int anInt     // Allocate space for an int object
anInt = 123; // Direct addressing
int *p;       // Allocate space to store the address of an int object
```

are graphically represented as follows:

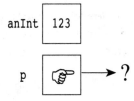

where ? signifies a pointer object has not been assigned a value yet. If we assign 0 to the pointer, we could picture the value like this:

But when the pointer is assigned an address, rather than writing the address, we move the arrow to point to the object stored at the address. So how can we make a pointer point to something?

Pointer objects may be assigned value through the & operator, which is called the *address of operator*. The address of operator returns the address of its operand, which is usually an object. This general expression

& *object-name*

evaluates to the address of *object-name*. For example, the following statement stores the address of anInt into the pointer object p (the expression &anInt is read as "address of anInt"):

```
p = &anInt; // &anInt returns the memory location (address) of anInt
```

This assignment is best presented pictorially by moving the arrow from ? to the object for which it holds the address:

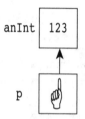

The arrow from p to anInt indicates that p is now pointing to the object anInt, and the actual value stored in p is an address.

The value of the object pointed to by a pointer object can also be altered indirectly. For example, we can change the state of anInt without even using its name. This *indirect addressing* with the *dereference*, or indirection operator *, allows us to inspect or change the memory pointed to by the pointer object. Here is an example of how the memory for the object pointed to by p may be altered:

```
*p = -654;     // Indirect Addressing stores -654 into anInt
               // because p is pointing to anInt
```

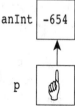

Programming Tip

It sometimes helps to give a name to a dereference operation. Try reading *p as "the object pointed to by p." Then, the assignment

```
*p = -654;
```

is read as "The object pointed to by p becomes -654."

Notice that the assignment to *p does not change p. Instead, it changes the value of the int pointed to by p. The * that precedes a pointer object indicates the object referenced, or pointed to, by the pointer object. To illustrate the differences between p (read as "p"), *p ("the object pointed to by p"), and &anInt ("the address of anInt"), consider the indirect addressing method of the following program that interchanges two pointers' values. By the end of the program, the two pointer objects p1 and p2 point to each other's original int object.

```
// Interchange two pointer values.  The pointers are
// switched to point to the other's original int objects.
#include <iostream.h>

int main()
{
  double *p1, *p2, *temp; // Three *s means 3 pointer objects
  double n1, n2;

  // Initialize the int objects
  n1 = 99.9;
  n2 = 88.8;
  // Let p1 point to n1 and p2 point to n2
  p1 = &n1;
  p2 = &n2;
  cout << "*p1 and *p2 before switch" << endl;
  cout << *p1 << "     " << *p2 << endl;

  // Let p1 point to where p2 is pointing and
  // let p2 point to where p1 is pointing to
  temp = p1;
  p1 = p2;
  p2 = temp;

  // Now the values of the pointers are switched to point
  // to each other's int object. The ints do not move.
  cout << "*p1 and *p2 after switch" << endl;
  cout << *p1 << "     " << *p2 << endl;
  return 0;
}
```

───────────────── **Output** ─────────────────

```
*p1 and *p2 before switch
99.9    88.8
*p1 and *p2 after switch
88.8    99.9
```

The values 99.9 and 88.8 are not moved in memory. Instead, the addresses stored in the pointer objects p1 and p2 are interchanged. The following graphic representation traces this program execution. First, all five objects—three of which are pointers—are declared but not initialized. (*Note:* All boxes represent memory storing the state of an object.)

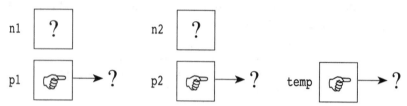

The next four program statements (n1 = 99.9; n2 = 88.8; p1 = &n1; p2 = &n2;) initialize four of the five main function objects—temp is still undefined.

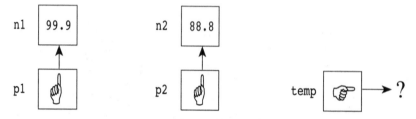

The statement temp = p1; means that the pointer object temp is set to point to the same memory location as p1. The address of p1 is stored into temp (at this point the expression temp == p1 would be true). This change is indicated by the fact that arrows from both p1 and temp point to the same location—the object named n1.

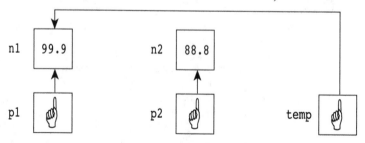

Next, the assignment p1 = p2 causes p1 to point to the same integer as p2. So p1 and p2 now store the same address—they are considered equal.

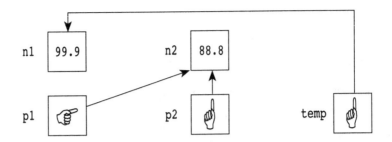

And finally, p2 = temp; causes p2 to point to the same int to which p1 was origi-nally pointing.

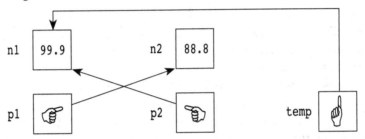

Now that p2 points to n1 and p1 points to n2, cout << *p1 displays 88.8, rather than the original 99.9.

This program illustrates the key problem to manipulating pointers: Are we chang-ing the pointer or the value to which it points?

Programming Tip

At first, working with pointers is not easy. It requires a shift from understanding an object as a named memory location that stores a value, to understanding objects that store an address of another object that holds a value. Algorithm design and debugging are different. One low-cost tool that helps is the use of arrows to repre-sent pointer values. We can trace through an algorithm by moving the arrow rather than writing the address. Also, when writing debugging code, the value being pointed to is usually more telling than the address of where that object is located. So debug with * as in cout << *aPointer; rather than cout << aPointer;. With this, you see the more useful value of the objects, not their addresses.

9.1.2 Addresses as Function Arguments

In Chapter 4, we first saw & used with parameters to pass arguments by reference rather than value. This is necessary to alter associated arguments. For example, when anInt is incremented here,

```
void inc(int & anInt)    // In-Out
{
  anInt++;
}
```

this associated argument (j) is also incremented:

```
int main()
{
  int j = 0;
  inc(j);    // j is now 1
  return 0;
}
```

With &, the parameter anInt is an alias (another name) for the argument j. That's because anInt receives the address of j, not the value of j. Without &, the associated argument (j) would not change.

References are also used for efficiency. Passing one address—a pointer of—an argument can often be less time consuming than copying all the values of that object. For example, if a large object consisting of thousands of bytes of memory were passed by value, the runtime system must first allocate that much memory and then copy every single byte to the function. Passing by value may noticeably slow down the system. To improve efficiency, a bank object is passed by reference to avoid copying potentially thousands of bankAccount objects:

```
// Pass a bank object by reference
#include "ourbank.h"

void someFunction(bank & aBank) // Passed by reference for efficiency
{
  // do something with aBank
}

int main()
{
  bank firstBank;
  someFunction(firstBank);
  // ...
  return 0;
}
```

Of course, the presence of & means that any change to bank inside someFunction will affect firstBank, and this may be the desired purpose of the function. But if no changes are to be made, the keyword const may be placed in front of the reference parameter. Then an attempt to change the object results in a compiletime error. The "safe" and efficient way to pass a bank that is not to be modified uses a *const reference* parameter:

```
void someFunction(const bank & aBank);
// The const reference parameter is efficient and prevents change to
// the associated argument.
```

Programming Tip

Any attempt to change a const object should be an error, and usually is. However, Turbo/Borland C++ incorrectly reduces this error to a warning and changes *do* occur. So if you are using Borland products, pay attention to the warning and don't rely on the system to prevent changes. The compiler allows the error to pass through.

```
// Pass a bank object by reference
#include "ourbank.h"

void someFunction(const bank & aBank)
{ // aBank is passed by const reference for efficiency and safety.
  // Changing the const object aBank should be an error...
  aBank.recordWithdrawal(50.00, 15);
  // ...but with Borland, this function call is only a warning

Warning: Non-const function recordWithdrawal(double, int) called for const object
```

Because pointer objects store addresses, a pointer argument ensures that the copied value is already an address; & is not required. For example, one pointer argument arises whenever an array argument is associated with an array parameter. This is because all array objects are actually a pointer to—or address of—the first array element! So you have been using pointers for some time now. Whenever the subscript operator is applied to an array object an address is computed. For example, if x is an array of ints where each int is 4 bytes long, and x has the value of address 60000, this formula

address of first array element + (subscript * size of one element)

computes x[3] as 60000 + (3*4). So x[3] is stored at address 60012.

When an array is passed to a function, it is actually the address of the first array element that is sent, so the associated parameter must use a different syntax. The array parameter is declared with the class and the parameter name followed by [ ]. These points are illustrated in a main function that passes an array to two different functions. Notice that when function inc alters the parameter anArray, the associated array argument x is also altered (each array element is incremented by +1). This occurs even though & is not used for the parameter anArray.

```
// Pass the address of the array
#include <iostream.h>

void inc(int anArray[ ], int n)  // [ ] signifies an array parameter
{
  for(int j = 0; j < n; j++)
    anArray[j] = anArray[j] + 1; // Increment each element by +1
}

void display(int anArray[ ], int n)
{
  for(int j = 0; j < n; j++)
    cout << anArray[j] << "  ";
}

int main()
{
  int x[3];
  int n = 3;
  x[0] = 90;
  x[1] = 95;
  x[2] = 99;
  cout << "Before calling inc(x,n), x = " << endl;
  display(x, n);
  cout << endl;
  inc(x, n);
  cout << " After calling inc(x,n), x = " << endl;
  display(x, n);
  cout << endl;
  return 0;
}
```

──────────────── **Output** ────────────────

```
Before calling inc(x,n), x =
90  95  99
 After calling inc(x,n), x =
91  96  100
```

Self-Check

1. Write the value of each of the four object attributes supplied by this initialization:

   ```
   float x = 987.65;
   ```

   a. Class   b. Name   c. State   d. Address

2. What do pointer objects store?

3. Name two methods for initializing a pointer object.
4. What is the value of floatPtr after this declaration?

```
float * floatPtr;
```

5. Use these statements to answer the questions below:

```
float * floatPtr;
float aFloat = 1.23;
floatPtr = &aFloat;
```

   a. What is the name of the pointer object?
   b. What is the value of the *floatPtr?
   c. Without using the object aFloat, write a statement that adds +1 to the memory storing 1.23.
6. Write the output generated by the following program.

```
#include <iostream.h>
int main()
{
   int *p;
   int j = 12;
   p = &j;
   // Note: The unary indirection operator * has higher prece-
   // dence than the addition + the multiplier operator *
   cout << ((*p) + (*p)) << "   " << ((*p) * (*p)) << endl;
   return 0;
}
```

7. Write the output generated by the following program.

```
#include <iostream.h>
void f(double & y)    // out
{
   y = y + 2;
}
int main()
{
   double x = 3.4;
   cout << x << "  ";
   f(x);
   cout << x << "  ";
   f(x);
   cout << x << "  " << endl;
   return 0;
}
```

8. Write the minimum declarations to store the address of ch, a char object, into a char pointer object named charPtr.

9. Write the minimum declarations and statements that declare and initialize all the objects as shown in the diagram below:

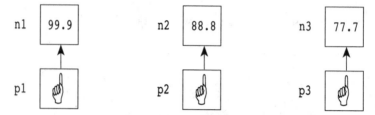

10. Using the code from Question 9, write a statement that displays the sum of all the float objects using * (the dereferencing operator). Do not use the object names n1, n2, or n3.

Answers

1. a. float   b. x   c. 987.65   d. Not known. The address cannot be determined with the information provided.
2. Addresses of other objects.
3. Assign it 0, assign it an address of another object with & (assign it the value of another pointer object).
4. Undefined (or garbage).
5. a. floatPtr   b. 1.23
    c. *floatPtr = *floatptr + 1.0;
        or (*floatPtr)++; // where due to the precedence rules, parentheses are necessary
6. 24   144
7. 3.4   5.4   7.4
8. char * charPtr;
    char ch;
    charPtr = &ch;
9. double n1 = 99.9, n2 = 88.8, n3 = 77.7;
    double *p1, *p2, *p3;
    p1 = &n1;
    p2 = &n2;
    p3 = &n3;
10. cout << (*p1 + *p2 + *p3) << endl;

9.2   char* Objects

A char* object can be used as the address of the beginning of a group of char objects. Commonly used in the absence of a string class, these pointers to char are declared as follows:

```
char * strPtr; // strPtr is a pointer to a char
```

A char* pointer is used in conjunction with *null-terminated* strings—a group of characters in contiguous (next to each other) memory that use the null char value '\0' as a marker to terminate the string. The null character is automatically appended to string literals as they are encountered in a program. The addresses of C++ string literals with their invisible null char are stored into pointer objects with assignments like this:

```
strPtr = "A null terminated string";
```

The pointer object strPtr now holds the address of the first char in the string literal—the byte that stores the char 'A' in this case. Consistently using char* (sometimes pronounced char star) objects with the terminating null char results in a quasi string class. In the case of the previous assignment, the memory required to store all the chars plus their terminating null is allocated automatically when the string literal is encountered.

Although it may appear as if the entire string is assigned to strPtr, it is the address of the string literal that is actually moved into the pointer object strPtr. The 25 characters of this particular literal (the 24 characters plus the terminating null) are located in some portion of the computer's memory. The pointer strPtr is the address used to locate these chars. This subtle distinction is represented pictorially as follows:

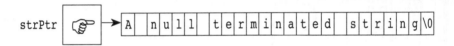

For instance, if the character 'A' is stored at address 5000, the ' ' is at address 5001, and the 'n' at 5002, the 'u' at 5003, and so on. The address stored in the pointer strPtr is 5000. This type of string requires all programmers and implementors of functions managing char* objects to adhere to this implementation detail:

Null-terminated strings must always be terminated with the null character '\0'

Sometimes the terminating null must be explicitly appended. But in most cases, the terminating null is appended automatically. For example, the terminating null automatically becomes part of all string literals when they are encountered within a program.

To illustrate that '\0' is indeed a part of string literals, first understand that all pointer objects, such as arrays and char*, may be subscripted to return the address of an object in the collection. In the case of a char* object, subscripts determine the addresses of individual characters. The first char pointed to by the char* object strPtr is referenced as strPtr[0]. Therefore, when strPtr is initialized with "abcd", the fourth char is strPtr[3] and the terminating null can be referenced as strPtr[4]. This is verified in

the following program that tests both values and displays a message that a null char
'\0' was indeed appended to the string literal "abcd":

```
#include <iostream.h>
int main()
{
  char * strPtr = "abcd";
  if((strPtr[3] == 'd') && (strPtr[4] == '\0'))
    cout << "A null char was appended to 'abcd'" << endl;
  return 0;
}
```

─── **Output** ───
```
A null char was appended to 'abcd'
```

A char* object is assigned a value through assignment with =, inserted into output
streams with <<, and extracted from output streams with >>. Some of these operations
are shown in the next program:

```
// Use char * pointer objects as a quasi-string class:
#include <iostream.h>

int main()
{
  char * wife;    // These two pointer objects store
  char * husband; // addresses of null-terminated strings

  wife = "Donna";
  husband = "Charlie";
  cout << "   The characters pointed to by wife: " << wife    << endl;
  cout << "The characters pointed to by husband: " << husband << endl;
  return 0;
}
```

─── **Output** ───
```
    The characters pointed to by wife: Donna
 The characters pointed to by husband: Charlie
```

Programming Tip

C++ defines << for char * objects. If the pointer itself is inserted, all chars up to the
terminating null are inserted. Inserting the dereference pointer shows only the first
char. Therefore, using the code above, this statement

```
cout << *wife;
```

displays D, while

```
cout << wife;
```

displays Donna.

As with other pointer objects, the values stored in `wife` and `husband` are addresses, not the entire null-terminated string. This is depicted in the following representation of the two pointers and the memory in which the null-terminated strings are stored (subsequent discussion presumes the two strings are stored next to each other, but this example may not work on all systems):

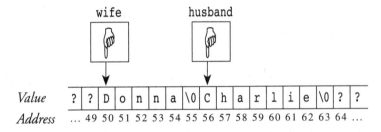

To illustrate we are dealing with addresses, this assignment of one pointer object to another

```
husband = wife;
```

does not move characters from one memory location to another. Instead the value of the pointer object `husband` is changed to point to the same byte of memory as `wife`:

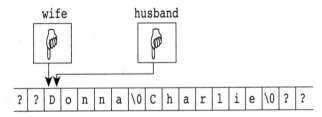

As you might expect, these two statements

```
cout << "   The characters pointed to by wife: " << wife    << endl;
cout << "The characters pointed to by husband: " << husband << endl;
```

generate output indicating the `char*` objects `wife` and `husband` are equal—they both store the same address.

```
The characters pointed to by wife: Donna
The characters pointed to by husband: Donna
```

But since these two quasistrings are pointing to the same memory, changes to one pointer object effectively alter the value pointed to by the other.

```
// This may cause an Segmentation fault runtime error on some systems:
husband[0] = 'X';   // Notice that wife is not being altered,
husband[3] = 'Y';   // But the memory pointed to by wife is.
husband[5] = 'Z';   // The output may be surprising especially
                    // if one terminating null is destroyed.
```

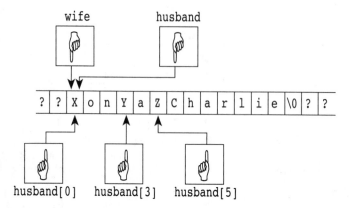

Self-Check

1. Using the state of memory illustrated above, evaluate the following expressions to true or false (1 or 0):

   a. wife[0] == husband[0]   d. wife[8] == husband[4]

   b. wife[3] == husband[4]   e. wife[1] == wife[1]

   c. husband == wife   f. wife[4] == husband[4]

Answers

1. a. True   d. True
    b. False   e. True
    c. True (the same address is f. True
        stored in both wife and husband)

Even though wife does not appear to change, the memory near the byte pointed to by wife is altered. The potentially surprising output of these statements is shown below

```
cout << "   The characters pointed to by wife: " << wife << endl;
```

---------- **Output** ----------
```
The characters pointed to by wife: XonYaZCharlie
```

As you can see, changes to one subscript pointer object (husband) effectively alter the other (wife). The reason Charlie appears to be appended to both strings is because the << operator is overloaded for char* objects; all characters are displayed beginning with the char pointed to by the pointer object until the null character '\0' is found. This is expressed in C++ as follows:

```
for(int j = 0; wife[j] != '\0'; j++) // Display each char until '\0'
    cout << wife[j];
```

Shortly we will see this as a major difference between quasistrings implemented as char* objects and the "safer" string class. Because the string class allocates separate memory for every string object, changing one string cannot alter another.

The following program presents one more example of how C++ passes addresses to functions. A char* object—an address—is passed to the makeUpper function. A change to the parameter (p) changes the argument (arg). Since the argument and associated parameter are both pointers (char* objects), no reference (&) is required. The argument is passed by value, which in the case of pointers like char* is an address.

```
// Illustrate a function call that passes a pointer as the argument
#include <iostream.h>
#include <ctype.h>     // for char toupper(char)

void makeUpper(char * p)     // p is an alias for the argument
{ // POST: The associated argument is changed to upper case
  for(int j = 0; p[j] != '\0'; j++)
    p[j] = toupper(p[j]);  // Convert each char to upper case
}

int main()
{
  char * arg = "Teague, David";
  makeUpper(arg);
  cout << arg << endl;
  return 0;
}
```

──────── **Output** ────────

```
TEAGUE, DAVID
```

The string.h file that accompanies all C++ compilers contains many functions designed for use with char* objects terminated with the null char '\0'. When combined with << and = operations, the string.h functions provide much of the functionality of the string class minus the safety features of string objects. The code shown next demonstrates a few commonly used functions: strlen, strcpy, strcmp, and strcat (*Note:* There is an intermittent runtime error present):

`char * s;`	Declare a char* object identified as s
`s = "string one!";`	Allocate memory for 12 chars, append '\0', let s point to them, s → "string one!\0"
`cout << strlen(s)` `    << endl;`	strlen returns the dynamic length of a char* object minus the 1 for '\0'. Output is 11
`strcpy(s, "new string");`	Write "new string\0" over memory pointed to by s, s → "new string\0"
`char * s2 = "another ";`	Initialize another char* object identified as s2, s2 → "another \0"

`if(strcmp(s2, s) < 0)`
`    cout << "s2 < s"`
`        << endl;`
	The strcmp functions returns 0 if its two arguments are equal, a negative if s2 < s and a positive if s2 > s. Output is s2 < s

`strcat(s2, s);`	Allocate more memory and append s to s2 with only one '\0'
`cout << s2;`	Output the concatenated chars pointed to by s2. Output is another new string

To demonstrate that char* objects are not safe, consider the following variety of results that occurred when the code in the left column above executed on several systems.

1. Nothing unusual.
2. Abnormal program termination error.
3. Told to save files, terminate applications, and reboot the computer.
4. Segmentation fault error.
5. Things worked for a while, and a later attempt to load a different application was unsuccessful.
6. Computer crashed, had to reboot.

The problem occurs at strcpy. We must declare the first argument large enough to hold the second argument. Declaring the first argument as an array of chars accomplishes this.

```
char * s = "string one!";
char s2[12];    // strlen(s)+1 is 12 so s2 can store 12 chars maximum
strcpy(s2, s);
```

The declaration of the array of `chars` named s2 allocates 12 new bytes of memory. This is enough to hold a copy of s. However, this approach requires us to declare the maximum size a `string` will reach at compiletime. To do this, declare the size of the array with either a constant such as 12, or with a named constant like MAX (assuming a declaration such as `const int MAX = 12;` has already occurred). There are other options. You could use a `string` class such as the one from this text, one that is available commercially (your system may have one), or one from freeware. Another option is to use the `new` operator covered in the following section.

Self-Check

1. Write the output generated by the following program:

```
#include <iostream.h>
int main()
{
  char * p = " abc";
  char * q = "0123";
  p[0] = 'T';
  for(int j = 0; j < 4; j++)
    cout << p[j] << q[j];
  return 0;
}
```

2. Write the output generated by the following program:

```
#include <iostream.h>
int main()
{
  char * p = "abcd";
  char * q = "1234";
  p = q;
  q = "A new string literal";  // <- A brand new literal
  cout << "p = " << p << " and q = " << q << endl;
  return 0;
}
```

Assuming #include <string.h> is present and these initializations:

```
char * s1 = "abc";
char * s2 = "123";
```

3. What is the value of `strlen(s1)`?
4. What is the value of `strlen(s2)`?
5. What output is generated by the statement `cout << s1 << s2 << s1;`?

6. What is the value of s2 after the statement `strcpy(s2, s1);`?
7. What is the value of s2 after the statement `strcpy(s2,"xyz");`?

Answers
1. `T0a1b2c3`
2. `p = 1234` and `q = A new string literal`
3. `3`
4. `3`
5. `abc123abc`
6. `"abc"`
7. `"xyz"`

9.3   Initializing Pointers with new

Pointer objects are frequently assigned values through the *new* operator. When the `new` operator precedes a class name, the resulting expression allocates a contiguous block of memory large enough to store one object of the given class. The same expression returns the address of, or a pointer to, this memory:

> `new` *class-name* ;

The memory is allocated at runtime from the *free store*—a portion of computer memory reserved for this purpose (the free store is sometimes called the *heap*). For example, the following expression allocates enough memory to store one `int` value. The expression is then replaced with a pointer to that memory.

```
new int;  // Allocate and get a pointer value, which is ignored here
```

Instead of ignoring the returned pointer value (the address of memory to store one `int` object), such pointer expressions can be combined with pointer objects in initializations.

```
int * intPtr = new int; // Allocate memory, store address into intPtr
```

Now we have `intPtr` holding the address of an `int` object. The only thing not currently assigned is the memory storing the `int` object. This is shown in the next figure where the undefined `int` value is signified as ? and the pointer value is represented as an arrow indicating a value that points to that undefined `int`:

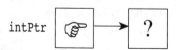

After the pointer object `intPtr` is initialized, we can store a value to the memory location pointed to by `intPtr` with an indirect assignment like this (`*intPtr` is the `int` object, not the pointer object):

```
*intPtr = 123;
```

This resulting representation shows that both the pointer object and the newly allo-cated memory now have been assigned values:

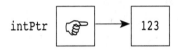

These new concepts are summarized in the following program that shows the differ-ence between a pointer object and the object that it points to.

```
// Illustrate one pointer object and one int object
#include <iostream.h>

int main()
{
  // Declare intPtr as an object that may point to an int
  int *intPtr;
  // Initialize intPtr to point to memory allocated through new int
  intPtr = new int;
  // Store 123 into the memory allocated for an int
  *intPtr = 123;
  //
  cout << " The address stored in the pointer object: " << intPtr << endl;
  cout << "The value of the int pointed to by intPtr: " << *intPtr << endl;
  return 0;
}
```

─────────── Output ───────────
```
The address stored in the pointer object: 0x6310
The value of the int pointed to by intPtr: 123
```

Note: The address shown in hexadecimal (base 16) format as `0x6310` equals decimal 25,360.

Notice that the pointer object, with value 25,360, is referenced as `intPtr`. The ac-tual `int` with value 123 is dereferenced as `*intPtr`.

9.3.1   Allocating More than One Object with new

There are many potential pitfalls with char* pointer objects such as this one related to the strcpy function.

```
char * str;
strcpy(str, "A string");   // Watch out!
```

As shown in the preceding section, this may result in a situation that could crash the system. It is an attempt to move characters into memory where none has been allocated—str does not have any new memory associated with it! This can be surprising, especially if you peruse the strcpy function prototype in string.h and discover that str, a char* object, is in fact the proper type to use as the first argument to strcpy:

```
char * strcpy(char * destination, char * source);
```

One way to avoid this problem is first to allocate the exact amount of memory to store the string argument passed to source. In the case of this string literal that appears to have 9 chars between " and "

```
"ten chars"   // Appears to be nine characters between " and "
```

we must allocate enough memory to store the 9 characters plus 1 extra to store the terminating null. The C++ new operator accomplishes this by allocating memory for many objects with [n], where n represents the number of objects to allocate:

```
new char[10]; // Allocate memory for 10 char objects and return
              // a pointer to this newly allocated memory
```

Again, because new also returns a pointer to the first byte of the 10 characters—an address—we can use it for pointer object initializations of this form:

class-name * *identifier* =   new   *class-name*[*number of elements*] ;

Example:
```
char * theChars = new char[10];
```

The pointer object theChars now points to the first of 10 bytes of memory where each byte may store one char object:

theChars

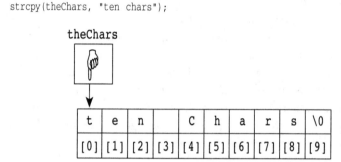

?	?	?	?	?	?	?	?	?	?
[0]	[1]	[2]	[3]	[4]	[5]	[6]	[7]	[8]	[9]

Since `strcpy` automatically appends a terminating null, we need a total of 10 chars to store the 9 chars of the string literal `"ten chars"` plus the automatically appended terminating null:

```
strcpy(theChars, "ten chars");
```

theChars

t	e	n		C	h	a	r	s	\0
[0]	[1]	[2]	[3]	[4]	[5]	[6]	[7]	[8]	[9]

This memory management technique—allocating the exact amount of memory, no more, no less—is utilized in the constructors of the `string` class. (*Note:* A portion of the `string` class declaration is provided here to put the private data members `int len` and `chars * theChars` into context.)

```
class string {
public:
   string::string(const char * initText);
   // POST: A string object is initialized using the char * argument
   //       when this constructor is called as string aStr("A string");
   // ...

private:
   int len;         // The dynamic length of any one string object
   char * theChars; // A pointer to the characters of a string object
};
```

For example, when we declare `string` objects like this:

```
string str("Any length string");
```

the following constructor function is called and the string literal `"Any length string"` is copied to the parameter `char* initText`:

```
string::string(char * initText)    // from ourstr.cpp
{ // len and theChars are private data members of the string class.
  // Construct one string object from a string literal:
  len = strlen(initText);          // Actual length without '\0'
  theChars = new char[len + 1];    // Allocate memory + 1 for '\0'
  strcpy(theChars, initText);      // Now theChars points to initText
}
```

This `string` constructor performs several actions to store the `chars` and a length for any `char*` argument passed to it. First, the call to `strlen` returns the length ('\0' is not counted) of the `string` literal pointed to by the pointer `initText`. This length is assigned to the private data member `len` to store the dynamic length of the `string` object.

Next, the `new` operator allocates the exact amount of memory from the free store required to store `initText` along with a terminating null (`len+1`). Finally, the characters are copied one by one into the newly allocated memory with the `strcpy` function stopping at the terminating null of `initText`. This generalized method guarantees that every `string` object stores the `char*` member of the `string` in its own space and places the terminating null into the correct position. These guarantees make the `string` class more user-friendly and safer than `char*` objects.

Self-Check

1. Write the output generated by the following program:

```
#include <iostream.h>
int main()
{
  int * p = new int;
  *p = 678;
  *p = *p + 111;
  cout << *p;
  return 0;
}
```

2. At the end of the next program, what can we say about the object p?

```
#include <iostream.h>
int main()
{
  double * p = new double;
  *p = 6.78;
  p = new double;
```

```
  cout << *p;
  return 0;
}
```

3. Write the output generated by the following program:

```
#include <iostream.h>
int main()
{
  double * p, * q;
  p = new double;
  q = new double;
  *p = 1.23;
  *q = 4.56;
  p = q;
  cout << *p << "  " << *q;
  return 0;
}
```

4. At the last statement of the preceding program, is it possible to retrieve the memory that stored 1.23?

5. Write the output generated by the following program:

```
#include <iostream.h>
#include <ouracct.h>
int main()
{
  bankAccount * bp = new bankAccount;
  char * name = "Hall";
  char * PIN = "1234";
  *bp = bankAccount(name, PIN, 100.00);
  cout << *bp << endl;
  return 0;
}
```

6. Write the output generated by the following program:

```
#include <iostream.h>
int main()
{
  int * x = new int[6];
  int j;
  for(j = 0; j < 6; j++)
    x[j] = 2 * j;
  for(j = 0; j < 6; j++)
    cout << x[j] << "  ";
  return 0;
}
```

7. Write one initialization using new to allocate memory for 1000 double objects that is pointed to by x.
8. Write the code to initialize to 0 all 1000 doubles of Question 7.
9. Write the code that allocates new memory for any string literal pointed to by charPtr and stores that string along with a terminating null char into memory pointed to by theChars. theChars and charPtr must be pointing to separate memory.

Answers
1. 789
2. p is undefined. The output is from some portion of memory, but it's not clear where or what that double value is.
3. 4.56   4.56
4. No, unless we had stored its address before resetting the pointer object p to point to the same double pointed to by q (before p = q).
5. { bankAccount: HALL, 1234, 100.00 }
6. 0 2 4 6 8 10 12
7. double * x = new double[1000];
8. for(int j = 0; j < 1000; j++)
       x[j] = 0.0;
9. int length = strlen(charPtr);
   char * theChars = new[length+1];
   strCpy(theChars, charPtr)

9.4 The delete Operator and Destructor Functions

So far, we have seen the new operator allocate only small amounts of memory from the free store. However, we should consider what happens when dynamic data grows to a large size. Using new without returning memory to the free store—a *memory leak*— limits the amount of memory available to a program. At some point, the dynamically allocated memory may no longer be needed. When this occurs, we should deallocate the unneeded memory back to the free store. This makes it available for other objects that have yet to be created. This return of memory, or *deallocation*, is accomplished with the C++ built-in *delete* operator. The delete operator has two general forms:

```
delete pointer-object ;
delete [ ] pointer-object ;
```

The first form returns the memory allocated for one dynamic object back to the free store while leaving an undefined value in that pointer object. The second form returns memory allocated for a group of objects allocated with new and [ ]. In the following program, the delete operator deallocates the memory for one double pointed to by p, ten chars pointed to by theChars, and 100 ints pointed to by x.

```
#include <string.h>              // for strcpy(char *, char*)
int main()
{
  double * p;
  p = new double;
  *p = 123;

  char * theChars;
  theChars = new char[10];
  strcpy(theChars, "ten chars");

  int * x;
  x = new int[100];

  // Use p, theChars, and x  ...
  // ...
  // When no longer needed, deallocate p, theChars, and x with delete:
  delete p;
  delete [ ] theChars;
  delete [ ] x;

  // All the bytes of memory pointed to by p, theChars,
  // and x is now returned to the free store
  return 0;
}
```

The three delete statements return the allocated memory back to the free store. All pointer objects now have undefined values that should not be used. Using them at this point results in undefined and therefore unpredictable behavior.

9.4.1   Destructors

Any class containing dynamic objects should also have the means to return the memory allocated with new back to the free store. Failure to use delete results in depletion of computer memory while the program is running. Although this may not produce any noticeable memory shortage in small programs, there are times when delete must be used to return the memory allocated with the new operator. One way to guarantee such memory deallocation and to avoid memory leaks is to add a *destructor* member function to any class that allocates memory with new. Whereas constructors are called at the point of object declaration, the class destructor (there can be only one) is automatically called when an object goes out of scope (at function returns, for example).

Within a class, a destructor prototype has the same name as the class, no arguments, and no return type. A class destructor prototype looks the same as a default constructor (no parameters) with a tilde character '~' preceding the prototype.

```
class class-name {
public:
    class-name::class-name();     // Constructor
    class-name::~class-name();    // Destructor
    //...
```

For example, a destructor for class myClass would be named ~myClass:

```
class myClass {
public
  myClass::myClass();  // constructor
  myClass::~myClass(); // destructor
  //...
```

The destructor member function is implemented like all other member functions with ~ written after the class name and scope resolution operator ::

```
myClass::~myClass()
{
   // ...  You will often see delete in class destructors
}
```

A destructor is called anytime an object goes outs of scope—the time at which a block is exited. So we do not need to call the destructor ourselves. In fact, we cannot. Instead, the runtime system does this automatically, and at the proper time—when the object is no longer needed. The following program uses a cout statement to illustrate how the destructor is called when the function is exited.

```
// Illustrate a class with a destructor
#include <string.h>    // for strlen(char *)
#include <iostream.h>  // for cout <<

class withDestructor {
public:
  withDestructor::withDestructor(char * initText);
  withDestructor::~withDestructor();
private:
  char * s;
};
```

```
withDestructor::withDestructor(char * initText)
{
  s = new char[strlen(initText) + 1];
  strcpy(s, initText);
  cout << "In constructor, s: '" << s << "'" << endl;
}

withDestructor::~withDestructor()
{
  cout << "'" << s << "' will be deleted by this destructor" << endl;
  delete [ ] s;
  // Memory allocated with s = new char[strlen(initText)+1];
  // has now been returned back to the free store.
}

void f()
{
  // Initialize dynamicObject by calling the constructor
  withDestructor dynamicObject("A string of any length");
  // When dynamicObject goes out of scope, the destructor is called
}

int main()
{
  cout << "Before f();" << endl;
  f();
  cout << "After f();" << endl;
  return 0;
}
```

Output

```
Before f();
In constructor, s: 'A string of any length'
'A string of any length' will be deleted by this destructor
After f();
```

The output shows that the private data member s is initialized in the constructor. The output of the argument

```
In constructor, s: A string of any length
```

infers that proper allocation of memory has occurred. Immediately after the call to the constructor, function f() is exited (there is only one statement in function f, the constructor call). This is the time at which the destructor is called, when dynamicObject goes out of scope. The output indicates that the private data member s is still valid at the time the destructor is called:

'A string of any length' will be deleted by this destructor

But immediately after this cout insertion, the statement

```
delete [ ] s;
```

is executed and s becomes undefined. Because this statement is in the destructor, memory allocated by the constructor is automatically returned to the free store for each and every object as it goes out of scope.

A similar approach to effective memory management is utilized in the string class. The constructor allocates memory with new and the destructor deallocates that memory with delete. The memory allocated for the private data member (theChars) is automatically deleted because the class destructor is called each time a string object goes out of scope. So we don't have to worry about returning memory when using a string class; it is done automatically. This prevents memory leaks.

```
// The string constructor and destructor are added here for easy
// comparison to the memory management exemplified in the code above

string::string(char * initText)
{ // The construct for string s("Initial text");
  len = strlen(initText);        // Actual length without '\0'.
  theChars = new char[len + 1];  // Allocate memory + 1 for '\0'.
  strcpy(theChars, initText);    // Let theChars point to initText
}

string::~string()
{ // The string destructor is called automatically to
  // deallocate memory as the object goes out of scope
  delete [ ] theChars;
}
```

9.4.2 Copy Constructors

One object of any class may be copied to another object. This is guaranteed by the C++ system for all classes. One object can be copied to another of the same class, either through assignment or argument/parameter association. The default copying process, called *memberwise copy*, copies the value of each data member of one object to another object. Although this may work fine for classes with no pointer members, we must override the defaults for classes with pointers. Consider these initializations and assignments for the withDestructor class:

```
withDestructor source("A string of any length");
withDestructor destination(source);
```

For assignments such as

```
destination = source;
```

the default memberwise copy situation is in effect. In the case of class `withDestructor`, the data member `s` is copied from `source` to the data member of `destination` in a manner that looks something like this:

```
destination.s = source.s;    // Memberwise copy
```

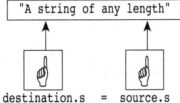

But since the lone data member `s` is a pointer object, we have an *address* that is copied. At this point the pointer data member of two objects (source and destination) are both pointing to the same memory.

We run into errors when the destructor is called to `delete` pointer data member(s). When memory for `destination.s` is deleted, `source.s` points to deleted memory! Now when the destructor is called for `source`, the attempt is made to delete memory that is already deleted. The result is undefined—usually a runtime error.

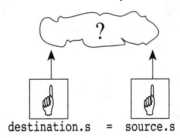

This detail of class implementation is summarized in the following program where function `processSome()` uses a few `withDestructor` objects. The default memberwise copy is now in effect.

```
// ... code for class withDestructor ...

void processSome()
{
  withDestructor source("Any length string, well this is longer");
  withDestructor destination(source);
```

```
            withDestructor aThirdObject(destination);
            // Do something with the objects
            // ...
            // When this function is done, the three objects will go out
            // of scope, the class destructor is called to delete the same
            // memory three times (Note: Errors may not always occur)
        }

        int main()
        {
          processSome();
          return 0;
        }
```

If one pointer is "deleted," the memory is deallocated to the free store. Then an attempt to delete the other memory is an attempt to delete memory that has already been deleted. You may see errors such as `'Null pointer assignment'` or other system-dependent behavior (and it may be an intermittent problem—the most insidious form of error). When pointers are involved in a class, we need allocation of separate memory for each pointer data member. But the default memberwise copy just copies addresses. As class implementors, we must override this situation.

For classes with no pointer data members, the default copy mechanism is acceptable for successful assignments, initializations, and pass by value. But in the case of classes with pointer objects, an overloaded assignment operator and a copy constructor should be added to the list of member functions (operator overloading is covered in the next section and Appendix B). Copy constructors are fairly easy to add to any class. A *copy constructor* takes exactly one argument. The general form of a copy constructor prototype for any class is as follows:

class-name::class-name (const *class-name* & *parameter-name*);

Because we are copying objects of the same class, the parameter must be the same class as the argument. For the sake of efficiency, the object is passed by reference with &. Finally, because we never want to alter the object being copied, the keyword const is added. For example, the string copy constructor prototype looks like this:

```
// Copy constructor:
string::string(const string & source);
// POST: source is copied during argument/parameter associations
//       during function returns, and when initialized like this:
//          string anotherStr(aStr);
```

The problem with class withDestructor disappears when the following copy constructor is added to the class declaration:

```
withDestructor::withDestructor(const withDestructor & source);
```

The action of the copy constructor function guarantees that two pointers to the same memory are not deleted by the destructor. This is accomplished for the class withDestructor by allocating new memory and using strcpy to create two distinct strings with their own memory.

```
withDestructor::withDestructor(const withDestructor & source)
{ // This copy constructor allocates new memory for s
  s = new char[strlen(source.s) + 1];
  // and then copies all characters into the new memory
  strcpy(s, source.s);
  // This is different from s = source.s; which would copy an address
  // and leave two pointers data members pointing to the same memory
}
```

The same memory management is used with the string class copy constructor where the len member is copied directly but new memory is allocated from the source to for theChars. The source argument and theChars will point to equivalent strings, but they will be stored in separate memory locations.

```
string::string(const string & source)
{ // Copy constructor:
  len = source.len;
  theChars = new char[len + 1];
  strcpy(theChars, source.theChars);
}
```

Copy constructors are frequently included as one of several constructors for a class, so it may help to remember this general rule:

Rule
Classes with pointer objects should have a copy constructor to override the default memberwise copy. Use new to allocate separate memory for each pointer data member.

Copy constructors have been covered here to emphasize some of the difficulties in working with pointer objects. Pointers carry their own set of unique problems along with their benefits of efficient memory management. In the next section and the next chapter, we will see pointers and dynamic memory allocation used to implement other classes. One allows improved arraylike objects of any maximum size. Another is a list class that grows itself when elements need to be added after the list is full. Both require dynamic memory management with pointers.

Self-Check

1. What does the `delete` operator do?
2. Why is the `delete` operator needed?
3. Describe the difference between these two uses of `delete`:

```
delete s;
delete [ ] x;
```

4. Write the code that allocates memory to store 100 `ints` pointed to by `quiz` and then deallocates that memory.
5. What should a destructor do?
6. What should a copy constructor do?

Answers

1. Deallocates memory allocated with `new` and makes the pointer object undefined.
2. It is used to return memory allocated with `new`. Without `delete`, we lose the advantages of allocating memory on an as-needed basis and we get memory leaks, a problem that is proportional to the size of the application.
3. `delete s` deallocates memory for one pointer object. `delete [ ] x` is used if x is pointing to memory allocated with class x = new class[*number of elements*].
4. `int * quiz = new int[100];    delete [ ] quiz;`
5. Roughly the opposite of the constructor in terms of memory allocation. Destructors should delete any memory allocated by `new` in the constructor.
6. Override memberwise copy and allocate memory for all pointer data members using the `new` operator.

9.5   A Safe Arraylike Class

We now examine an arraylike class that performs subscript range checking. The `intArray` class

1. uses a pointer variable as its major data member,
2. is another example of dynamic memory management (`new` and `delete`) similar to the `string` class,
3. acts as a preview to the major topic of the next chapter,
4. gives us the opportunity to examine operator overloading—specifically we overload the subscript operator [ ] to allow references to individual elements in the same manner as the C++ built-in array.

An `intArray` object stores any number of `int` objects. The maximum size is set by the user with the initialization of the `intArray` object during the call to the initializer constructor:

```
#include "intarr.h"  // for class intArray with set and sub
                     // functions. There is no copy constructor
int main()
{
  intArray scores(9); // store up to 9 ints
  // Use scores...
```

Individual intArray elements may be indexed with the integers 0 through maximum size minus one. References to intArray elements will eventually be made through subscripts, like the C++ array. But first, we see what the class could look like without the ability to overload the subscript operator. In this case, references to individual array elements could be made through the two member functions intArray::set and intArray::sub. These member functions prototypes are shown in the file that declares the class:

```
//-----------------------------------------------------------------
// SPECIFICATION FILE intarr.h
//
// Declares: class intArray using set and sub members
//           functions for individual element access
//-----------------------------------------------------------------
#ifndef INTARR_H  // avoid duplicate compilations
#define INTARR_H

class intArray {
public:
  intArray::intArray(int initMax);
  // POST: Memory for initMax ints, pointed to by x, is allocated

  intArray::~intArray();
  // POST: Memory for max ints, pointed to by x, is deallocated

  void intArray::set(int position, int newInt);
  // POST: If(0 <= position < max ), newInt is stored at the pos-
  //       ition element of x. Otherwise the program is terminated.

  int intArray::sub(int position);
  // POST: If(0 <= position < max), x[position] is returned.
  //       Otherwise, the program is terminated.

private:
  int * x;   // A pointer to int
  int max;   // Maximum number of int objects that can be stored
};

#include "intarr.cpp"  // Include the member function implementations

#endif
```

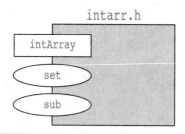

Figure 9.1   Interface diagram for module intarr.h

The following program constructs an `intArray` object of maximum size 9 and makes a few set and submember function calls:

```
// Use an intArray object to store some bowling scores. The
// set and sub member functions reference individual elements
#include "intarr.h"     // for class intArray
#include "ourstuff.h"   // for round(x)
#include <iostream.h>   // for cout <<

int main()
{
  intArray scores(9);   // store up to 9 ints with
                        // indices 0 through 8

  scores.set(0, 149);   // set scores[0] to 149
  scores.set(1, 165);   // set the second intArray element to 165
  scores.set(2, 203);   // set the third to 203

  // Total three bowling scores
  int total = 0;
  for(int j = 0; j < 3; j++)
    total = total + scores.sub(j); // <- Sum three intArray elements
  cout << "Bowling average: " << round(total / 3.0);

  return 0;
}
```

─────────────── **Output** ───────────────
```
Bowling average: 172
```

If the index is outside of the allowable range, as in `scores.sub(-1);` or as in `scores.set(9, 300);`, `intArray::set` displays an error message before terminating the program:

```
**Error** Subscript [9] is not in the range of 0 through 8
**Program terminated**
```

Let's now look at the implementation of intArray. The individual elements are pointed to by x, the pointer to ints declared in the private data member section. The constructor must allocate the proper number of ints from the free store:

```
intArray::intArray(int initMax)
{ // The constructor
  max = initMax;
  x = new int[max];
}
```

The intArray constructor also sets max as the maximum number of ints that can be stored under any intArray object. So, after initialization and setting the first three elements of scores, the data store looks like this:

Current State of Scores

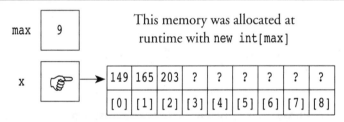

Because there is a pointer member, the destructor deallocates memory:

```
intArray::~intArray()
{ // The destructor
  delete [ ] x;
}
```

and this class should have a copy constructor.

The other two member functions are intArray::set and intArray::sub. The underlying pointer variable x cannot alter other memory. This is prevented with an if statement that makes sure the array subscripts are in bounds. If the value of position is outside the proper range, an error message is displayed and the program is terminated with exit(0).

```
void intArray::set(int position, int newInt)
{
  if(position < 0 || position >= max)
  {
    cout << "\n**Error** Subscript [" << position
         << "] is not in the range of "
         << "0.." << (max-1) << endl;
```

```
    cout << "**Program terminated**" << endl;
    exit(0); // Terminate program
  }
  // Only reaches this code if position is in the proper range
  x[position] = newInt;
}
```

The implementation of sub shows that users cannot reference memory outside the memory allocated for x.

```
int intArray::sub(int position)
{
  if((position < 0) || (position >= max))
  {
    cout << "\n**Error** Subscript [" << position
        << "] is not in the range of "
        << "0.." << (max-1) << endl;
    cout << "**Program terminated**" << endl;
    exit(0); // Terminate program
  }
  // Only reaches this code if position is in the proper range
  return x[position];
}
```

In summary, because this intArray class uses a pointer variable and dynamic memory allocation, we must consider these items:

1. Allocate with new [ ] in the constructor like this.

```
int * x = new int[max];
```

2. Deallocate with delete [ ] in the destructor.
3. Add a copy constructor, even if its absence may not be noticed at first.

Even though the intArray class currently has no copy constructor, it may cause no problems for some time. Try running this program on your system to see what happens:

```
#include <iostream.h>
#include "intarr.h"  // for intArray with set and sub members
                      // and no copy constructor
const int MAX = 10;

void aCopyFunction(intArray aCopyOfOne)
{
  // Any class with a pointer data member should have
  // a copy constructor for pass by value
```

```
    int j;
    for(j = 0; j < MAX; j++)
      cout << aCopyOfOne.sub(j) << endl;
}

int main()
{
  intArray one(MAX);

  int j;
  for(j = 0; j < MAX; j++)
    one.set(j, 2 * j);

  aCopyFunction(one);
  return 0;
}
```

The output is questionable.

To be on the safe side, the copy constructor should be added. Its prototype is in the class declaration and the following definition is in the implementation file:

```
intArray::intArray(const intArray & source)
{
  max = source.max;
  x = new int[max];
  for(int j = 0; j < max; j++)
    x[j] = source.x[j];
}
```

This copy constructor overrides default memberwise copy. The source's max data member is copied into the parameter's max data member with

```
max = source.max;
```

Now, if the source object is declared with 1000 elements, the new operation allocates an additional 1000 memory locations with this statement:

```
x = new int[max];
```

and every one of source's objects are copied into the parameter with this for loop:

```
for(int j = 0; j < max; j++)
  x[j] = source.x[j];
```

When an `intArray` object is now copied by value, we no longer have a memberwise copy statement that would look like this pointer assignment:

```
x = source.x;  // Default not in effect when copy constructor is added
```

Although more efficient, this default situation leads to other errors.

The copy constructor just shown will be added to the `intArray` class that is declared and implemented in two other files: `"intarray.h"` and `"intarray.cpp"`, respectively. This class will also replace the `set` and `sub` members in favor of the more familiar subscript operator.

9.5.1 Operator Overloading and an Alternate intArray class

Although we have already seen how `set` and `sub` reference individual `intArray` objects, an overloaded `[ ]` operator for `intArray` objects would make it look more like the built-in C++ array. We would then have a "safer" arraylike class that is used in the same manner. This process of applying new meaning to existing operators is called *operator overloading*. In general, overloading operators requires a function prototype with the reserved word *operator*. When declared as a member function, the keyword `operator` must be preceded by a return type such as `int`, `float`, `string`, or `intArray`, and followed by one of the "overloadable" C++ operators such as `+`, `/`, `=`, or `[ ]`. Using this general form,

return-type class-name`::operator` *operator* (*single-operand*) ;

we can add this member function prototype to the `intArray` class:

```
int intArray::operator [] (int subscript);
```

This allows any of the `intArray` values to be returned if implemented something like this:

```
int intArray::operator [] (int subscript)
{ // Terminate program if subscript is not in range
  if((subscript < 0) || (subscript >= max))
    exit(0);
  else
    return x[subscript];
}
```

and expressions like this are now allowed:

```
sum = scores[0] + scores[1] + scores[2];
```

However, this overloaded operator does not allow for assignment. Instead, we need to return a reference to the int. We can allow for both expressions and an lValue when the overloaded [ ] operator is declared to return a reference to an int (int &) like this:

```
int & array1::operator [ ] (int subscript);
```

The return value is not an int; it is a reference to an int. Now we can use the subscript in expressions to the right of = as well as a location value (lValue) to the left of =, for example

```
scores[3] = 278;      // requires int & return type for assignment
```

Without the & in the return type, this assignment would not be allowed. We cannot store 278 into an int. We can, however, store that value into the location of an int (int &). In addition to the copy constructor, the improved intArray class includes this overloaded [ ] operator.

```
//------------------------------------------------------------
// SPECIFICATION FILE intarray.h
//
// Declares: class intArray
//------------------------------------------------------------
#ifndef INTARRAY_H   // avoid duplicate compilations
#define INTARRAY_H

class intArray {
public:
  intArray::intArray(int initMax);
  // POST: Memory for max ints, pointed to by x, is allocated

  intArray::intArray(const intArray & source);
  // POST: Allocates new memory and copies source to target
  //       during pass by value argument/parameter associations
  //       and initializations like this:  intArray two(one);

  intArray::~intArray();
  // POST: Memory for max ints, pointed to by x, is deallocated

  int & intArray::operator [] (int subscript);
  // POST: If(0 <= subscript && subscript < max), return a
  //       reference to an individual array element. If the
  //       subscript is out of range terminate the program.
```

```
private:
  int * x;    // A pointer to int
  int max;    // Maximum number of int objects that can be stored
};

#include "intarray.cpp"

#endif
```

Self-Check

1. Write the output from the following program:

    ```
    #include <iostream.h>
    #include "intarr.h"  // for intArray with set and sub members
    int main()
    {
      const int MAX = 6;
      intArray test(MAX);
      int j;
      for(j = 0; j < MAX; j++)
        test.set(j, (10 * j + 50));
      for(j = 0; j < MAX; j++)
        cout << test.sub(j) << "  ";
      return 0;
    }
    ```

2. Name all the classes of data that stored intArray objects can manipulate.
3. Write the output of the following program:

    ```
    #include "intarr.h"  // for intArray with set and sub members
    int main()
    {
      const int MAX = 6;
      intArray test(MAX);
      test.set(6, 123);
      cout << test.sub(6);
      return 0;
    }
    ```

4. What four things must the copy constructor do to properly copy an intArray argument to an intArray parameter by value?
5. Does this function prototype allow a subscripted intArray object to appear on the left side of an assignment operator?

    ```
    int intArray::operator [ ] (int index);
    ```

Chapter Summary

Pointer objects store addresses of other objects. Objects are given meaningful values through assignment of one pointer to another, or with the & (address of) operator that returns the address of its operand. Pointers, used with the new and delete operations, allow programmers to better utilize computer memory. For example, the string class is designed to allocate the minimum amount of memory at the instant it is needed. When the object is no longer needed, the memory is deallocated back to the free store for use by other objects.

Using pointers to chars (char* objects) and functions of the string.h file provides a quasi string class that must be used carefully and with function calls. The safer string class defines operators to make it look more like built-in classes such as int and float.

Pointers and dynamic memory allocation were used in an arraylike class (intArray1) to provide array capabilities with subscript range checking. We also saw an example of operator overloading.

Working with pointers and dynamic memory allocation can prove tricky. One helpful tool is to use arrows to represent address values. Pointer objects can be inserted for output, but it is their use with the dereference operator * that helps the debugging process.

The new operator allocates memory from the free store. The delete operator deallocates memory. If more than one object is allocated, as in

```
char * name = new char[10];
```

it should be deallocated with [ ], as in

```
delete [ ] name;
```

Because of the inherent problems with pointers, this section gives several suggestions that relate to the use of pointers.

1. Remember the difference between a pointer object and the object it points to.
A pointer object points to another object. That object is referenced with the special symbol *. In the following example, `ptr` is the pointer object and `*ptr` is the object being pointed to.

```
float * ptr;
float x
ptr = &x;
* ptr = 1.234;
```

2. Note that memory for dynamic objects must be allocated before values can be stored into them.
The `new` operator is used to allocate memory from the free store and to initialize the pointer object. An assignment to a pointer object not properly allocated with `new` will cause that value to be stored anywhere in the free store. This can cause the program to crash or the computer to hang.

3. When in doubt, use diagrams when debugging a program's pointer objects.
The value of a pointer object represents a location in the memory of the computer. These values are difficult to use in a program trace. A diagram with arrows and boxes can make the program execution much clearer.

4. Be aware that even after a pointer object is deleted, its value can still point to the same dynamic object.
Don't trust these values. Consider the following code and output:

```
int * ptr;
cout << *ptr << endl;  // Should display garbage
ptr = new int;
* ptr = 123456;
cout << * ptr << endl; // Should display 123456
delete ptr;            // ptr is undefined, but may still point
cout << * ptr << endl; // to the same place, output may be 123456
                       // or any other bytes storing any int
```

The first line of output is garbage since neither `ptr` nor `*ptr` have been assigned a value yet. Both the pointer object and the dynamic object have meaningless values. After both objects have been assigned a value, the proper value of 123456 is displayed. Notice that the same value is displayed even after `ptr` is deleted. Even if `ptr` and `*ptr` still have the same value, they would probably be altered at some later point in a more complex program. This is usually beyond our control.

Exercises

1. Write the value of each of the four object attributes supplied by this initialization:

   ```
   float x = 987.65;
   ```

   a. Name   b. Class   c. State   d. Address

2. Declare a pointer to an `int` and initialize it.
3. Use these statements to answer the questions below:

   ```
   int * intPtr;
   int anInt = 123;
   intPtr = &anInt;
   ```

   a. What is the name of the pointer object?
   b. What is the value of the `*intPtr`?
   c. Without using the object `anInt`, write a statement that adds 100 to the memory storing 123.

4. Write the output generated by the following program:

   ```
   #include <iostream.h>
   void huh(double & parm)    // Out
   {
     parm = parm + 1;
   }
   int main()
   {
     double aFloat = 99.9;
     huh(aFloat);
     cout << aFloat << " ";
     huh(aFloat);
     cout << aFloat << " " << endl;
     return 0;
   }
   ```

5. Write the minimum declarations and statements that declare and initialize all the objects as shown below:

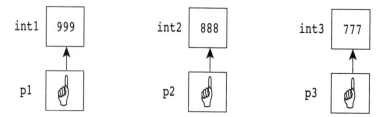

6. Using the code from Exercise 5, write the statements that will have a pointer object named `largestPtr` pointing to the largest `int` no matter where it is stored among `int1`, `int2`, or `int3`.

7. Using the declarations shown, which of the following are valid assignments that do not generate an error?

```
int j;
int *p;
```

a.	p = j;	e.	j = 123;	i.	*p = "abc";
b.	p = &j;	f.	*p = j;	j.	*j = 123;
c.	p = 0;	g.	p = &p;	k.	j = &p;
d.	j = p;	h.	p = 123;	l.	*p = *p;

8. Write the output generated by the following program:

```
#include <iostream.h>
int main()
{
    int * intPtr;
    int anInt = 987;
    intPtr = &anInt;
    *intPtr = (*intPtr) + 111;
    cout << (*intPtr) << "  " << (anInt);
    return 0;
}
```

9. Write the output generated by the following program:

```
#include <iostream.h>
#include "ouracct.h"
int main()
{
    bankAccount *p1, *p2, *temp;
    bankAccount a1, a2;
    p1 = new bankAccount("Hall", "1234", 111.11);
    p2 = new bankAccount("Simpson", "4321", 999.99);
```

```
// Note: cout << bankAccount("Hall", "1234", 111.11);
// generates this output { bankAccount: HALL, 1234, 111.11 }
cout << "p1 points to " << *p1 << endl;
temp = p1;
p1 = p2;
p2 = temp;
cout << "p1 now points to " << *p1 << endl;
cout << "p2 now points to " << *p2 << endl;
return 0;
}
```

10. Write the output generated by the following program:

```
#include <iostream.h>
int main()
{
  double * x = new double[5];
  int j;
  for(j = 0; j < 5; j++)
    x[j] = (j + 0.1 ) + (j * 0.1);
  for(j = 0; j < 5; j++)
    cout << x[j] << "   ";
  return 0;
}
```

11. Starting with the representation of memory shown below and after these objects have been declared

```
int n1, n2, *p1, *p2, *p3;
```

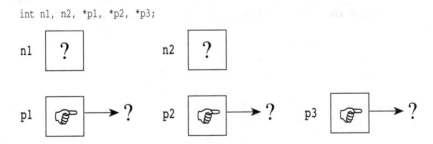

a.   Trace the following program segment by showing the values of int objects or arrows indicating the values of the pointer objects:

```
n1 = 123;
p1 = &n1;
*p1 = *p1 + 111;
```

b. Trace the following program segment by showing the values of int objects or arrows indicating the values of the pointer objects:

```
n2 = 999;
p3 = &n2;
p2 = p3;
```

c. Trace the following program segment by showing the values of int objects or arrows indicating the values of the pointer objects:

```
int * intPtr;
intPtr = p3;
```

Lab Projects

9A   Using Objects

Using only indirection, write a complete C++ program that extracts three ints from cin and displays the sum of those three ints. Do not use any int objects. Use only int* objects with new to allocate memory to store ints.

9B   Using Objects

Write a function called lowerCase that converts any char* argument into its lowercase equivalent. First find the difference between 'A' and 'a' on your system (32 on some) and recall that - and + can be applied to char operands like this:

```
#include <iostream.h>

int main()
{
  cout << ('a' - 'A') << endl;
  cout << char('A' + 32) << endl;
  return 0;
}
```

```
----------------------- Output -----------------------
32
a
```

Use this exact function prototype that returns a char* value but will not let you alter the argument because of the const signature.

```
char * toLower(const char * s);
```

Then test your function with the following `main` function using the output as a test oracle:

```
int main()
{
  cout << toLower("AbCdEfG") << endl;
  cout << toLower("ABC!@#$XYZ") << endl;
  char * str = "<def123GHI-+'?>";
  cout << toLower(str) << endl;
  return 0;
}
```

──── **Output** ────
```
abcdefg
abc!@#$xyz
<def123ghi-+'?>
```

9C   Implementing a Class

Write a complete class named `mystery` that has one constructor, one destructor, and one `char *` data member named `message` (do not use the `string` class, which has its own destructor). Implement the constructor to allocate memory for the data member with the message `"Constructor message goes here"` and the destructor to display the message `"Destructor message goes here"`. Test your class to see if you have properly managed memory using the following program:

```
// You must declare and implement the mystery class

void f()
{
  mystery source;
}

int main()
{
  f();
}
```

──── **Output** ────
```
Constructor message goes here
Destructor message goes here
```

Your output should be the same as that shown above. If it is not, make it so. If you get a runtime error, make sure you are properly allocating and deallocating memory with new and delete, respectively.

9D   Modifying a Class

Modify the stringList class to meet the specification of the class declaration given below. The major difference is that the array str is changed to a pointer object. It is the responsibility of the default constructor to establish a list of the default size MAX. The other constructor must allocate memory for the number of string objects supplied by the users. Both constructors will have to allocate memory like this:

```
str = new string [MAX];      // Place this in the default constructor
str = new string [initMax];
```

Remember that the private data member str is available to the constructors.

- Put the file ourstrli.h into your editor.
- Modify the class declaration to look like this (get rid of init if it's still there, add another constructor, add a destructor, and change the private data):

```
// ... The file ourstli.h:
const int MAX = 3;

class stringList {
public:
  stringList::stringList();
  // POST: This default constructor sets lastOne to MAX,
  //       allocates memory for MAX elements,
  //       and the size of the list to 0

  stringList::stringList(int initMax);
  // POST: This default constructor sets lastOne to initN,
  //       allocates memory for initN elements,
  //       and the size of the list to 0

  stringList::~stringList();
  // POST: The memory allocated with new in the constructor
  //       has been returned to the free store.

  void stringList::add(string newString);
  // POST: The string is added at the end of the array
  //       and the size of the list is increased by 1.
  //       If the array is full, a message is displayed.
```

```
void stringList::display();
// POST: All string objects currently stored in the array are dis-
//       played after a heading indicating the size of the list.
//       If no strings have been added, no strings are displayed.

void stringList::remove(string searchString);
// POST: If searchString is found, the string is removed from list.
//       If searchString is not found, a message is displayed.
// NOTE: The array of strings (str) and the number of string elements
//       added (size) are accessible from this member function.

private:
    string * str;    // <-- CHANGE THIS LINE*******
    int lastOne;     // <-- Add this new data member to store MAX********
    int size;
};
```

- Save the header file and edit the implementation file ourstrli.cpp to meet the specification.
- Use the following program to test your modified class:

```
int main()
{
    stringList nameListOne;         // Store up to MAX elements. MAX = 3
    stringList nameListTwo(50);     // Store up to 50 elements
    nameListOne.add("Tim");
    nameListOne.add("Sue");
    nameListOne.add("Hollie");
    // Should not be able to add a fourth when MAX = 3;
    nameListOne.add("Viv");
    cout << "list one: " << endl;
    nameListOne.display();

    nameListTwo.add("Anton");
    nameListTwo.add("Kellin");
    nameListTwo.add("Harold");
    nameListTwo.add("Catrina");
    cout << "\nlist two: " << endl;
    nameListTwo.display();
}
```

```
─────────────────── Output ───────────────────
stringList is full! 'Viv' could not be added

list one:
0. Tim
1. Sue
2. Hollie

list two:
0. Anton
1. Kellin
2. Harold
3. Catrina
```

9E   Modifying a Class

Completely implement class `floatArray` to perform subscript range checking with an overloaded subscript operator [ ]. `floatArray` objects store only `float`s. The user may set the maximum size.

10

Templates

C++ arrays are flexible enough to handle collections of any type (class), capable of manipulating a large number of elements, general enough to store almost any object, and useful in a wide variety of applications. But with the help of the C++ class and the template mechanism—the major focus of this chapter—improvements can be made to the primitive C++ array structure. In this chapter we will examine a programmer-defined class named `array1` that provides the benefits of the C++ array with some improvements.

Our first view of `array1` objects will be from the user's side as we see it compared to the built-in C++ array. For example, we will see some of the problems caused by C++'s inability to perform subscript bounds checking. To alleviate this, we will write the `array1` class to perform subscript bounds checking automatically. But at this point, we would have to implement an array class for each class of data—one for `int`, one for `float`, one for `string`, one for `bankAccount`, and so on. However, we will see that the template mechanism permits a safe array class that stores *any* class of data—one array class for all existing classes and any new programmer-defined class.

Later we will look at the implementation side of the array class as we explore the C++ template mechanism. Templates allow us to pass a class name as an argument, allowing for arrays and lists of any class. In future study, you will find templates a useful tool for implementing other data structures known as ordered lists, stacks, queues, and trees.

The same approach (use, then implement) is followed for a parameterized `list` class with operations like the `stringList` class first encountered in Chapter 7. The major difference is that the `list` class manages collections of any type, not just `string`. We will also see how the `list` class applies the `new` operator to allocate additional memory during an `add` operation when there is not enough memory. This approach is one solution to the maximum size issue—`list` objects grow themselves to store as many objects as memory allows. And it occurs with no requirements imposed on users of the class.

After studying this chapter, you will be able to:

- Understand why out-of-bounds subscripts can cause errors that are difficult to fix and detect.
- Use a "safe" array class that performs subscript range checking.
- Implement function and class templates.
- Implement parameterized classes that manipulate collections of any type.

10.1 The Trouble with Arrays

Consider this innocent-looking little program and the trouble it caused:

```
#include <iostream.h>
int main()
{
  int x[20];
  x[20] = 123;
  cout << x[20];
}
```

Output
```
123123123123123123123123123123123123123123123123123123123123123
123213123123123123123123123123123123123123123123123123123123123
123123123123123123123123123123123123123123123123123123123123123
123123123123123123123123123123123123123123123123123123123123123
123123123123123123123123123123123123123123123123123123123123123
12312
```
. . . the system crashed, the keyboard locked up so rebooting was necessary,
unsaved work was lost . . .

On two other systems, this less dramatic error occurred:

```
Segmentation fault
```

And on yet another system, everything seemed okay—a situation potentially more troublesome than any of the obvious errors. The error occurred when 123 was assigned to an array element with an out-of-bounds subscript. Now, try to detect the error in the following program (or is there one?):

```
// Error or not?
#include <iostream.h>

int main()
{
  int x[2], y[2];
  x[0] = 999;
  cout << "x[0]: " << x[0] << endl;
  y[2] = 123;
  cout << "y[2]: " << y[2] << endl;
  cout << "x[0]: " << x[0] << endl;
}
```

There are no compiletime errors or warnings. It links and an executable program is generated. When the program runs there are no runtime errors. The system thinks everything is okay. But with no apparent error reported by the compiler or runtime system, try to explain this output:

```
x[0]: 999
y[2]: 123
x[0]: 123
```

How can x[0] have the value of 999 and then be changed to 123 with no apparent cin or assignment statement?

The trouble occurs when 123 is assigned to the array named y. Recall that the subscript range for primitive C++ arrays is 0 through the maximum declared size minus 1. Therefore, the valid subscript range for y is 0 through 1. We are not to use out-of-bounds subscripts. Specifically, the assignment to y[2] altered the state of x[0]!

To explain the unexpected change to x[0] we must accept that individual array elements are stored in contiguous (next to each other) memory locations. So the memory layout of the two array objects and the state at all four elements might look this (y comes before x in memory even though y came after x in the declaration):

Object	Value
y[0]	?
y[1]	?
x[0]	999 123 y[2] was computed to be the memory for x[0]; no error was flagged
x[1]	?

The attempt to store 123 into y[2] was interpreted by the system as x[0]. Instead of storing 123 into the last element of y, it was stored into the first element of x.

Even if we always remember that subscripts must be in the proper range, it is still possible to let slip an occasional subscript referring to memory that is not part of the array. To truly appreciate the trouble with arrays, you need to lose several hours' work through a system crash or lose data that can never be retrieved—telephone reservations or sales entered into the computer, for example. The errors could even be much more disastrous and certainly unpredictable.

C++ arrays were designed to allow out-of-bounds subscripts. The upside to not checking subscript range is runtime efficiency. A program that does not check subscripts runs faster. And this can be important when arrays are traversed during a sort, search, or some other operation that requires a lot of looping. If the C++ array were implemented to check subscripts, every single reference to an array element would require evaluation of a logical expression like the one for class intArray of the preceding chapter:

```
(subscript >=0) && (subscript < max)
```

So the programmer must ensure array subscripts cannot get out of bounds, or be convinced that it doesn't matter if one does.

At a cost of this runtime efficiency, we could implement our classes to check the subscript ranges, which usually involves evaluation of a logical expression to avoid out-of-bounds subscripts. This has already been done with one of our programmer-defined classes. For example, the `stringList` class will not add an element to its private array data member if there is no more room. Instead, a message is generated so the program may keep running. But if we eliminate the subscript range checking in `stringList::add`, we might eventually add a string to the array when `size` is out of bounds (`size >= MAX`, the last available memory location):

```
// A modified add operation that no longer
// tries to avoid out-of-bounds subscripts
// Size will get arbitrarily big.
void stringList::add(string newString)
{
   // Remember, str[MAX] should not be altered!
   // That memory does not belong to the array!
   if(size >= MAX)
      cout << endl << "stringList is full! '" << newString
                   << "' could not be added" << endl;
   else
   {
      // Store the argument into the array of string objects...
      str[size] = newString;
      // ...and make sure the size is always increased by +1:
      size++;
   }
}
```

Using `MAX=3` and running this program shows what went wrong on one system:

```
// This program was run with a string stored into str[MAX]
// A general protection fault shut down the system after
// displaying the first three valid strings and 29 other
// garbage strings thought to be part of the list.
// Apparently, the fourth add destroyed the true value of size.
#include <iostream.h>
#include <ourstrli.h> // a modified "non-safe" stringList class

int main()
{
   stringList aList;
   aList.add("one");
   aList.add("two");
   aList.add("three");
   aList.add("When MAX=3, this is added (sort of): VERY UNSTABLE!");
   aList.display();
}
```

```
──────────────────── Output ────────────────────
The number of string objects in this object is 42:
0. one
1. two
2. three
3. When MAX=3, this is added (sort of): VERY UNSTABLE!
4.
5. ÜéD!A!N!Z!¥²¿ç
6. d trying to create
```

(20 lines of garbage are not shown here)

```
28.
29. çg to create
                    General Protection Fault
```

A general protection fault occurred after dumping the garbage. The first line of output indicates that the value of `size` was destroyed. When `size` should have not gone beyond 3—the declared maximum size of the array data member `str`—the now "unsafe" `stringList` class allowed an inappropriate modification to `size`. It let `size` go to 4 during the fourth call to `add`. Then, because `str[3]` was out-of-bounds, this statement

```
str[size] = newString;
```

wiped out some portion of memory. Apparently, `aList`'s private data member `size` was one of those destroyed objects. As a result `size` picked up the garbage value 42! This unstable behavior indicates that moving a `string` of unpredictable length into some unpredictable memory location may result in some unpredictable error. And those errors may be difficult to detect, locate, and fix. All of this trouble arose from an out-of-bounds subscript.

10.1.1 array1: A Safe, Parameterized, Singly Subscripted Array Class

The C++ class and the ability to overload operators such as [ ] allows us to make up our own improved array class. In much the same manner as the primitive C++ array, the programmer-defined, singly subscripted, *array1 class* of this section manages collections of `chars`, `ints`, `floats`, `doubles`, `strings`, `bankAccounts`, and so on (the 1 in `array1` is for 1 subscript). Individual `array1` elements are referenced in exactly the same manner with subscripts [ ], like C++ arrays. There are also a fixed number of elements. Here are two of the differences:

1. array1 objects can be declared with greater flexibility in the subscript ranges, such as starting at 1, ranging from 1995 through 2001, or using negative subscripts.
2. Subscript range checking is performed on all references to all array1 elements.

Templates make the array1 class general enough to manage collections of any type. This is a big improvement over class intArray of Chapter 9, which only stores ints. We will see that templates allow us to implement one class rather than one class for every data type.

An array1 object is declared with a general form that requires a class between < and > to be passed as an argument. A lower and an upper subscript range must also be supplied:

array1< *class-name* > *object-name* (*lower-subscript, upper-subscript*) ;

The *class-name* is used like an argument to the array1 class. The user declares the type of elements that the array1 object must store. The *class-name* can be any of the fundamental classes or programmer-defined classes that have a default (no argument) constructor—the same restriction that applies to primitive C++ arrays. The lower and upper subscripts define the range of subscripts and the maximum number of objects that may be stored under the array1 object, thereby providing greater flexibility in subscript ranges. For example, the following array1 object allows management of up to 100 ints through the following declaration, where the first element is referenced as intArray[1] and the last element as intArray[100]:

```
array1<int> intArray(1, 100);  // Subscript range is 1 through 100
```

The next two array1 objects show that we can supply negative int expressions and more meaningful subscripts such as those that represent a range of years for lower and upper subscript arguments:

```
array1<float> time(-10, 10);          // Subscript range is -10..10
array1<double> population(1995, 2001);  // Subscript range 1995..2001
```

10.1.2 Using array1 Objects

To use class array1, the file arrays.h must be included before declaring these array1 objects:

```
#include "arrays.h"   // for class array1
#include "ouracct.h"  // for class bankAccount
#include "ourstr.h"   // for class string
```

```
int main()
{                                       // Singly subscripted arrays of:
  array1<int> intArray(0, 19);          // 20 int objects
  array1<bankAccount> acct(1, 100);     // 100 bankAccount objects
  array1<string> champion(1984, 1994);  // 7 string objects
  //
  // Use intArray, acct, and champion...
```

Through subscripts, the intArray object shown above manages up to 20 ints with a subscript range of 0 through 19, acct manages 100 bankAccount objects with a subscript range of 1 through 100, and champion stores up to 7 variable-length string objects with a subscript range of 1984 through 1994. The major difference between the primitive C++ array and the programmer-defined array1 class is that our array1 class performs range checking for each and every subscript reference. So instead of destroying other memory or crashing the system, the expressions intArray[-1] and acct[101] generate runtime errors. You may appreciate this difference only after spending hours debugging a program with intent errors that would have been avoided with the array1 class. The array1 class also provides greater flexibility in the subscript ranges for array1 objects.

An array1 object can be sized at runtime. The int expression setting the maximum size of an array1 object may be an int expression such as size:

```
int size;
cout << "Enter number of bankAccounts: ";
cin >> size;
array1<bankAccount> acct(1, size); // Runtime array sizing
```

Dialogue

```
   Enter number of bankAccounts: 100
```

When this code begins to execute and the user enters 100, the array1 object named acct manages 100 bankAccounts with the subscript range 1 through 100.

With array1 objects, any attempt to reference memory through out-of-bounds subscripts results in a runtime error message followed by program termination. This was deemed a preferable course of action to the alternative: destruction of objects, loss of work due to system restarts, and hours of unnecessary debugging. Therefore, this attempt to modify a nonexistent 101st bankAccount object,

```
emp[101] = bankAccount("No", "Good", 0.0); // Runtime error
```

results in the following runtime error message that immediately precedes program termination:

```
**Error** Subscript [101] is not in the range of 1..100
**Program terminated**
```

Programming Tip

It is recommended that you develop programs using this template-based `array1` class. Bugs are more easily detected and therefore avoided than with primitive C++ arrays. The error message is meant to indicate what went wrong and is fairly easy to track down. This will also tend to help you avoid system crashes. The trade-off is runtime efficiency—programs run more slowly.

10.1.3 Simplifying class names with typedef

Passing an `array1` object to a function requires this general form:

> *return-type function-name* (`array1` < *class-name* > *identifier*)

For example, to pass by value, an `array1` object storing `int` elements to function `sum`, this prototype could be used:

```
int sum(array1<int> x);
```

An `array1` object storing `bankAccount` objects could be passed to function `display` like this:

```
void display(array1<bankAccount> accountList);
```

But `array1<Type>` can be given another name with a C++ `typedef` declaration. A *typedef* allows us to give a single meaningful name to what might otherwise be too long or awkward. The general form of a `typedef` is given as

> `typedef`   *class-definition   identifier* ;

where the keyword `typedef` is followed by a class-definition such as `int`, `string`, `bankAccount`, or

> `array1`< *Type* >

The class-definition is followed by an identifier that can be used later in place of a class name. Some example `typedef`s include:

```
                                     // Example declarations...
typedef string nameType;             // nameType first, last;
typedef char letterGradeType;        // letterGradeType cmpSc103;
typedef array1<bankAccount> bankType; // bankType firstNational;
```

So given this declaration,

```
typedef array1<bankAccount> accountType;
```

the previous function prototype of display can be simplified as shown in this program:

```
// This code compiles with a new name for a type: listType
// Function implementations are not given (so it won't run)
#include "ouracct.h"
#include "arrays.h"

typedef array1<bankAccount> listType;

void init(listType & accounts);   // Modify the object in main

void display(listType accounts); // Get a copy of the object in main

int main()
{
  listType accounts;
  init(accounts);
  display(accounts);
  return 0;
}
```

It should be noted that a class declaration also creates a new type. The class name itself is automatically treated as a type by the compiler.

10.1.4 array1::firstSubscript and array1::lastSubscript

Two other array1 member functions include firstSubscript and lastSubscript. They return the lower and upper bounds of the array1 object, respectively.

```
int array1::firstSubscript();
// POST: The lower subscript bound is returned

int array1::lastSubscript();
// POST: The upper subscript bound is returned
```

These operations represent improvements over the built-in C++ array, which requires this information to be managed separately from the array and always passed as arguments to functions. All array1 objects always keep track of and pass on this information automatically.

```cpp
// Illustrate use of all array1 class operations
#include <iostream.h>
#include "arrays.h"

typedef array1<double> popType;

const double GROWTH_RATE = 0.035;

void showGrowth(popType pop) // Pass array and subscript range together
{ //
  // Use the member functions
  // array1::firstSubscript, array1::lastSubscript
  //
  cout << "The years from "
       << pop.firstSubscript() << ".." << pop.lastSubscript()
       << " assuming a " << GROWTH_RATE*100
       << "% per year increase"
       << endl;

  // Show predicted population growth
  int j;
  double currentPop;
  cout << "Enter this years population: ";
  cin >> currentPop;

  // Initialize first year's population
  pop[pop.firstSubscript()] = currentPop;

  // Compute future populations
  for(j = pop.firstSubscript() + 1; j <= pop.lastSubscript(); j++)
    pop[j] = pop[j-1] + GROWTH_RATE * pop[j-1];

  // Display population growth
  for(j = pop.firstSubscript(); j <= pop.lastSubscript(); j++)
    cout << "population in " << j << " = " << long(pop[j])
         << endl;
}

int main()
{ // Declare an array1 object and pass it to function showGrowth
  double firstYear, lastYear;
```

```
cout << "Enter this year: ";
cin >> firstYear;
cout << "Enter ending year: ";
cin >> lastYear;

// Declare an array1 object...
popType population(firstYear, lastYear);

// ...and pass it along with its subscript range and size
showGrowth(population);

return 0;
}
```

─────────────────────────── **Output** ───────────────────────────

```
Enter this year: 1995
Enter ending year: 2001
Enter this years population: 123456789

The years from 1995..2001 assuming a 3.5% per year increase
population in 1995 = 123456789
population in 1996 = 127777776
population in 1997 = 132249998
population in 1998 = 136878748
population in 1999 = 141669504
population in 2000 = 146627937
population in 2001 = 151759915
```

Self-Check

Use this declaration to answer the following questions:

```
array1<int> y(1, 5);
```

1. How many ints can be stored in y?
2. What integer subscript is used to reference the first element in y?
3. What integer subscript is used to reference the last element in y?
4. Write the code that stores 89 into the first element of y.
5. Write the code that stores 91 into the second through last elements of y.
6. Write the code that sums all elements of y.
7. What value is returned by y.firstSubscript(); ?
8. What value is returned by y.lastSubscript(); ?
9. Write the output generated by the following code fragment:

```
array1<float> x(0, 9);
x[10] = 1.234;
```

10. Declare an `array1` object that can manage up to 500 `bankAccount` objects.
11. Write the output generated by the following program:

```cpp
#include "arrays.h"
#include "ourstr.h"

int main()
{
  array1<string> name(1, 4);
  name[1] = "Chuck";
  name[2] = "Marylin";
  name[3] = "Megan";
  name[4] = "Jonathon";

  int j = 1;
  for(j = 1; j <= 4; j++)
  {
    name[j].toUpper();
    name[j] = "!" + name[j] + "! ";
  }
  for(j = 1; j <= 4; j++)
    cout << name[j];
}
```

Answers

1. 5
2. 1
3. 5
4. y[1]=89
5. `for(int j = 2; j <= 5; j++ )`
   `   y[j] = 91;`
6. `int sum = 0;`
   `for(int j = 1; j <= 5; j++)`
   `   sum = sum + y[j];`
7. 1
8. 5
9. `**Error** Subscript [10] is not in the range of 0..9`
   `**Program terminated**`
10. `array1<bankAccount> acct(1, 500);`
11. `!CHUCK! !MARYLIN! !MEGAN! !JONATHON!`

10.2 Function Templates

The C++ *template* mechanism permits class names to be passed to a class. In much the same manner as we pass expressions such as x or 1.5 as arguments to functions, we can pass class names such as int, float, string, and bankAccount as arguments to a class utilizing templates. In this case, the class is said to be *parameterized* because it is has a parameter that can be associated with an argument that is a class name. Parameterized classes can manipulate a variety of classes.

The template mechanism proves useful when implementing *container* classes—data structures such as lists, stacks, queues, and trees that are designed to manage collections of objects in a specific and useful manner. These data structures are mentioned here (without explanation) only to suggest an alternative implementation in your future studies. The main goal now is to provide enough information to let you implement classes with templates if you so choose. Rather than being required to implement a list, stack, queue, or tree for each class, templates can be used to implement classes that may be declared with a class argument like this:

```
list<bankAccount> acct;
list<string> str;
stack<double> operand;
stack<char> operator;
queue<automobile> car;
queue<person> inLine;
tree<double> searchTree;
tree<inventoryItem> inventory;
```

With templates, one class may be implemented to manage many different classes. In the previous section, we saw the user side of templates when declaring an array1 object.

```
array1<bankAccount> acct(1, 100);    // An array of 100 bankAccounts
```

The implementation side of such classes requires an understanding of C++ function template and class template declarations.

10.2.1 Function Templates: An Example

Any class where > has meaning could have one object considered to be larger than another. If we were to implement a function to return the larger of any two data objects, we have several choices. We could implement a different function for every class (here are some prototypes):

```
int largerInt(int a, int b);
float largerFloat(float a, float b);
string largerString(string a, string b);
char * largerCharStar(char * a, char * b);
long largerLong(long a, long b);
```

or we could use function overloading and implement one function for each class. This leads to many functions with the same name.

```
int larger(int a, int b);
float larger(float a, float b);
string larger(string a, string b);
char * larger(char * a, char * b);
long larger(long a, long b);
// and so on...
```

Although function overloading lets us have the same name for many functions, an alternate solution is to use a *function template* to make the compiler do the work for us by creating many overloaded functions. The general form of template declarations used in this text is as follows:

template < class *identifier* >
declaration

where the *declaration* must be either a class declaration or a function declaration. For each function call encountered with a noticeably different class, the compiler uses the function template declaration to construct a different function. Here is one example of a template declaration and a complete function declaration:

```
template<class Type>
void display(Type anyObject)
{
    cout << anyObject << endl;
}
```

The identifier Type is a parameter with scope that extends to the entire function declaration that follows. This includes the parameter list and the function body, { through }. At this point, display may be called with any Type argument where << is defined for the class. Roughly speaking, for each unique argument class encountered in a call to display, a function with that type is generated. So if these three function calls are encountered in function main:

```
int main()
{
  display(123);
  display("A string literal");
  bankAccount anAccount("Name", "PIN", 0.00);
  display(anAccount);
  return 0;
}
```

the compiler generates three overloaded functions (same name, different class of parameters) similar to these:

```
void display(int anyObject)
{
  cout << anyObject << endl;     // Display an int object
}

void display(char * anyObject)
{
  cout << anyObject << endl;     // Display a char * object
}

void display(string anyObject)
{
  cout << anyObject << endl;     // Display a bankAccount object
}
```

This `display` and a `larger` function are demonstrated in the following program where we see the keyword template followed by the class parameter named `Type`. The template declarations are required for both functions because the scope of the parameter `Type` extends only to the declaration immediately following.

```
// Demonstrate two template functions with a variety of Type arguments

#include <iostream.h>
#include "ourstr.h"
#include "ouracct.h"

template<class Type>
Type larger(Type a, Type b)
{
  if(a > b)
    return a;
  else
    return b;
}

template<class Type>
void display(Type anyObject)
{
  cout << anyObject << endl;
}

int main()
{
  // Use different class arguments (float, char, and char*)
  cout << "Demonstrate the larger function: " << endl;
  cout << larger("abcd", "defg") << endl;
  cout << larger(99.9999, 99.9998) << endl;
  cout << larger('A', 'B') << endl;
```

```
// And some programmer-defined class names
string s1 = "abc";
string s2 = "xyz";
cout << larger(s1, s2) << endl;

cout << endl;
cout << "Demonstrate the display function: " << endl;
display("A string literal");
display(123);
display(4.56);
bankAccount anAcct("Hall", "1234", 100.00);
display(anAcct);
return 0;
}
```

──────────── **Output** ────────────

```
Demonstrate the larger function:
defg
99.9999
B
xyz

Demonstrate the display function:
A string literal
123
4.56
{ bankAccount: HALL, 1234, 100.00 }
```

In summary, a function template acts as a model for constructing many distinct functions. This is accomplished by replacing the parameter named Type by the class (such as int, float, string, or bankAccount) of the argument in each function call. A function template provided by us gives the compiler a model for other functions. We will now see that one class can also be declared as a template for other classes.

10.3 Class Templates

Recall that the declaration part of a template declaration

> template < class *identifier* >
> *declaration*

must either be a function declaration or a class declaration. Template declarations written before a class give the class *identifier* a scope that extends throughout the entire class declaration. For example, the array1 template of arrays.h begins something like this:

```
template<class Type>
class array1 {
public:                              // Constructor
    array1::array1(int first, int last); // array1<class> name(int,int);
```

The array1 class declaration is preceded with the keyword template and the keyword class is followed by the parameter named Type between < and >. (*Note:* Other programmers use parameter names such as T instead of Type.) Then, in subsequent declarations and implementations of array1 member functions, the parameter Type is used instead of a specific class. The array1 class makes frequent use of the parameter Type. But just what does this template mechanism and the Type parameter buy us?

We are in the process of examining a class that builds on the existing data structures of C++ to produce a better product—a "safe" array. Without the Type parameter made possible through the template mechanism, we would have to build a class for every type: stringArray1, floatArray1, bankAccountArray1, and so on. We saw one implemented in Chapter 9: the class intArray. What the template and Type parameter buys is this: we can build just one template class that stores objects of any type that "unsafe" C++ arrays do.

```
array1<string> name(1, 100);
array1<bankAccount> firstBank(1000, 3000);
array1<bank> branch(1, 17);
array1<ATM> consortium(-1, 2902);
```

It works like this. At some point, the parameter Type is replaced by the class name that was passed as the argument to the array1 class between angle brackets. For example, to allow for prototypes of this form:

```
void display(array1<string> name)
```

the copy constructor for array1 uses Type as the class name.

```
array1::array1(const array1<Type> & source);
// POST: This copy constructor allows array1 objects to be passed to
//       functions by value and to allow array1 return types
```

When float is passed as an argument to the array1 class,

```
array1<float> x(0, 9);
```

C++ replaces Type with float:

```
array1::array1(const array1<float> & source);
```

When string is passed as an argument to the array1 class,

```
array1<string> x(1, 20);
```

C++ replaces Type with string:

```
array1::array1(const array1<string> & source);
```

And when bankAccount is passed to the array1 class,

```
array1<bankAccount> x(1, 500);
```

C++ replaces Type with bankAccount:

```
array1::array1(const array1<bankAccount> & source);
```

With the array1 declared as a template class, it can be used by the compiler as a model for any number of other classes. The class parameter named Type has scope that extends to the end of the class declaration. This means that Type may be used anywhere in the class declaration, such as the public section for the copy constructor above or in the private data member section. For example, writing the Type parameter before the pointer data member x in the array class declaration is critically important to the array1 class:

```
// ...
private:
  Type * x;  // x is a pointer to any Type: char*, int*, bankAccount*
  int maxEls;
  int lower, upper;
};
```

The parameter named Type in the private data section becomes the class of objects that x will store. At declaration, the Type identifier is replaced with the argument specified at declaration. For example, these object declarations cause x to point to int, string, and bankAccount objects, respectively:

```
array1<int> a1(1, 5);     array1<string> a2(1, 6);     array1<bankAccount> a3(1, 7);
           ↓                          ↓                              ↓
       Type * x;                  Type * x;                      Type * x;
           ↓                          ↓                              ↓
        int * x;                  string * x;                   bankAccount * x;
```

In the array1 class, once the Type pointed to by x is known, the new operator allocates the proper amount of memory. Because a Type argument must be passed during the call to the array1 constructor, the class of data allocated by new is known immediately. The Type parameter specifies not only the class of data pointed to by x but also the amount of memory to allocate for each object of that class (each object requires a specific number of bytes for each data object). For example, with this declaration

```
array1<int> intArray(1, 6);
```

memory is allocated to store 6 elements of class int—not double, string, or bankAccount. The class name, int here, is passed to the array1 class as an argument. Then the constructor is able to allocate memory for maxEls elements of class Type with the new operation. Although the first few statements that store the lower subscript, the upper subscript, and the maximum number of elements do not need to know about Type, the new operation definitely does.

```
// array1 constructor implementation in arrays.cpp
template<class Type>
array1<Type>::array1(int first, int last)
{
  lower = first;
  upper = last;
  maxEls = upper - lower + 1;
  x = new Type[maxEls];  // Type is known throughout the entire class
}
```

In general, when x = new Type [maxEls] executes, the parameter Type is replaced with the argument passed to a parameterized class, which in this particular case is int.

The class parameter Type in the declaration:
```
//...
  x = new Type[maxEls];
}
private:
  Type * x;
//...
```

After replacing Type with int:

```
//...
  x = new int[maxEls];
}
private:
  int * x;
// ...
```

10.3.1 array1 class Memory Management with new and delete

Memory is managed in the array1 class with the pointer object x, the new and delete operators, and subscripts. Recall from Chapter 9 that the new operator with [ ] allocates any number of objects pointed to by x. The following representation shows how the private data of intArray can be referenced through subscripts.

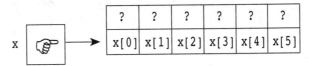

Because x is a pointer to the argument associated with the class parameter Type, the subscript notation can be used for any class associated with Type. So x[1] may be a reference to an int, float, string, or bankAccount object that is stored in an array1 object. The array1 class overloads [ ] to allow for references to individual array1 objects. Because of the flexible subscripts, a reference to an individual array1 element requires a translation. For example, with this array declaration

```
array1<double> population(1995, 2001);
```

population[1995] is actually stored in the private data member x[0] and population[1996] is stored in x[1]. The actual member function shows from arrays.cpp shows the formula that returns the correct element from x. This happens only after the subscript range is checked to ensure it is within the range of lower and upper:

```
template<class Type>
Type & array1<Type>::operator [] (int subscript)
{ // Terminate program if subscript is not in range
  if((subscript < lower) || (subscript > upper))
  {
    cout << "\n**Error** Subscript [" << subscript
         << "] is not in the range of " << lower << ".." << upper
         << endl;
    cout << "**Program terminated**" << endl;
    exit(0);
  }
  return x[subscript - lower];
}
```

Because array1 objects may consume large chunks of memory, there is a destructor to deallocate all unneeded memory when the array1 object goes out of scope. Because x was allocated with [ ], delete must be followed by the [ ] before the pointer object name.

```
// Destructor
template<class Type>
array1<Type>::~array1()
{
  delete [ ] x;
}
```

10.3.2 Member Function Templates

Classes such as array1 are referred to as a *parameterized* class—one that has a parameter in scope for the purpose of passing a class argument. After the class has been declared:

```
template<class Type>
// The scope of parameter Type extends to the end of class declaration
class array1 {
public:
  array1::array1(int first, int last);
  // ...
private:
  Type * x;
  // ...
};
```

all member functions of a class are considered to be template functions. Their implementation must be preceded with the same template declaration that precedes the class declaration:

```
template<class Type>
member-function definition
```

In implementations of parameterized classes, you will see the template<class Type> repeated often—before every member function implementation. Additionally, the parameter name must be added to the qualifier between < and >. So a member function without templates written like this

```
array1::array1(int first, int last)          // <- Error
```

is an error in parameterized classes. The parameter name must be added in-between < and >.

```
array1<Type>::array1(int first, int last)   // add <Type> to class qualifier
```

These two points are summarized by two more `array1` member function implementations. They both show the template declaration preceding the member function. Also notice that the parameter `<Type>` is added to the qualifier so `array1::` becomes `array1<Type>::` (the extra overhead involved in defining member functions is displayed in boldface):

```
template<class Type>
int array1<Type>::firstSubscript()
{ // POST: Return the smallest int in the valid subscript range
  return lower;
}

template<class Type>
int array1<Type>::lastSubscript()
{ // POST: Return the largest int in the valid subscript range
  return upper;
}
```

The complete declaration and implementation of the `array1` class can be seen in the files `arrays1.h` and `arrays1.cpp`, respectively.

10.3.3 A Simple Parameterized Class

A simple class is presented here to summarize the previous discussion of template declarations for classes and functions. In this class we see the `Type` parameter used to store precisely one object of class `Type`. The data member value is initialized when the constructor is called and `one<Type>::display` simply displays the three objects in a manner appropriate to the class.

The implementation of both the constructor and the display member functions are given immediately after the class `one` declaration. Also included is a `main` function that creates four objects of different classes. Each of these objects is a request to the compiler for unique classes, one each of type `int`, `float`, `string`, and `bankAccount`. All four classes are based on the template class named `one`.

```
#include <iostream.h>
#include "ourstr.h"
#include "ouracct.h"

// Declare parameterized class one
template<class Type>
class one {
```

```
public:
  one(Type initValue);      // Constructor
  void display();
private:
  Type value;
};

// Implement the parameterized class one
template<class Type>
one<Type>::one(Type initValue)
{
  value = initValue;
}

template<class Type>
void one<Type>::display()
{
  cout << value << endl;
}

// This main function will cause four classes to be generated by the
// compiler with Type replaced by int, float, string, and bankAccount
int main()
{
  one<int> intObject(-999);
  one<float> floatObject(1.23e4);
  one<string> stringObject("abcdefg");
  one<bankAccount> bankAccountObject(bankAccount("Hall", "1234", 100));
  intObject.display();
  floatObject.display();
  stringObject.display();
  bankAccountObject.display();
  return 0;
}
```

──────────────── **Output** ────────────────

```
-999
123000
abcdefg
{ bankAccount: HALL, 1234, 100.00 }
```

In summary, a class template acts as a model for constructing many distinct classes, just as a class is used to construct many distinct objects. Specifically, class one acted as a template for the four classes specified in function main: int, float, string, and bankAccount.

10.4 A Safe, Parameterized list Class That Grows Itself

Imagine computer-based management of address books, appointment calendars, reservation systems, college course registrations, catalogue orders, test scores, and so on. We could use either the C++ array or the parameterized array1 class with subscripts to help manage these collections. Or, if the objects to be stored were only strings, we could use the stringList class of Chapter 7. Although the stringList class is a step up from lower level arrays with subscripts, it suffers from this restriction: stringList objects only manage a collection of string objects. Lists of ints, floats, bankAccounts, or other classes are not allowed.

In Chapter 7, stringList member functions were introduced:

```
stringList names;
names.init();
names.add("Sally Small");
names.add("Linda Ewall");
names.display();
```

Then in Chapter 8, a constructor was added to avoid requiring users of the class to call init. We will now see the template mechanism used to implement a class that is general enough to manage lists of any class through add and remove operations. The parameterized *list* class introduced here combines add and remove member functions (like stringList) with the *genericity* (general enough to manage many classes) of the array1 class for a class that allows list adds and removals of ints, floats, strings, bankAccounts, and so on.

A list object is declared with this general form:

list < *class-name* > *identifier* ;

One of the advantages of this list class, and an issue that becomes important in many applications, is the number of elements that may be stored with one list object. We will see that this cannot be determined exactly. The number of objects that may be stored under one list object depends on the size of the objects and the amount of available memory on the free store. The best answer is this: A list object will store as many objects as memory allows—there is no fixed maximum size, as previously seen in primitive C++ arrays and in the stringList and array1 classes. We will return to this maximum size issue. For now, here are some examples of list declarations in function main, which shows the construction of four list classes, each managing different classes of objects:

```
#include "ourlist.h"   // for list<Type>
#include "ourstr.h"    // for class string
#include "ouracct.h"   // for class bankAccount

int main()
{
  list<int> intList;
  list<float> floatList;
  list<string> stringList;
  list<bankAccount> acctList;

  ...
```

A list class (or something similar to it) is useful when many additions and deletions are being made—in a reservation system, for example. We could manage a list of airlineReservation, rentalCar, or concertGoer objects. We could also have a list of bankAccounts by passing the class name as an argument to the list. The genericity is implemented with templates.

The following program illustrates the behavior of a list object with the relatively small set of list operations (as you continue with your study of computing beyond this text, you will likely encounter lists described and/or declared with even more operations):

```
// Use the parameterized list class to manage a small list of
// bankAccounts. Four additions and two removals are performed.
#include "ourlist.h"   // for list<Type>
#include "ouracct.h"   // for class bankAccount

int main()
{
  // Pass the bankAccount class as an argument to the list class
  list<bankAccount> acctList;

  bankAccount a("Sally Small", "1234", 987.56);
  bankAccount b("Kerry Holstein", "4324", 100);
  bankAccount c("Jose Gonzalez", "0098", 879.99);

  // Use all list operations:
  acctList.add(a);
  acctList.add(b);
  acctList.add(c);
  acctList.display();
  acctList.remove(a);
  acctList.remove(b);
  acctList.add(bankAccount("Zung Nguyen", "4643", 876.98));
  acctList.display();
  return 0;
}
```

```
──────────────── Output ────────────────
1. { bankAccount: SALLY SMALL, 1234, 987.56 }
2. { bankAccount: KERRY HOLSTEIN, 4324, 100.00 }
3. { bankAccount: JOSE GONZALEZ, 0098, 879.99 }
1. { bankAccount: JOSE GONZALEZ, 0098, 879.99 }
2. { bankAccount: ZUNG NGUYEN, 4643, 876.98 }
```

Unlike the array1 class, the class of list elements has been restricted to make it easier to demonstrate. The class restrictions are due to the higher level list operations named list::remove and list::display. To remove an object from a list, the == operator needs to be defined for the class. Also, because the display operation inserts objects to cout, the << operator must be defined for the class. (*Note:* Most classes in this text have == and << defined.) In short, the class name passed to the list class constructor must have these two operations defined (these restrictions allow us to avoid discussion of iterators and other related issues that are beyond the scope of this textbook):

Restrictions on types managed by class list

<< must be defined to allow elements to be displayed.

== must be defined to allow elements to be located and/or removed.

One class that cannot be managed by list is array1<Type>. A list of array1<Type> objects is not currently allowed only because the << and == operators have not been overloaded for array1<Type>. However, these overloaded operations could be added to array1<Type> when the meaning of == and << becomes useful.

Self-Check

Use this declaration to answer the following questions:

```
list<int> intList;
```

1. How many ints can be stored in intList?
2. What integer subscript is used to reference the first and last element in intList?
3. Write the code that stores 89 as the first element of intList.
4. Declare a list object that manages at least 200 float objects.
5. Write the output generated by the following code fragment:

```
    #include "ourlist.h"    // for class list<Type>
    #include "ourstr.h"     // for class string
    int main()
    {
      list<string> strList;  // a list of string objects

      strList.add("John");
      strList.add("Wendy");
      strList.add("Brooke");
      strList.add("Jared");
      strList.display();
      return 0;
    }
```

Answers
1. It is not clear from the description of the list class, so "I don't know" is a good answer. We will address the size issue later in this chapter.
2. The subscript operator is not currently defined (although it could be)—so one answer is "No subscript can be used."
3. `y.add(89);`
4. `list<float> anyName;` // For now, presume anyName manages at least 200 floats
5. `Number of objects in this list is 4`
   ```
   1. John
   2. Wendy
   3. Brooke
   4. Jared
   ```

10.5 Class list Implementation

In this section, we show how pointers and genericity are combined to implement the list class. A list object is one that is

1. Safe: No subscript-out-of-range error can occur.
2. Generic: Manages data of most classes (some restrictions do apply).
3. Without a fixed maximum size: Allocate memory as long there is some on the free store.

Imposed on this list class is the precondition that the class argument has defined the << and == operators. The intentionally limited set of operations is summarized by the class declaration as it exists in the file ourlist.h. The class parameter named Type is used where a specific class would be, so the extra overhead involves the addition of this class template declaration:

```
template<class Type>
```

which extends the scope of Type throughout the entire class. We must also remember to use the class parameter named Type rather than a specific class such as string. This applies to the use of Type as a parameter or as the class of elements pointed to by x of the private section.

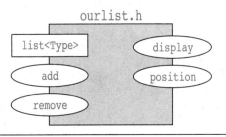

Figure 10.1   Interface diagram for module ourlist.h

```
//-------------------------------------------------------------------
// DECLARATION File "ourlist.h"
//
// Precondition: The class passed to class list must define << and ==
//       Declares: A generic class list initialized like this
//                 list<int> intList;
//                 list<string> stringList;
//                 list<bankAccount> bankAccountList;
//-------------------------------------------------------------------
#ifndef OURLIST_H
#define OURLIST_H

const int GROW_BY_SIZE = 20;

template<class Type>
class list {
public:
  list::list();
  // POST: The size of the list is set to 0

  ~list();
  // POST: All memory allocated in add is returned to the free store

  void list::add(Type newElement);
  // POST: The new object is added at the end and the size of the
  //       list is increased by 1. The number of elements that may
  //       be added, is limited by the size of the free store.

  void list::remove(Type removeElement);
  //  PRE: The class Type has defined the equality operator ==
  // POST: Remove any element from the list where == is defined
```

```
    void list::display();
    //  PRE: The Type of the elements managed by this list object
    //       has defined the stream insertion operator <<.
    // POST: All objects currently stored in the array are dis-
    //       played after a heading indicating the size of the list.
    //       If no objects have been added, no strings are displayed.

    int list::position(Type searchElement, int & found);
    //  PRE: class Type has defined the equality operator ==
    // POST: If searchElement is in the list, position becomes
    //       the subscript of searchElement and found is returned
    //       as true. If searchElement is not in the list, position
    //       becomes -1 and found is returned as false.

private:
  Type * x;      // x stores the base address of list elements.
  int size;      // Always store how many have been added.
  int maxSize;   // The maximum size before increasing the size.
};

#include "ourlist.cpp"   // Add the member function implementations

#endif   // #ifndef OURLIST_H
```

Although a pointer object and subscripts are employed as the major behind-the-scenes data structure for the list class, we use list objects without subscripts. For example, the member function display is called to display all the elements in a list. With a primitive C++ array, we need a for loop and subscript references. Rather than performing sequential search with a loop and subscript referencing during a search or remove operation, the position and/or remove member functions are called. size—encapsulated as a data member of the list class—is automatically updated during each add and each remove (this important piece of data would have to be managed separately from a primitive C++ array). These differences represent a step up in abstraction.

Because we saw the stringList member functions used in an earlier section, we should be somewhat familiar with their use with list objects. The algorithms should also be familiar since they were all studied with primitive arrays in Chapter 7 (pointers and arrays are both subscripted variables). In particular, the stringList class used similar algorithms to manage a fixed-size collection of string objects with the C++ array. The significant differences between the stringList class and this generic list class include:

1. The list class manages collections of any class rather than just string.
2. The list::add no longer limits the number of objects stored by a list object. This list grows itself through careful use of the new and delete operators and subscripted pointer objects.

3. The major data store is a subscripted pointer data member rather than a C++ singly subscripted array (see the private data section here for `Type * x;` where `x` is the pointer object name that may be subscripted).

We concentrate on these differences: the constructor, the destructor, and the `list::add` member function.

10.5.1 list::list()

As with the `stringList` constructor, the `list` constructor initializes the size of the list to 0. In this way we always start with an empty list. But since we are using a pointer object with `new` and `delete`—and the reason for this should become clear shortly—`x` is initialized to point to `maxSize` elements of class `Type` during the `new` operation.

```
template<class Type>
list<Type>::list()
{ // Create an empty list with an initial size of GROW_BY_SIZE
  size = 0;
  // Allocate some memory: space to store GROW_BY_SIZE objects
  maxSize = GROW_BY_SIZE;
  x = new Type[maxSize];
}
```

10.5.2 list::add()

If `GROW_BY_SIZE` is declared to be 20, we can add up to 20 objects before removing any object. But when a 21st object is added, we don't tell the user it can't be done. Something different happens. The `new` operator allocates additional memory for `GROW_BY_SIZE` (20) more objects. In general, each newly added object is appended at the end of the subscripted pointer object named `x`. When the value of `size` is less than `maxSize`, new objects are added with little fuss. This code from `list::add`'s implementation might look familiar because it is the same as the `stringList` class.

```
// Store the argument into the array of <Type> objects
x[size] = newElement;
// And make sure the size is always increased by +1
size++;
```

But the `list` class prevents adds that would otherwise result in the destruction of other objects stored in memory. If there is no more room to add an object, several steps are taken to increase the amount of memory. We will see the `list` grow itself. How this is done is summarized here as comments:

```
// Check to see if we need to grow the list:
if(size + 1 > maxSize)
{
  // Increase maxSize
  // Allocate memory to store another GROW_BY_SIZE objects
  // Copy old elements into the temporary array
  // Deallocate memory that is no longer needed
  // Let x point to the new larger array
}
```

Assuming GROW_BY_SIZE and therefore maxSize are initialized to 3 with this initialization:

```
list<int> intList;  // Presume const int GROW_BY_SIZE = 3
                    // maxSize will start as 3
```

and three adds are executed:

```
intList.add(90);
intList.add(80);
intList.add(70);
```

the portion of memory storing the state would look something like this (size=3, maxSize=3):

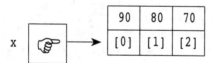

Then, an attempt to add a fourth results in this expression being true:

```
if(size + 1 > maxSize)
  (  3  + 1 >    3    )
  (     4   >    3    )
            true
```

The fourth add first grows the list by 3 elements and then stores the fourth at x[3]:

```
intList.add(60);
```

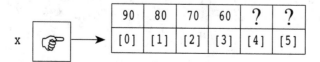

Two more adds

```
intList.add(50);
intList.add(40);
```

do not create a need to grow the list. Memory would look something like this (size=6, maxSize=6):

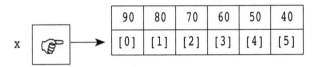

But to add another three

```
intList.add(30);
intList.add(20);
intList.add(10);
```

the list must grow by another 3 objects of class Type. The list object would look like this after these nine adds:

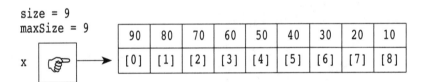

The code of list::add below shows that an attempt to add a tenth object will make room for 9 + GROW_BY_SIZE (12) objects with size incremented to 10 and maxSize to 12. Next a temporary pointer (named extraData) allocates room for all objects currently in the list plus GROW_BY_SIZE for subsequent adds. With all the existing objects copied into the newly allocated memory, we end up with two copies of the list, but extraData points to memory that can store three more elements.

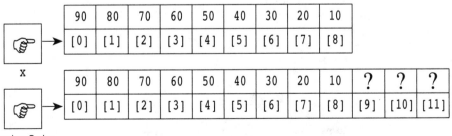

With `extraData` available, the memory pointed to by x can be deleted to return the old `list` memory to the free store.

```
delete [ ] x;
```

We must then assign the address to x with this statement:

```
x = extraData;
```

The list is now back to its original state, except x is pointing to memory with room for GROW_BY_SIZE more elements.

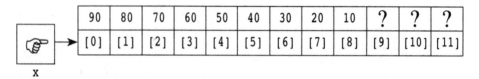

GROW_BY_SIZE elements can now be added at the end of memory pointed to by x. Here is the C++ code that accomplishes these tasks:

```
template<class Type>
void list<Type>::add(Type newElement)
{
  // Check to see if we need to increase
  // number of objects x can point to
  if(size + 1 > maxSize)
  {
    // Increase maxSize
    maxSize = size + GROW_BY_SIZE;
    // Allocate memory to store another GROW_BY_SIZE objects
    Type * extraData = new Type[maxSize];
    // Copy elements into the temporary array
    for(int j = 0; j < size; j++)
      extraData[j] = x[j];
    assert (extraData);
    // Deallocate old memory that is no longer needed
    delete [ ] x;
    // Let x point to the new larger array
    x = extraData;
  }

  // Store the argument into the array of <Type> objects
  x[size] = newElement;
  // And make sure the size is always increased by +1
  size++;
}
```

Programming Tip

The memory of the free store can become exhausted. One way to check to see if a memory allocation was successful is to use the assert function, declared in assert.h, immediately after new:

```
Type * extraData = new Type[maxSize];
assert(extraData);
```

The assert function will provide you with a message and then terminate the program whenever its argument is false. The new operator returns 0 whenever there is not enough memory to fulfill the request or the address; otherwise, a nonzero value is returned. So when there is not enough memory, assert terminates the program with the expression as the message, the name of the file, and the line number where the assertion failed. Incidentally, the assert function can be used to assert almost anything. For example, to check if a subscript is in bounds, we could write an assert function call like this:

```
assert(subscript >= 0 && subscript <= maxSubscript);
```

10.5.3 list::~list()

The third member function that needs consideration in light of this dynamically sized list is the destructor. Since we have been careful to copy all list elements into memory pointed to by x and to delete all memory in the temporary memory pointed to by extraData, x is pointing to all the data elements allocated, no matter how many there were. The single statement in the list destructor returns any remaining memory back to the free store as the list goes out of scope.

```
template<class Type>
list<Type>::~list()
{
  delete [ ] x;
}
```

There are better ways to implement a list class and there should be more operations—list::retrieve, for example. However, the implementation given was intended only to illustrate class templates, and how pointers, along with new and delete operations, hold promise for effective memory management. Parameterized classes offer an alternative to implementation of container classes in future studies.

Self-Check

1. How many classes are constructed when this `main` function is compiled?

    ```
    int main()
    {
        list<int> tests;
        list<int> quizzes;
        list<string> name;
        // ...
    }
    ```

2. Assuming `GROW_BY_SIZE = 20`, what is the value of the `maxSize` data member after each of these situations (assume each situation occurs immediately after declaration)?

    a. 10 adds and 5 removals   d. 44 adds
    b. 20 adds and 5 removals   e. 0 adds
    c. 21 adds and 5 removals   f. 2000 adds and 1999 removals

Answers
1. Two: One for a list of `ints` and one for a list of `strings`
2. a. 20   b. 20   c. 40   d. 60   e. 20   f. 2000

Chapter Summary

We saw that out-of-bounds subscripts can cause problems. Sometimes they are obvious; sometimes your program will not work properly because of them. The `array1` class makes it obvious that array subscripts are out bounds by terminating the program. This can actually save time during program development.

Parameterized classes allow the user to pass a class name as an argument to the class. This gives us the ability to have arrays and lists that manage data objects of any class. The `array1` class is similar to the C++ array but the `array1<Type>` class offers subscript range checking and greater flexibility with the lower and upper bounds of subscripts. Whereas the C++ array puts the onus of subscript range checking on the user, the `array1<Type>` class has a safety net that terminates the program if the user is not careful. There are advantages and disadvantages to both classes. The `array1` was designed to mimic C++ array usage with the additional subscript range checking feature. Only the declaration is different.

Function templates act as a model for the compiler to use when creating other functions. A class template also permits the compiler to create many different classes. The compiler does the work, the class has the same name. We do not need separate `stringList`, `intList`, and `bankAccountList` classes, for example.

The `list` class was used to demonstrate memory management that can be hidden to users of a class.

Exercises

1. Use this declaration to answer each of the questions below:

    ```
    include "arrays.h"
    array1<double> x(1, 20);
    ```

    a. How many doubles may be referenced by subscripting x?
    b. Which integer is used as the subscript to reference the first double in x?
    c. Which integer is used as the subscript to reference the last double in x?
    d. Write the code that displays the elements of x from the first element to the last on separate lines.
    e. Write code that initializes all elements of x to 0.0.
    f. Write a code that increments every element of x by 1.0.

2. Use this declaration to answer the following questions below:

    ```
    array1<bankAccount> account(1, 72);
    ```

    a. How many bankAccount objects can be stored in account?
    b. Which integer is used as the subscript to reference the first bankAccount in account?
    c. Which integer is used as the subscript to reference the last bankAccount in account?
    d. Write code that initializes the first element of account to a bank account with the name "Kieran", a PIN of "9876", and an initial balance of 1500.00.
    e. Write the code that displays all elements of account on separate lines.

3. Show the output of the following program:

    ```cpp
    #include <iostream.h>
    #include "arrays.h"
    int main()
    {
      const int MAX = 6;
      array1<int> x(1, MAX);
      int j;
      x[MAX] = 95;
      for(j = MAX-1; j >= 3; j--)
        x[j] = x[j+1] - 15;
      for(j = 1; j <= 2; j++)
        x[j] = x[j+2];
      for(j = 1; j <= MAX; j++)
        cout << x[j] << "   ";
    }
    ```

4. Write the code that determines the smallest value of the following `array1` object, assuming all 20 values are initialized:

```
array1<double> x(1, 20);
```

5. Write the code that determines the average value in `y`, assuming all 7 values are initialized.

```
array1<double> pop(1995, 2001);
```

6. Declare an `array1` object named `floatArray` that references 11 `float`s with subscripts -5 through 5.

7. Write a complete program that initializes all `testScore` elements to -1:

```
array1<int> testScore(1, 10)
```

8. Write code that finds the range (highest–lowest) of `x`. Assume this declaration of `x` and the fact that only the first *size* elements of `x` are initialized:

```
array1<int> x(1, 20);
```

Lab Projects

10A   Implementing Function Templates

Implement a generic function that returns the smaller of any two of these objects: `char`, `int`, `float`, `double`, and `string`. If the objects are equal, return either one.

10B   Modifying a Class

Modify the `remove` member function of the `list` class (stored in `ourlist.cpp`) such that it checks to see if some memory can be returned to the free store. If possible, do it and return `GROW_BY_SIZE` elements back to the free store.

10C   Modifying a Class

Add a `currentSize` member function to the `list` class so it always returns the current size of the `list`. Write a `main` function to test `currentSize` before and after declaration, after a few adds, and after a few more adds and some removals.

10D   Modifying a Class

Overload the subscript operator to allow retrievals of any single list element. You will need the files "ourlist.h" and "ourlist.cpp". Use the intArray class of Chapter 9 as an example.

10E   Using Objects

Implement a menu-driven reservation system that adds and removes reservations for exactly three hotels. The string class can be used to represent one reservation—the person's last name only. The user of your program must be able to make a reservation, cancel a reservation, and display lists of all reservations for any one hotel. Assume the list contains unique names (make it a precondition to simplify things). Use three list objects where each list is named after a hotel.

10F   Implementing a Class

Implement a parameterized class that implements a generic stack. A *stack* class allows elements to be added and removed in a last in/first out (LIFO) manner. Stacks have an operation called push to place elements at the "top" of the stack and another operation called pop to remove elements from the top of the stack. The only element on the stack that may be referenced is the one on the top of the stack. This means that if two elements are pushed onto the stack, the topmost element must be popped (removed) from the stack before the first pushed element can be referenced. To demonstrate the stack operations, we initialize a stack to store up to 10 char objects:

```
// Declare s as a stack object that can store up to 10 elements
stack<char> s(10);
// Push one element onto the empty stack
s.push('a');
```

The stack started as empty, but now has one char element on it. The current state of the stack is represented as follows:

'a'   *Top of the Stack*

After two more push operations, the charStack would contain three elements where the top one has the value of 'c':

```
charStack.push('b');
charStack.push('c');
```

```
'c'    Top of the Stack
'b'
'a'
```

Use the following template class declaration to completely implement a generic stack class. Make sure you declare and implement the entire class in one file called "stack.h".

```
template <class Type>
class stack {
public:
  stack::stack(int max);
  // Initializes a stack to an empty state

  void stack::push(Type element);
  //  PRE: There is room to add an element on top
  // POST: Inserts El onto the top of the stack.

  //... you declare stack::pop and stack::empty...

private:
  Type * bottom;   // Pointer to the bottom most element
  int size;        // The number of elements on the stack
  int max;         // The maximum number of elements
};
```

Implement the member functions in the same file (some systems don't allow separate declaration and implementation files).

```
template <class Type>
stack<Type>::stack(int initMax)
{
  size = 0;
  max = initMax;
  bottom = new Type [max];
}

template <class Type>
void stack<Type>::push(Type element)
{
  bottom[size] = element;
  size++;
}

//... You implement stack::pop and stack::empty
```

Then use the following program to test your stack class:

```cpp
#include <iostream.h>
#include "stack.h"

int main()
{
  char element;
  stack<char> charStack(10);
  cout << "After initialization, stack::empty() returns: "
       << charStack.empty() << endl;

  charStack.push('a');
  charStack.push('b');
  charStack.pop(element);
  // 'b' is on top of the Stack
  cout << element << " popped from stack" << endl;
  charStack.push('c');
  charStack.push('d');
  charStack.push('e');
  charStack.push('f');
  // 'f' is on top of the Stack
  charStack.pop(element);
  cout << element << " popped from stack" << endl;

  cout << "Before popping, stack::empty() returns: "
       << charStack.empty() << endl;
  // Pop and display all remaining elements
  while(! charStack.empty())
  {
    charStack.pop(element);
    cout << element << endl;
  }
  cout << "First in, last out!" << endl;
  return 0;
}
```

---------- **Output** ----------

```
After initialization, charStack::EmptyStack() returns: 1
b popped from stack
f popped from stack
Before popping, charStack::EmptyStack() returns: 0
e
d
c
a
First in, last out!
```

10G   Modifying a Class

Note: Complete Lab Project 10F first. Modify some of the preconditions written in the declaration of the generic `stack` class. Then change the implementation to disallow stack overflows (`size >= max`) during a `push` operation or stack underflows (`size < 0`) on a `pop` operation. If either happens, issue one of the following error messages:

```
**Error** Stack overflow

**Error** Stack underflow
```

whichever is appropriate. Write a complete program that attempts to perform a stack overflow and a stack underflow.

11

Doubly Subscripted Arrays

We have now seen a singly subscripted `array1` class as the major data storage object for a variety of collections. These objects manage collections of ints, chars, doubles, students, bankAccounts, phone listings, golfers, and so on. We now examine a doubly subscripted array class that manages data logically stored in a table-like format—in rows and columns. Although we may declare arrays with many subscripts, the focus is on arrays with two subscripts. This data structure proves useful for storing and managing data in applications such as electronic spreadsheets, games, topographical maps, student record books, and many other data best viewed as a collection of rows and columns. For example, this table of data represent a lab attendance sheet for 10 students over a 15-week semester.

An Attendance Sheet

Student#	Week# 1	2	3	4	5	6	7	8	9	10	11	12	13	14	15
1	1	1	1	1	1	0	1	1	1	1	1	1	1	0	1
2	1	1	1	0	1	1	1	1	1	1	1	1	1	1	1
3	1	1	1	1	1	1	1	0	1	1	1	1	1	1	1
4	1	1	1	1	1	1	1	1	1	1	1	1	1	1	1
5	1	1	1	1	1	1	1	1	0	1	1	0	1	1	1
6	1	0	1	0	1	1	1	0	1	1	1	1	1	0	0
7	1	1	1	1	1	1	1	1	1	1	1	1	1	1	1
8	0	1	1	0	1	1	1	1	1	1	0	1	1	1	1
9	1	1	1	1	1	1	1	1	1	1	1	1	1	1	1
10	1	1	1	1	1	1	1	1	1	1	1	1	1	1	1

Code: 1 represents attendance, 0 indicates absence.

This data can be processed in a variety of ways, such as:

- Use Column 5 as the attendance record for Week #5.
- Use Row 9 to determine the number of absences for Student #9.
- Use the entire table to determine the ratio of class attendance to absences.
- Use the table to determine whether or not any student was present or absent for any recorded week.

After studying this chapter, you will be able to:

- Process arrays with two subscripts (two-dimensional arrays).
- Perform row by row and column by column processing of two-dimensional array objects.

11.1 A Doubly Subscripted Class: array2

The array2 class is similar to the array1 class, except that array2 objects use two subscripts. The first subscript represents a row and the second subscript represents a column. Declarations of the array2 class must specify exactly four int arguments to represent the range of rows and columns. Here is the general form:

```
#include "arrays.h" // for class array2
```

array2 < *class-name* > *identifier* (*firstRow, lastRow* , *firstCol, lastCol*);

Examples

```
// An array2 object with 20 rows containing 10 columns each
array2<int> unitsSold(1,20 , 1,10);

// An array2 object with 10 rows and 15 columns
array2<int> student(1,10 , 1,15);

//----------------------------------------------------------------------
// SPECIFICATION file arrays.h
// Declares: A generic (parameterized) array2 class, a double
//           subscripted array of any type
//
// By default (if no argument is passed after array-name), instances of
// array have 0 as the first subscript and 20 as the last (size 21).  In
// this case, only array-name[0] through array-name[20] may be referenced.
//
//   Implements: A generic table class allowing doubly subscripted
//               arrays of any type. Range checking is active for both
//               row and column. There are no defaults subscript bounds
//               each table object must specify the first row, last row.
//               followed by the first columns last column
//
// The default constructor allows for a 21 x 21 table were the row ranges
// anywhere from 0 through 20 and the columns from 0 through 20. If the
// default constructor is not used, exactly four arguments are required
// The first two are the lower and upper bounds on the rows, respectively
// the third and fourth are the lower and upper bounds on the columns.
//
// Example array2 declarations:
//    array2<string> student(1,40, 1,10); // 40 students, 10 elements each
//    array1<double> matrix(1,5, 1,8);    // a 5 x 8 matrix
//
```

```
// References to this array2 object ranges from matrix[1][1] through
// matrix[5][8]. If either the row or column subscript is out of bounds,
// the program is terminated as shown in these two errors:
//
// cout << matrix[6][8];
// First subscript [6] is not in the range of 1..5
// **Program terminated**
//
// cout << matrix[5][9];
// Subscript [9] is not in the range of 1..8
// **Program terminated**
//
//-----------------------------------------------------------------------

#ifndef ARRAYS_H    // Avoid duplicate declaration and implementation
#define ARRAYS_H

const int DEFAULT_LOW = 0;
const int DEFAULT_HIGH = 20;

template <class Type>
class array2 {
public:
  // Default constructor:
  array2::array2();
  // POST: Memory is allocated for an array of arrays of Type elements.
  //       The default subscripts are declared as constant in ourarray.h

  // Initializer constructor:
  array2::array2(int initFirstRow, int initLastRow,
                 int initFirstCol, int initLastCol);
  // POST: Memory is allocated for an array of arrays of Type elements
  //       using the specified row and column subscripts

  // Destructor:
  array2::~array2();
  // POST: Deallocate all memory that was allocated for the array2 object

  int array2::firstRow();
  // POST: The upper subscript bound is returned

  int array2::lastRow();
  // POST: The upper subscript bound is returned

  int array2::firstCol();
  // POST: The upper subscript bound is returned

  int array2::lastCol();
  // POST: The upper subscript bound is returned
```

```
arrayl<Type> & array2<Type>::operator [] (int subscript);
// POST: Returns a reference to an entire row (the first subscript).
//       Note: The second subscript of an array2 object calls the
//       overloaded subscript operator [] in the arrayl class.

void array2::resize(int initFirstRow, int initLastRow,
                    int initFirstCol, int initLastCol);
// POST: Destroys the data of the array2 object and creates a new
//       array2 object using the subscripts specificied as arguments

private:
  // Use an array of arrays to store tabular data
  arrayl< arrayl<Type> * > rowPtr; // This array of pointers points
                                   // to maxRow arrays of any Type
  int lowerRow, upperRow;
  int lowerCol, upperCol;
};

#include "arrays.cpp"

#endif // ifndef ARRAYS_H
```

A reference to an individual element of array2 requires two subscripts (row and column) of this general form:

array2-object [*row*] [*column*]

Each subscript must be bracketed individually. For example, if student stores the attendance data shown earlier, the value of student[8][1] is 0 and of student[8][2] is 1. Student #8 was absent in week 1, week 4, and week 11. The sum of these three elements is 0:

```
// Because columns 1, 4, and 11 of row 8 are 0, attend is assigned 0
int attend = student[8][1] + student[8][4] + student[8][11];
```

In general, we use the first subscript of an array2 object to specify the row and the second subscript to specify the column. For example, the attendance percentage of Student #1 is found with this loop where row 1 refers to the data for one student:

```
float present = 0;
int column;
for(column = 1; column <= 15; column++)
{
  if(student[1][column] == 1)
    present++;
}
```

```
float attendanceRate = present / 15.0;
cout << "Student #1 attended " << (attendanceRate * 100)
    << " percent of the time";
```

─────────────────────────── **Output** ───────────────────────────

```
Student #1 attended 93.3 percent of the time
```

11.1.1 Nested Looping with Doubly Subscripted Arrays

Nested looping is commonly used to process the data of array2 objects. If we start with this declaration:

```
array2<int> table(1,5 , 1,8);
```

enough memory is allocated to store 40 ints—a table with 5 rows and 8 columns. All 40 entries initialize to 0 with these nested loops:

```
for(row = 1; row <= 5; row++)
{
  // Initialize one row
  for(col = 1; col <= 8; col++)
  {
    // Reference each column in the row
    table[row][col] = 0;
  }
}
```

After these assignments:

```
table[1][1] = 53;
table[2][2] = 64;
table[3][3] = 75;
table[4][4] = 86;
table[5][5] = 97;
table[5][6] = 106;
table[5][7] = 117;
table[5][8] = 128;
table[1][8] = -1;
```

nested for loops display each row on a separate line:

```
for(row = 1; row <=5; row++)
{
  // Display one row
  for(col = 1; col <= 8; col++)
  {
    // Display each column of the row
    cout.width(6);
    cout << table[row][col];
  }
  cout << endl;
}
```

─────────────────────── **Output** ───────────────────────

53	0	0	0	0	0	0	-1
0	64	0	0	0	0	0	0
0	0	75	0	0	0	0	0
0	0	0	86	0	0	0	0
0	0	0	0	97	106	117	128

Self-Check

1. Which class more accurately manages lists of data, array1 or array2?
2. Which class more accurately manages data viewed in a row/column format, array1 or array2?
3. array2 objects must be constructed with how many arguments?
4. Declare array2 with identifier sales such that 120 float elements are managed in 10 rows.
5. Declare array2 with identifier sales2 such that 120 float elements are managed in 10 cols.

Answers
1. array1
2. array2
3. four
4. array2<float> sales(1, 10, 1, 12);
5. array2<float> sales(1, 12, 1, 10);

11.2 Row and Column Processing

Doubly subscripted arrays manage tabular data that is processed by row, by column, or in totality. These forms of processing are examined in an example that manages a grade book where the data consist of six quizzes for each of the eleven students. The 66 quizzes shown next are used throughout this section to demonstrate several forms of processing the data of array2 objects.

Quiz Data for a Semester

Student Number	Quiz 1	Quiz 2	Quiz 3	Quiz 4	Quiz 5	Quiz 6
1	67.8	76.4	88.4	79.1	90.0	66.0
2	76.4	81.1	72.2	76.0	85.6	85.0
3	87.8	76.4	88.7	83.0	76.3	87.0
4	86.4	54.0	82.6	82.5	95.6	98.4
5	76.8	79.0	58.0	77.0	80.0	87.7
6	94.4	63.0	92.9	45.0	75.6	99.5
7	85.8	75.0	78.1	100.0	60.0	65.8
8	76.4	84.4	100.0	94.3	75.6	74.0
9	67.9	79.5	98.8	76.4	80.0	96.0
10	86.1	76.0	72.0	88.1	55.6	71.3
11	87.2	95.5	68.1	67.0	89.0	76.8

The quiz average is computed for each student by processing this tabular data one row at a time (row by row processing), the average, highest, and lowest score of each quiz by processing one column at a time (column by column processing), and the overall quiz average by referencing all array elements. But before any processing occurs, the array2 object must be declared and given a defined state.

11.2.1 Initializing array2 Objects with File Input

In programs with little data required, interactive input suffices. Initialization of structured objects such as array1 and array2 involves larger amounts of data. The input would have to be extracted from the keyboard many times during the implementation and testing phase of the programming process. Because so much interactive input is tedious and error prone, the ifstream class is used here to obtain data from an external file through extraction operations—no keyboard data entry is required. Before examining several doubly subscripted array processing algorithms, we take care of some housekeeping chores such as #include directives, and giving a simpler name for array2 subject declarations with typedef.

```
#include "arrays.h"     // for class array2
#include <iostream.h>   // for cout <<
#include <fstream.h>    // for class ifstream
#include "ourstuff.h"   // for decimals(cout, 1)

typedef array2<double> quizType; // Default size of 20 X 20 in effect

void init(char * fileName, quizType & quiz);
//  PRE: fileName represents an existing file with the proper format
// POST: An array2 object is returned that is the exact size of the
//       data stored in fileName (the array2 object is resized)
```

```
void display(const quizType & quiz);
// POST: The entire two dimensional array is displayed

void studentStats(const quizType & quiz);
// POST: A row by row report of student's scores is displayed

void quizStats(const quizType & quiz);
// POST: A Column by column report of quiz statistics is displayed

double average(const quizType & quiz);
// POST: The overall quiz average is returned

int main()
{
  quizType quiz;
  decimals(cout, 1);
  init("quiz.dat", quiz);
  // Verify proper array2 initialization by echoing the input
  display(quiz);
  studentStats(quiz);
  quizStats(quiz);
  cout << "Average of all quizzes (no quizzes dropped) " << average(quiz)
       << endl;
  return 0;
}
```

If the file is found, we can begin to initialize an array2 object using the file data. The first line specifies the number of rows and columns contained in the input file:

```
11     6
67.8   76.4   88.4    79.1   90.0   66.0
76.4   81.1   72.2    76.0   85.6   85.0
87.8   76.4   88.7    83.0   76.3   87.0
86.4   54.0   82.6    82.5   95.6   98.4
76.8   79.0   58.0    77.0   80.0   87.7
94.4   63.0   92.9    45.0   75.6   99.5
85.8   75.0   78.1   100.0   60.0   65.8
76.4   84.4  100.0    94.3   75.6   74.0
67.9   79.5   98.8    76.4   80.0   96.0
86.1   76.0   72.0    88.1   55.6   71.3
87.2   95.5   68.1    67.0   89.0   76.8
```

The ifstream object inFile will be associated with this external file in the init function, and the number of rows and columns will be extracted from the first line in the file (11 and 6) with this statement:

```
inFile >> lastStudent >> lastQuiz;
```

The default size for the array2 object (20 rows by 20 columns) will be immediately resized for maximum memory efficiency:

```
quiz.resize(1, lastStudent, 1, lastQuiz);
```

Thus quiz can from this point forward communicate its subscript ranges for both row and column at any time and in any function. Like the array::firstSubscript and array1::lastSubscript functions, array2 has several member functions to report the number of rows and columns. These four members of array2 will now return the values shown:

Member function call	*Will now return*
quiz.firstRow()	1
quiz.lastRow()	11
quiz.firstCol()	1
quiz.lastRow()	6

Now that we have an array2 object exactly large enough to store 11 (lastStudent) rows of data with 6 (lastQuiz) doubles in each row, the array2 object extracts file data for all elements with nested for loops. Because quiz is a reference parameter (&), quiz is returned to function main completely initialized.

The arrays.h module contains the related array1 and array2 classes.

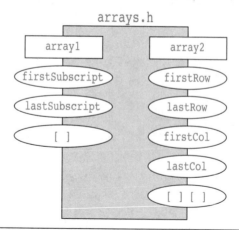

Figure 11.1   Interface diagram for module arrays.h

```
void init(char * fileName, quizType & quiz)
{
  // Initialize quiz
  ifstream inFile(fileName);
  if(!inFile)
  {
    cout << "**Error** opening input file 'quiz.dat'" << endl;
    cout << "**Program terminated**";
    exit(0);
  }
  else
  {
    int lastStudent, lastQuiz, row, col;
    inFile >> lastStudent >> lastQuiz;
    quiz.resize(1,lastStudent , 1,lastQuiz);

    // Initialize a lastStudent by lastQuiz two-dimensional array
    for(row = quiz.firstRow(); row <= quiz.lastRow(); row++)
      for(col = quiz.firstCol(); col <= quiz.lastCol(); col++)
        inFile >> quiz[row][col];
  }
}
```

As with arrays, the antibugging technique of displaying all initialized elements of an array2 object can help prevent errors. This echo of the input data is accomplished again with the help of nested loops. The output is meant to look just like the input file.

```
void display(const quizType & quiz)
{
  int row, col;
  for(row = quiz.firstRow(); row <= quiz.lastRow(); row++)
  {
    for(col = quiz.firstCol(); col <= quiz.lastCol(); col++)
    {
      cout.width(6);
      cout << quiz[row][col];
    }
    cout << endl;
  }
}
```

--- **Output** ---

The output looks exactly like the input file (quiz.dat) shown above after the line with 11   6.

This array2 object is now correctly initialized and stores 66 quiz scores, where each row represents the record of one student and each column represents the record of one quiz.

Programming Tip

When working with arrays, take a little extra time to output all elements and the number of assigned elements. Do this immediately after the code that initializes the objects. Do not continue until you are satisfied the array has been properly initialized. Otherwise, a lot of debugging effort could be wasted on the wrong portion of a program. It may appear that there is a bug later on in the program, when, in fact, the array1 or array2 object has never been initialized correctly to begin with.

11.2.2 Student Average (Row by Row Processing)

The average for one student is found by adding all the elements of one row and dividing by 6 (the number of quizzes taken by each student). Dropping the lowest quiz score provides an interesting twist. To drop the lowest, we have to find the column with the lowest score and subtract it from the total of all six quizzes (before dividing by 5 instead of 6). Since the data for each student are stored in one row of the array2 object, the doubly subscripted array is processed in a row by row manner.

Row by row processing is characterized by nested loops where the row subscript changes in the outer loop and the column subscript changes more quickly in an inner loop. The column subscript increments faster than the row to process one complete row of data before proceeding to the next. The following code is an example of row by row processing where each row of data is used to sum every column of data in a row to find the average quiz score.

```
void studentStats(const quizType & quiz)
{
  // An example of row by row processing
  double sum, lowest, average;
  int row, col;
  cout << endl;
  cout << "   Student        Average" << endl;
  cout << "   =======        =======" << endl;
  for(row = quiz.firstRow(); row <= quiz.lastRow(); row++)
  {
    // Assume the first quiz is the lowest
    lowest = quiz[row][1];
    // Assign sum the value of the first quiz
    sum = lowest;
    // Process the remaining quizzes
```

```
for(col = quiz.firstCol()+1; col <= quiz.lastCol(); col++)
{
    sum = sum + quiz[row][col];
    if(quiz[row][col] < lowest)
        lowest = quiz[row][col];
} // End inner loop
// Drop the lowest quiz
sum = sum - lowest;
// PRE: lastQuiz > 1
// Compute number of quizzes per student
int n = quiz.lastCol() - quiz.firstCol() + 1;
// Average is based on dropping lowest so Divide by one less than n
average = sum /(n - 1);
cout.width(10);
cout << row;
cout.width(15);
cout << average << endl;
} // End outer loop
}
```

---- **Output** ----

Student	Average
=======	=======
1	80.3
2	80.8
3	84.6
4	89.1
5	80.1
6	85.1
7	80.9
8	86.1
9	86.1
10	78.7
11	83.3

11.2.3 Quiz Average (Column by Column Processing)

Column by column processing occurs when data of a doubly subscripted array are processed such that all the rows of one column are referenced before proceeding to the next column. The row subscript changes faster than the column subscript. Since each element in quiz is represented as one column, processing the data column by column generates quiz statistics such as the lowest, highest, and average scores for each quiz.

```
void quizStats(const quizType & quiz)
{
   // An example of column by column processing
   float sum, highest, lowest, average;
   int row, col;
   cout << endl;
   cout << "       Quiz      High       Low   Average" << endl;
   cout << "      =====     =====     =====   =======" << endl;
   for(col = quiz.firstCol(); col <= quiz.lastCol(); col++)
   {

     highest = quiz[quiz.firstRow()][col];
     lowest  = highest;
     sum = lowest;
     for(row = quiz.firstRow() + 1; row <= quiz.lastRow(); row++)
     {
       sum = sum + quiz[row][col];
       if(quiz[row][col] < lowest)
         lowest = quiz[row][col];
       if(quiz[row][col] > highest)
         highest = quiz[row][col];
     }
     average = sum / 11 ;// (quiz.lastRow() - quiz.firstRow() + 1);
     cout.width(10);
     cout << col;
     cout.width(10);
     cout << highest;
     cout.width(10);
     cout << lowest;
     cout.width(10);
     cout << average << endl;
   }
}
```

——————————————— **Output** ———————————————

Quiz	High	Low	Average
=====	=====	=====	=======
1	94.4	67.8	81.2
2	95.5	54.0	76.4
3	100.0	58.0	81.8
4	100.0	45.0	78.9
5	95.6	55.6	78.5
6	99.5	65.8	82.5

The above code illustrates column by column processing. The outer loop increments the column only after all the statements necessary to process each row are completed. The inner loop changes the row subscript more quickly to sum all the scores and compare each to the current highest and lowest before proceeding to the next quiz. Now that we've seen examples of row by row and column by column processing, let's look at an `array2` object that is processed in its entirety.

11.2.4 Overall Quiz Average (Processing All Elements)

Finding the overall average without dropping any quiz scores is a simple matter of summing every single element in the `array2` object and dividing by the total number of quizzes.

```
double average(const quizType & quiz)
{
  double sum;
  int row, col;
  sum = 0;
  for(row = quiz.firstRow(); row <= quiz.lastRow(); row++)
    for(col = quiz.firstCol(); col <= quiz.lastCol(); col++)
      sum = sum + quiz[row][col];
  int n = (quiz.lastRow() * quiz.lastCol());
  return sum / n;
}
```

Output
from function main

Average of all quizzes (no quizzes dropped) 79.9

Most students should appreciate the fact that they appear to have done better than the class average. This is because the report by student saw the lowest quiz dropped whereas the overall average included all quiz scores including the lowest for each student.

Programming Tip

If you use the `array2` class as a data member of another class, you will have to use the default constructor as shown in the private section of class `matrix`:

```
class matrix {
public:
  matrix::matrix(int rows, int columns);
  // ...
private:
  array2 <double> m;  // Use any subscript from 0 through 20
};
```

If you need to alter the subscripts to anything else, the `array2::resize` member function must be called immediately:

```
matrix::matrix(int rows, int columns)
{
  m.resize(1, rows, 1, columns);
  //...
```

This function will destroy any old data before resetting the subscripts, so use caution. On the other hand, the default of 20 rows by 20 columns is more than sufficient for all examples in this text. Resizing is not necessary.

Self-Check

1. In row by row processing, which subscript increments more slowly, row or column?

2. In column by column processing, which subscript increments more slowly, row or column?

3. Justify the use of an external file and class ifstream to initialize an array2 object of 110 rows and 8 columns while a program is being tested.

Using this beginning of a program

```
#include "arrays.h"    // class array2
int main()
{
  int r, c, rows=10, cols=5;
  array2<int> t(1, rows, 1, cols);
  // Assume all 50 elements of t are initialized
```

and assuming all elements have been properly initialized somehow, answer the following questions.

4. Write code that determines the sum of all array2 elements

5. Write code that displays the largest element in each column.

Answers

1. row
2. column
3. An external file of 880 elements need be created only once. Input need not be entered manually every time the program executes. This is less error prone and is more likely to guarantee the same data each time the program is run.
4.
```
int sum = 0;
for(r = 1; r <= rows; r++)
{
  for(c = 1; c <= cols; c++)
    sum = sum + t[r][c];
}
cout << "sum:" << sum;
```

```
5.  int large;
    for(c = 1;  c <= cols; c++)
    {
      large = t[1][c];
      for(r = 1; r <= cols; r++)
      {
        if (t[r][c] > large)
          large = t[r][c];
      }
      cout << endl;
      cout << "Largest in column " << c << " is " << large;
    }
```

Exercises

1. Write the output generated by the following program:

```cpp
#include <iostream.h>
#include "arrays.h"

typedef array2 <int> matrix;

void init(matrix & m)
{
  for(int row = m.firstRow(); row <= m.lastRow(); row++)
  {
    for(int col = m.firstCol(); col <= m.lastCol(); col++)
    { // Give each quiz a value using a meaningless formula
      m[row][col] = row + col;
    }
  }
}

void show(const matrix & m)
{
  for(int row = m.firstRow(); row <= m.lastRow(); row++)
  {
    for(int col = m.firstCol(); col <= m.lastCol(); col++)
    {
      cout.width(4);
      cout << m[row][col];
    }
  cout << endl;
  }
}
```

```
int main()
{
  matrix m;
  m.resize(1,4 , 1,4);
  init(m);
  show(m);

  return 0;
}
```

2. Using the `typedef` shown above, write function `showDiagonal` that displays the diagonal of any `array2` object where the number of columns equals the number of rows. The diagonal is the elements `m[1][1]`, `m[2][2]`, `m[3][3]`, ... , `m[m.lastRow()-1][m.lastCol()-1]`, `m[m.lastRow()][m.lastCol()]`. Align your output so it looks like a diagonal. When used with the program in Question 1, the output from `showDiagonal` should look like this:

```
2
  4
    6
      8
```

3. Using the `typedef` shown above, write function `addOne` that adds +1 to every element in the `matrix` object.
4. Using the `typedef` shown above, write function `rowSum` that *returns* the sum of all columns in the row supplied as the first argument. A valid call to `rowSum` is shown in this `cout` statement:

```
cout << rowSum(2, m);
```

Lab Projects

11A   Using Objects

Write a program that extracts data from an external file to initialize an `array2` object. The first line of the file contains the number of rows and columns for the table data that follows.

*   First, create the following file:

```
2 3
 -7.5   8.1   12.3
22.19  16.7   -9.99
```

This file store represents a doubly subscripted array that is 2 rows by 3 columns where 12.3 is the 3rd element in row 1. Your program should be able to store doubly subscripted arrays with a maximum size of 15 rows and 15 columns of ints, floats, or doubles. The output should show the elements of the array2 object. Using the file shown above, your output should look exactly like this:

Initialized Table

```
    -7.50    8.10   12.30
    22.19   16.70   -9.99
```

Now create a data file named table.dat with 5 rows of data where each row has 3 columns of any numeric data. To indicate a 5 x 3 array2 object, the first line of data must look like this:

```
5  3
```

IIB   Using Objects

An m by n matrix is a doubly subscripted array of numeric values stored in m rows and n columns. The sum of two matrices a and b stored into matrix c is defined as follows:

```
c[j][k] = a[j][k] + b[j][k]  for j ranging from 1 to m and k ranging from 1 to n
```

Write a program that initializes two array2 objects named a and b through file extraction. The sum of the two matrices must be stored into an array2 object named c, which must then be displayed to the screen. Since a and b must have the same number of rows and columns, the first line of the input file will be used to specify the number of rows followed by the number of columns.

• First create the following input file:

```
3  4

1    2    3    4
5    6    7    8
9   10   11   12

-1    2    0    0
 3    0   -1    3
 3    2    1    0
```

- Then complete the code to generate output like this:

```
matrix a:
  1   2   3   4
  5   6   7   8
  9  10  11  12

matrix b:
 -1   2   0   0
  3   0  -1   3
  3   2   1   0

matrix c: (a + b)
  0   4   3   4
  8   6   6  11
 12  12  12  12
```

11C   Using Objects

Write a complete program that initializes an array2 object through file extraction. The row and column size are located as the first two ints in the file. The maximum size of the array2 object cannot exceed 20 rows by 20 columns. The output should include the entire array with the highest and lowest written to the right of each row. A sample input file is shown with the output that should be generated.

- First create the following input file:

```
3 5
11  53   6  -1   5
21  34   6  12   0
31  91   3 -12  55
```

- Then complete the code to generate output that appears as close to the following as possible (assuming you use the previous input file):

```
    Col# 1    2    3    4    5    Hi    Lo
Row#  -----------------------    --    --
  1|   11   53    6   -1    5    53    -1
  2|   21   34    6   12    0    34     0
  3|   31   91    3  -12   55    91   -12
```

I I D   Implementing a Class

A magic square is an n by n array where the integers 1 to n² appear exactly once, and the sum of the integers in every row, column, and on both diagonals is the same. For example, the following magic square results when n = 7. Notice that each row, column, and both diagonals total 175:

30	39	48	1	10	19	28
38	47	7	9	18	27	29
46	6	8	17	26	35	37
5	14	16	25	34	36	45
13	15	24	33	42	44	4
21	23	32	41	43	3	12
22	31	40	49	2	11	20

Implement class square with two member functions: a constructor and display. The following code should generate output like that shown above:

```
square magic(7);
magic.display();
```

You should be able to construct an n by n magic square for any odd value n from 1 to 15. When j is 1, place the value of j in the middle of the first row. Then, for a counter value ranging from 1 to n², move up one row and to the right by one column and store the counter value unless one of the following events occurs:

1. When the next row becomes 0, make the next row equal to n (this assumes you used 1 for the first row).
2. When the next column becomes n+1, make the next column equal to 1 (this assumes you used 1 for the first column).
3. If a position is already filled, or the upper right corner element has just obtained a value, place the next counter value in the position that is one row below the position where the last counter value had been placed.

11E   Modifying a Class

After implementing the magicSquare class, add a test member function to verify the sums of all the rows, columns, and both diagonals to ensure that each sum is the same. When n= 7, the output generated by square.test() should look like this (assuming 1 is first row and column):

```
Sum of row 1 = 175
Sum of row 2 = 175
Sum of row 3 = 175
Sum of row 4 = 175
Sum of row 5 = 175
Sum of row 6 = 175
Sum of row 7 = 175

Sum of col 1 = 175
Sum of col 2 = 175
Sum of col 3 = 175
Sum of col 4 = 175
Sum of col 5 = 175
Sum of col 6 = 175
Sum of col 7 = 175

Sum of diagonal one = 175

Sum of diagonal two = 175
```

11.3 Case Study: Visibility Study Report

A research study by the Electric Power Research Institute (EPRI) was conducted to investigate factors contributing to decreasing visibility in pristine and near-pristine areas. A large amount of data was collected for the following reasons:

- To help determine why we can't see as far as was once possible.
- To establish measurement techniques for environmental impact studies.
- To establish baseline data for future comparisons of visibility.

The data included human-observed estimates of visibility that were compared to nephelometer (an instrument that measures light refraction in a closed unit) and teleradiometer (an instrument that measures radiance generated by far-off targets) electronic visibility estimates collected at the same time. Human-observed visibility measurements for one day were also recorded:

One-Day Human Estimates of Visibility in Three Directions

```
          8:00   9:00  10:00  11:00  12:00  13:00  14:00  15:00
Path +-------------------------------------------------------
   1 |   40.0   35.0   38.0   40.0   40.0   40.0   35.0   35.0
   2 |    2.5   15.0   23.0   50.0   50.0   65.0   65.0   50.0
   3 |   52.0   60.0   35.0   35.0   20.0   60.0   60.0   60.0
```

Every hour on the hour, from 8:00 a.m. to 3:00 p.m., a site technician used known targets such as ridges and mountains in the distance to estimate visibility. There were three paths numbered 1, 2, and 3. The estimates of visibility by the site technician were recorded to the nearest tenth of a mile for distances less than 4 miles and were rounded to the nearest mile for distances greater than 4 miles. With this background, a report is now described that produces statistics for one day's worth of human-observed estimates of visibility.

11.3.1 Analysis

Problem: *Using data such as those shown above, produce a report of human-observed visibility. The visibility report should display the input in a manner similar to the one above. The following four statistics should be repeated for each path and for the day:*

1. Farthest estimate of visibility
2. Shortest estimate of visibility
3. Range of visibility (range = farthest – shortest)
4. Average of the visibility estimates

The visibility report should look like the following (with question marks replacing the correct output):

```
17-JUNE-81
SITE 2
ESTIMATES OF HUMAN-OBSERVED VISIBILITY

          8:00   9:00  10:00  11:00  12:00  13:00  14:00  15:00
       +-------------------------------------------------------
Path 1 |   40.0   35.0   38.0   40.0   40.0   40.0   35.0   35.0
     2 |    2.5   15.0   23.0   50.0   50.0   65.0   65.0   50.0
     3 |   52.0   60.0   35.0   35.0   20.0   60.0   60.0   60.0

          Farthest    Shortest     Range    Average
          ========    ========     =====    =======
Path 1      40.0        35.0        5.0       43.3
Path 2      ??.?        ??.?        ??.?      ??.?
Path 3      ??.?        ??.?        ??.?      ??.?
   Day      60.0         2.5       57.5       ??.?
```

The input comes from a file named as site# + h (for human-observed) + Day + Month + Year + . + dat. For example, the data for site# 2's human-observed estimates of visibility for the seventeenth of June, 1981 are stored in the file 2h170681.dat.

```
2 17-JUNE-81
  40.0   35.0   38.0   40.0   40.0   40.0   35.0   35.0
   2.5   15.0   23.0   50.0   50.0   65.0   65.0   50.0
  52.0   60.0   35.0   35.0   20.0   60.0   60.0   60.0
```

The data in this file are shown differently from the actual raw data. This is done to keep input simple and avoid more details in the study. In reality, there was much more data for each day such as electronic measurements, hourly anemometer (wind speed and direction) readings, and the potential for a large number of codes to describe anomalous conditions such as snow on the mountain and dark clouds behind.

11.3.2 Design: Component Reuse

Nine sites were involved in this study, each site collecting hundreds of data items per day over a two-year period. But the problem statement reduces this huge database to a report on one day's human-observed visibility captured in a file with a meaningful name. Performing a complete analysis of all data at all nine sites requires a much larger view of this narrowed case study. To accomplish a larger scale problem we might need the ability to

- Find the range of visibility in the western United States on any given day by comparing all nine sites.
- Compute average visibilities at any site when the humidity was less than 20% (or greater than 80%).
- Compare human-observed estimates to teleradiometer estimates at any particular time of day, or on any path, or at all sites.

plus many, many other views of the data, including some operations that have not been anticipated. This is quite complex, but reusing other software such as an object-oriented database management system (OODBMS) would reduce the complexity of the system while saving money. Also, we would be starting with a fairly well-tested and debugged system—another advantage of software reuse. A scaled-down version of software *reuse* helps us with our scaled-down problem.

But which software components *can* we reuse? We could, for instance, reuse any objects identified in the vocabulary of the problem statement. We notice data is stored in a file and we need to extract that input. So once again, having the file stream class saves us a lot of work. We can use an ifstream object named inFile. We avoid much work that would otherwise be necessary to implement extraction and insertion operations that handle input and output for a large variety of systems. The stream classes were implemented with reuse in mind. Both manage the built-in classes. The stream classes are also capable of managing objects of programmer-defined classes that have not even been implemented. The `array2` class was also designed for reuse.

Visualize a `site` object with a `reportHOV` member function that takes a file name as an argument. This external file contains the site number and date on the first line followed by three rows of the human-observed estimates of visibility (eight valid numeric data per line). These data are extracted from the file stream and stored into an `array2` object. With an initialized doubly subscripted array, we have the ability to manage the data in a variety of ways. We can produce a report, determine statistics for each path, for each hour, and/or for the entire day. To do this, we must also maintain the number of paths (`rows`) and observations (`cols`) as part of each class object. The member functions and data members of the `site` class can now be summarized as follows:

Member Functions of Class site	*Data Members of Class site*
`reportHOV(string fileName)`	An `array2` object which knows its own number of initialized rows and columns

11.3.3 Implementation

Although the complete implementation of the `site` class is left as a lab project at the end of the chapter, the file provided on disk is shown here to indicate how a `site` class might appear. Each `site` object has an `array2` object named `vis` (no arguments) of the default row and column dimensions, which for our purposes are more than large enough.

```
// File name: mysite.h
// Required file in the working directory: 2h170681.dat
//
// This file contains a partially implemented site class
// and a main function as a short test driver. With all
// necessary data encapsulated in every site object,
// the two-dimensional array processing is self-contained.

#include <fstream.h>    // for class ifstream
#include "arrays.h"     // for class array2
#include "ourstr.h"     // for class string
#include "ourstuff.h"   // for decimals(cout, 2);

class site {
public:
  void site::reportHOV(string fileName);

private:
  array2 <double> vis; // This gives us a large enough array2 object
};
```

```
void site::reportHOV(string fileName)
{ // PRE: fileName represents a file in the working directory
  //
  // Note, string::chars() is a new function. fileName.chars()
  // returns the string literal of the string object.  The argument
  // to the ifstream constructor cannot be a string object. It must
  // be an object that we have not yet discussed (see Chapter 10).
  ifstream inFile(fileName.chars());
  if(! inFile)
  {
    cout << "**Error opening input file '"
         << fileName.chars() << "' " << endl;
  }

  // If the file is not opened, the report is meaningless
  int nRows = 3;
  int nCols = 8;
  int siteNumber;
  string date;
  inFile >> siteNumber;
  inFile >> date;
  // Incomplete: Now extract the data from inFile.
  // Note: the doubly subscripted array name is vis
  // -->
  // -->
  // -->

  decimals(cout, 1);
  clearScreen();
  cout << "Site #" << siteNumber << endl;
  cout << date << endl;
  cout << "ESTIMATES OF HUMAN-OBSERVED VISIBILITY" << endl
       << endl;
  cout << "        8:00  9:00 10:00 11:00 12:00 13:00 14:00 15:00"
       << endl;
  cout << "Path +------------------------------------------------+"
       << endl;
  // Incomplete: Now display the table, use 6 columns
  // for each human estimate of visibility.
  // -->
  // -->
  // -->

  // Incomplete: Now compute and output statistics for one day:
  // -->
  // -->
  // -->
}
```

Modifying and testing this class is discussed in the associated lab project.

Programming Tip

The `array2` data member of class `site` is declared without arguments because most systems simply do not allow arguments to exist in the class declaration. This awkward constraint led to a decision to allow `array2` objects with no arguments. For these declarations the default constructor is called. In cases such as this, the default subscript bounds are in effect. Row and column subscripts are limited to 0 through 19.

Self-Check

1. Name two classes that you have reused to this point.
2. The farthest, shortest, range, and average statistics for paths 1, 2, and 3 are an example of row by row or column by column processing?

Answers
1. Possible answers include `ostream`, `istream`, `ifstream`, `string`, `array1`, `array2`
2. row by row

11.4 C++ Arrays with Two Subscripts

The previous concepts of row by row and column by column processing also apply to primitive C++ arrays declared with two subscripts. However, there are a few differences between our `array2` class and a doubly subscripted C++ array that uses the first subscript to declare the maximum number of rows rather than the row subscript range. The second subscript in a C++ array declaration represents the maximum number of columns rather than the column subscript range. The reason that primitive C arrays cannot be declared to specify subscript ranges is because they also have a default subscript of 0 for the first row and a default subscript of 0 for the first column. So a C++ array declared with two subscripts has `int` expressions that specify the *number* of rows and columns. For example, x is declared here to store 10 rows and 5 columns of data for a total of 50 `floats`:

```
float x[10][5];   // Row subscripts = 0..9 and column subscripts = 0..4
```

The other important difference is that the C++ array has no subscript range checking for either the row or the column. The following is a comparison of the `array2` class to the primitive C++ array declared with two subscripts.

	The array2 class declared in "arrays.h"	*Doubly subscripted C++ array*
General Form	`array2` < *class-name* > *identifier* (*firstRow, lastRow, firstCol, lastCol*);	*class-name identifier* [*# rows*] [*# columns*];
Example	`array2<int> unitsSold(0, 8, 0, 11);`	`int unitsSold[9][12];`
Range Checking	Yes	No
First Row	Any `int`	0
Last Row	Any `int` >= First Row	*# rows* − 1
First Column	Any `int`	0
Last Column	Any `int` >= First Column	*# columns* − 1
Required `#include`	`#include "arrays.h"`	no include required

The `array2` object `unitsSold` manages 9 rows and 12 columns of `int`s (108 elements altogether). The equivalent primitive C++ array of the same name (declared in the right column above) manages the same number of `int`s with the same subscript range but does not perform subscript range checking. The `array2` class was purposely designed to be used in the same manner as primitive doubly subscripted C arrays. This was possible through overloaded subscript operators and flexibility with subscript ranges so `array2` objects could be declared with any `int` subscript including 0 as the first row and first column. Now, using either the primitive C++ array or the `array2` class, individual array elements are referenced in the same manner. Subscripts can be made to start at 0. This means that the following code may be used with either an `array2` object or a doubly subscripted C++ array:

```
int r, c;
for(r = 0; r < 8; r++)
{
  for(c = 0; c < 12; c++)
    unitsSold[r][c] = r + c;
}
```

If you prefer to count from row 1 column 1, you desire more meaningful subscripts, or you want the safety of subscript range checking, use the `array2` object rather than the primitive C++ array with two subscripts. On the other hand, if your compiler does not have templates, you can use the same algorithms discussed earlier.

11.4.1 Arrays with More Than Two Subscripts

Singly and doubly subscripted arrays occur more frequently than do arrays with more than two subscripts. However, arrays with three and even more subscripts are sometimes useful. Triply subscripted arrays are possible because C++ does not limit the number of subscripts. For example, the declaration

```
float q[3][11][6]
```

could represent the quiz grades for three courses, since 198 (3 x 11 x 6) grades can be stored under the same name (q). This triply subscripted object

```
q[1][9][3]
```

is a reference to quiz index 3 of student index 9 in course index 1. In the following program, an array with three subscripts is initialized (with meaningless data). The first subscript—representing a course—changes the slowest. So the array object q is initialized and then displayed in a course-by-course order.

```
// Declare, initialize and display a triply subscripted array
// object. The primitive C subscripted object is used here, but
// we could also use an array of array2 objects to do the same thing.

#include <iostream.h>

int main()
{
  const int courses = 3;
  const int students = 11;
  const int quizzes = 6;
  int q[courses][students][quizzes];

  int c, row, col;

  for(c = 0; c < courses; c++)
    for(row = 0; row < students; row++)
      for(col = 0; col < quizzes; col++)
        // Give each quiz a value using a meaningless formula
        q[c][col][row] = (col+1) * (row+2) + c + 25;

  for(c = 0; c < courses; c++)
  {
    cout << endl;
    cout << "Course #" << c << endl;
    for(row = 0; row < students; row++)
    {
      for(col = 0; col < quizzes; col++)
      {
        cout.width(5);
        cout << q[c][col][row];
      }
      cout << endl;
    }
  }
  return 0;
}
```

```
─────────────────────── Output ───────────────────────
Course #0
    27    33    41    49    57    65
    28    34    43    52    61    70
    29    35    45    55    65    75
    30    36    47    58    69    80
    31    37    49    61    73    85
    32    39    46    53    60    67
    33    41    49    57    65    73
    34    43    52    61    70    79
    35    45    55    65    75    85
    36    47    58    69    80    91
    37    49    61    73    85    97

Course #1
    28    34    42    50    58    66
    29    35    44    53    62    71
    30    36    46    56    66    76
    31    37    48    59    70    81
    32    38    50    62    74    86
    33    40    47    54    61    68
    34    42    50    58    66    74
    35    44    53    62    71    80
    36    46    56    66    76    86
    37    48    59    70    81    92
    38    50    62    74    86    98

Course #2
    29    35    43    51    59    67
    30    36    45    54    63    72
    31    37    47    57    67    77
    32    38    49    60    71    82
    33    39    51    63    75    87
    34    41    48    55    62    69
    35    43    51    59    67    75
    36    45    54    63    72    81
    37    47    57    67    77    87
    38    49    60    71    82    93
    39    51    63    75    87    99
```

The table below provides another view of the object declaration. The first subscript is the same for each course. For example, every quiz for course #0 has 0 as the first subscript. The second and third subscripts represent the student (row) and quiz (column), respectively.

An Array with Three Subscripts

		Course #2					
		q[2,0,0]	q[2,0,1]	q[2,0,2]	q[2,0,3]	q[2,0,4]	q[2,0,5]
	Course #1	q[2,1,0]	q[2,1,1]	q[2,1,2]	q[2,1,3]	q[2,1,4]	q[2,1,5]
	q[1,0,0]	q[1,0,1]	q[1,0,2]	q[1,0,3]	q[1,0,4]	q[1,0,5]	q[2,2,5]
Course #0	q[0,1,0]	q[1,1,1]	q[1,1,2]	q[1,1,3]	q[1,1,4]	q[1,1,5]	q[2,3,5]
q[0,0,0]	q[0,0,1]	q[0,0,2]	q[0,0,3]	q[0,0,4]	q[0,0,5]	q[1,2,5]	q[2,4,5]
q[0,1,0]	q[0,1,1]	q[0,1,2]	q[0,1,3]	q[0,1,4]	q[0,1,5]	q[1,3,5]	q[2,5,5]
q[0,2,0]	q[0,2,1]	q[0,2,2]	q[0,2,3]	q[0,2,4]	q[0,2,5]	q[1,4,5]	q[2,6,5]
q[0,3,0]	q[0,3,1]	q[0,3,2]	q[0,3,3]	q[0,3,4]	q[0,3,5]	q[1,5,5]	q[2,7,5]
q[0,4,0]	q[0,4,1]	q[0,4,2]	q[0,4,3]	q[0,4,4]	q[0,4,5]	q[1,6,5]	q[2,8,5]
q[0,5,0]	q[0,5,1]	q[0,5,2]	q[0,5,3]	q[0,5,4]	q[0,5,5]	q[1,7,5]	q[2,9,5]
q[0,6,0]	q[0,6,1]	q[0,6,2]	q[0,6,3]	q[0,6,4]	q[0,6,5]	q[1,8,5]	q[2,10,5]
q[0,7,0]	q[0,7,1]	q[0,7,2]	q[0,7,3]	q[0,7,4]	q[0,7,5]	q[1,9,5]	
q[0,8,0]	q[0,8,1]	q[0,8,2]	q[0,8,3]	q[0,8,4]	q[0,8,5]	q[1,10,5]	
q[0,9,0]	q[0,9,1]	q[0,9,2]	q[0,9,3]	q[0,9,4]	q[0,9,5]		
q[0,10,0]	q[0,10,1]	q[0,10,2]	q[0,10,3]	q[0,10,4]	q[0,10,5]		

The array1 and array2 classes were designed to manage collections with either one or two subscripts, with this overriding consideration: Because some compilers do not have templates, the array1 and array2 classes were designed to mimic primitive C++ arrays with one or two subscripts, respectively. You can use the same algorithms to perform doubly subscripted array processing. Only the declarations differ.

This makes the transfer of knowledge concerning array1 and array2 object usage and their C++ array counterparts interchangeable.

Self-Check

Use these declarations to answer the questions that follow

```
int a[3][4];
array2<int> b(1, 3, 1, 4);
array2<string> names;
```

1. Which object has the row subscript begin at 1, a or b?
2. Which object has range checking, a or b?
3. How many int elements are properly managed by a?
4. How many int elements are properly managed by b?

5. How many `string` elements are managed by `names`?
6. What is the row (first) subscript range for `names`?
7. What is the column (second) subscript range for `names`?
8. Write code to initialize all elements of `b` to 999.
9. Write code to display all rows of `b` on separate lines with 8 spaces for each element.

Use this declaration to answer the questions that follow:

```
int x[3][4][5];
```

10. How many elements are properly stored under the array `x`?
11. Which of the following references to `x` can be properly used as the object to the left of an assignment operator?

    a. `x[0][0][0]`   d. `x[3][4][5]`

    b. `x[1][2][3]`   e. `x[2][2][2]`

    c. `x[-1][0][1]`   f. `x[3]`

Answers

1. b   2. b   3. 12   4. 12
5. 400 (Default size is 20 rows by 20 columns)
6. 0 through 19
7. 0 through 19
8.
```
for(row = 1; row <=3; row++)
   for(col = 1; col <= 4; col++)
      b[row][col] = 999;
```
9.
```
for(row = 1; row <=3; row++)
{
   for(col = 1; col <= 4; col++)
   {
      cout.width(8);
      cout << b[row][col];
   }
}
```
10. 60
11. a, b, e (Note: c and d may not cause compiletime errors but may cause runtime errors, therefore, c and d can not be considered to be proper usage.)

Chapter Summary

The new concept introduced in this chapter was an `array2` class replete with row- processing algorithms written in C++ code. The `array2` class is similar to the C++ array declared with `[ ][ ]` but the `array2<Type>` class offers subscript range checking and greater flexibility with the lower and upper bounds for the rows and columns. Whereas the C++ array puts the onus of subscript range checking on the user, the `array2<Type>`

class has a safety net that terminates the program if the user is not careful. There are advantages and disadvantages to both classes.

Some of the new ideas presented with the `array2` class include:

- A doubly subscripted array manages data that is logically organized in a tabular format—that is, in rows and columns.
- The first subscript of a doubly subscripted array specifies the row of data in a table; the second represents the column.
- The elements stored in an `array2` object can be processed row by row, column by column, or by rows and columns.
- `for` loops are commonly used to process arrays. In the case of a doubly subscripted array being processed row by row, the outer loop usually increments the row index and the inner loop usually increments the column index.

The `array2` classes were designed to mimic C++ array usage with the additional subscript range checking feature. Only the declaration is different. Individual elements in both classes are referenced with two consecutive subscript operators.

Exercises

5. For each doubly subscripted array declaration below, determine
   a. the total number of elements.
   b. the first row subscript.
   c. if range checking will be performed to assure the subscripts are in bounds.

   ```
   array2<double> x(1, 5, 1, 10);      array2<string> teacher(1, 40, 1, 6);
   double budget[6][1000];             int y[12][20];
   array2<int> test(1, 1, 1, 1);       string children[100][9];
   ```

6. Detect the error(s) in the following attempts to declare a doubly subscripted array:
   a. `int x(5,6);`
   b. `double x[5,6];`
   c. `array2 <int> x[1, 5, 1, 6];`
   d. `array2 <int> x(5, 6);`

7. Using the `array2` class, declare a doubly subscripted object identified as a matrix with three rows and four columns of `float` elements.

8. Write the C++ code to accomplish the following tasks:
   a. Declare an `array2` object called `aTable` that stores 10 rows and 14 columns of `float` elements.
   b. Set every element in `aTable` to 0.0.
   c. Write a `for` loop that sets all elements in row 4 to -1.0.

9. Show the output from the following program when the input is

   a. 2 3   d. 1 1
   b. 3 2   e. 1 2
   c. 4 4   f. 2 1

```
#include "arrays.h"
#include <iostream.h>
int main()
{
  int maxRow, maxCol;
  cout << " # rows? ";
  cin >> maxRow;
  cout << " # cols? ";
  cin >> maxCol;
  array2<int> aTable(1, maxRow, 1, maxCol);
  int row, col;

  // Initialize array2 elements
  for(row = 1; row <= maxRow; row++)
  {
    for(col = 1; col <= maxCol; col++)
      aTable[row][col] = row * col;
  }

  // Display table elements
  for(row = 1; row <= maxRow; row++)
  {
    for(col = 1; col <= maxCol; col++)
    {
      cout.width(5);
      cout << aTable[row][col];
    }
    cout << endl;
  }
}
```

10. Using this code

```
#include "arrays.h"    // for class array2
int main()
{
  int r, c, rows=10, cols=5;
  array2<int> t(1, rows, 1, cols);
  // Assume all 50 elements of t are initialized
```

and assuming all elements of t have been properly initialized, write code that displays the range of elements (highest–lowest) in each row on its own separate line.

Lab Projects

11F   Implementing and Modifying a Class

Complete class site that was begun in the case study of this chapter. Make the report appear as shown there. First create a test oracle so you can test class site independently with a calculator or by hand. The high, low, and range for each path and for the day are easily determined by inspecting the input file. You can create these files from the case study or use the following files on the disk that accompanies this textbook:

```
mysite.h
2h170681.dat
```

Test your changes with the following main function:

```
#include "mysite.h"
int main()
{
  site two;
  two.reportHOV("2h170681.dat"); // File must be in working directory
  return 0;
}
```

11G   Modifying Classes

During the visibility study described in the case study, radiance measurements were made by an electronic instrument called a teleradiometer. Two measurements were taken—the radiance emitted by a mountain target, and the radiance emitted from the sky directly above the mountain target. The electronic estimate of visibility (visEst) is computed using this formula:

$$visEst = distance \times \frac{skyRad - tarRad}{1 + log(skyRad - tarRad)}$$

where

tarRad is the teleradiometer reading of the mountain target
skyRad is the radiance measurement of the sky above
distance is the distance to the mountain target:

1. Distance for Target 1 on Path 1 = 16 miles
2. Distance for Target 2 on Path 2 = 23 miles
3. Distance for Target 3 on Path 3 = 15 miles

For example, the electronic visibility estimate for Path 1 at 10:00 when `tarRad=203` and `skyRad=211` is evaluated as:

```
visEst = 16 * ( 211 - 203 ) / ( 1 + log( 211 - 203 ) )
         16 * 8 / ( 1 + log ( 8 ) )
         16 * 8 / ( 1 + 2.079441542 )
         16 * 8 / 3.079441542
         16 * 2.597873637
visEst = 41.565978190
```

The data for one day's radiance measurements are stored in a file shown next. Two consecutive integers determine the value of one `array2` element.

File name: 2r170681.dat

```
2 17-6-1981
 654 671 483 501 203 211 604 615 406 416 203 212 359 372 505 513
  45  43 107 108 230 230  44  49 105 114 127 140  43  49 101 109
 400 411 200 212 225 234 400 403 200 212 235 254 401 418 200 215
```

Two `ints` in a row represent one mountain-target and sky-reading pair. The first line of the file above represents target one, line 2 is the data collected for target 2, and line 3 is the data for target 3. For example, the fifth and sixth values of row one represent the target (203) and sky radiance measurements (211) for path 1 recorded at 10:00 (this produced an electronic estimate of 41.6 miles in the example above).

To class `site` add `site::reportRAD("file-name.dat")` such that it also reports the electronic estimates of visibility using the data file shown above. Given this program:

```
int main()
{
  site two;
  two.reportRAD("2r170681.dat"); // File must be in working directory
  return 0;
}
```

the output format should be similar to this (the question marks should be replaced with the correct visibility estimates):

```
17-06-81
SITE 2
ESTIMATES OF ELECTRONICALLY MEASURED VISIBILITY

              8:00   9:00 10:00 11:00 12:00 13:00 14:00 15:00
    Path    -----------------------------------------------
       1 |  ??.?  ??.?  41.6  ??.?  ??.?  ??.?  ??.?  ??.?
       2 |  ??.?  ??.?  ??.?  ??.?  ??.?  ??.?  ??.?  ??.?
       3 |  ??.?  ??.?  ??.?  ??.?  ??.?  ??.?  ??.?  ??.?
```

Make sure you avoid function calls to `log(x)` when `x <= 0.0`. The `log` function is undefined for values less than or equal to 0.0. If the sky radiance measurement is less than or equal to the target, set the visibility estimate to be the distance to the target. This should occur for the path 2 8:00 and 10:00 data.

I I H   Implementing a Class

Implement a `gradeBook` class. Design the file and the C++ class yourself. Responsibilities must include at least these:

1. Constructor to initialize an `array2` object from an external file. Declare the object in the private section of the class.
2. High, low, and average of any one student.
3. High, low, and average of any one quiz.
4. Overall high, low, and average.

- Create the input data file.
- Implement the `gradeBook` class with at least the constructor to initialize the `array2` object.
- Declare the class in a file named `mygrade.h`.
- Implement class `gradeBook` in a file named `mygrade.cpp`.
- Include the dot cpp file at the end of your dot h file.
- Test your class with this code's functions:

```cpp
#include "mygrade.h"
#include "ourstuff.h"
#include <iomanip.h>

int main()
{
  gradeBook  fall;
  decimals(cout, 1);
  // Show statistics for student #1
  cout << "Student   Hi   Lo   Ave" << endl;
```

```
    cout << setw(8) << 1;
    cout << setw(6) << fall.studentHi(1);
    cout << setw(6) << fall.studentLo(1);
    cout << setw(6) << fall.studentAve(1) << endl;
    // Show statistics for quiz #2
    cout << "  Quiz   Hi   Lo   Ave" << endl;
    cout << setw(8) << 2;
    cout << setw(6) << fall.quizHi(2);
    cout << setw(6) << fall.quizLo(2);
    cout << setw(6) << fall.quizAve(2) << endl;

    cout << "Overall highest grade: " << fall.highest() << endl;
    cout << "Overall  lowest grade: " << fall.lowhest() << endl;
    cout << "Overall average grade: " << fall.average() << endl;
}
```

11   Implementing a Class

The Game of Life was invented by John H. Conway to simulate the birth and death of cells in a society. The following rules govern the birth and/or death of these cells between two consecutive time periods of the society. At time T:

1. A cell is born if there was none at time T–1, and exactly 3 of its neighbors were alive.
2. An existing cell remains alive if at time T–1 there were either 2 or 3 neighbors.
3. A cell will die from isolation if at time T–1 there were fewer than 2 neighbors.
4. A cell will die from overcrowding if at time T–1 there were more than 3 neighbors.

A neighborhood consists of the 8 elements around any other element:

```
                    O O O
                    O   O
                    O O O
```

The following patterns would occur for T=1 to 5, if the first society was that shown for T=1. O represents a live cell; a blank indicates that no cell exists at the particular location in the society.

```
    T=0     T=1     T=2     T=3     T=4

    O O     O O
    OOO     O O     O O      O                // Society dies off at T=4
             O       O       O
```

Other societies stabilize like this:

```
T=0     T=1     T=2     T=3     T=4

        O               O
000     O      000      O      000     // This pattern repeats
        O               O
```

Implement a class named gameOfLife that works with the following driver:

```cpp
int main()
{
  gameOfLife myGame("society1.dat");
  do {
   society.display();
   society.update();
  } while(! society.done());
}
```

Here are some suggestions:

1. Use a three-dimensional C++ array to represent two consecutive societies. The first subscript is either 0 or 1 to represent changing societies. This array is given next in the context of a class declaration:

```cpp
const int LASTROW = 22;
const int LASTCOL = 72;

class gameOfLife {
public:
   gameOfLife::gameOfLife(string fileName);
   // POST: The 3-d array is initialized ignoring row 0 and 23
   //       and column 0 and 71. Cells exist only in rows 1..22
   //       and columns 1..72. First all cells = ' ', then certain
   //       cells are set to 'O' based on the input file specified
   //       as filename.theChars(). Here is an example file
   //                      O
   //                      000
   //                      000
   //                      O

   void display();
   // POST: The current society is displayed
```

```
    void update();
    // POST: Change to the next society (the most difficult task)

    int done();
    // POST: Asks the user if he or she wants to quit and returns true
    //       when the user responds positively, or false otherwise.

  private:
    society[2][LASTROW+2][LASTCOL+2];
    // You may need some other data members or member functions.
    // ...
  };
```

2. Allow the user to view a society for as long as he or she wishes, but clear the
    screen between successive societies so the patterns can be observed. (*Hint:* Use
    clearScreen and causeApause from ourstuff.h.)
3. The input should consist of an initial society contained in an external file with
    no more than 72 columns and 22 lines (rows) where a live cell is represented by
    '0'.
4. Allow rows 0 and 23 along with columns 0 and 73 to be used as a border where
    no cell may be placed. The rules no longer apply once the border is in a neigh-
    borhood. When this occurs, display a meaningful message and terminate the
    program with exit(0) (from stdlib.h).
5. The input file(s) used to represent an initial society should include organisms
    around the middle of the available space.
6. Implement the constructor first, the display member function second, update
    as a do-nothing function third, and finally implement quit. Your program should
    display the same society until the user desires to quit. Once you get the bugs out
    of the non-changing society, concentrate on the update operation.

Appendices

Appendix A

Additional Lab Projects

5H   Modify a Class

In this lab, you are asked to modify a copy of the existing class bankAccount. To protect the original class bankAccount, you will be modifying an equivalent class called myBankAccount, which is declared and implemented in the file myacct.h. Objects of class myBankAccount currently allow negative withdrawals and deposits, and withdrawals greater than the available balance. In this lab, you are asked to disallow these transactions. Currently there are no preconditions stated, and without safeguards, withdraw(-100.00) subtracts -100.00 from the balance. This is like adding 100.00 when 100.00 should have been subtracted from the account balance—a difference of 200. Also, deposit(-100.00) reduces rather than increases the balance. Finally, withdrawal amounts greater than the balance are also allowed. You are asked to modify class myBankAccount and prevent these practices. The end result is similar functionality with some built-in safeguards. This relieves the programmer of some responsibility.

- First read the following program and predict the output.

```
#include <iostream.h>
#include "myacct.h"     // for class myBankAccount
#include "ourstuff.h"   // for decimals(cout, 2);

int main()
{
  myBankAccount anAcct("Hall", "1234", 100.00);
  decimals(cout, 2);
  cout << "          Initial balance: " << anAcct.balance() << endl;
  anAcct.withdraw(200.00);
  cout << " After withdrawing 200.00: " << anAcct.balance() << endl;
  anAcct.withdraw(-100.00);
  cout << "After withdrawing -100.00: " << anAcct.balance() << endl;
  anAcct.deposit(-50.00);
  cout << " After depositing -50.00: " << anAcct.balance() << endl;
  return 0;
}
```

- Create a new file and retype the preceding program into it.
- Save, compile, link, and run this program.
- Verify that your prediction was correct. If your handwritten results disagree, reread the program and make sure you made withdrawals of 200 and -100, and one deposit of -100.
- Place the file myacct.h into your editor (if this is not available, ask your instructor for the file).
- Modify the postconditions of the withdraw member function. This documentation should state that withdraw amounts less than 0 or greater than the customer's balance will not affect the balance.
- Modify the postconditions of the deposit member function. This documentation should state that deposit amounts less than 0 will not affect the balance.
- Save the specification file myacct.h.
- Load the implementation file myacct.cpp into your editor.
- Find the following implementation of the deposit member function (near line 21):

```
void myBankAccount::deposit(double amount)
{ // This allows negative deposits. Modify myBankAccount::deposit
  // so negative amounts have no affect on accountBalance.
  accountBalance = accountBalance + amount;
}
```

- Add selection control to prevent any negative amount from incrementing the accountBalance. If amount is less than 0.00, don't allow a change to accountBalance. Modify the comment to reflect the change.
- Find this implementation of myBankAccount::withdraw immediately below the deposit member function (near line 28):

```
void myBankAccount::withdraw(double amount)
{ // This allows overdrafts and negative withdrawals. Modify
  // myBankAccount::withdraw so negative amounts have no affect
  // on accountBalance. Also make sure withdrawals greater than
  // accountBalance are prevented.
  accountBalance = accountBalance - amount;
}
```

- Add selection control to prevent any negative amount from decrementing accountBalance. Also disallow a change to accountBalance if the withdrawal amount passed to this member function is greater than the accountBalance.
- Save the file myacct.cpp.

- Run your program with function `main` as shown earlier.
- Verify that improper transactions are not taking place by noting that the balance is unaffected.

The `withdraw` and `deposit` member functions of class `myBankAccount` are currently implemented as `void` member functions. They do not return a value. But such functions typically return `int`s to indicate failure or success of the operation. You are now asked to convert these two `void` member functions so that they may be used as a logical expression in an `if` or `if...else` statement such as this:

```
if(deposit(-100.00))
  cout << "deposit succeeded" << endl;
else
  cout << "deposit failed" << endl;
cout << " After depositing -100.00: " << anAcct.balance() << endl;
```

- Open `myacct.h` and convert the class declaration so that `myBankAccount::withdraw` and `myBankAccount::deposit` return `int` values (modify the function prototypes).
- Modify the postconditions of the class declaration to indicate that the function returns true or false. Explain why.
- Save the file.
- Edit the file `myacct.cpp`. Convert the member function implementations of `myBankAccount::withdraw` and `myBankAccount::deposit` to return an `int` (modify the function headers by changing the return type from `void` to `int`).
- Modify the bodies of these two member functions so that 1 is returned for nonnegative amounts and withdrawal values not greater than `accountBalance`. If an improper amount is passed to the function, return 0.
- Write a program to try all possible proper and improper arguments to both `withdraw` and `deposit`. Use `if...else` statements and a balance call to `myBankAccount::balance` as shown above. You should have five `if...else` statements, similar to the one above, to test for the following conditions:

1. negative deposit as shown above (this should fail)
2. negative withdrawal (this should fail)
3. positive withdrawal that is greater than the account balance (this should fail)
4. positive withdrawal that is less than or equal to the account balance (this should succeed)
5. positive deposit (this should succeed)

51   Modifying a Class

During this lab, you will be asked to update class `myWeeklyEmp` to reflect more recent United States tax laws. This class is declared in the file named `myemp.h` and implemented in the file `myemp.cpp`. It is similar to the `weeklyEmp` class. This allows free modification of class `myWeeklyEmp` without altering the original `weeklyEmp` class.

There have been several changes to the laws since the example shown earlier. The weekly allowance has increased, FICA (Social Security) tax was split into two separate taxes, and the tax tables have changed. Let's look at these changes one at a time and perform some maintenance.

51.1   Maintain WEEKLY_ALLOWANCE

After many years of no increase, each of the past several years has seen an increase in the annual allowance. The value of one annual withholding allowance was $1,000.00 per year for each person in a family. This tax deduction was increased to $2,350.00 in 1993. The value of the allowance to subtract from the gross wages depends on the payroll period. For employees paid once a year, the allowance is $2,350.00 per exemption. For employees paid on a monthly basis, it is $195.83. The weekly withholding allowance for each exemption is approximately 1/52 of the annual allowance or precisely $45.19. This value is maintained as the constant object `WEEKLY_ALLOWANCE` in the file `myemp.h`. Use the following instructions to update the weekly allowance.

- Load the specification file `myemp.h` into your editor.
- Go to line 13 (approximately) to find the line

  ```
  const double WEEKLY_ALLOWANCE = 39.42;
  ```

- Change `WEEKLY_ALLOWANCE` to `45.19`.

51.2   Maintain FICA_TAX_RATE

Recently, the FICA (Social Security) tax has been divided into two taxes—FICA and Medicare. Both taxes are a set percentage of the gross pay to total the previous percentage for FICA tax alone. This means we have one additional tax to add, one percentage to add, and another percentage to decrease. You are now asked to modify the FICA tax rate, add the Medicare tax rate, and add a member function prototype named `medicareTax`.

- Go to the constant object `FICA_TAX_RATE` (approximately line 15) and change the 7.65% tax rate to 6.2%. (*Note:* This reduction will be transferred to the `medicareTax` member function.)
- Immediately after the constant object `FICA_TAX_RATE`, add a new line and then add the constant object `MEDICARE_TAX_RATE` equal to 1.45%. You will be adding the `medicareTax` member function that uses this new constant object.

51.3   Declare the medicareTax() Member Function Prototype

- Go to line 42 (approximately) of `myemp.h` and you should see this line:

```
// Line 42: Write the medicareTax prototype and postcondition here
```

- Delete the comment at line 42 and add the `medicareTax();` function prototype (don't forget the semicolon) and the postcondition as shown here:

```
double myWeeklyEmp::medicareTax();
// POST: The Medicare tax is returned
```

- Save the file.
- Load the implementation file `myemp.cpp` into your editor.
- Go to line 105 (approximately) in the file "myemp.cpp" to find this line. It is near the end of the file.

```
// Line 105: add myWeeklyEmp::medicareTax() implementation here
```

- Delete this comment that starts with `// Line 105:`
- Implement a function that returns the `MEDICARE_TAX_RATE` * the employee's gross pay rounded to two decimal places. Make sure the function becomes a member of `myWeeklyEmp` by qualifying it with the scope resolution operator `::`, as shown here:

```
double myWeeklyEmp::medicareTax()
{
  return round (MEDICARE_TAX_RATE * grossPay(), 2);
}
```

- Save this file.

51.4   Maintaining the Tax Tables

The IRS tax tables have changed almost every year since 1986. The most recent tax tables in effect until the end of 1993 are reflected in the tables below. Update class `myWeeklyEmp` to reflect these changes.

- If necessary, reload the implementation file into your editor.
- Go to line 60 (approximately) to locate the `incomeTax` member function:

```
// Line 60: Modify this incomeTax member function
double myWeeklyEmp::incomeTax()
{
    double taxableIncome, tax = 0.0;

    taxableIncome = grossPay() - exemptions * WEEKLY_ALLOWANCE;

    if( single() //...
```

- The number of categories has been shrinking for some time. Most recently the number of tax categories changed from five to four. This is reflected in the difference between the tax table shown earlier and the one shown next. Using the table below, modify the incomeTax member function. *Note:* You will have to delete one of the categories from the file that you are modifying. This is true for both filing statuses.

```
              Tables for Percentage Method of Withholding
                        (For Wages Paid in 1993)

                        Table 1—Weekly Payroll Period

(a) SINGLE person--including head of household:    (b) MARRIED Person--

If the amount of wages                             If the amount of wages
(after subtracting       The amount of income tax  (after subtracting       The amount of income tax
withholding allowances) is:  to withhold is:       withholding allowances) is:  to withhold is:

Not over $49  . . . .     $0                        Not over $119 . . . .     $0

Over--   But not over--       of excess over--      Over--   But not over--       of excess over--
$49      --$451........ 15%            --$49         $119     --$784..........15%           --$119
$451     --$942........ $60.30  plus 28%  --$451     $784     --$1,563........$99.75  plus 28%  --$784
$942     ................. $197.78  plus 31%  --$942  $1563    ................. $317.87  plus 31%  --$1,563
```

- Once you have made all necessary changes, save the implementation file again.

51.5   Test the Maintenance

You are now asked to perform branch and boundary testing for both the single and married filing status by writing a program modeled after the earlier example that tested the older tax tables. That program used twelve myWeeklyEmp objects. We start with six single status taxpayers.

Note: Write down your answers to the numbered questions on a separate piece of paper.

1. Use the table above to determine the income tax to be withheld for each of the following adjusted wages. Assume that all employees have a single filing status and zero exemptions. Write down your answers for future use (label your answers with the letters a through f).

    a. 49   b. 50   c. 451   d. 452   e. 942   f. 943

- Create a new file and implement a program creating six `myWeeklyEmp` objects all working one hour but at the various rates of pay as shown above (a through f). For each employee, display the gross pay, income tax, and name. (*Hint:* Use the testing program from the Analysis, Design, and Implementation section in Chapter 5 as a model for your testing program.)

2. Does your output match your hand-calculated results written as your answer to the previous question?

- If your answer is no, recheck the hand-calculated results that do not match the program output. If they are correct, check your code for bugs. Do not continue until you have adequately tested the single taxpayers.

Now that you have tested the single taxpayer categories, perform branch and boundary testing for the married filing status.

3. Use the table above to determine the income tax to be withheld for each of the following adjusted wages. Assume that all employees have a married filing status and zero exemptions. Write down your answers for future use (label your answers with the letters g through l).

    g. 119   h. 120   i. 784   j. 785   k. 1563   l. 1564

- To your `main` function, add six `myWeeklyEmp` objects who all work one hour but at the rates of pay as shown above (g through l). For each employee, display the gross pay, income tax, and name.

4. Does your output match your hand-calculated results written as your answer to the previous question?

- If your answer is no, recheck the hand-calculated results that do not match the program output. If they are correct, check your code for bugs.
- Before quitting this lab project, make sure you have performed branch and boundary testing. Also make sure that employees with exemptions have the correct income tax calculation.

51.6   Write a Simple Payroll Program

• Write a payroll program that produces a simple paycheck for one myWeeklyEmp object. The program must input the employee's first name, last name, filing status ('S' or 'M'), number of exemptions, hourly rate of pay, and hours worked. Use this data and the concatenation feature of string to initialize an object in which the name is initialized as last name first, a comma, and the first name last. The paycheck should be formatted to always show currency amounts rounded to the nearest hundredth. The paycheck must include the employee's name, the gross pay, all taxes, and the net pay. Here is one sample dialogue and an example paycheck with headings:

```
      First Name: Steph
       Last Name: Walker
     Hourly Rate: 10.00
    Hours Worked: 40
      Exemptions: 2
S)ingle M)arried: M


      Employee: Steph Walker

  Gross  Income   FICA   Medic      Net
    Pay     Tax    Tax     Tax      Pay
  ======  ======  ======  ======  =======
  400.00   28.59   24.80    5.80   340.81
```

6F   Modifying a Class

In this lab project, you are asked to add a complete member function to the class myBankAccount declared in the file myacct.h. The function is to be implemented in the file myacct.cpp. You will be extracting a set of floats contained in a file to determine an average daily balance for the bank account. The member function is to be named myBankAccount::applyInterest(). It must apply the monthly interest to an average daily balance of the account and then add this interest to the current account balance.

• Add one private data member to class myBankAccount. Identify this float data member as annualInterestRate.

• Use the constructor to initialize this annualInterestRate to 6% (0.06). No extra arguments are necessary. Just initialize the data member annualInterestRate to the float constant 0.06.

• To myBankAccount, add a public member function called applyInterest. Type its void function prototype in the class declaration with no parameters. The interest should be applied with a call such as anAcct.applyInterest();.

- After the class declaration, completely implement myBankAccount::applyInterest, which pays a monthly interest rate on the average daily balance for the month. The following algorithm summarizes the behavior of the applyInterest member function. It is followed by some details intended to help in its implementation.

  1. Compute the average daily balance
  2. Calculate the monthly interest.
  3. Increment accountBalance by the interest earned for the month.

The monthly rate is the annual interest rate divided by the number of months in a year. The average daily balance requires knowledge of the balance for every single day in a month. We accomplish this by extracting data from a file containing 28, 29, 30, or 31 daily balances. A test file called balances.dat should be available. If it is not, create one that contains any 30 floats that appear to represent a bank account balance. Here is a refinement of the first step:

1. Compute the average daily balance
   a. Initialize inFile an object associated with the external file "balances.dat".
   b. Extract, sum, and count the all individual balances in the file.
   c. Set the average daily balance as the sum of the balances divided by the number of balances.

Adjust the balance by adding the interest determined by multiplying the average daily balance by annualInterestRate/12.0.

- Test your modifications with this program. The output depends on the value of the average daily balance.

```
#include "ourstuff.h"
#include "myacct.h"
int main()
{
  myBankAccount myAcct("ME", "1234", 1000.00);
  decimals(cout, 2);
  cout << myAcct.balance() << endl;
  myAcct.applyInterest();
  cout << myAcct.balance() << endl;
  return 0;
}
```

- Using a calculator, determine the average daily balance of all balances in the file.
- Determine the interest by multiplying the average daily balance by $0.06/12$.
- Verify that this interest is added to the account balance by comparing this result with program output.

6G   Modifying a Class

In this lab project, you are asked to enhance class `stats` to provide a wider array of statistics than currently exist. The `stats` constructor currently extracts a set of `float`s from a file and sets the private data member `n` to the size of the set. The size of the set is returned through the public function `stats::size()`. Other private data members and public member functions are implemented so you can concentrate on computing and storing a variety of statistics such as the largest. Other statistical measures on a set of data include the mean and measures of dispersion around the mean such as the variance and the standard deviation.

$$\text{a. Mean} = \frac{1}{n}\sum_{j=1}^{n} x_j$$

$$\text{b. Variance} = \frac{1}{n}\sum_{j=1}^{n} x_j^{\,2} - \frac{1}{n^2}\left(\sum_{j=1}^{n} x_j\right)^{\!2}$$

$$\text{c. Standard Deviation} = \sqrt{\text{Variance}}$$

In total, these statistics are accessible through public member functions. Without modification, all but one (`size`) return garbage:

Member Function	Description
int size()	The number of elements in the set of `float`s
float mean()	The average element
float high()	The largest element in the set
float low()	The smallest element
float variance()	The variance (see description below)
float standardDeviation()	The standard deviation (see description below)

All you have to do is compute and store the correct values into the correct private member data. The following steps are intended to help you modify class `stats`:

- First, create the following input file called `stats.dat` in your current working directory:

```
76   65   93  100   84
85  100   76   65   76
86   82   68   79   83
```
← The file `stats.dat`

- Make sure the files "`mystats.h`" and "`mystats.cpp`" are in your current working directory.

- Copy the following program and run it. You should notice most member functions return garbage (except `size`).

```
// Call all members of class stats
#include <iostream.h>
#include "mystats.h"        // for class stats

int main()
{
  stats tests;
  cout << "Statistics for a set of tests"    << endl;
  cout << "     Size: " << tests.size()       << endl;
  cout << "     Mean: " << tests.mean()       << endl;
  cout << "     High: " << tests.high()       << endl;
  cout << "      Low: " << tests.low()        << endl;
  cout << " Variance: " << tests.variance()  << endl;
  cout << "Stand Dev: " << tests.standardDeviation() << endl;
  return 0;
}
```

─────────── **Output** ───────────

Note: Except for the input data and size, most output is garbage.

```
Begin input data
        76       65     93     100      84      85     100      76
        65       76     86      82      68      79      83
End input data

Statistics for a set of tests
     Size: 15
     Mean: 2.349635e-32
     High: 391167.5625
      Low: 0
 Variance: 6.83896e-33
Stand Dev: 2.510205e-10
```

- Complete a test oracle for the given data. Currently, only `size` is correct (15).
- If you do *not* see any input data or you *do* see the following error message, make sure you have the `stats.dat` file stored in the correct directory.

```
    **Error opening file 'stats.dat'
```

- Open the file `mystats.h`. It begins like this (the first two compiler directives ensure the same file is not compiled twice)

```
//************************************************************
// SPECIFICATION FILE: mystats.h
// Declares: class stats
//
// stats is a class capable of reading data from a file while
// computing and storing several statistics which are accessible
// through member functions as summarized in the class definition.
//
// It is your job to store the correct values
// into the proper private data members.
//
//************************************************************/

#ifndef MYSTATS_H          // Avoid duplicate compilation
#define MYSTATS_H
#include <fstream.h>
#include <iostream.h>
```

- Locate the class definition, which includes all public member functions (these have been completely implemented later in the file but are not shown here):

```
class stats {
public:
        stats::stats();   // Constructor
  int   stats::size();
  float stats::mean();
  float stats::high();
  float stats::low();
  float stats::variance();
  float stats::standardDeviation();

private:
  int n;        // Returned by stats::size()
  float ave;    // Returned by stats::mean()
  float hi;     // Returned by stats::high()
  float lo;     // Returned by stats::low()
  float var;    // Returned by stats::variance()
  float sd;     // Returned by stats::standardDeviation()
};
```

- Peruse the definition and the comments indicating stats::size returns n and ave is returned by stats::mean.
- Close the declaration file and open the implementation file named "mystats.cpp".
- Locate the following constructor, which generated the output shown earlier and sets n to its proper value so it can be returned by stats::size:

```
stats::stats()
{ // This constructor extracts data from an input file and sets n as
  // the size. Each float is displayed to verify input is occurring.
  ifstream inFile("stats.dat");
  if(!inFile)
    cout << "**Error opening file 'stats.dat'" << endl;
  else
  {

    n = 0;
    float x;
    cout << endl << "Begin input data" << endl << endl;
    while( (inFile >> x) !=0 )
    {
      n = n + 1;

      // Display each float, up to eight per line.
      cout.width(8);
      cout << x;
      if (n % 8 == 0)  // Output a newline for every 8 floats
        cout << endl;
    }
   cout << endl << endl << "End input data" << endl;
  }
}
```

- Now modify the constructor such that ave, hi, lo, var, and sd are correctly computed and initialized. You may need to declare some local objects inside the constructor, but remember that all member functions have access to all private data members. In this class, n, ave, hi, lo, var, and sd are accessible and need not be redeclared. In fact, they must not be redeclared locally in the constructor.
- If you have not already done so, complete your test oracle based on the data shown in the file above.
- Run the preceding test program and compare your result to the test oracle.
- If necessary, debug your modifications to class stats.

6N   Using Objects

Implement a program that displays the shape of a diamond. The user must input the height of the diamond where height is the total number of rows displayed (and the number of characters in the middle row). The height must be an odd integer in the range of 1..23. The dialogue should look like this:

```
Enter the height as an odd integer from 1 to 23: 6
**Error - Height entered is even.
Enter the height as an odd integer from 1 to 23: 24
**Error - Height is out of range.
Enter the height as an odd integer from 1 to 23: 7

    #
   ###
  #####
 #######
  #####
   ###
    #
```

As you will see, the division of this problem is a simple example of *top-down design*—a form of divide and conquer. Top-down design involves the decomposition of a problem into smaller, more manageable subproblems. The idea is that several subproblems are more easily managed than one large problem. In even larger problems, each subproblem may also in turn be decomposed into other subproblems. On multiperson programming projects, one or more subproblems may be assigned to one individual programmer or to a team of programmers.

This problem and the resulting program pale in comparison to programs requiring 10,000 to over one million lines of code or others with hundreds of classes and thousands of member functions. But for those of us new to loops and programming, by dividing this problem into the smaller subproblems, we derive the benefits of reduced complexity and increased manageability. The top-down design approach encourages us to recognize problems as collections of smaller problems. In this case, there are four.

The following main function is supplied to preview the implementation as a solution in phases. It recognizes the four problems summarized by the function names getSize, top, middle, and bottom.

```cpp
int main()
{
  int size;
  getSize(size); // Get an odd size from 1 to 77
  top(size);     // Display the top portion of the diamond
  middle(size);  // Display the middle portion of the diamond
  bottom(size);  // Display the bottom portion of the diamond
  return 0;
}
```

You will be asked to implement your solution in four phases where each phase is accomplished by the completion of four void functions:

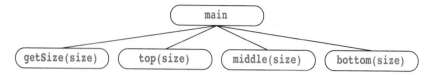

6N.1   Diamond: Phase One

Begin by obtaining the height and displaying its value. Implement this as function getSize with a reference. Be sure you show the error message when the height is either out-of-range or even. Use this main function to test getSize:

```
int main()
{
  int size;
  getSize(size);
  cout << "You entered: " << size;
  return 0;
}

  Enter the height as an odd integer from 1 to 23: 6
  **Error - Height entered is even.
  Enter the height as an odd integer from 1 to 23: 24
  **Error - Height is out of range.
  Enter the height as an odd integer from 1 to 23: 7
  You entered: 7
```

Do not proceed until getSize is tested!

6N.2   Diamond: Phase Two

Implement function middle so it displays the middle row of the diamond. Use size as an argument to middle. Test middle with the following program using 7 as input:

```
int main()
{
  int size;
  getSize(size);
  middle(size);
  return 0;
}

  Enter the height as an odd integer from 1 to 23: 7
  #######
```

Do not proceed until middle is tested!

6N.3   Diamond: Phase Three

Implement function top so it displays the top portion of the diamond. Use size as an argument to top. Notice that each new line has two extra characters displayed. Do not try to get the spacing on the left that makes the diamond. For now, let the output show a triangle instead. You will be asked to correct this later. Test top with the following program using 7 as input:

```
int main()
{
  int size;
  getSize(size);
  top(size);
  middle(size);
  return 0;
}

Enter the height as an odd integer from 1 to 23: 7
#
###
#####
#######
```

Do not proceed until top is tested!

6N.4   Diamond: Phase Four

Implement function bottom so it displays the bottom portion of the diamond. Use size as an argument to bottom. Do not try to get the spacing on the left that makes the diamond. For now, let the output show a triangle instead. You will be asked to correct this later. Test bottom with the following program:

```
int main()
{
  int size;
  getSize(size);
  top(size);
  middle(size);
  bottom(size);
  return 0;
}

Enter the height as an odd integer from 1 to 23: 7
```

```
#
###
#####
#######
#####
###
#
```

Do not proceed until `bottom` is tested!

6N.5   Diamond: Phase Five

Modify the `top` function such that a blank space is displayed with enough columns to push over each row the proper number of columns. Use a statement such as

```
cout.width(n); cout << ' ';
```

where n is *decremented* by one for each row displayed. Modify your program and run it until your output looks like this:

```
   #
  ###
 #####
#######
 #####
  ###
   #
```

6N.6   Diamond: Phase Six

Using what you learned to modify the `top` function, modify the `bottom` function such that a blank space is displayed with enough columns to push over each row the proper number of columns. Use

```
cout.width(n); cout << ' ';
```

where n is *incremented* by one for each row displayed. Your final output should look like the diamond shown next when 7 is entered as the height.

```
Enter the height as an odd integer from 1 to 23: 7

   #
  ###
 #####
#######
 #####
  ###
   #
```

Appendix B

Class complex with Operator Overloading

Prerequisite: Completion of Chapters 1 through 8.

The complex number system is reviewed as a prelude to the implementation of a complex number class. As you read through this introduction, think of a complex number as one point on the complex plane. The point is usually written as (1,2) where 1 is the number on the real axis and 2 is a value on the imaginary axis.

The complex class will be used to provide simple solutions to finding the center of a line and the center of a triangle. Let's first examine the following program and discover that the center of a line represented by two points, a and b, is the average of those two complex numbers $((0,0) + (1,1))/2 = (0.5,0.5)$. The center of a triangle, represented by points a, b, and c, is the average of those three complex numbers.

```cpp
// This program assumes that the file ourcmplx.h has class complex and
// the division and addition operators (/ and +) have been overloaded
#include "ourcmplx.h"

int main()
{
  complex a(0, 0);
  complex b(1, 1);
  complex center;

  center = (a + b) / 2;
  cout << "\n Center of the line " << a << ", " << b << ": "
       << center << endl;

  complex c (0.5, 2);
  center = (a + b + c) / 3;
  cout << "\n Center of triangle " << a << ", " << b << ", " << c << ": "
       << center << endl;
  return 0;
}
```

```
━━━━━━━━━━━━━━━━ Output ━━━━━━━━━━━━━━━━
   Center of the line (0, 0), (1, 1): (0.5, 0.5)
   Center of triangle (0, 0), (1, 1), (0.5, 2): (0.5, 1)
```

Notice that a complex number is displayed as two numbers separated by ',' and enclosed in '(' and ')'. This is made possible by overloading << for output.

B.1   A Complex Class

The following specification of a complex number class is well short of a full complex class, which would define subtraction, multiplication, and many other functions such as absolute value, complex conjugate, square root, and so on. This keeps the discussion shorter and simpler. Additional operations could be given as lab projects.

Project: *Implement a complex number class that computes the average of a set of complex numbers as easily as if they were one of the fundamental numeric classes like int or float. Users should be able to construct complex objects and perform complex addition and division. Users should also have I/O operations available.*

The set of real numbers contains solutions to many, but not all equations. For example, the real solution of the equation $X^3 = -1$ is -1. On the other hand, there is no real solution of the equation $X^2 = -1$ since the square of any real number is always positive. To work around this, mathematicians invented the complex number system by introducing the symbol i as the solution of the equation $X^2 = -1$ such that $i = sqrt(-1)$ or $i^2 = -1$. A complex number is expressed in the form $a + bi$ where a and b may be double objects. For the complex number c,

```
c = a + bi
```

a is the real part and b is the imaginary part. A number such as $a + bi$ where $b = 0.0$ has a real number equivalent since there is no imaginary part. When the coefficient of i is zero, the number is real.

The following is a representation of the complex numbers $3+2i$, $-2+i$, $3.5+0i$, $1.5-2i$, and $-3-3i$ written as points on the *complex plane:*

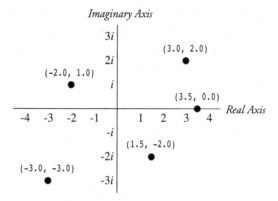

Many of the familiar arithmetic operators are also defined for complex numbers. For example, addition and division operations are defined for complex numbers. The meaning, however, is different. Complex addition and division obey the following rules (the subtraction and multiplication operations are discussed later as a lab project).

Addition Example

$$(a+bi)+(c+di)=(a+c)+(b+d)i$$

$$(3+4i)+(5+6i)=(3+5)+(4+6)i=8+10i \text{ or } (8,10)$$

Division Example

Note: Complex division is undefined when $c^2 + d^2 = 0$.

$$\frac{a+bi}{c+di}=\frac{a*c+b*d}{c^2+d^2}+\frac{b*c-a*d}{c^2+d^2}i$$

$$\frac{3+4i}{5+6i}=\frac{3*5+4*6}{5^2+6^2}+\frac{4*5-3*6}{5^2+6^2}i$$

$$=\frac{15+24}{25+36}+\frac{20-18}{25+36}i$$

$$=\frac{39}{61}+\frac{2}{61}i$$

$$=0.63934+0.03279i$$

$$=(0.63934,0.03279)$$

To perform tasks requiring complex arithmetic, we could have a class that can handle operations such as addition and division as easily as if the operands were int, float, or double. The less desirable design is to keep track of the four components involved—the four objects a, b, c, and d. With the latter design, the user is always responsible for making sure that the arithmetic is done properly. We also do not take advantage of the abstraction made possible by implementing a complex class as a natural part of the language. For example, without a complex class we might need to remember the complex arithmetic rules and to code all of the following statements each time complex arithmetic is required:

```cpp
// This is the difficult way of doing things. Without a complex class,
// we must remember many details (especially with division). Also, this
// approach increases the probability of errors.
#include <iostream.h>
#include <math.h>

main()
{
  // Find the center of a line the hard way:
  double a, b, c, d;
  a = 0.0;
  b = 0.0;
  c = 1.0;
  d = 1.0;
  // First, add two complex numbers
  double realSum = a + c;
  double imaginarySum = b + d;
  // The sum is now  (realSum + imaginarySum * i)
  // so to divide by (   2    +     0     * i)
  // we need this:
  a = realSum;
  b = imaginarySum;
  c = 2.0;          // c and d represent the real and imaginary
  d = 0.0;          // parts of the divisor.

  // Determine the common denominator as c squared plus d squared
  double denominator = pow (c, 2) + pow (d, 2);

  // Now create a new complex number which is the
  // average of (0,0) and (1,1).
  double numerator1 = (a * c + b * d);
  double numerator2 = (b * c - a * d);
  double real = numerator1 / denominator;
  double imag = numerator2 / denominator;

  // Output
  cout << "Center of line: " << "(" << real << ", " << imag << ")";
}
```

─────────────────── **Output** ───────────────────
```
Center of line: (0.5, 0.5)
```

Or, with a `complex` class, we could use the much simpler abstract view of complex numbers as shown here with a `complex` class stored in `ourcmplx.h`:

```
// If someone has done all the work of implementing
// a complex class, we should use it. This program
// solves the same problem in a simpler manner.
#include <iostream.h>
#include "ourcmplx.h"

main()
{
  complex c1(0, 0);
  complex c2(1, 1);
  cout << "Center of line: " << (c1 + c2) / 2 << endl;
}
```

```
──────────── Output ────────────
  Center of line: (0.5, 0.5)
```

This second, more elegant solution uses abstraction to hide many of the details from the user and to provide appropriate operations such as + and /. This makes `complex` objects as easy to use as `int` and `float` objects. The second solution is the preferred method, at least from the user's perspective, but it requires a class declaration and implementation. Once a `complex` class is completed, it exists for continued use. So the goal here is to implement a complex number class. In the process, we review the C++ class construct, cover operator overloading, and develop a deeper appreciation of the importance of abstraction in computer science.

Although there are many other complex operations required for a full `complex` class, the complex number specification restricts the operations to two basic arithmetic operations (addition and division), constructor functions for initialization, a member function for displaying a complex number as shown in the preceding output, and a member function for input of complex numbers.

B.2   Implementation

A complex number has a real part and an imaginary part. The real part could be represented as a `float`, but to obtain maximum precision, a `double` data member is preferred. The imaginary part is also best represented by a `double` that acts as the coefficient of i. For example, the complex number $a + bi$ is represented by a and b as `double` objects. Two private data members, identified as `realPart` and `imagPart`, successfully represent a complex number.

As for member functions, access functions are included that return the real and imaginary parts (called `real` and `imag`, respectively) for two reasons. One, there are applications when it is necessary to reference only the real part or only the imaginary part of a `complex` object. Two, `real()` and `imag()` allow us to implement the overloaded operator functions.

As for the constructor(s), we make a design decision to allow objects that cannot be assigned a value until later. This is accomplished by adding a default constructor for declarations such as `complex c1;`. Another constructor is required for complete initialization such as `complex c2(1.5,2.5)`. Another constructor will be added to allow a second default argument of `0.0` for legal initializations as `c3(2.0)`. This is a real number with the complex equivalent of $2.0 + 0.0i$. This leads to a class declaration with five public member functions and two private data members:

```
class complex {
public:                     // Constructors
  complex();                // 1. Default for complex a;
  complex(double initReal)  // 2. Initializer for complex b(1.0);
  complex(double initReal,  // 3. Initializer for
          double initImag); //      complex c(1.0. 2.0);
  // Accessing functions
  double real();
  double imag();

private:
  double realPart, imagPart;
};
```

If no arguments are supplied, the default constructor `complex::complex()` is called to initialize the real and imaginary parts of the class arbitrarily making the complex value (0, 0). Such is the case in an initialization such as `complex a;`. This constructor is called when no arguments are supplied:

```
complex::complex()
{ // Default constructor
  realPart = 0.0;
  imagPart = 0.0;
}
```

The second constructor with one parameter provides initialization of complex numbers where 0.0 is assumed to be the imaginary part (a real number). This constructor uses 0.0 as the argument for `initImag`.

```
complex::complex(double initReal)
{
  realPart = initReal;
  imagPart = 0.0;
}
```

When two arguments are supplied at instantiation, the real and imaginary parts are initialized with the values of the first and second arguments, respectively.

```
complex::complex(double initReal, double initImag)
{
  realPart = initReal;
  imagPart = initImag;
}
```

In summary, complex objects are constructed in these three ways:

```
complex a;            // realPart = 0.0, imagPart = 0.0
complex b(1.0);       // realPart = 1.0, imagPart = 0.0
complex c(2.5, 3.5);  // realPart = 2.5, imagPart = 3.5
```

The other two members are accessor functions that simply return the private data:

```
double complex::real()
{
  return realVal;
}

double complex::imag()
{
  return imagVal;
}
```

B.2.1 Operator Overloading

The implementor of a class should make the class intuitive and easy to use. For example, we can implement operators such as +, /, <<, and = for complex objects. The process of applying new meaning to existing operators is called *operator overloading*. For example, instead of requiring the users of our class to remember to make two assignments (one to the real part, another to the imaginary part), the following assignments are preferable:

```
complex a, b;
a = complex(1, 4);
b = a;
```

These assignments are allowed because the C++ compiler automatically gives us an over-loaded = operator. But to overload other operators such as + and /, we must add other functions. Instead of requiring the user to remember all the rules of complex division, overloading / and + allows expressions that are more intuitive:

```
complex center, a(0, 0), b(1, 1);
center = (a + b) / 2;
```

Users of the class immediately recognize the meanings of these three operations (=, +, and /). These are operations common to other numeric classes. Let's first look at how operators are overloaded so that we can make complex a natural part of the language.

Binary operators are treated as functions with two arguments. For example, a non-member function prototype used to implement the + function to add two complex numbers could look like this:

```
complex operator + (complex leftOperand, complex rightOperand);
```

Assuming a and b are complex objects, this function would be called with these operator function calls:

```
a + b      b + a      a + complex(1, 2)      complex(1, 2) + b
```

In general, overloading operators requires a function prototype containing the reserved word *operator*. The reserved word operator must be preceded by a return type such as int, float, string, or complex and followed by one of the "overloadable" C++ opera-tors such as +, /, =, or <<. The left and right operands are declared as parameters after the operator:

return-type operator *an-operator* (*left-operand* , *right-operand*) ;

We will be implementing these overloaded operator functions in the same file as the member functions (making them member functions is another possible scenario). So the complex arithmetic functions become stand-alone functions in the same files as the complex class. The overloaded operators will be available along with the complex class by including the file ourcmplx.h.

The parameter list for binary operators declared outside a class must contain exactly two parameters. The first parameter represents the operand to the left of the operator and the second parameter represents the operand to the right of the operator. For ex-ample, when given an implementation such as this:

```
complex operator + (complex left, complex right)
{ // Complex addition
  // (a + bi) + (c + di) = (a + c) + (b + d)i
  double tempReal = left.real() + right.real();  // a+c, the real part
  double tempImag = left.imag() + right.imag();  // b+d, imaginary part
  complex temp(tempReal, tempImag);
  return temp;
};
```

and the following expression is encountered:

```
complex(1, 2) + complex(3, 4)
```

the parameter `left` is given a copy of `complex(1,2)` and the parameter identified as `right` gets a copy of the value `complex(3,4)`. The rules of complex addition are applied and a temporary complex value (`temp`) is created using the constructor. This temporary complex is returned to the point of the complex addition.

C++ also allows for implicit conversions (number promotions). For example, when the following expression is encountered, the left operand (2) is implicitly converted into a `complex` (with `0.0` as the coefficient of the imaginary part) by calling the constructor function with one parameter:

```
2 + a    // 2 is replaced by complex(2.0, 0.0);
b / 2.0  // 2.0 is replaced by complex(2.0, 0.0);
```

B.2.2 Overloading the / Operator for Complex Division

Because / is a binary operator, a function designed to overload / for complex division also requires two parameters. So the function prototype is very similar to the one used to overload binary +. In both functions, the return type is complex since both addition and division of complex numbers result in complex numbers. The algebra used to do division is more involved than addition, so we simplify things by calculating the denominator and numerators separately before creating and returning the temporary complex number `temp`. The resulting complex value is again created via the constructor function.

```
complex operator / (complex left, complex right)
{ // Complex division:
  //                    a * c + b * d      b * c - a * d
  // (a+b*i)/(c+d*i) = -------------- + -------------- * i
  //                      c*c + d*d          c*c + d*d

  double den;       // c squared + d squared (denominator)
  double nuR, nuI; // The Real and Imaginary numerators
```

```
// c * c + d * d
den = pow(right.real(), 2) + pow(right.imag(), 2);
// a * c + b * d
nuR = left.real() * right.real() + left.imag() * right.imag();
// b * c - a * d
nuI = left.imag() * right.real() - left.real() * right.imag();

// Create a temporary complex number and return it:
complex temp(nuR / den, nuI / den);
return temp;
};
```

The following program shows complex division with two complex operands and one division in which an implicit conversion is applied to the operand 2.

```
#include <iostream.h>
#include "ourcmplx.h"

main()
{
  complex a(1.0, 1.0), b(2.0, 2.0);
  cout << b / a << endl;
  cout << a / b << endl;
  cout << a / 2 << endl; // Implicit conversion from int to complex
}
```

———— **Output** ————
```
(2, 0)
(0.5, 0)
(0.5, 0.5)
```

B.2.3 Overloading the << Operator for Complex Output

In an effort to make our classes easier to use, the insertion operator << is also overloaded to provide appropriate output format for the class. For example, we may wish to show a complex number as 1+5i, 1.000+5.000j, or as was previously shown: (2, 0). As with the + and / operators, the stream insertion operator << is also a binary operator—one that requires two operands. While it may be obvious that the right operand should be a complex number, what may not be so obvious is that the left operator is a reference to an output stream—an ostream object.

```
cout << c1; // Left operand is an ostream object
```

The identifier cout is just one example of an ostream object. Whenever we include iostream.h in a program, cout is automatically initialized and associated with the computer screen. Whenever `ostream` objects occur as a parameter or a return type, it is essential that they be passed by reference, rather than by value. Since updates occur behind the scenes during input and output operations, it is necessary to make sure the object is allowed to change. Therefore, anytime we overload the << operator, we will pass `ostream` by reference (& is added). Here is the prototype as declared in `ourcmplx.h`:

```
ostream & operator << (ostream & os, complex c);
```

Now in the operator << function shown next, `os` is a parameter declared as an `ostream` object. When `cout` is passed by reference in a statement like this:

```
cout << complex(1.0, 2.0);
```

any change to `os` alters the associated argument, which in this case is `cout`.

```
ostream & operator << (ostream & os, complex c)
{
  os << "(" << c.real() << ", " << c.imag() << ")";
  return os;
}
```

After the first statement of this overloading function executes with a statement like this

```
complex c1(2.0, 3.0);
cout << c1;   // call ostream & operator << (ostream &, complex)
```

the function call `cout << c1;` inserts these expressions into the output stream:

1. An opening (left) parenthesis
2. The real part (2)
3. A comma and a space
4. The imaginary part
5. The closing (right) parenthesis

to generate this output:

```
(2, 3)
```

Any change to the output stream associated with `os` (`cout` in this case) makes the proper change to the correct stream. Any change to `os` in the function is a change to `cout` where the function was called because the parameter (`os`) is associated with the argument (`cout`) by reference (&).

Chain insertions are made possible by returning a reference to the ostream object involved in the original function call. Upon close examination of the operator << function, you will notice a reference used in the return type:

```
ostream & operator << (...
```

The value that is returned to the point of the function call (cout << c1) is a reference to the output stream object passed as the first parameter: cout. The return value is used as the next argument for another insertion operation. Whenever there are more than one << operators in a cout statement, the expressions are inserted into the output stream in a left to right order. The reference in the return type is necessary to allow the chaining of insertions as in the following statement (c1, c2, c3 are complex objects):

```
cout << c1 << c2 << c3;
```

The first function call is cout << c1. To allow for subsequent << operations, the value that replaces (cout << c1) must be a reference to the same output stream. This allows for a second function call (ostream & << c2), which in turn allows for a third function call (ostream & << c3). The entire expression can also be written with parentheses indicating the three function calls to the ostream & operator << function in a left to right order.

```
(((cout << c1) << c2) << c3);  // Insert c1, return reference to cout

((   cout      << c2)  << c3 ); // Insert c2, return reference to cout

(        cout          << c3 ); // Insert c3, return reference to cout

         cout                   // This reference to cout is ignored
```

B.2.4 Overloading the >> Operator for Complex Input

We can also allow input of complex values with the cin statement. To do this, we overload the extraction operator for complex objects such that the real and imaginary components of a complex number are entered as two consecutive double values. This code:

```
complex c1;
cout << "Enter a complex number: ";
cin >> c1;
```

requires a dialogue such as this:

```
Enter a complex number: 3.75  -1.5
```

One difference between overloading << and >> is the consideration of the class from which cin and cout are constructed. The following function prototype uses istream in place of ostream and is in place of os.

```
istream & operator >> (istream & is, complex & c);
```

Another difference is the fact that the right operand, a complex object, must be passed by reference. This makes sense because the state of the right operand is the one we wish to change. Without the reference before c, the expression cin >> c1 would call this function but not alter the state of c1.

```
istream & operator >> (istream & is, complex & c)  // c must be &
{
  double r, i;
  is >> r >> i;      // The arguments associated with
  c = complex(r, i); // parameters is and c are altered
  return is;
};
```

As was the case for overloading <<, the return type for the function that overloads >> must be a reference to the input stream. The reference in the return type (istream &) allows the chaining of extraction operations as in this expression:

```
cin >> c1 >> c2 >> c3;
```

The return type of operator >> is a reference to the same input stream passed as the first argument (istream & is). The first function call (cin >> c1) returns a reference to cin—the left operand for istream & >> c2. This is the second function call, which again returns an istream & to allow output of the third complex number c3. The entire expression can also be written with parentheses indicating the function calls occur in a left to right order.

```
(((cin >> c1) >> c2) >> c3);
```

Self Check

1. Determine the complex numbers that result from each of the following arithmetic operations.

   a. (1.0, 3.0) + (2.0, 4.0)   c. (-1.0, -1.0) + (-2.0, -2.0)

   b. (4.0, 3.0) + (-1, -1)   d. (4.0, 4.0) / (1.0, 1.0)

2. What error would you expect with the operation (2.0, 3.0) / (0.0, 0.0)?

3. Write the output of the following program:

```
#include <iostream.h>
#include "ourcmplx.h"
main()
{
  complex c1(3.5, 6.25);
  cout << c1.real() << "   " << c1.imag();
}
```

4. Write the output of the following program:

```
#include <iostream.h>
#include "ourcmplx.h"
main()
{
  complex c2(-1.0, -2.0);
  c2 = c2 + 6.0;
  cout << c2;
}
```

5. Rewrite the function that overloads << for complex objects such that output appears without parentheses with the symbol i. The + or - operator should always be between the real and imaginary parts. These statements

```
complex c1(1.1, 3.5);
cout << c1;
```

should generate this output:

```
1.1+3.5i
```

Answers
1. a. (3,7)   b. (3,2)   c. (-3,-3)   d. (4,0)
2. Division by zero.
3. 3.5 6.25
4. 5-2i
5. ```
   ostream & operator << (ostream & os, complex c)
     {
       os << c.real();
       if(c.imag() >= 0) // Avoid showing + and - for negative coefficients of i
         os << '+';
       os << c.imag() << 'i';
       return os;
     }
   ```
   ```

Lab Projects

BI   Modifying a Class

Modify mycmplx.h by overloading the - operator for complex subtraction and * for complex multiplication, respectively. Test your program by hand-calculating some complex expressions and comparing them with C++ program output. Find the definition of these two complex operations in your math book or the library.

B2   Using Objects

Write a function that returns the complex roots of a quadratic equation using the quadratic formula:

$$\frac{-b \pm \sqrt{b^2 - 4ac}}{2a}$$

where a, b, and c represent the coefficients of a quadratic equation in the form $ax^2 + bx + c$. If the discriminate (b*b - 4*a*c) is positive, two distinct real roots exist. If the discriminant equals 0.0, then two nondistinct real roots exist. In both of these cases, the imaginary part is 0.0, indicating the roots are real. If the discriminant is negative, two distinct complex roots exist. In this third case, we factor out i (sqrt(-1)) by taking the absolute value of the discriminate before applying the square root function. In all cases, the roots should be returned as complex numbers. Real roots have 0.0 as the imaginary part; imaginary roots have nonzero coefficients of i. For real roots with 0.0 as the imaginary part, call the one argument constructor like this:

```
r1 = complex( (-b + sqrt(disc)) / (2 * a) );
r2 = complex( (-b - sqrt(disc)) / (2 * a) );
```

For the nonreal roots, return these two complex numbers as the roots:

```
r1 = complex( -b/(2*a), +sqrt(abs(disc))/(2*a) );
r2 = complex( -b/(2*a), -sqrt(abs(disc))/(2*a) );
```

Use the following program and output as a test oracle:

```
#include <iostream.h>
#include <math.h>
#include "ourcmplx.h"

//
// Include function roots here. Remember to use references
// for both complex parameters representing the roots.
//

int main()
{
  complex r1, r2;
  roots(1.0, 2.0, 3.0, r1, r2);
  cout << r1 << " and " << r2 << endl;
  roots(1.0, 0.0, -1.0, r1, r2);
  cout << r1 << " and " << r2 << endl;
  roots(1.0, 1.0, -6.0, r1, r2);
  cout << r1 << " and " << r2 << endl;
  roots(1.0, 1.0, 2.0, r1, r2);
  cout << r1 << " and " << r2 << endl;
  return 0;
}
```

──────────────── **Output** ────────────────

```
(1, 1.414214) and (-1, 1.414214)
(1, 0) and (-1, 0)
(2, 0) and (-3, 0)
(-0.5, 1.322876) and (-0.5, -1.322876)
```

Appendix C

C++ Reference Section

C.1   C++ Keywords

asm	continue	float	new	signed	try
auto	default	for	operator	sizeof	typedef
break	delete	friend	private	static	union
case	do	goto	protected	struct	unsigned
catch	double	if	public	switch	virtual
char	else	inline	register	template	void
class	enum	int	return	this	volatile
const	extern	long	short	throw	while

Keywords are wordlike tokens with predefined meaning. They cannot be redeclared to mean anything else.

C.2   One Character Special Symbols

!	%	&	'	:	-	=	.	¦
[	^	;	(	"	+	?	{	/
]	\	*	)	<	>	,	}	~

One character special symbols are used for punctuation or operators.

C.3   Two Character Operators

->	*=	.*	<<	+=	&=	==	^=
¦¦	--	%=	>>	<<=	>=	!=	&&
++	/=	->*	-=	>>=	<=	¦=	::

All two character operands are used as operators only.

C.4   Precedence Rules of C++ Operators (Complete List)

Rank 1 has the highest precedence. Rank 16 has the lowest precedence. Operators within each rank have equal precedence.

Category	Operator	Description	Associativity (Grouping Order)
1. Highest	::	Scope resolution	Left to right
	()	Function call	
	[]	Array subscript	
	->	Indirect member selector	
	.	Direct member selector	
2. Unary	!	Logical negation (not)	Right to left
	+	Unary plus	
	-	Unary minus	
	~	Bitwise (1's) complement	
	++	Pre- or postincrement	
	--	Pre- or postdecrement	
	&	Address	
	*	Indirection	
	sizeof	Returns operand size in bytes	
	new	Allocates storage	
	delete	Deallocates storage	
3. Member Access	.*	Dereference	Left to Right
	->*	Dereference	
4. Multiplicative	*	Multiplication	Left to right
	/	Division	
	%	Remainder	
5. Additive	+	Binary plus	Left to right
	-	Binary minus	
6. Shift (over- loaded for I/O)	<<	Shift left	Left to Right
	>>	Shift right	
7. Relational	<	Less than	Left to right
	>	Greater than	
	<=	Less than or equal to	
	>=	Greater than or equal to	
8. Equality	==	Left to right	
	!=	Not equal	
9.	&	Bitwise AND	Left to right

10.	^	Bitwise XOR	Left to right
11.	¦	Bitwise OR	Left to right
12.	&&	Logical AND	Left to right
13.	¦¦	Logical OR	Left to right
14. Conditional	?:	A ternary operator like `if...else`	Left to right
15. Assignment	=	Assign lValue to rValue	Right to left
	*=	Assign product	
	/=	Assign quotient	
	%=	Assign remainder (modulus)	
	+=	Assign sum	
	-=	Assign difference	
	&=	Assign bitwise AND	
	^=	Assign bitwise XOR	
	¦=	Assign bitwise OR	
	<<=	Assign left shift	
	>>=	Assign right shift	
16. Comma	,	Evaluate	Left to right

The following operators are not covered in this textbook:

```
->   sizeof .*     ->*    ^      ¦     ?:    <<=    >>=
*=   /=    %=     +=     -=     &=    ^=    ¦=     ,
```

C.5   Numeric Classes (Data Types)

There are a large number of numeric classes that must be available with each C++ system. The ranges are implementation specific so the ranges shown in the right column vary among systems. On many systems the range of `int` is -2,147,483,648 through 2,147,483,647.

Class	Range for Turbo C++, a DOS-Based System
unsigned char	0 to 255
char	-128 to 127
enum	32,768 to 32,767
unsigned int	0 to 65,535
short int	-32,768 to 32,767
int	-32,768 to 32,767
unsigned long	0 to 4,294,967,295
long	-2,147,483,648 to 2,147,483,647
float	$3.4 * (10^{-38})$ to $3.4 * (10^{+38})$
double	$1.7 * (10^{-308})$ to $1.7 * (10^{+308})$
long double	$3.4 * (10^{-4932})$ to $1.1 * (10^{+4932})$

C.6   Escape Sequences

When an escape sequence is encountered as a char constant or inside a string literal, the escape sequence has special meaning. For example, the escape sequence \a will sound the speaker.

Escape Sequence	Meaning
\n	newline
\t	horizontal tab
\v	vertical tab
\b	backspace
\r	carriage return
\f	form feed
\a	alert
\\	backslash
\?	question mark
\'	single quote
\"	double quote
\ooo	octal number
\xhhh	hexadecimal number

The escape sequence \\ is a special case. Because the compiler interprets a backslash and the character(s) following as an escape sequence, it would assume a directive such as

```
ifstream inFile = "c:\tests.dat"   // File not found
```

would mean to open a file named c:<Tab>ests.dat and the file would not be found. Instead, the escape sequence \\ must be used to represent the \ character:

```
ifstream inFile = "c:\\tests.dat"
```

Appendix D

C Style I/O: printf and scanf

Much of the material in this text applies to the C programming language. The major difference between C and C++ is that C, which predates C++, does not have the class construct. Even C++'s early name of "C with Classes" indicates this difference. Because you are likely to encounter C programs in the future, you will notice the absence of cout << and cin >> operations. These two objects require the C++ classes ostream and istream, respectively.

This appendix is not intended to be a complete discussion of C style input/output with stdio.h functions. Instead, the example programs are intended to highlight a major difference between C and C++ style I/O. You are likely to encounter C++ code sprinkled with printf and scanf statements because many programmers still mix C style I/O in their C++ programs.

C++ is a superset of C. All C++ compilers must be able to compile C code. Therefore, you may test the code in the discussion that follows on your C++ compiler since it is also a C compiler. Input and output are handled though the functions printf and scanf, both of which are declared in the header file stdio.h.

D.1   printf

The printf function writes output to the standard output device, which is usually the screen. From this standpoint, it is roughly equivalent to cout. Here are some example calls shown in the context of a program:

```
#include <stdio.h>    // for printf
#include <string.h>   // for strncpy

int main()
{
  int anInt = 123;
  char aChar = 'M';
  float aFloat = 4.56e-3;
  char * aString;
  aString = new char[10];
  strncpy(aString, "Ten chars", 10);
```

```
printf("Hello world\n");
printf("  anInt: %i \n", anInt);   // Use format specifier %i (integer)
printf("  aChar: %c \n", aChar);   // Use format specifier %c (character)
printf(" aFloat: %f \n", aFloat);  // Use format specifier %f (floating)
printf("aString: %s \n", aString); // Use format specifier %s (string)
return 0;
}
```

─────────────── **Output** ───────────────

```
Hello world
  anInt: 123
  aChar: M
 aFloat: 0.004560
aString: Ten chars
```

The printf function takes two arguments: a string (char*) containing text such as "Hello world", escape sequences such as \n and format specifiers such as %i and %f. For each format specifier, objects of the proper class are supplied as additional arguments. Any number can be supplied. The additional arguments may be expressions with operators. The following program illustrates these points. It also shows floating point values formatted in the form

> %W.Df

where W is an integer representing the number of columns and D is the number of decimal places. The descriptor 4.1f means that the associated expression (t1+t2+t3)/3.0 is displayed in the next four columns rounded to 1 decimal place.

```
#include <stdio.h>  // for printf

int main()
{
  int t1 = 76, t2 = 93, t3 = 85;
  printf("t1, t2, and t3 are: %i, %i, and %i \n", t1, t2, t3 );
  printf("    The average is: %4.1f \n", (t1+t2+t3)/3.0 );
  return 0;
}
```

─────────────── **Output** ───────────────

```
t1, t2, and t3 are: 76, 93, and 85
    The average is: 84.7
```

D.2   scanf

The scanf function declared in stdio.h reads input from the standard input device, usually the keyboard. It is roughly equivalent to cin >>. The first argument is a string containing format specifiers for the arguments that follow. The address of the operator & is explicitly used with the C scanf function. This means we are passing the address of the variable to the scanf function (see Chapter 9). For each input variable, we need a format specifier of the proper type.

```
printf("Enter an int, a char and a float: ");
scanf("%i %c %f", &anInt, &aChar, &aFloat);
```

Here is another example of interactive I/O using stdio.h functions rather than C++'s iostream.h functions:

```
#include <stdio.h>   // for printf and scanf

int main()
{
  int t1, t2, t3;
  printf("Enter three ints: ");
  scanf("%i %i %i", &t1, &t2, &t3);
  printf("  The average is: %5.2f \n", (t1+t2+t3)/3.0 );
  return 0;
}
```

——————————— **Dialogue** ———————————

```
Enter three ints: 76 93 85
  The average is: 84.67
```

Appendix E
Module Interface Diagrams

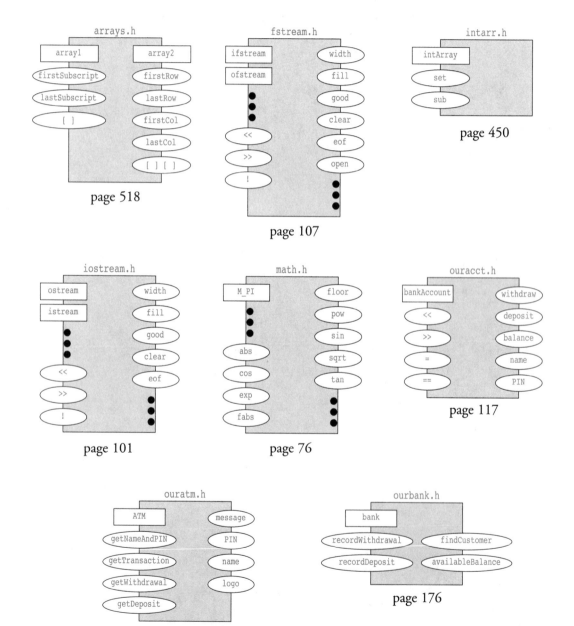

arrays.h

array1
firstSubscript
lastSubscript
[ ]

array2
firstRow
lastRow
firstCol
lastCol
[ ] [ ]

page 518

fstream.h

ifstream
ofstream
●
●
●
<<
>>
!

width
fill
good
clear
eof
open
●
●
●

page 107

intarr.h

intArray
set
sub

page 450

iostream.h

ostream
istream
●
●
●
<<
>>
!

width
fill
good
clear
eof
●
●
●

page 101

math.h

M_PI
●
●
●
abs
cos
exp
fabs

floor
pow
sin
sqrt
tan
●
●
●

page 76

ouracct.h

bankAccount
<<
>>
=
==

withdraw
deposit
balance
name
PIN

page 117

ouratm.h

ATM
getNameAndPIN
getTransaction
getWithdrawal
getDeposit

message
PIN
name
logo

page 163

ourbank.h

bank
recordWithdrawal
recordDeposit

findCustomer
availableBalance

page 176

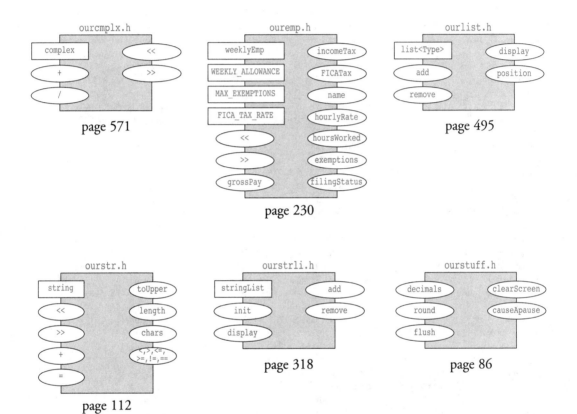

ourcmplx.h

complex
<<
+
>>
/

page 571

ouremp.h

weeklyEmp   incomeTax
WEEKLY_ALLOWANCE   FICATax
MAX_EXEMPTIONS   name
FICA_TAX_RATE   hourlyRate
<<   hoursWorked
>>   exemptions
grossPay   filingStatus

page 230

ourlist.h

list<Type>   display
add   position
remove

page 495

ourstr.h

string   toUpper
<<   length
>>   chars
+   <,>,<=,
=   >=,!=,==

page 112

ourstrli.h

stringList   add
init   remove
display

page 318

ourstuff.h

decimals   clearScreen
round   causeApause
flush

page 86

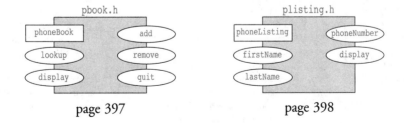

pbook.h

phoneBook   add
lookup   remove
display   quit

page 397

plisting.h

phoneListing   phoneNumber
firstName   display
lastName

page 398

Index